The Transition to Democracy in Hungary

Unlike in other countries of Eastern Europe where the opposition to Communism came in the form of single mass movements led by charismatic leaders such as Václav Havel and Lech Wałęsa, in Hungary the opposition was very fragmented, brought together and made effective only by the authoritative, significant but relatively unknown Árpád Göncz, who subsequently became Hungary's first post-Communist president. This book charts the political career of Árpád Göncz, outlining the outstanding contribution he made to Hungary's transition to democracy. Drawing on a wide range of sources, including archives and interviews with Göncz himself and others, it shows how Göncz, unlike Havel who was a playwright and whose political role was largely symbolic, was a campaigning politician all his life, consistently advocating social democratic, but not communist, values. Imprisoned from 1956 for his participation in the 1956 uprising, Göncz was a highly-effective political operator in the transition period around 1989, and as president wielded real power effectively. As politics in Hungary are again marred by deep division and fragmentation, Göncz's success in bringing rival groups together is even more pronounced.

Dae Soon Kim is a Lecturer in Politics at Hankuk University of Foreign Studies, Korea

BASEES/Routledge series on Russian and East European Studies

Series editor:
Richard Sakwa
Department of Politics and International Relations, University of Kent

Editorial Committee:
Roy Allison, *St Antony's College, Oxford*
Birgit Beumers, *Department of Theatre, Film and Television Studies, University of Aberystwyth*
Richard Connolly, *Centre for Russian and East European Studies, University of Birmingham*
Terry Cox, *Department of Central and East European Studies, University of Glasgow*
Peter Duncan, *School of Slavonic and East European Studies, University College London*
Zoe Knox, *School of Historical Studies, University of Leicester*
Rosalind Marsh, *Department of European Studies and Modern Languages, University of Bath*
David Moon, *Department of History, University of York*
Hilary Pilkington, *Department of Sociology, University of Manchester*
Graham Timmins, *Department of Politics, University of Birmingham*
Stephen White, *Department of Politics, University of Glasgow*

Founding Editorial Committee Member:
George Blazyca, *Centre for Contemporary European Studies, University of Paisley*

This series is published on behalf of BASEES (the British Association for Slavonic and East European Studies). The series comprises original, high-quality, research-level work by both new and established scholars on all aspects of Russian, Soviet, post-Soviet and East European Studies in humanities and social science subjects.

1. **Ukraine's Foreign and Security Policy, 1991–2000**
   Roman Wolczuk

2. **Political Parties in the Russian Regions**
   Derek S. Hutcheson

3. **Local Communities and Post-Communist Transformation**
   Edited by Simon Smith

4. **Repression and Resistance in Communist Europe**
   J.C. Sharman

5. **Political Elites and the New Russia**
   Anton Steen

6. **Dostoevsky and the Idea of Russianness**
   Sarah Hudspith

7. **Performing Russia – Folk Revival and Russian Identity**
   Laura J. Olson

8. **Russian Transformations**
   Edited by Leo McCann

9. **Soviet Music and Society under Lenin and Stalin**
   The baton and sickle
   Edited by Neil Edmunds

10. **State Building in Ukraine**
    The Ukranian parliament, 1990–2003
    Sarah Whitmore

11. **Defending Human Rights in Russia**
    Sergei Kovalyov, Dissident and Human Rights Commissioner, 1969–2003
    Emma Gilligan

12. **Small-Town Russia**
    Postcommunist livelihoods and identities: a portrait of the Intelligentsia in Achit, Bednodemyanovsk and Zubtsov, 1999–2000
    Anne White

13. **Russian Society and the Orthodox Church**
    Religion in Russia after Communism
    Zoe Knox

14. **Russian Literary Culture in the Camera Age**
    The word as image
    Stephen Hutchings

15. **Between Stalin and Hitler**
    Class war and race war on the Dvina, 1940–46
    Geoffrey Swain

16. **Literature in Post-Communist Russia and Eastern Europe**
    The Russian, Czech and Slovak fiction of the changes, 1988–98
    Rajendra A. Chitnis

17. **The Legacy of Soviet Dissent**
    Dissidents, democratisation and radical nationalism in Russia
    Robert Horvath

18. **Russian and Soviet Film Adaptations of Literature, 1900–2001**
    Screening the word
    Edited by Stephen Hutchings and Anat Vernitski

19. **Russia as a Great Power**
    Dimensions of security under Putin
    Edited by Jakob Hedenskog, Vilhelm Konnander, Bertil Nygren, Ingmar Oldberg and Christer Pursiainen

20. **Katyn and the Soviet Massacre of 1940**
    Truth, justice and memory
    George Sanford

21. **Conscience, Dissent and Reform in Soviet Russia**
    Philip Boobbyer

22. **The Limits of Russian Democratisation**
    Emergency powers and states of emergency
    Alexander N. Domrin

23. **The Dilemmas of Destalinisation**
    A social and cultural history of reform in the Khrushchev era
    Edited by Polly Jones

24. **News Media and Power in Russia**
    Olessia Koltsova

25. **Post-Soviet Civil Society**
    Democratization in Russia and the Baltic States
    Anders Uhlin

26. **The Collapse of Communist Power in Poland**
    Jacqueline Hayden

27. **Television, Democracy and Elections in Russia**
    Sarah Oates

28. **Russian Constitutionalism**
    Historical and contemporary development
    Andrey N. Medushevsky

29. **Late Stalinist Russia**
    Society between reconstruction and reinvention
    Edited by Juliane Fürst

30. **The Transformation of Urban Space in Post-Soviet Russia**
    Konstantin Axenov, Isolde Brade and Evgenij Bondarchuk

31. **Western Intellectuals and the Soviet Union, 1920–40**
    From Red Square to the Left Bank
    Ludmila Stern

32. **The Germans of the Soviet Union**
    Irina Mukhina

33. **Re-constructing the Post-Soviet Industrial Region**
    The Donbas in transition
    Edited by Adam Swain

34. **Chechnya – Russia's "War on Terror"**
    John Russell

35. **The New Right in the New Europe**
    Czech transformation and right-wing politics, 1989–2006
    Seán Hanley

36. **Democracy and Myth in Russia and Eastern Europe**
    Edited by Alexander Wöll and Harald Wydra

37. **Energy Dependency, Politics and Corruption in the Former Soviet Union**
    Russia's power, Oligarchs' profits and Ukraine's missing energy policy, 1995–2006
    Margarita M. Balmaceda

38. **Peopling the Russian Periphery**
    Borderland colonization in Eurasian history
    Edited by Nicholas B. Breyfogle, Abby Schrader and Willard Sunderland

39. **Russian Legal Culture Before and After Communism**
    Criminal justice, politics and the public sphere
    Frances Nethercott

40. **Political and Social Thought in Post-Communist Russia**
    Axel Kaehne

41. **The Demise of the Soviet Communist Party**
    Atsushi Ogushi

42. **Russian Policy towards China and Japan**
    The El'tsin and Putin periods
    Natasha Kuhrt

43. **Soviet Karelia**
    Politics, planning and terror in Stalin's Russia, 1920–1939
    Nick Baron

44. **Reinventing Poland**
    Economic and political transformation and evolving national identity
    Edited by Martin Myant and Terry Cox

45. **The Russian Revolution in Retreat, 1920–24**
    Soviet workers and the new communist elite
    Simon Pirani

46. **Democratisation and Gender in Contemporary Russia**
    Suvi Salmenniemi

47. **Narrating Post/Communism**
    Colonial discourse and Europe's borderline civilization
    Nataša Kovačević

48. **Globalization and the State in Central and Eastern Europe**
    The politics of foreign direct investment
    Jan Drahokoupil

49. **Local Politics and Democratisation in Russia**
    Cameron Ross

50. **The Emancipation of the Serfs in Russia**
    Peace arbitrators and the development of civil society
    Roxanne Easley

51. **Federalism and Local Politics in Russia**
    Edited by Cameron Ross and Adrian Campbell

52. **Transitional Justice in Eastern Europe and the former Soviet Union**
    Reckoning with the communist past
    Edited by Lavinia Stan

53. **The Post-Soviet Russian Media**
    Conflicting signals
    Edited by Birgit Beumers, Stephen Hutchings and Natalia Rulyova

54. **Minority Rights in Central and Eastern Europe**
    Edited by Bernd Rechel

55. **Television and Culture in Putin's Russia: Remote Control**
    Stephen Hutchings and Natalia Rulyova

56. **The Making of Modern Lithuania**
    Tomas Balkelis

57. **Soviet State and Society Under Nikita Khrushchev**
    Melanie Ilic and Jeremy Smith

58. **Communism, Nationalism and Ethnicity in Poland, 1944–1950**
    Michael Fleming

59. **Democratic Elections in Poland, 1991–2007**
    Frances Millard

60. **Critical Theory in Russia and the West**
    Alastair Renfrew and Galin Tihanov

61. **Promoting Democracy and Human Rights in Russia**
    European organization and Russia's socialization
    Sinikukka Saari

62. **The Myth of the Russian Intelligentsia**
    Old intellectuals in the new Russia
    Inna Kochetkova

63. **Russia's Federal Relations**
    Putin's reforms and management of the regions
    Elena A. Chebankova

64. **Constitutional Bargaining in Russia, 1990–93**
    Institutions and uncertainty
    Edward Morgan-Jones

65. **Building Big Business in Russia**
    The impact of informal corporate governance practices
    Yuko Adachi

66. **Russia and Islam**
    State, society and radicalism
    Roland Dannreuther and Luke March

67. **Celebrity and Glamour in Contemporary Russia**
    Shocking chic
    Edited by Helena Goscilo and Vlad Strukov

68. **The Socialist Alternative to Bolshevik Russia**
    The Socialist Revolutionary Party, 1917–1939
    Elizabeth White

69. **Learning to Labour in Post-Soviet Russia**
    Vocational youth in transition
    Charles Walker

70. **Television and Presidential Power in Putin's Russia**
    Tina Burrett

71. **Political Theory and Community Building in Post-Soviet Russia**
    Edited by Oleg Kharkhordin and Risto Alapuro

72. **Disease, Health Care and Government in Late Imperial Russia**
    Life and death on the Volga, 1823–1914
    Charlotte E. Henze

73. **Khrushchev in the Kremlin**
    Policy and government in the Soviet Union, 1953–1964
    Edited by Melanie Ilic and Jeremy Smith

74. **Citizens in the Making in Post-Soviet States**
    Olena Nikolayenko

75. **The Decline of Regionalism in Putin's Russia**
    Boundary issues
    J. Paul Goode

76. **The Communist Youth League and the Transformation of the Soviet Union, 1917–1932**
    Matthias Neumann

77. **Putin's United Russia Party**
    S. P. Roberts

78. **The European Union and its Eastern Neighbours**
    Towards a more ambitious partnership?
    Elena Korosteleva

79. **Russia's Identity in International Relations**
    Images, perceptions, misperceptions
    Edited by Ray Taras

80. **Putin as Celebrity and Cultural Icon**
    Edited by Helena Goscilo

81. **Russia – Democracy Versus Modernization**
    A dilemma for Russia and for the world
    Edited by Vladislav Inozemtsev and Piotr Dutkiewicz

82. **Putin's Preventative Counter-Revolution**
    Post-Soviet authoritarianism and the spectre of Velvet Revolution
    Robert Horvath

83. **The Baltic States from the Soviet Union to the European Union**
    Identity, discourse and power in the post-communist transition of Estonia, Latvia and Lithuania
    Richard Mole

84. **The EU–Russia Borderland**
    New contexts for regional cooperation
    Edited by Heikki Eskelinen, Ilkka Liikanen and James W. Scott

85. **The Economic Sources of Social Order Development in Post-Socialist Eastern Europe**
    Richard Connolly

86. **East European Diasporas, Migration and Cosmopolitanism**
    Edited by Ulrike Ziemer and Sean P. Roberts

87. **Civil Society in Putin's Russia**
    Elena Chebankova

88. **Post-Communist Poland – Contested Pasts and Future Identities**
    Ewa Ochman

89. **Soviet Economic Management under Khrushchev**
    The Sovnarkhoz reform
    Nataliya Kibita

90. **Soviet Consumer Culture in the Brezhnev Era**
    Natalya Chernyshova

91. **The Transition to Democracy in Hungary**
 Árpád Göncz and the post-Communist Hungarian Presidency
 Dae Soon Kim

92. **The Politics of HIV/AIDS in Russia**
 Ulla Pape

93. **The Capitalist Transformation of State Socialism**
 The Making and Breaking of State Socialist Society, and What Followed
 David Lane

94. **Disability in Eastern Europe and the Former Soviet Union**
 History, policy and everyday life
 Edited by Michael Rasell and Elena Iarskaia-Smirnova

The Transition to Democracy in Hungary
Árpád Göncz and the post-Communist Hungarian Presidency

Dae Soon Kim

LONDON AND NEW YORK

First published 2013
by Routledge
2 Park Square, Milton Park, Abingdon, Oxfordshire OX14 4RN

Simultaneously published in the USA and Canada
by Routledge
711 Third Avenue, New York, NY 10017

Routledge is an imprint of the Taylor and Francis Group, an informa business

First issued in paperback 2015

© 2013 Dae Soon Kim

The right of Dae Soon Kim to be identified as the author of this work
has been asserted in accordance with sections 77 and 78 of the Copyright,
Designs and Patents Act 1988.

All rights reserved. No part of this book may be reprinted or reproduced
or utilised in any form or by any electronic, mechanical, or other means,
now known or hereafter invented, including photocopying and recording,
or in any information storage or retrieval system, without permission in
writing from the publishers.

Trademark notice: Product or corporate names may be trademarks or
registered trademarks, and are used only for identification and
explanation without intent to infringe.

British Library Cataloguing in Publication Data
A catalogue record for this book is available from the British Library

Library of Congress Cataloging in Publication Data
Kim, Dae Soon.
 The transition to democracy in Hungary: Árpád Göncz and the post-communist
Hungarian presidency / Dae Soon Kim.
 pages cm.—(BASEES/Routledge series on Russian and East European studies ; 91)
 Includes bibliographical references and index.
 1. Göncz, Árpád. 2. Göncz, Árpád–Political and social views.
 3. Presidents–Hungary–Biography. 4. Post-communism–Hungary–History–20th century.
 5. Democracy–Hungary–History–20th century. 6. Social change–Hungary–History–
20th century. 7. Hungary–Politics and government–1989- 8. Hungary–Politics
and government–1945-1989. I. Title.
 DB958.6.G66K56 2013
 943.905'41092–dc23
 [B]
 2012047753

ISBN 978-0-415-63664-3 (hbk)
ISBN 978-1-138-64335-2 (pbk)
ISBN 978-0-203-69425-1 (ebk)

Typeset in Times New Roman
by Swales & Willis Ltd, Exeter, Devon

To my parents and younger brother

Contents

Foreword by Vaclav Havel	xvi
Foreword by Nigel Swain	xvii
Preface	xx
Acknowledgements	xxii
List of abbreviations	xxiv
Introduction	1

PART I
The development of Göncz's political views   13

1	Beginnings	15
2	The 1956 Hungarian Revolution	39
3	Dissidence in the 1980s	68

PART II
The post-Communist presidency   87

4	Development of the post-Communist presidency in Hungary	89
5	The first presidency (1990–1995)	108
6	The second presidency (1995–2000)	157
	Conclusion	197

Notes	209
Bibliography	223
Index	253

Foreword

I remember vividly the moment in January 1990 when – less than a month after I was elected president of Czechoslovakia – I first met Árpád Göncz, the well-known Hungarian writer, in Budapest. Such a meeting had been inconceivable until then, as I had to be elected president to become eligible for a passport. At the time, Göncz did not hold any political office, and I had not yet been absorbed in my duties as president. Today, state visits are strictly [planned] and supervised by the presidential staff, and such informal meetings at the spur of the moment are no longer possible. Back then, almost anything could happen. At the same time, a meeting with a member of the anti-totalitarian resistance movement was more than a warm-hearted conversation with a fellow writer. The meeting signalled that even though we were prepared to engage in negotiations with those in power [the ruling Communists], we remained committed to overarching political changes. A few months later, my Hungarian colleague was elected president of Hungary. I, as the president of Czechoslovakia and later the Czech Republic, could not have dreamed of a better partner and friend than Árpád Göncz.

Vaclav Havel
1 December 2011

Foreword

There are few biographies of Eastern European post-socialist presidents. Vaclav Havel, dissident playwright, turned cowboy president, turned elder statesman, has merited several; while marginally fewer have been written about Slobodan Milošević, reforming communist, turned nationalist communist, turned war criminal. Lech Wałęsa has written two autobiographies, although only one covers his period as president. But that is it, so far. So why write a biography on Árpád Göncz?

Dae Soon Kim establishes the case very effectively. Göncz was Hungary's first post-socialist president; he was, according to the polls, Hungary's most popular post-socialist president; he was Hungary's only uncontentiously appointed post-socialist president; and he made some important and contentious rulings. More important than that, he was perhaps the only person who could have been Hungary's first post-socialist president, and that in itself reveals a great deal about the nature of Hungary's post-socialist politics and its unbridgeable divide between a national, Christian vision of Hungary, reinforced by a populist rhetoric, and those who do not share it – the socialists, liberals, 'progressives'.

What distinguishes the politics of post-socialist Hungary from that of its neighbours is that the non-communist field was already deeply divided long before the first democratic elections. In Czechoslovakia and Poland, socialist governments were overthrown by umbrella organisations, such as Solidarity and its Civic Committee, Civic Forum and Public Against Violence. These campaigned in their country's first free elections, which they won. It was only subsequently that they split into parties of the left, right and centre. In Hungary, however, the opposition to socialism was split from the start and the electorate during the first free elections was faced by competing anti-socialist programmes.

Hungarians conventionally distinguish between 'populist' and 'urbanist' traditions in twentieth century thought, and it was a distinction that fed through into the dissident movement during the socialist years. The 'democratic opposition', which traces its roots back to protests against the invasion of Czechoslovakia in 1968 and was producing a regularly published, samizdat journal, *Beszélő*, by the 1980s, was located squarely in the 'urbanist' camp. Key 'populist' writers made their peace with the Kádár regime after 1956, and the 'populist' opposition to the regime tended to keep its powder dry, except on the potentially explosive issue of the treatment of ethnic Hungarians in the neighbouring fellow socialist states of Romania and Czechoslovakia. These two traditions came together in 1985 for a three-day meeting in Monor, which also included some reform communists. But there was no lasting unity. When the Hungarian Democratic Forum held its very first meeting in Lakitelek in 1987 (before it turned itself into a political party), the 'democratic opposition' was conspicuous by its absence, even though reform communists, including Imre Pozsgay, were present.

The creation of the Opposition Round Table in March 1989 was directed not at unifying this already divided opposition but at preventing the communist party from using 'divide and rule' tactics to destroy it. This worked until well into the National Round Table negotiations, when, in late July and August, the idea began to germinate that the Polish solution of a socialist president but an opposition prime-minister might be appropriate for Hungary, with Pozsgay being the socialist candidate for president. The issue ultimately divided the opposition. The 'urbanists' in September refused to sign the agreement which was to conclude the National Round Table negotiations and began collecting signatures to hold a referendum on areas where agreement had not been reached, including the manner of the election of the president. Thus, not only was the opposition split before the first democratic elections were held, the population had also been forced to the ballot box to decide between the 'urbanists' who rejected a direct election (because they feared Pozsgay) and the 'populists' who, although they had nominated their own presidential candidates, were known to be unconcerned about a Pozsgay presidency. The populists lost this referendum in November 1989, but they won, in the form of the Hungarian Democratic Forum, the first free parliamentary elections held in two rounds in March and April 1990. A coalition government was formed with like-minded political parties, but this first post-socialist government had many 'cardinal laws' to pass which required a two-thirds majority. Co-operation across the divide was essential in order to achieve this, and at the end of April a coalition pact was signed with the 'urbanist' Alliance of Free Democrats.

Post-socialist politicians were not just divided in the spring of 1990, but bitterly divided; their divisions had been put to the ballot box twice, with different outcomes. Yet they had to somehow make the new political system work; and they had to elect a president who was acceptable to them all. The divide between them seemed unbridgeable. But there was one man who had a foot in both camps, and that man was Árpád Göncz.

I leave it to Dae Soon Kim to explain how and why this was the case. One of the many merits of this book is the author's careful tracing of the life of a man with impeccable anti-Communist credentials and both 'populist' and 'urbanist' experience. A Christian, he was attracted by the populists in his youth and he encountered both József Antall senior and József Antall junior as Smallholder politicians. But after his imprisonment for his activities in 1956, his concerns became more 'urbanist', and he was a founder member both of the Network of Free Initiatives (which became the Alliance of Free Democrats) and the Committee for Historical Justice (which was instrumental in organising the reburial of Imre Nagy on 16 June 1989). If Göncz's election to the presidency was uncontested, those of subsequent incumbents were considered partisan. Over the almost two and a half decades of post-socialist politics, political parties have come and gone; but a deep chasm in Hungarian politics has remained, still essentially the 'populist'–'urbanist' divide. Fidesz has taken over the national, Christian, populist mantle from the Hungarian Democratic Forum. The Alliance of Free Democrats has disappeared from the political spectrum, leaving the socialists and former socialist leader Ferenc Gyurcsány's Democratic Coalition to represent the 'urbanist' alternative.

Árpád Göncz was the right man for the moment, perhaps because of his relative obscurity; his humanity transcended the 'populist'–'urbanist' divide. Dae Soon Kim presents us with the life of a truly remarkable man and in doing so provides a lens through which to examine deep-seated tensions which have bedevilled post-socialist Hungarian politics.

Nigel Swain
Liverpool, June 2012

Preface

This book offers an introduction to the fascinating but relatively lesser known life and political activities of Hungary's first post-Communist president, Árpád Göncz. Originally, the manuscript was written in fulfillment of the requirements for the degree of Doctor of Philosophy and submitted to the University of Glasgow in January 2011. Upon successful defence of the thesis, the text was submitted to Routledge on the suggestions of Prof. Nigel Swain, Prof. Geoffrey Swain, Prof. Terry Cox, and later Prof. Stephen White. I am sincerely grateful for their support and encouragement.

Ever since Hungary's political transformation to democracy, politics in Hungary has been marked by division between the conservatives and the liberals. Unlike in Poland and Czechoslovakia where the opposition to Communism developed within united social movements (*Solidarność* and the Civic Forum), which only later began to split, the opposition to the Communists in Hungary was divided from the very beginning. In particular, political tension centred on the so-called 'national-populists' (*népi-nemzetiek*) and the 'urbanists' (*urbánusok*), whose origin dated back to the 1930s. Given that this political divide was entrenched in Hungary's political system, the figure elected as the country's first president was expected to take non-partisan stance and had to be capable of bridging that political divide.

Göncz espoused the ideals of 'peasant populism' which was so significant in Hungary during the inter-war period. He also embraced the values of liberal democracy, a view which had resulted from his first hand experiences in the struggle against autocratic rule. These factors gave rise to an image of Göncz: he was seen not as a figure who would represent the narrow interests of a party, but as one who might act as mediator between the two oppositional camps.

Thus, appointed as a consensus builder, Göncz presided over bitterly fought political squabbles and intervened decisively in important events and issues that the first transitional post-Communist government had to face. As current politics in Hungary is once again marred by political polarisation, and is in fact moving towards authoritarianism, the consensus-based democracy that Göncz sought to achieve during his presidential term in office carries even more significance.

For those with an interest in the problems of political transition in Hungary, especially with respect to the role undertaken by the president in a parliamentarian system, I hope that this first English scholarly biography lays the groundwork for comparative studies in the discipline of Communist and post-Communist politics in Central and Eastern Europe.

Dae Soon Kim
Seoul, June 2012

Acknowledgements

As a non-native English and Hungarian speaker, writing this book has been one of the greatest challenges I have ever undertaken. There were numerous times when I questioned my motivations for undertaking this research and, sometimes, I was sceptical about my chance of completing this book. It has, at times, felt like a rather lonely and uncertain journey with an end that seemed far from clear. Yet an end of one sort or another is always inevitable and this journey has reached its conclusion; I was never completely alone. My first thanks must go to my academic advisors, Prof. Terry M. Cox and Dr Clare McManus. They have consistently provided constructive comments and critical feedback on my work from the outset of my research. I am hugely grateful for their sincerity and kindness.

My special thanks go to Prof. Stephen White. His encouragement and support for my research has been one of the main impetuses for its completion. I am also obliged to thank Dr Zsuzsánna Varga, who kindly provided me with Hungarian language support.

I would also like to thank all my respondents who accepted my interview requests during my field work in Budapest. My special thanks go to the former president of Hungary Árpád Göncz and his wife Zsuzsánna Göntér, who responded so positively to interview requests themselves and who acted as gatekeepers enabling me to secure subsequent interviews with others vital to the narrative I present here. My thanks also go to Katalin Szánthó, the secretary of the 1956 Institute in Hungary who encouraged and supported me during my fieldwork in Budapest. She was always ready to listen, offering invaluable advice and a home away from home to which I could retreat when the need arose. I will always remember her kindness and generosity.

I have been fortunate to get to know some genuine and lovely people and to make durable, important friendships over the course of my time in Glasgow Sophie Mamattah, Jeffrey Richard Meadowcroft, Rebecca Reynolds, Ada-Charlotte Regelmann, David Green, Colin Vernall, Elizabeth Dunlop, Tibor Codileen Fülöp Réka, Agnieszka Katarzyna Uflewska-Watson, Timofey Agarin and Muhammed Kaleemhave consistently encouraged me to complete my research They acted as vigorous debating partners providing a forum in which I could discuss the progress of my research and writing. I am sincerely grateful for their kindness, spirit of solidarity and friendship.

Finally, the completion of this book would not have been possible without the support and love of my parents and younger brother. Although they have never understood why I became interested in Hungarian studies, they showed consistent interest in, and enthusiasm for, my research. I am truly grateful for their endless love and I dedicate this book to them.

List of abbreviations

Parliamentary parties

AFD	Alliance of Free Democrats
AYD*	Alliance of Young Democrats
CDP	Civic Democratic Party
CDPP	Christian Democratic People's Party
CP	Communist Party
HDF	Hungarian Democratic Forum
HJLP	Hungarian Justice and Life Party
HPP	Hungarian People's Party
HRP	Hungarian Radical Party
HSDP	Hungarian Socialists Democratic Party
HSP	Hungarian Socialist Party
HSWP	Hungarian Socialists Workers' Party
ISP	Independent Smallholders' Party
NPP	National Peasant Party
SDP	Social Democratic Party

* Since 1993, the AYD has gradually shifted its ideological orientation from the centre-left to the centre-right wing of the political spectrum. At the 1995 party convention, the AYD officially declared this change by renaming itself as the Alliance of Young Democrats and Hungarian Civic Party.

State institutions, civil and social organisations

AB	Agricultural Bank
ACC	Allied Control Commission
ECJ	European Court of Justice
FFHS	Freedom Front of Hungarian Students
FFHY	Freedom Front of Hungarian Youth
HBC	Hungarian Brotherly Community
HF	Hungarian Front
MOJ	Ministry of Justice
MTB	Mihály Táncsics Brigade

List of abbreviations xxv

NAACP	National Association of Agricultural Cooperatives and Producers
OPM	The Office of the Prime Minister
OR	Opposition Roundtable
PCC	Parliamentary Constitutional Committee
PTWG	Pál Teleki Work Group, later renamed the Democratic Alliance of Hungarian Intellectuals (DAHI)
RTN	Round Table Negotiation
SPPMC	State Privatisation and Property Management Corporation

Others

EECR	East European Constitutional Review
MPs	Members of Parliament

Introduction

Reminiscing about the political transition of 1989, Péter Tölgyessy – the former president of the Alliance of Free Democrats – stated that 'unlike Poland and the Czech Republic, there were no heroes representing the idea of political transformation to democracy in Hungary' (interview with Tölgyessy, 15 October 2007).

Perhaps, this observation is true as Hungary's political transformation of 1989 was generally regarded as a peaceful 'negotiated revolution or transition' between the ruling Communists and the opposition (Bozóki, 2002; Bruszt, 1990; Bruszt and Stark, 1991; Linz and Stepan, 1996; Sajó, 1996; Tőkés, 1996) and there were no high-profile figures, such as Vaclav Havel and Lech Wałęsa in Czechoslovakia and Poland, representing the interests of society. This is not to imply that the transformation in Hungary was any less dramatic and far-reaching than in the Czech Republic or Poland. Hungary's role has far greater significance than is suggested by purely internal events. After all, it was the decision of Hungary's government to open its border with Austria and let East German asylum seekers flee to West Germany (Kontler, 2002: 467; Lewis, 1994: 246; Romsics, 2007: 242–43) which in turn catalysed 'the fall of the Berlin Wall' (Swain, 1993: 66) and the collapse of 'the dominoes in the socialist camp' (Okey, 2004: 85). Gyula Horn – the foreign minister of Hungary at the time – recalled the consequence of the decision thus: 'It was quite obvious to me that this would be the first step in a landslide like series of events' (Isaacs and Downing, 1998: 382) across the whole of the Soviet Bloc.

Moreover, these historical changes could not be achieved without those who dedicated their lives to the pursuit of democracy and upheld its values. One of those contemporaries, a 'non-hero' according to Tölgyessy, who experienced the major events of Hungarian history, including having been sentenced to life imprisonment due to his participation in the 1956 Revolution, was Árpád Göncz. He subsequently became the first post-Communist president of the Republic of Hungary. Speaking at a ceremony welcoming Göncz to the United States, the former president of the United States Bill Clinton introduced him as a safeguard of democracy in Hungary:

> In the past year, I have had the privilege to welcome to the White House extraordinary leaders who risked their lives in the struggle for liberty, were imprisoned for their beliefs and activism, and now emerged in freedom's

sunlight as the presidents of their nations: Kim Dae Jung of South Korea, Vaclav Havel of the Czech Republic, Nelson Mandela of South Africa. Today, with freedom at last shining brightly in Hungary, I have the great honour and pleasure to welcome President Árpád Göncz.[1]

As a survivor of this period (he was born in 1922 and lived through the inter-war period, three years of a brief democratic interlude, Communist era and finally transition and post-transition periods), Göncz had a unique social background and experiences including participation in student resistance movements against the Nazis, as a junior politician in the Independent Smallholders' Party, as an agronomist, steelworker, and political prisoner in Communist prison, a literary translator, and a dissident (*Esti Hírlap*, 20 June 1995; Feitl and Kende, 2007: 204; *New York Times*, 3 May 1990; Okolicsanyi, 1990: 21). Though not born into a political family, Göncz, who witnessed the key events of the twentieth century, subsequently became involved in some of the key social and political movements of the age, proposing particular solutions to the political problems of those eras.

In a speech on the role of politics and literature, Göncz recounted an important moment in his life and its impact on his political development:

> I started my political and literary career at the age of twenty three [1945]. What happened before that – a few poems, literary dreams, armed resistance to the Nazis – were rather emotional affairs and *not the planned self-testing of a young man or the prudent acts of a politician*. The war started when I finished my secondary education and I was at university when Hungary entered as a belligerent. In those years Hungary was drowning in a deluge of injustice, social inequality, racial and ethnic discrimination . . . The end of the war promised the ardently awaited return of national independence . . . [and] the coming of democracy . . . But it soon became clear that liberation meant Soviet occupation and the Cold War brought the formal Communist take-over in its wake . . . [Then] *1956 swept me back into politics* with a much deeper understanding of social and political matters [. . .]
>
> (Tóth, 1999: 228–9, my emphasis)

Recalling these events and issues, Göncz recorded his experiences and views through his unpublished personal Oral History and in his essays, monologues and speeches. These documents contain a rich vein of detailed information with regard to Göncz's understanding of Hungary's social and political developments and offer a unique insight into the events and issues of the age. One of Göncz's essays entitled '1956', for example, unveils a previously recondite story of the 1956 Hungarian Revolution which includes details of the Indian leadership's mediation in the conflict between Hungarian democratic forces and the Soviet leadership (Göncz, 1991: 269–83). Despite such content, documents directly or indirectly related to Göncz have been largely untapped and have remained under-researched. At present, there are no autobiographies or biographies of Göncz either in English or Hungarian although an attempt to write a biography was made. The

Hungarian political commentator, László Lengyel, noted that 'Timothy Garton Ash once thought about writing a biography of Göncz but he did not do so in the end' (interview with Lengyel, 13 September 2007).

Göncz's Oral History, two sizeable volume of unpublished writing that forms a record of a series of interviews conducted between 1985 and 1986 and augmented in 1990, was and remains the first port of call for biographical research on Göncz. These books contain ground-breaking information regarding Göncz's life and his personal testimony and views on the key events and issues of the age. Inspite of their potential importance, these documents have been under-researched partially due to their limited accessibility,[2] but also because of sheer volume (around 430 pages in Hungarian) discouraging a wider readership at home and abroad. Recently, an abridged version of these books has become available through the official website of the Institute for the History of the 1956 Hungarian Revolution.[3] However, neither the original nor the newly edited and condensed version deals with the period of Göncz's presidency and his presidential role as a whole.

'Conversation with the President' (*A beszélgetések az elnökkel*), a compilation of Göncz's interviews, aired on Kossuth Radio between 1991 and 1993, does constitute an important contribution to the biographical data available to the general public. It presents Göncz's recollection of some historical events and his views and opinions regarding important issues and events that took place – primarilyduring the early part of the 1990s. In 2007, this book was reissued with the inclusion of additional interviews with Göncz and his wife under the title of *Looking Back* (*Visszanézve*). However, these publications are far from biographical in their contents and structure to enable researchers to trace Göncz's intellectual and political development as they evolved through his life. As Pimlott notes, the most fascinating aspect of biography is that 'it links together human events in the way human beings actually experienced them' (Pimlott, 1999: 34) and draws insights into the lives and thoughts of the individuals in question. The existing documentation, however, is not structured in a way that enables researchers to see and reconstruct Göncz's life within the context in which he lived and experienced contemporary events. Pimlott further explains the inherent nature of biographical research and what biographers should bear in mind when conducting research:

> Writing a biography is like entering a deep cavern. The cavern is a human life, the walls of the cavern are the evidence. From the lie of the land, you can tell that the cavern is likely to be an interesting one. But until you light your lamp and crawl around, you do not know what you will find. You will never get the whole picture; there will always be crevices out of reach. But the project is finite and when your exploration is finished you will have not only a unique appreciation of the particular cave, but a better feeling for geology in general.
> (Pimlott, 1999: 34)

In view of this, the research–as the first English language scholarly biography on Göncz–addresses a gap in the literature through the narration of the story of Göncz's life; an expansive account of Göncz's life, within the wider history, politics and social concerns of his generation is attempted. Biography, by definition, is 'person-centred' (Chamberlayne, Bornat and Wengraf, 2000: 22) and foregrounds individuals' personal accounts and their views; this is indicative of the fact that the focus of analysis is upon particular individuals and, it is then told against a backdrop of broader social, economic and political developments. Yet this does not necessarily mean that biographers do not consider the social and political context in their research. On the contrary, Roger Gough – the prominent English biographer of János Kádár – notes that 'biography can illuminate not only an individual life but also the forces and events that shaped it' (Gough, 2006: 12). This biography does consider the social and political contexts in which individuals lived. Bearing this in mind, this research reconstructs the key events and issues taking place in twentieth century Hungarian history, refocusing them through Göncz's experience.

Designing research: the main framework of research, its questions and methods

Within the framework of this type of biographical enquiry, the book seeks to answer the following research questions. First, from where did Göncz's political ideals originate and what form did they take? Second, in which ways did Göncz seek to translate his political ideals into practice? Last, with regard to Hungary's transformation to democracy, what did Göncz seek to achieve and what did he actually accomplish as the first post-Communist president of the Republic of Hungary? These questions have been identified during my field work in Budapest where I conducted archival research and undertook a series of interviews with Göncz and those who directly or indirectly became involved in the political decision making process. Despite the fact that, prior to the field work, I had a general picture of important phases of Göncz's life and related questions, it was only during the field work that I was able to set the boundaries of research. For example, the documents I accessed before the field work indicate that Göncz's visit to the United States in 1982 might have carried certain political importance.[4] During the field work, however, it became evident that, other than some fragmentary information on Göncz's observations and general impressions of the social atmosphere of the United States and his pursuit of a literary career, there was not sufficient information demonstrating the importance of his activism during this period (between the 1970s and the first half of 1980s). In my interview with Göncz, he explicitly stated that his visit to the US did not carry political significance:

Kim: As far as I know, you travelled to the US in 1982. What was the main aim of this visit?

Göncz: This visit did not have a political meaning . . . At the invitation of my old friends, we [Göncz and his wife] travelled to America. This visit, however, did not have any political aims or significance. We had known many friends who were previously active in the Smallholders' Party and they invited us. This visit was entirely a personal matter.

(Interview with Göncz, 18 June 2006)

In a subsequent interview with me, Göncz's wife, Zsuzsánna Göntér, reaffirmed the fact that Göncz's visit to the United States was for the purpose of nothing more than seeking a reunion with his old friends:

Göntér: A letter of invitation came from Göncz's friends. Tibor Hám, István Csicsery-Rónay and those who emigrated to the US between 1947 and 1948 [in the wake of the dissolution] of the Smallholders' Party invited us . . . Hám waited for us at Washington Airport and from that point, we had a wonderful time there for two months. Hám took us to [various events] organised by American–Hungarian associations . . . and this was the first big gathering we had had together since [after 1948].
(Joint interview with Göncz and Göntér, 10 January 2008)

In this way, by recording Göncz's answers to each detailed question inspired by my field work and cross-checking the information with published sources as well as with those who had known him, I was able to frame the research themes for the book presented here. It transpired that the research could be broadly classified into two main analytical themes: the development of Göncz's political beliefs during his early years and the ten years of his presidency. Moreover, it became clear to me that Göncz's presidency is definitively the main focus of the research. This is not simply because his presidency is the major gap in the literature to be addressed, but also beacuse it was through his presidency that Göncz ultimately embodied his political beliefs. A set of important events and issues with which Göncz dealt during the term of his presidency are thus selected, arranged and critically assessed against his desire to pursue his political beliefs. In so doing, this enables us to analyse Göncz's actions in the presidential role in the context of the time at which they were undertaken and assess them within a coherent framework. Having set the central themes and main questions of the research, it is necessary to discuss the key framework and its methods.

Underpinned by established, biographical research as earlier mentioned in relation to Chamberlayne *et al.* (2000) and Gough (2006), this book examines Göncz's life chronologically, as his political development cannot be understood fully in isolation from the time and the context in which he lived. Roberts notes that: Lives have to be understood . . . as lived within time and time is experienced according to narrative. Narratives – of past, present [and] future – are the means by which biographical experience is given an understandable shape (2002: 123).

Thus, a chronological framework leads us to reconstruct Göncz's life as it related to social and historical processes through which he lived. The intention of the research, however, is not to narrate every detail as determined by slavish adherence to a time line. This is a *political* biography of Göncz with particular concentration on his presidential role and activity and its implications for the understanding of post-Communist politics in Hungary. Given the focus of the research, details of Göncz's non-political activities and any other background information will only be presented where appropriate as additional to his intellectual and political developments. For this reason, his literary work, primarily based upon the translation of American and English literature, is not dealt with in detail in this book.[5]

Text-based data

During my preliminary research (July–August 2006) and the subsequent field work conducted in Budapest (2 May 2007–10 February 2008), a considerable amount of documentation relating to the research topic was gathered. Video and audio media, leaflets, manuscripts, magazines, archives and, above all, newspaper articles relating to Göncz and other useful background materials were systematically collected, analysed and utilised for the research. The four major Hungarian dailies – *Magyar Hírlap*, *Magyar Nemzet*, *Népszabadság* and *Népszava* – were the major sources of information, but other relevant Hungarian periodicals (as listed in the bibliography) were also scrutinised. Given the different political orientations of each newspaper, I endeavoured to collect newspaper articles while, at the same time, taking the political leanings of the papers into account. Over the course of my archival research, however, it soon became apparent that a comprehensive treatment of the newspapers would not be viable. This was partially because of the internal procedures which are routinely carried out when requesting newspapers in archives and libraries but, primarily, because of the sheer amount of material in circulation.[6] It transpired that there were an enormous number of articles published in periodicals pertaining to the subject of my research.[7] In order to deal with these articles effectively, material which fitted into the set of themes upon which this research was based was selected and collected during the field work period. Overall, the press data provided me with valuable background information which formed the basis for identification of the main issues and events on the Hungarian political scene and therefore laid the basis for the formulation of research questions for the subsequent interviews.

In addition to the press data, archives that directly and indirectly related to Göncz were located in the major archival centres of Budapest: the Hungarian National Archive, the Open Society Archives and the Institute for the History of the 1956 Hungarian Revolution. The Historical Archives of the Hungarian State Security were, however, inaccessible for my research,[8] and some of documentation concerned with Göncz's imprisonment and dissident activities of the 1980s could not be obtained. Similarly, the Library of the Presidential Office which holds an array of original documents composed by Göncz and his successors was not – and is still not – accessible to researchers for ethical and security reasons.[9] Consequently, Göncz's personal documents which include letters, notes, memoranda, speeches and any other writings, could not be obtained. Despite these restrictions, the Oral History of Göncz held in the 1956 Institute provided essential information regarding Göncz's life and his political development; this source was examined in depth and employed as the primary source for my research. Additionally, speeches written by Göncz were compiled in the book entitled *Göncz Árpád: Sodrásban* and later published in an English edition under the title of *Árpád Göncz in Midstream* (see Göncz, 2004a, b). In order to examine Göncz's thoughts as they were expressed in the speeches that he delivered, these publications were used as additional important sources.

Narrative analysis

The main analytical tool for interpreting textual data utilised in this book was narrative analysis. This research approach is 'concerned with the search for and analysis of the stories' that subjects tell in order to try to understand their life and 'the world around them' (Bryman, 2004: 412), and it has been employed for the reasons that follow. First, narrative analysis is advantageous for looking at an individual's life experience as a unified whole and it allows the researcher to set their analysis within the context that their subject lived and experienced their life; it is for this reason that the method was considered appropriate for the purposes of interpreting Göncz's views and experiences and reconstructing the inner world that he envisaged. Josselson and Lieblich note that:

> Narrative approaches to understanding bring [the] researcher more closely into the investigative process than do quantitative and statistical methods. Through narratives, we come in contact with our participants as people engaged in the process of interpreting themselves. We work then with what is said and what is not said, within the context in which life is lived and the context of the interview in which words are spoken to represent that life.
>
> (1995: ix)

Second, narrative analysis is beneficial for eliciting insights regarding a subject's life experiences and the meaning that they give to these experiences. Mitchell captures the fundamental utility of the narrative approach for the social and natural sciences concisely: 'the study of narrative is no longer the province of literary specialists or folklorists borrowing their terms from psychology and linguistics but has now become a positive source of insight for all the branches of human and natural science' (Mitchell, 1981: 9–10). As Caine notes, 'the most important contribution of biography to history is the insight that it offers into the lives and thought of significant individuals' (Caine, 2010: 1); thus, narrative analysis which highlights the importance of incisiveness is apposite to this type of biographical research.

However, this is not to suggest that narrative analysis is not without disadvantages. As Roberts points out, narrative analysis has weaknesses in terms of 'quantification, generalisability, hypothesis-testing and validity and objectivity' (Roberts, 2002: 117). Thus if the focus of study is concerned to any great extent with the replicability of finding, narrative analysis may not be an appropriate research method. Despite these limitations, as Wisniewski and Hatch note, in addition to the positivist scientific research methods which stress the importance of standardisability and replicability of data, one of the alternative ways to find the truth is to 'go beyond the standardised notion of reliability, validity and generalizability' that is established in the tradition of quantitative research (Wisniewski and Hatch,

1995: 128). Therefore, the use of narrative analysis in this biographical study is justifiable.

Elite interviewing

In addition to narrative analysis for scrutiny of text-based data, in-depth interviews with the elite who were directly or indirectly involved in politics and knew Göncz personally were conducted. The semi-structured interview is employed in this research, because it is not only advantageous for interviewers to 'exercise some form of control' during the interview (Robert, 1998: 4), but also gives interviewees leeway to respond to questions and prioritise themes and raise issues important to them (Bryman, 2004: 321; Peabody *et al.*, 1990: 452). The selection of interviewees was made largely based upon three elite groups in society – politicians, academics and journalists – who had first-hand experience and expertise in history, law, politics, economics and who were familiar with Göncz. This sampling was purposeful rather than representative, as it cannot be said that my select interviewees represented the majority opinion, perceptions, beliefs or the values and knowledge of the institutions to which they belonged. Despite this limitation, such interviewing has strengths and advantages which are central to this research. The elite interview is suitable for eliciting insights into events and issues that were little known to the general public and for the enrichment of the quality of information that could be obtained in any other form of published resource (Lilleker, 2003: 208; Peabody, *et al.*, 1990: 454; Richards, 1996: 200; Robert, 1998: 5). As stated above, certain sections of archival resources on Göncz were subject to access restrictions, thus interviewing elites was considered and employed as an alternative method for gaining access to relevant information and opinions where necessary.

It is necessary to mention a number of disadvantages and limitations that are associated with interviewing elites and possible ways to address the issues concerned. First, there is the question of power relations between the researcher and the interviewee. As Richards points out, 'by the very nature of elite interviews, it is the interviewee who has the power' and controls 'the information the interviewer is trying to eke out' (Richards, 1996: 201). Insufficiently well prepared researchers would find it difficult to engage in discussion and to establish a good rapport with interviewees. Second, there is the issue of reliability in elite interviewing. Interviews are subjective in nature and in terms of interviewees' position, they are under no obligation 'to be objective and to tell [interviewers] the truth' at all time (Berry, 2002: 680). In fact, in the extreme instances, interviewing is counterproductive to research as interviewees 'may deliberately set out to mislead or falsify an issue or event' in question (Richards, 1996: 201).

With these caveats and guidelines in mind, I tried to address the issues of elite interviewing in following way. In an attempt to reduce the power differential between myself and the selected elites, prior to conducting an interview, I undertook thorough background research on my interviewee and their area of speciality. The main interview questions were formulated in accordance with the discoveries of this prior research and these were put forward during the interview with particular attention paid to the way in which questions related to Göncz. For example, legal experts were asked more specific questions regarding the constitutional and legal issues that arose during Göncz's presidency. As Dexter notes, building up a decent level of background knowledge should precede elite interviews in order for it to be successful (Dexter, 1970: 20). Similarly, to address the question of reliability, information provided by my respondents was cross-checked with published resources. In the event that relevant information was not available in the form of documentation, the same questions were raised with other interviewees in an attempt to further verify the given data. In this way, to some extent, I was able to address some of the issues that arise in elite interviewing and, in total, 52 interviews were completed over the course of my field work. On average, the interviews lasted between thirty minutes and one hour. All respondents who agreed to be interviewed were extremely helpful in providing me with valuable opinions, counter-opinions, judgements on and insights into the issues and events in Hungarian politics in which Göncz became involved. While they differed considerably in their views and in their attitudes toward Göncz, there was also a certain convergence in their opinions. I found interviewing to be a useful and effective research method for data generation.

Ethical considerations

Ethics, the primary concern of which is to protect individual rights from any sort of transgressions caused by research (Bryman, 2004: 509), are a key issue to be addressed before, during and after conducting field work. Given that my research project involved interviewee participants, before conducting my field work, I applied for ethical approval from the Departmental Ethical Committee. Approval was granted with the guideline of ethical principles, which I read carefully.[10] The most important aspect of these guidelines in relation to my project concerned the requirement to gain informed consent from my potential interviewees and to provide them with essential information regarding my project and their entitlements and rights regarding their involvement in, or non-participation in, the research. With this in mind, I made contact with my interviewees on an individual basis (primarily through e-mail) and informed them of the basis for my research project and their rights therein. Some respondents refused to be interviewed (the majority of these were the current representatives of the Alliance of Young Democrats and Civic Party) and, in certain cases, the interviewees who initially agreed to be interviewed changed their minds before the interview. Overall, however, the vast majority of my respondents were willing to give interviews and, in fact, some of them undertook the role of gatekeeper and helped me to secure subsequent interviews (for example, Göncz himself). On the condition that interview materials would be used exclusively for my research project, no interviewee objected to their words being quoted and none requested anonymity.[11]

The overview of the book

This book is composed of six chapters and broadly divided into two parts. The first part of the book is composed of three background chapters that examine the processes through which Göncz's political beliefs were developed. His first hand experiences in the Second World War, the 1956 Hungarian Revolution and the political transition of 1989 are selected as the focus of analysis, as they were the key events in which Göncz not only became involved, but they were also those which contributed to his intellectual and political development. Having examined these factors which contributed to shaping his political beliefs, the second part of the book is devoted to exploring the main characteristics of Göncz's presidency by examining his role, actions and decisions that he undertook during the decade of his presidency.

Chapter 1 explores the early years of Göncz's life and the development of his political outlook. Göncz's family background, education, peer group and other social movements in which Göncz became involved and with which he interacted are examined as the basis for understanding his political origins. The focus of investigation is upon identifying the key factors for the early development of his political beliefs. The inter-war years' democratic organisation known as the Pál Teleki Work Group, his first hand experience of struggle against the Nazis, his involvement in one of the key social movements of the 1930s, the so-called peasant populism, and his first political activity in the Independent Smallholders' Party are examined in depth, as they were the most important activities that Göncz undertook at this time.

Chapter 2 examines Göncz's first-hand experience of the 1956 Hungarian Revolution and his time in prison and thereafter. Where Chapter 1 examined the key factors shaping Göncz's early political leanings, Chapter 2 goes on to trace his first-hand experience of the Revolution and its impact on his political development. Göncz's motivations for involvement in the resistance that followed the suppression of the Revolution and his views on and interpretation of the significance of this movement are investigated in depth. This examination leads us to understand the proactive role and activities that Göncz undertook during the resistance and why he retrospectively defended the memory of the Revolution during his imprisonment.

Chapter 3 continues the exploration of Göncz's political development during which he participated in dissident movements in the late 1980s. The focus of investigation is upon Göncz's thoughts on and his interpretation of the changing social and political circumstances and the process through which his political beliefs were developed at this time. The chapter examines the significance of Göncz's involvement in the dissident movements in terms of the development of his political views and his career at this time.

Chapter 4 critically reviews the process through which the presidency was established. This includes an examination of political bargaining, the actual negotiations among the political elites as they exerted their vested interests during the national Round Table Talks and negotiations that followed thereafter. Given that these political negotiations were *de facto* a key to shaping the main attributes of the presidency and their results were codified in the Constitution, the chapter analyses the presidential competences through scrutinising the Constitution itself. This examination leads us to understand the president's position in Hungary's political system and provides an essential background to the context in which Göncz interpreted and exercised his vested constitutional powers during the term of his presidency.

Having examined the main characteristics of the presidency, Chapters 5 and 6 explore the way in which Göncz interpreted his constitutional powers and fulfilled the presidency. The decisions and actions that Göncz undertook during the decade of his presidency are critically assessed against a framework provided by a set of issues and events with which he became involved. Motivations for his involvement in dealing with important transitional issues and events are investigated, particularly in connection with his desire to pursue his liberal political values. This investigation leads us to understand why Göncz intervened in certain governmental matters and attempted to influence politics. Ultimately, the chapters question the consistency of his values and explore their significance for an understanding of Hungarian politics.

In what follows I will address the first and second research questions through an exploration of the early years of Göncz's life and his intellectual and political development. The final question then will be addressed through an examination of the way in which Göncz sought to realise his liberal political beliefs.

Part I
The development of Göncz's political views

1 Beginnings

This chapter charts and examines the development of Göncz's political views over the course of his adolescence and early adulthood. First, the influences of family, peer group, education and other social environments in which Göncz grew up, and with which he interacted, are examined. These are assessed in terms of their influence on the development of his social and political views. As noted by Károly Vígh, the Hungarian biographer of Endre Bajcsy-Zsilinszky, 'the social environment in which one has grown up is one of the most important elements of influence and it determines one's later life choices' (Vígh, 1992: 8).

Second, the chapter seeks to examine the impact that the democratic social organisation, known as the Pál Teleki Work Group, and one of the key social movements of 1930s – peasant populism – had on the shaping of Göncz's political beliefs. Iván Vitányi, a veteran of anti-fascist movements and an old friend of Göncz's, notes that:

> The awakening of Göncz's political idea [occurred] not in his workplace, but in the circles, groups and movements in which he had conscientiously participated. The first, and perhaps the most important, was the Pál Teleki Work Group . . . Next, interconnected with this, there was the influence of populist writers [. . .].
>
> (Vitányi, 2002).

Third, Göncz's experience in the fight against the autocratic rule of the age and the influence of Hungarian intellectuals are considered in connection with his intellectual and political development. In an interview with Kossuth radio in 1993, Göncz specifically mentioned 'my experience of fighting against Nazi inhumanity' as one of the main factors explaining the liberal political views he later adopted (Wsinger and László, 1994: 71). Concerning the political impact on his thinking of the Hungarian intellectuals who laid the foundation for Hungary's democracy, in his presidential inaugural address, Göncz revealed:

> I am thinking of such guardians . . . Béla Kovács, the one-time general secretary of the Smallholders' Party, kidnapped and held prisoner for years in the

Gulag . . . István Bibó, the embodiment of the noblest democratic ideals, of Christian tolerance and patriotism and the independence of a true citizen.

(Tóth, 1999: 19–20)

Examining these multiple explanatory factors will enable us to see the process through which Göncz's political beliefs developed and later informed his term as the first post-Communist president of Hungary.

Thus, sections 1 and 2 of the chapter explore the effect that Göncz's immediate family and peer groups had on the formation of his political ideas. The subsequent two sections then examine the impact of Göncz's first hand experience in the armed student resistance movements and, that of social movements or idea elaborated by the so-called 'populist writers'. The remainder of the chapter examines Göncz's first political activity, his role in the Independent Smallholders' Party and Kovács's influence on his political development.

1.1. The early years

Árpád Göncz was born on 10 February 1922 in Budapest to Lajos Göncz and Ilona Heimann (Hegedűs, 1985). The Göncz family originally hailed from Csáktornya in Zala county, southern Hungary. Göncz's great-great-grandfather worked as a pharmacist in Csáktornya, where he later participated in the 1848 Revolution, serving in the Zala Battalion (Wisinger and László, 2007: 14). Originally, he was an officer in the military of the Austrian Emperor but, during the Revolution, he changed sides and began supporting the idea of Hungarian independence (Hegedűs, 1985). Injured in the battle of Vág, Göncz's great-great grandfather was imprisoned for nine years after the defeat of the Revolution (Wisinger and László, 1994: 6–7). In one of his essays Göncz described his predecessor as an anonymous hero who facilitated the laying of the foundations of modern Hungarian democracy:

> In 1956, people rose up and the revolution broke out. It was inseparably linked to the spirit of anonymous Hungarians who fought in 1848. When my great-great grandfather [fought] against the Austrian [monarchy], he fought for our country's independence. He paved the way for the first democratic Republic of Hungary.
>
> (Göncz, 1991: 7)

The above extract suggests that Göncz's great-great grandfather's story remained a source of pride in Göncz's memory. Göncz foregrounds the continuity of the democratic ethos between two pivotal revolutions in Hungary's modern history, taking pride in his great-great grandfather's participation in the 1848 Revolution. In fact, when discussing the matter in interview in 2006, Göncz confirmed the assertion that, despite the fact that he had little information on his great-great grandfather (other than knowing of his participation in the battle and his subsequent imprisonment), his influence on Göncz's political outlook was important.

Göncz:	Originally, he was a pharmacist . . . later joined the Zalai Battalion. He was injured in the battle but I do not know where he was imprisoned. I do not have precise information on this. I cannot confirm it.
Kim:	Are you saying that your great-great grandfather's story did not affect you?
Göncz:	Well, *everyone [including him] who fought [in the battle] influenced me* [. . .]

(Interview with Göncz, 18 June 2006, my emphasis)

Göncz's mother, Ilona Heimann, was born in the small village of Tusty in the southern part of Transylvania (currently this territory lies in Romania). Her father was Jewish and her mother came from Székely, an ethnic Hungarian region in Transylvania. The cause of her parents' death is unknown, but Heimann lost them both at the same time. Initially she was sent to an orphanage but was soon placed in foster care with the Báthy family. According to Göncz, the Báthy family had a good educational background and a social democratic disposition (Hegedűs, 1985). They made a living from the wood and textile trades until the end of the First World War. With the conclusion of the Treaty of Trianon,[1] the Báthy family fled to Pest where Heimann met with her future spouse, Lajos Göncz. Thereafter, Heimann settled in Pest permanently; she never took paid employment, but instead dedicated herself to caring for Lajos and their son, Árpád Göncz.

Information on Lajos Göncz is scant. He was the youngest child and only son in a family of five children, as a result of which (according to Göncz), he was spoiled by his parents. Initially, Lajos was a postman but later became one of the best tennis players in Hungary and even wrote a tennis instruction manual (Papp, 2002). When Göncz turned six, Lajos divorced his wife. After the divorce, Heimann and her son lived in Lajos' parents' house. The time spent living with his father's parents, however, was not the basis of pleasant memories for Göncz. Heimann had not been treated like a member of the family.

> In reality, my mother never became an independent person. We lived in my father's parents' house, and this was a very bitter situation. My mother was always considered to be a second-rate family member. This hurt her and she could not overcome this obstacle. This burden also [affected] me.
>
> (Hegedűs, 1985)

This suggests that the way in which Heimann was treated by her ex-husband and his parents laid the foundation for a lifelong remoteness between father and son. In fact, Göncz expressed strong feelings of dislike for his father noting that:

> 'In general, one takes after one's father. [But], I have a hatred of my father . . . For me, the role of father does not mean authority. My father was a source of pain to me . . . There was no intimate, close and loving relationship between us'.
>
> (Hegedűs, 1985)

18 The development of Göncz's political views

Thus, it is hardly surprising that Göncz did not wish to resemble his father and, consequently, Lajos Göncz's role in shaping his son's political views was marginal. Heimann's influence is, however, acknowledged. Göncz confirmed this position in his response to my questions about his mother's influence on his future ideas and political beliefs.

Kim: It is known that during one's adolescence, parents, teachers and friends have important impacts on shaping one's ideas. Could you tell me how your parents affected the development of your ideas? In particular, how influential were they on your political ideas?

Göncz: In terms of political view, their impact on me was modest . . . My mother's influence [remained] *in all aspects*, but my father was mainly abroad. I can say my father's impact was insignificant. My nature was similar to my father's *but I consciously followed, and still follow my mother's example.*

(Interview with Göncz, 18 June 2006, my emphasis)

Given the absence of intimacy between Göncz and his father, Göncz's comments regarding his mother's influence might derive from his affection for her. Thus Göncz's apolitical mother's sense of decency and kindness is what ultimately seems to have embedded itself in his politics.

In 1932, after the completion of four years' primary schooling, Göncz began his secondary education at the *Werbőczy Gimnazium* and, during his eight years' of education that Göncz undertook at the *Werbőczy*, he joined in Boy Scouts activities. Hungary was at the forefront of the Boy Scout movement at this time. Since the translation of Lord Baden-Powell's *Scouting for Boys* had been published in 1909 (Ablonczy, 2006: 131), the idea of scouting had taken hold in Hungary. From 1909 onwards, the number of Scout troops rapidly increased and by 1930, the International Scout Bureau and other associated organisations had been founded.[2] In 1933, Hungary hosted the fourth World Jamboree which took place at Gödöllő, a small city 11 miles away from the capital. While the scouting movement regards its role as one of forging good and well-rounded citizens from adolescent men as dictated in the founding precepts of the Movement,[3] for Göncz participation in scouting had a different significance. Scouting opened Göncz's eyes to social reality, particularly with regard to the problems of the poor peasantry.

The thing which determined the way of thinking for the entirety of Hungarian youth was the demand for land reform and peasant radicalism . . . We knew the necessity of land reform at the age of 14 or 15; we came to know the poverty of the peasantry. Through camping, we – the children who came from cities – encountered the [lives] of villages. This [scouting] was really a determining [factor].[4]

The given account does not present us with the solid context in which the Hungarian peasants lived, let alone the meaning of 'peasant radicalism'. However, the urban peer group to which Göncz belonged and with which he interacted, shared experience in and knowledge of the situation in Hungary's rural society. For Göncz, it is evident that his scouting experience functioned as an influence which awakened his political ideas and social sensibility. Göncz's wife, Zsuzsánna Göntér, noted this significance thus:

> Ultimately, in the days of his youth, his social and political interest came from the Boy Scout Movement. This was the time before the Second World War, when the German threat was beginning to take shape . . . During the time when he was going to secondary school, the awakening of his political ideas took place in the Boy Scout Movement. After that, when he was a university student, this happened in the Pál Teleki Work Group.
> (Joint interview with Göncz and Göntér, 10 January 2008)

Göntér's observation underscores the fact that Göncz's participation in the Boy Scouts was crucial in increasing his political and social awareness. Although this does not provide us with concrete information regarding the Pál Teleki Work Group (PTWG), during the early stage of Göncz's adolescence, his scouting experience and later work in the PTWG were pivotal for the shaping of his political outlook. Moreover, it is likely that Göncz's joining the PTWG was not coincidental. Having discovered some common ground or continuity between his scouting experience and the PTWG, Göncz may have decided to join the latter. Substantiation of this reasoning is in the subject of the next section of this chapter, in which I examine the main characteristics of the PTWG, and ask what it meant for the development of Göncz's political ideas.

1.2. The Pál Teleki Work Group (*Teleki Pál Munkaközösség*)

The PTWG was formed in the autumn of 1936 by Piarists (Papp, 2002: 3),[5] who organised a series of social seminars for university students. The seminar was intended to foster a future leadership which would hold a certain world view and uphold a certain sense of morality. Count Pál Teleki was the programme's chief supporter; he envisioned that the direction of and initiative for the lives of Hungarians would not come from politicians, but from society itself (Lukács, 1992: 57). Enlightening the Hungarian population became the PTWG's main goal; national education was considered the key means through which a good social basis for future leadership could be nurtured. A good knowledge of Hungarian history, geography and a sense of responsibility towards family, friends, community and nation were seen as essential to the preservation of Hungarianness (*Magyarság*) (Mészáros, 1993: 57–64). The PTWG was intended to play the part of educational provider or forum where university students could gather to discuss various social issues that Hungary faced at the time. According to Göntér, the discussions centred on issues which affected the poor Hungarian peasantry and possible remedies. Göntér recalled: 'The PTWG was one of the programmes [which sought] a political solution to the problem of agricultural poverty and the poverty of rural peasants' (joint interview with Göncz and Göntér, 10 January 2008). The PTWG also had links to the National Alliance of People's Colleges,[6] which functioned as an educational provider for peasant children, and was intended to provide a platform for ingress into the intelligentsia.

In 1941, the PTWG expanded its membership through the absorption of leading politicians and their associations into its organisational structure. One prominent historian, Gyula Szekfű, and key figures from the Independent Smallholders' Party (ISP), József Bognár and Endre Bajcsy-Zsilinszky joined the PTWG at this time. In the following year, a draft of the Self-Education Programme for the members of the PTWG was also composed. The Programme's main objective was the realisation of the basic founding principle: to help young intellectuals identify various social problems that Hungary was experiencing and to find adequate solutions for them (Lukács, 1992: 58).

After the German invasion of Budapest on 19 March 1944, the PTWG widened its purview. It was no longer just a discussion forum, but also joined other civic resistance movements to fight the Nazi occupation. The vice-president of the PTWG, István Csicsery-Rónay, circulated an underground newspaper, while another member of the PTWG, Pál Játzkó, directed sabotage against Nazi Germany. At this time, Göncz also participated in students' armed resistance movements as a member of the PTWG (discussed in Section 1.3).

With the end of the Second World War, the PTWG was reorganised as the Democratic Alliance of Hungarian Intellectuals (DAHI). The DAHI issued a manifesto and drew up a new action plan. According to the manifesto, the DAHI's main objective was the mobilisation of Hungarian intellectuals in the expectation that they would play a key role in reconstructing democratic Hungarian society. The manifesto proclaimed:

> Hungarian Intellectuals! To build a new society, enormous work awaits you . . . It is you who must reconstruct, organise and lead destroyed Hungarian industry. It is you who must undertake the education of a new generation.
> Let your expertise flourish for the reconstruction of new Hungary.
> Workers and peasants! Fight and arbitrate against the oppression of the fascists for an independent, sovereign Hungary; for democratic human rights; for the freedom of religion and consciousness; for land reform [. . .].[7]

To realise these aims, plans which set out the individual intellectual tasks which, together, would result in the successful fulfilment of DAHI's manifesto pledges were formulated. For instance, multilateral talks held with people of various social backgrounds contributed to enriching the mutual understanding and knowledge of the DAHI's membership. Those who had an expertise in foreign policy were assigned the task of formulating the DAHI's syllabus on the topic;[8] as a result, a comprehensive course on foreign policy and, subsequently, a professional lecturing panel were set up.[9] The foreign minister himself, János Gyöngyösi, gave the opening lecture on 25 May 1945 (*Kis Újság*, 26 May 1945; *Kossuth Népe*, 27 May 1945; *Népszava*, 27 May 1945; *Szabad Szó*, 27 May 1945).

In addition to serving as a key organ of education and building the social basis for a democratic Hungary, the DAHI played a role on the conventional political stage. This was demonstrably realised when the central leaders of DAHI joined the ISP. The chairman of the DAHI, Tibor Hám, became the general secretary of the Political Committee of the ISP,[10] while the vice-president of the DAHI, Csiszery-Rónay, was in charge of the Department of Foreign Affairs within it (Saláta, 1989: 100). According to Lukács, one of the most important activities that the DAHI performed was the preparation for the municipal election in Budapest and the general election (Lukács, 1992: 62). At this time, Göncz also joined the ISP, where he served as secretary to the general secretary of the party, Béla Kovács (discussed in Section 1.5).

Despite successfully negotiating the transition to the national political stage, between 1947 and 1948, the DAHI, along with other political forces, was forced to dissolve. It was at this time that Communists came to power in Hungary, employing so-called 'divide and rule tactics' (*szalámi taktika*) to eliminate their political opponents. Most members of the DAHI's leadership were arrested and either sent to prison or compelled to leave the country in connection with an alleged conspiracy against 'the Republic of Hungary' (discussed in Section 1.5). As Göncz eloquently asserted, the PTWG (later DAHI) which existed during and after the inter-war period, 'fought for an independent and democratic Hungary with pen and sword' (Lukács, 1992: 64), but neither instrument protected the organisation from oblivion.

The PTWG thus laid an intellectual foundation and paved the way for Göncz's subsequent political development. In his personal Oral History, Göncz recounted what the PTWG meant for him:

> I identified [myself] in spirit and practice with the PTWG. For one thing, this was the only group to have perfected its ideas of a democratic system of institutions, to have a tangible history of resistance and hold specific notions of democratic transformation and its methods, consequences, popular basis and system of law and education. We had been working on this for years, thrashing it out. Reading the ideas of the 1945 PTWG today, they may seem naive and ill-expressed, but there's nothing in them I could not espouse now.
>
> (Tóth, 2009)

This suggests that the PTWG laid the fundamental foundation for Hungary's democratic transformation. Göncz is clearly of the view that the PTWG's political ideals are not obsolete but have a contemporary relevance. In particular, the way in which the PTWG strove for their political ideals during the inter-war period remained – and remains – a significant legacy for him. While the extract above does not detail the way in which the PTWG had an influence on the shaping of Göncz's political beliefs, Göncz certainly shared (and still shares) its founding ideas. In essence, Göncz asserted that he was able to expand his world view through his participation in the PTWG discussion forum:

22 The development of Göncz's political views

> The PTWG was the creature of the Boy Scout squad arising out of the liberal political movement and activity of the old Piarist students. The executive consisted of Tibor Hám, Pál Jaczkó, and Kálmán Saláta . . . [It] had an outlook very close to me in its efforts towards universality, its openness . . . It was organised quite democratically, with free debate and a constant flow of information from educated people . . . who were clearly expecting a German defeat when the war broke out . . . The whole thing, with its liberalism and openness came as a kind of refreshment to me.
>
> (Tóth, 2009)

The extract above highlights the fact that the central atmosphere Göncz encountered in the PTWG was free, democratic and open. Göncz felt that the PTWG served not only as a venue where intellectuals gathered to share available information, but also as a forum in which cultivated people vigorously debated the future of the country. Political and social problems of the age, including Hungary's engagement in the Second World War, were dealt with in the PTWG discussions. According to Göncz's account, the forum seemed to have been organised in such a way as to create a constructive ground in which independent thinking and progressive ideas could be fermented. Indeed, in an interview with György Litván, Göncz reaffirmed the reasoning that the PTWG was not only significant in his intellectual advancement but also in his subsequent political developments.

Litván: In 1945, you worked at the ISP as a parliamentary secretary. Was this the beginning of your political career?

Göncz: No. The beginning was when I was a university student, which means [at] the PTWG. The older [generation] of the PTWG constituted the so-called centre [force] of the ISP, which Béla Kovács and Béla Varga formed. I worked for Béla Kovács.

Litván: So, the beginning of your political career was not bound to a party but to a place in which your intellectualism originated.

Göncz: Yes. It was the PTWG that endeavoured to find a solution to the country's problems and sought democracy. Even today I accept all the ideas that we adopted there. [When] I read old pieces on the PTWG's works, they are still moving for me. They were composed by those people who had nothing to do with power anywhere on earth . . . In its spirituality, there were [elements] of experience in [our generation]: Christianity, the acceptance of democracy and the sense of social responsibility . . . It embraced the important elements of liberalism, the sense of Hungarianness, Europeanness and Christianity.

(4 × 4, 1997)

In view of this, it can be argued that the PTWG played a central role in the foundation of Göncz's intellectual and political development. As was established in Section 1.1 of this chapter, during Göncz's adolescence, if his scouting experience was momentous for arousing his political and social consciousness, it was the PTWG that contributed to the shaping of his democratic ideas thereafter. Evidence of such a connection was seen through the establishment of four values that Göncz embraced at this stage in his life, in which the PTWG had an enduring impact on his political beliefs. Having noted the PTWG's significance to Göncz's democratic beliefs, especially with reference to his first political career in the ISP, the role and activities that Göncz undertook in this party will be discussed. Before embarking on this task, the following section of the chapter explores the democratic activities in which Göncz was engaged in the student resistance movements.

1.3. Resistance: the Freedom Front of Hungarian Students

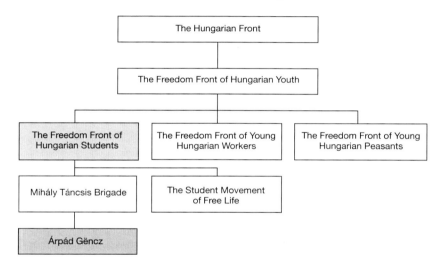

The Freedom Front of Hungarian Students (FFHS) was officially formed on 7 November 1944 under the joint leadership of László Kardos, Sándor Kiss, Tibor Zimányi, Ferenc Szűcs, Imre Farkas, György Szabó and Péter Pintér.[11] They all signed the FFHS's founding manifesto (Kiss and Vitányi, 1983: 100). Initially the FFHS was not a sub-unit of armed resistance but, under the command of the Hungarian Front, it was subsequently transformed into an underground armed resistance group. The Hungarian Front (HF) constituted leaders of the left-wing political parties which had been disbanded under the fascist Szalási regime (Kontler, 2002: 384).[12] The Front was the prime association of those aiming to unify and direct the various underground resistance groups which existed at this time (Romsics, 1999: 213, 2005: 546). For example, the presidents of the Smallholders' Party and the Social Democrats, Zoltán Tildy and Árpád Szakasits, were the leaders of the HF (Feitl and Kende, 2007: 199–200). In its manifesto, the HF called for national unity and for the creation of an independent, peaceful and democratic Hungary:

In the most crucial time of our history, we speak [before] the nation. The German conqueror smashed our country. Our lives, freedom, nation and the fate of future Hungarian generations are at risk . . . We feel great responsibility for the fate of our country and for the perpetuation of our nation. . . . We create the unit for the fight for Hungarian freedom – the Hungarian Front. The [aims] of the HF [are as follows]: the expulsion of the German conquerors and their accomplices, peace with the allies, [to] lay the foundations for the basis of free and democratic Hungary.

(Romsics, 2000: 62–4)

The main task assigned to the Freedom Front of Hungarian Youth (FFHY), a sub-unit of the HF, was to coordinate the unorganised and sporadic student resistance movements. However, the FFHY's coordinating role did not function as intended. Different sub-groups conceived different strategies of extrication from the war and this was particularly true in respect to the differing approaches proposed for fighting against the German occupiers. Furthermore, members of the sub-groups had varied political orientations meaning that each association wished to develop political affiliations with different parties. For instance, both the Győrffy College students (*Győrffy Kollégium*)[13] and the Movement of Student Unity (*A Diák Egység Mozgalom*) positioned themselves on the left of the political spectrum. Yet the former had links to the Communists and Social Democrats, whereas the latter preferred to build their affiliations with the Smallholders (Kiss and Vitányi, 1983: 104–9). Thus, although the different groups were tentatively unified and coordinated through their allegiance to organisations higher up in the organisational hierarchy of resistance movements, once anti-Nazi sentiment was removed from the equation they were politically incompatible. In Deák's terms, the anti-German resistance movement was 'a small movement consisting of a few hundred individuals from the most varied political backgrounds, [and, moreover] their fundamental differences could barely be bridged by their common determination to oppose the Germans' (Deák, 1995: 210).

The Mihály Táncsis Brigade (MTB), one of the sub-groups in the resistance movement to which Göncz belonged, was founded in December 1944 (Kiss and Vitányi, 1983: 122–3). At this time, Horthy's Regency was still in control of the conservative Hungarian government, and during this period (March 1920–November 1944), a paramilitary unit, known as the *Levente*, operated in Hungary. Young male students between the ages of 12 and 21 were required to participate in regular military exercises or physical training.[14] The intended goal of the programme was to equip them with basic military skills in an attempt to complement and augment the country's self-defence system (Kontler, 2002: 357–8). As the Treaty of Trianon banned Hungary from forming a national army, the Hungarian government introduced this Levente system in an attempt to overcome the limits which had been placed it in this regard. The Levente was later transformed into a paramilitary unit which was renamed the National Guard (*Nemzetőr*) (Kiss and Vitányi, 1983: 123). The National Guard was composed of different units constituted from university students. József Várhelyi, a medical student at the Budapest Sciences

University, was appointed as one of the captains during the Lakatos government (between 29 August 1944 and 16 October 1944).[15] Similarly, Kálmán Szenpétery was chosen a captain of the Economics Faculty of the Budapest Engineering University. Under orders from the leadership of the HF to form a unified structure, on 1 December 1944, these two captains decided to amalgamate the two groups into one unit, creating the MTB (Kiss and Vitányi, 1983: 124).

The founding of the MTB was important to Göncz at this time since he deserted his military posting and joined this student resistance group instead. Göncz had been conscripted into the Hungarian army after the German occupation began (Göncz's interview with Bartok Radio, 12 July 2002), but had been exempt from enlistment while he attended university. Upon the completion of his studies, he was drafted into and later deployed by the 25th Reserve Mountain Infantry Battalion (Hegedűs, 1985). At the time of Göncz's deployment, the Red Army had already crossed the border of Eastern Front and Göncz's regiment was given an order to retreat to Germany but, realising that neither his conscience nor his military pledge would allow him to leave the country, Göncz soon decamped from his barracks (Papp, 2002). Göncz stated:

> I took an oath to myself, because as I see it, one should not leave one's country when the country is in trouble. It is only acceptable to leave your country when your country is doing well . . . With a rifle and a hand grenade, I set off in the opposite direction [to Budapest].
> (Wisinger and László, 1994: 13)

Upon his return to Budapest, Göncz joined the MTB with the help of his friend, Miklós Szűr, a former member of the PTWP.

According to MTB records, Göncz belonged to the first platoon led by Tamás Székely. The majority of the First Platoon's members were from the Arts and Law Faculties of Budapest University and particularly, they were students of Eötvös College, and the Horthy Dormitory. The First Platoon (members of which called themselves 'Leprosy') was always in the vanguard of any action; its members assumed risky and difficult tasks, such as stealing weapons from the Nazis and helping to acquire identity cards for refugees (Kiss and Vitányi, 1983: 127). Göncz himself participated in an operation to disarm the local military unit of the Arrow Cross in Rákos Hill (Göncz's interview with Bartok Radio, 12 July 2002).[16] Göncz reminisced about the time:

> We returned to the Rákos Hill and there, in collaboration with the illegal [cell] of the Communist Party, we liberated one village. Along with two 17-year-old boys, I stole weapons from the house of the Arrow Cross . . . I was injured and one comrade was killed.[17]

Göncz's involvement in this movement was important for him, since through it he came to realise how basic democratic values – freedom, national independence and humanity – were critical to those people who had been deprived of them.

Göncz stated explicitly in an interview that a cooperative network of resistance movements was established by people of different political affiliations so as to help extricate the country from the vortex of war:

> We were bound together and interconnected [by our] hatred of inhumanity, [and we felt] a sense of responsibility to save the country. We hardly asked who our fellow resistance fighters were. Especially, it was not appropriate to ask whether one was Communist, because it [represented] a life-threatening danger . . . *The common spiritual denominator that bound us together was a commitment to freedom, a sense of social responsibility and humanism . . .* The essence of the fight that we carried on was against inhumanity which meant that Hungary should escape from the War as soon as possible . . . Our common goal was to save as many people as we could.
>
> (Wisinger and László, 2007: 24–5, my emphasis)

This suggests that the civil resistance movement which Göncz joined was a genuine manifestation of the will of those Hungarians who were willing to devote themselves to the realisation of a free, socially responsible and humane society. According to Göncz, these three fundamental values underpinned the idea of modern democracy which was threatened by the War. Thus, those individuals felt the necessity to end the War gathered together and formed resistance groups. As Iván Vitányi pointed out, during the time of the resistance movements' activities the only question they asked the people who wished to join was whether they would accept Hitler. Vitányi said: 'We did not ask whether one was a communist or a social democrat. We asked people about Hitler . . . Do you accept Hitler? If not, come to us' (interview with Vitányi, 23 November 2007). Moreover, as Göncz commented in an interview with a Hungarian political weekly, *168 Óra*, it was because of his awareness of the country's predicament that he felt he had to join the resistance movement. Göncz stated:

> [The] inhumanity surrounding [us] led me [to join] the armed resistance [movement]. If you had lived at that time, perhaps you would have done the same thing. In these circumstances it was not possible for the people to stand there [without] doing something.
>
> (*168 Óra*, 8 May 1990)

In this light, it can be said that Göncz's participation in the resistance movement can be seen as a singular move neither driven by ardent patriotic sentiment nor inspired by the pursuit of a future political career. There is little doubt that through his participation in the anti-fascist movement, Göncz distinguished himself from individuals who either – reluctantly or willingly – compromised themselves by engaging with Nazi Germany. As we will see in Chapter 4, Göncz's anti-fascist credentials were fundamental to the subsequent public perception of him as a politician of moral authority. Much later, this would be an important factor in Göncz's nomination to the post of Hungary's first post-Communist president. Despite this fact, it is fair to suggest that the plurality of the movement – though a product of dire necessity to struggle against the Nazi inhumanity – was Göncz's principal motivation for participation in the resistance and subsequently, in politics. Bearing this in mind, the way in which Göncz struggled for democracy and that impact on his political development will be further examined. Before then, the following section examines another important factor contributing to the shaping of Göncz's political beliefs: so-called radical peasant populism.

1.4. Peasant populism

In the mid-1930s in Hungary there emerged group of intellectuals known as the 'populist writers' (*népi írok*) who attempted to represent the traditional values of the Hungarian peasantry (Némedi, 1995: 69; Kiss, 2002: 749). While these writers had differing political leanings or orientations,[18] the one common element intellectuals shared was a desire to see radical change in the under-developed, backward agricultural regions of rural Hungary. For these intellectuals the peasants were 'the source of morality' (Mudde, 2001: 35) and the root of Hungarianness, and these ideas formed the philosophical foundation of their mission. The populist writers considered drawing the attention of the ruling elites towards the reality of the poor peasantry to be their top priority. To this end, these writers, along with a number of sociologists who felt a moral imperative to discover the reality of the situation and the social milieu in which the Hungarians peasantry lived, conducted so-called 'village explorations' (Held, 1980: 335–36; Kontler, 2002: 359; Romsics, 1999: 172, 2005: 523). They travelled from county to county to uncover the real circumstances under which the peasants lived, and tried to formulate a solution to the destitution of the Hungarian peasantry. Between 1936 and 1938 a series of essays was published, vividly describing the pauperised peasantry and the oppressive attitude of the ruling elite towards 'the fate of three million beggars', and arousing public awareness of peasants' poor social conditions (Némedi, 1995: 70).[19] As Molnár points out, this number is rather exaggerated but considering that the vast majority of the rural population did not possess cultivable lands,[20] it is highly indicative of the fact that the question of the Hungarian peasantry was viewed as the critical social issue of the time (Molnár, 2001: 271–2). In Rainer's terms, the one thing that bound the populist writers together was 'moral outrage or indignation' over the indifference of ruling elites towards the landless peasants (Rainer, 1993: 34). It is not surprising therefore that 'at the heart of the populist movement there lay a demand for radical land reform' (Held, 1980: 336) and, with this aim, the populists considered that it was necessary to undertake political actions in order to further their aims and agenda. In March 1937 they formed a popular front, the so-called March Front, followed later by the founding of the National Peasant Party (NPP).

The March Front had a 'twelve-point manifesto' demanding radical political and socio-economic reforms (Tőkés, 1970: 87). The guarantee of universal suffrage, individual and political freedoms, land reform, the elimination of *latifundia*, the abolition of industrial cartels, a guarantee of workers' rights, educational reform and the realisation of self-determination for the people of the Danube valley among others were outlined in the Front's manifesto (Litván and Varga, 1995: 166–7; Romsics, 2000: 282–3), which called upon the Hungarian government to take radical action. However, these radical and progressive ideas were neither supported by the conservative government, nor successful in prompting the mobilisation of urban intellectuals and the peasantry. Consequently, the first fundamental transformation of the established structure of land-ownership (Kónya, 2000: 262) and political enfranchisement only took place in Hungary after the end of the Second World War, only to be undermined almost immediately by the imposition of Soviet style of communism (Held, 1996: 16).

However, even though the era of peasant populism was relatively short-lived, the populist movement was a significant social phenomenon, as the intellectuals of those days strove to address the question of impoverished peasantry. As Tőkés notes, populist movements in Hungary were the genuine manifestation of provincial intellectuals efforts to 'search for realistic, non-revolutionary [methods of] socio-political modernisation and democratisation at home' (Tőkés, 1970: 87) or 'a third road to incorporate the best and reject the worst features of fascism and communism'(Tőkés, 1996: 6).

At the height of the Hungarian populist movement (which culminated in the formation of the March Front), Göncz was still a young man (15 years old) and one who had yet to formulate his ideas definitively. However, Göncz's own reflection on this period of his life suggests that the populist movement had an important impact on his intellectual development:

> *Look, the impact of the populist writers was so significant in our generation.* [They] deeply influenced us . . . I knew the populist writers very well because [one of the] exam questions in my secondary school graduation [paper] was also about them . . . I read the populist writers' work and these were the most important things to read. The populist writers represented the view of the peasantry . . . In practice, I knew none of them in person . . . but *their influence on my intellectual development was very important.*
>
> (Interview with Göncz, 18 June 2006, my emphasis)

This suggests that Göncz's access to the populist writers' publication opened his eyes to the world and reality of the peasantry and it is clear that the influence of populist writers' ideas was entrenched in Göncz's memory. Of course, the idea of peasant populism was not only transmitted to Göncz through his reading activity, but also through his direct and first-hand experience, as discussed earlier, in his scouting activity. The particular social issues that drew Göncz's intellectual curiosity concerned the question of peasantry and land reform.

There is wealth of other evidence to support the contention that Göncz's outlook was deeply influenced by the populist movement and the writers at its helm. In an interview he gave on Kossuth Radio, for example, Göncz emphasised the role of peasant populism in the genesis of his political outlook. Furthermore,

Göncz claimed that his political views were already well developed by the time he reached his early twenties:

Radio Interviewer: What idea of society influenced your political belief at the time?
Göncz: In the PTWG, we constantly followed the most important social phenomena. By the age of twenty, I already had a political notion which was organically linked. [My outlook was concerned with] the nature of democracy, the way of democracy, the question of the peasantry and the question of land [reform]. We believed the key to the future of Hungary lay in land reform. This was the thinking among the young intellectuals at the time – my thinking as well. *The ideas of the populist radicals influenced [me] most deeply.*

(Wisinger and László, 2007: 17, my emphasis)

Göncz's emphatic statement suggests that his political beliefs were significantly affected by the idea of peasant populism. The precise concept of democracy Göncz envisaged was not detailed in the interview (as will be discussed in Chapter 3), but he believed that the core of peasant populism lay in land reform and this would pave the way for the future of Hungary's democracy. According to Göncz's exposition, it is clear that peasant populism was a crucial social movement, and he was also under its influence.

Another important component which demonstrates Göncz's populist leanings is related to his preferred literature and his later academic pursuits in agriculture. Göncz noted:

I was influenced by the populist writers, perhaps László Németh most of all. My favourite poet was Mihály Babits, [who] almost excluded the influence of László Németh, but embraced the political [idealying] at the root of land reform, that is, radical peasant politics.

(Tóth, 2009)

Göncz's interest in agriculture led him to acquire expertise in this related area. This was realised in 1952 when he entered the Gödöllő Agricultural University.[21]

Finally, given Göncz's interest in peasant populism, it is not surprising that the leading Hungarian intellectuals who had the most impact upon shaping his later political ideas were also involved in populist movements. For example, István Bibó, whom Göncz met personally, espoused the idea of peasant populism. Bibó was at the forefront of populist movements. He not only became involved in the drafting of the March Front (Litván and Varga, 1995: 166–7; Szilágyi, 1991: 532), but was also one of the key founding members of the National Peasant Party (Berki, 1992: 514). Göncz's own comment regarding Bibó's intellectual legacy is indicative of Bibó's influence on him:

30 The development of Göncz's political views

Göncz: My political view is identical with that of Bibó.
Kim: You mean, [in terms of] the liberal, social aspect?
Göncz: Yes, and populist [ideas], Bibó attached himself to the Peasant Party, whereas I attached myself to the Smallholders' Party [. . .]

(Joint interview with Göncz and Göntér, 10 January 2008)

Göncz's comments on Bibó's intellectual legacy are too brief to estimate the significance of Bibó's role in shaping Göncz's populist ideology. However, when Göncz later became the first post-Communist president, in an opening speech delivered at the foundation of New Peoples' College, he reiterated the fact that Bibó played a key role in shaping his political beliefs, including populist ideas. As Göncz explicitly stated, 'Bibó was my role model':

> I cut my teeth in the late 1930s under the spell of populist culture, at the time of the radical peasant movement, when a pressing need was felt for land reform. István Bibó contributed much to my understanding, putting into focus for me the component elements which have determined my political beliefs to this day. He was my role model with his gentle radicalism, genuine Hungarianness, European liberalism.
>
> (Tóth, 1999: 10)

Thus, it can be reasonably argued that Bibó's intellectual influence and peasant populist ideology had become entrenched in Göncz's political beliefs. Having recognised this significance, the next chapter further explores and traces Bibó's intellectual influence on Göncz characterised throughout the latter stage of Göncz's life. The views of the head of the 1956 Institute, János Rainer are apposite with regard to concluding this exploration of Göncz's early political and intellectual development:

> The populist movement was Göncz's political school. Indeed, it had a big impact on him . . . One should not forget that in the beginning, the populist movement was a radical left-wing movement. The cause of this [radicalism] was moral indignation over the peasantry who live in misery, because they did not have land, [access to] credit, or job opportunities [. . .]. They lived in unjust circumstances. The village was backward . . . and the populist movement fought against this. It was a left-wing movement of social critique . . . It separated [itself] from the legacy of Horthy's Hungary.
>
> (Interview with Rainer, 22 August 2007)

With the end of the War, Göncz found his role within the ISP, which embraced the idea of peasant populism and represented the interests of a small land-owning peasantry. Göncz believed that the ISP would serve as the main platform through which he could pursue his ideals in politics. The substantiation of this reasoning is the subject of the following section of this chapter, in which I examine the main characteristics of the ISP and its political context in post-War Hungary. This is followed by a brief biographical sketch of Béla Kovács – the general secretary of the party – with whom Göncz established his first political career as a personal secretary.

1.5. Independent Smallholders' Party

On 4 November 1945, the first free, unfettered general election was held in Hungary. Among the six parties entered into Parliament, the ISP secured an absolute majority of votes cast and won a landslide victory.

The significant portion of seats that the ISP secured in Parliament enabled the party to form its own government. However, partially due to a pre-election intraparty agreement, regardless of the electoral result, they were to form a coalition government (Crampton, 1997: 222) and, more importantly, through the pressure of the Marshall of the Allied Control of Commission (ACC), Kliment Voroshilov, the ISP was compelled to establish a coalition with three left-wing parties: the CP, the SDP and the NPP (Argentieri, 2008: 217; Cartledge, 2006: 440). This power-sharing structure is interesting and, in fact, clearly representative of the disadvantageous political circumstances that the first post-war electoral victor – the ISP democratic government – had to face at the time. Founded in 1930, the ISP was initially a left-wing-orientated opposition party to the conservative government which existed during the inter-war period (Körösényi, Tóth and Török, 2003: 192). Its constituency lay in rural areas and represented the interests of a small land-owning peasantry, today considered as 'small farmers' (Tőkés, 1997: 116). The end of the war did not alter this original platform on which the ISP stood, but there was a shift in its political orientation. It became something of a catch-all party, an amalgam of anti-Communist conservative forces (Körösényi et al., 2003: 192). 'The party united several different political lines stretching from the clerical right to the national left' (Bozóki and Karácsony, 2002: 73), indicating that the ISP had a broader appeal to the electorate than the party's name might have suggested. The ISP, however, could not translate legitimate power into its actual legislative programme without the Soviet leadership's consent. Despite the fact that the Soviet leadership's approach towards Hungary was relatively tolerant and permissive; as such, free elections were permitted. However, there was a limit to the Soviet leadership's tolerance of Hungary's democratic experience; this was demonstrated by the ACC's direct and indirect intervention in domestic affairs.

Table 1.1 The electoral result of the 1945 parliamentary election.

Parties	Votes (ratio)	Number of seats
The Independent Smallholders' Party	57.03	245
Social Democratic party (SDP)	17.41	70
Communist Party (CP)	16.95	69
National Peasant Party (NPP)	6.87	23
Civic Democratic Party (CDP)	1.62	2
Hungarian Radical Party (HRP)	0.12	—

Source: Adapted from Bihari (2005: 74)

For example, the post of interior minister – the key to the control of the police and security apparatus – should have been allocated to the ISP. The portfolio, however, was assigned to the Communists owing to pressure from Voroshilov (Kontler, 2002: 396), and was 'thereafter never to be relinquished' (Rothschild and Wingfield, 2000: 99). The consequence of this was the Communists' misuse of security force to threaten and coerce oppositional forces under the guise of law enforcement. As I shall discuss below, Kovács and Göncz also became victims of this abuse, albeit on different charges.

In brief, the overall political situation in which the ISP democratic government found itself was in character that of a 'constrained sovereignty' (Bihari, 2005: 60–2) or 'tentative democracy' (Gyarmati, 2005: 551); in reality, it was unable to wield and exercise power. As Göncz, a young member of the ISP, neatly observed; real power lay with the Communists backed by the Soviet army. The weakness of this power relation was exemplified by the ISP's leniency towards and concession to the demands of the Soviet leadership. Göncz asserted that the reason for conceding was the ISP's naive expectation that the Paris Peace Treaty would bring about a political turn-around with the withdrawal of Soviet troops:

> The ISP could not enjoy 100 percent power, because the source of power lay in the presence of the Soviet army. I remember inter-party agreements were concluded between [the coalition parties]. [But], the next day, Voroshilov announced that if this and that did not happen in eight days, Hungary must pay off the arrears of reparation. To prevent civil war and famine, the ISP gave way again and again . . . The ISP leaders believed the country's occupation would cease . . . [They believed] once the Peace Treaty was concluded, the occupying force would withdraw and if there were democratic parties about when this happened, they could take over power.
>
> (Hegedűs, 1985)

However, the Peace Treaty was not concluded as the ISP leadership expected. On the contrary, the Treaty allowed the Russian army onto Hungarian territory;[22] under its protection, the Communists could lay the foundation for the consolidation of their power. This process developed *gradually* until 1949, when Hungary became Sovietised with the proclamation of the Hungarian Peoples' Republic.[23]

It is not known precisely when Göncz joined the ISP, but his decision to become a member of the party was influenced by his friends. Having realised those PTWG members who struggled together during the anti-Nazi resistance movements had found a role in the ISP, Göncz also decided to join the party. Initially, the PTWG leaders requested that Göncz run for the general election and become a parliamentarian, but he refused reasoning that he was not ready for that position. Instead Göncz took on a secretarial job for Béla Kovács (Hegedűs, 1985).

Béla Kovács was born on 20 April 1908 to a small peasant family (Palasik, 2002: 9). During his adolescence, Kovács was under the influence of peasant populism. He took the question of the peasantry seriously, and felt the improvement of their social environment was essential. On 12 October 1930 at Békés, where the ISP was founded, Kovács was influenced by a visionary speech delivered by the party leader, Ferenc Nagy (Palasik, 2002: 10). This was the most crucial moment for him, as Kovács not only decided to join the party but later came to a leading position through Ferenc Nagy's sponsorship. In 1932, he briefly assumed a post of associate-judge in Mecsekalj and, after four years, was appointed as the general secretary of ISP's Barany constituency.[24] In Kovács's political conviction, the peasantry was considered a national tribe (*nemzet törzse*) whose virtue had to be preserved, and he strongly advocated the interests of the peasantry (Vida, 2002).

During the German occupation of Hungary, Kovács took an anti-Nazi stance and supported resistance movements, establishing contact with the leaders of the HF as well as the PTWG. With the end of the war, he briefly assumed the post of minister of agriculture, but on 23 February 1946, he resigned from this post to dedicate himself to being the general secretary of the ISP.[25] Kovács was a straightforward, resolute and intransigent personality (Palasik, 2002: 12) who considered the Communist's monopoly on power to be inadmissible (Vida, 2002). His anti-Communist line caused a conflict with the Communists; according to Göncz, Kovács was audacious enough to stand against the future Hungarian Stalinist leader Mátyás Rákosi. Göncz recounted that: 'In a meeting, Kovács once said to Rákosi, "Hey Mátyás, haven't you got a neck. [If not], how can we hang you?" People thought [saying] this sealed his fate' (Hegedűs, 1985). On 25 February 1947, Kovács was arrested for his implication in an alleged conspiracy against the Republic and taken to a Soviet labour camp. From 1948 onwards, he was transferred to several camps in the Soviet Union and, on 7 September 1955, by the decision of the Supreme Presidium Council, Kovács was handed over to the Hungarian authorities. He was subsequently imprisoned in Jászberény and in April 1956, through the mediating roles of ISP politicians, he was released.[26]

Göncz fulfilled the secretarial position until Kovács's arrest by the Hungarian authorities. According to Göncz's account, however, this period of work was an unpleasant time in his life. Göncz recalled it thus:

> When I undertook the job of secretary, I had no idea what it would entail. A secretary, after all, is a personal assistant, there to clean and feed the boss and so on. This kind of work is not my cup of tea. Nor did I like calling my boss 'Sir'. The time I spent alongside Kovács was [one of the most] unpleasant period[s] in my life.
>
> (Hegedűs, 1985)

Perhaps, Göncz's independent personality and the assignments he undertook were incompatible. However, Göncz's sense of dissatisfaction with his professional work does not necessarily mean that it did not have an important impact on the shaping of Göncz's political outlook. For example, in an interview with Demszky, Göncz remembered Kovács as a statesman who was endowed with all qualities that he respected and still respects:

> I think, among the peasant MPs within the ISP, Kovács was the most influential figure. In my opinion, he was a man who had the gifts to be a great statesman: energy, readiness to learn, his vision of the [future], decisiveness and others . . . I was a witness on the day when he was taken away to the [Soviet Union]. It was at the time that the entire coalition government was in crisis, and when Communists used salami tactics to [eliminate their opponents]. Kovács struggled almost alone to protect the party – even [confronting] Zoltán Tildy [the party chairman] – from those threats which came from outside the party . . . In my opinion, he lived an unfulfilled political life. [His abduction meant] the significant loss of his [vision] on peasants and its accompanying democratic [ideals].[27]

Göncz noted that Kovács was an important politician who lived through during the inter-war period. Göncz was clearly of the view that because of the firmness of Kovács' own political principles and beliefs, his integrity and above all, his courage, which had been displayed to him, to party members and to political opponents, Kovács remained a moral authority. The practical meaning of Kovács's vision of the peasantry and his ideals remains open to question, but Kovács's influence on Göncz's political development is firmly established. In an interview with me, Göncz reaffirmed the argument, noting that:

> Béla Kovács was the general secretary of the ISP. He was an extremely important politician who came from a peasant [background]. He was imprisoned for nine years in the Soviet Union. I learnt politics from him and saw politics from his eyes. He had a significant impact on me, because Kovács was the first serious politician whom I had ever met . . . I learnt a lot from Kovács not only from the perspective of politics, but also from his personality . . . Kovács constantly read books and had a strong sense of responsibility as the minister of agriculture . . . *In a word, my encounter with Kovács was a critical juncture in my life.*
> (Interview with Göncz, 18 June 2006, my emphasis)

This still does not tell us in what way Kovács had an impact on Göncz's subsequent political developments. However, according to Göncz's account, it is clear that he saw Kovács as a teacher or reference figure for a good statesman role model. As Göncz mentioned, he may have disliked his work as an assistant secretary but his position certainly was part of his apprenticeship in building up his political career next to the person to whom he deferred and paid respect at the time, and still does so.

Aside from his role as secretary, another important activity performed by Göncz in this period was undertaking the editorship of the weekly party magazine, *The Generation* (*Nemzedék*). According to Göncz, *The Generation* was not successful at the time, partly because the ISP did not have sufficient funds to support it, but primarily because the readership of magazine was not clearly established. Göncz observed: 'I think, we could not really decide who this magazine was for. Was it for the youngsters or the senior citizens or the peasants or the students?' (Wisinger and László, 2007: 27). Among those articles published, the first issue contained one, 'The Crisis of Democracy', written by István Bibó. The central theme of the article dealt with the abstract concept of 'reactionaries' (*reakciósok*). The article is too brief to elicit an underlying message; however, Bibó and Göncz diverged in their opinions over the question of how they defined and saw reactionaries.

Göncz interpreted Bibó's view as being that reactionaries were those individuals who openly and consciously stood against democracy and human needs (Göncz, 1946). Göncz, however, contended that the reactionaries were not all identical and in his opinion, they fell into two distinct categories: the 'objective' and 'subjective' reactionaries. The first category referred to those individuals appointed to privileged positions in terms of economic resources and political power, so-called 'aristocrats'. The second type were not originally aristocrats, but behaved as if they were. Among the subjective reactionaries, there was a significant economic gap between the wealthy peasants and the poor ones. The wealthy peasants behaved like the gentry, whereas the poor peasants, who lacked economic assets, tried to overcome their disadvantaged position through education. The critical issue was, however, that the vast majority of the Hungarian population belonged to the latter category; a reasonable solution had to be found to narrow this disparity. One of the ways to bridge the material gap conceived by Göncz was to hold social discourse or dialogue, in the expectation that it would provide some idea or solution to tackle the problem. One could infer that the idea of holding social dialogue could be related to the influence that the PTWG had on Göncz. As discussed in Section 1.2, the PTWG held social seminars where university students and intellectuals gathered to discuss social issues and exchange ideas regarding the question of the peasantry. In this article, however, Göncz did not detail the way in which social discourse could be organised, not to mention that no probable connection between the PTWG and his idea was mooted; this therefore remains open to question. Nevertheless, Göncz's editorship of the party magazine was an important activity undertaken at this time. It not only demonstrated Göncz's capacity for critical thinking on the issue of the peasantry, but also highlighted the fact that his own approach to politics was already well formed by this time.

Göncz's editorial activity did not last long, as the ISP was gradually dissolved. The State Security Authority led by the Communists arrested the key leadership of the ISP in connection with an alleged conspiracy against the Republic. The pretext for this was the ISP's complicity in an illegal, secret organisation of Hungarian nationalists, which had existed since before the War, the so-called the Hungarian Brotherly Community (HBC). The HBC was founded in the 1920s by a group of Calvinist gentry who mainly came from Transylvania (Palasik, 2000). At the core of their thought, Hungary was perceived as a distinguished nation but the development of this nation was hampered by foreign influence. In particular, German expansionism was considered as a major threat; the HBC took an anti-German and later an anti-Nazi stance. Bálint Arany, a nationalist ISP politician, was the HBC's spiritual leader but, according to Göncz, the centrists within the party – Kálmán

Saláta, István Csicsery-Rónay and even the prime minister, Ferenc Nagy – were secret members (Hegedűs, 1985). The main goal the HBC aspired to achieve was preparation for a time when they could form a democratic government, but 'without the participation of Communists' (Kenez, 2006: 220). The HBC was also known to have a secret military cell whose strength was insignificant when measured against that of the Red Army (Kenez, 2006: 221). However, uncovering the existence of this secret society gave a sufficient pretext for the Communists, who claimed that the HBC conspired to overthrow a democratically elected coalition government to act. A wave of arrests in the HBC leadership ensued, and with fabricated evidence and extorted confessions, it was soon claimed that the ISP was behind the alleged conspiracy.

In particular, the Communists targeted Béla Kovács who was seen as an obstinate, intransigent and anti-Communist figure (Cartledge, 2006: 443). Despite his legal immunity, on 25 February 1947, Kovács was arrested by the Soviet authorities on the grounds that he had masterminded the formation of a secret anti-Soviet armed terrorist group (Palasik, 2002: 66) and for 'espionage against the Soviet army' (György, 1947: 309). Briefly tried in the Soviet military court, Kovács was imprisoned in a Soviet labour camp (Romsics, 1999: 234). Other leaders of the ISP suffered a similar fate: they were forced to resign or sent into exile. As Göncz noted, Kovács had nothing to do with the HBC; on the contrary, he stood against it: 'Kovács loathed the HBC . . . [He] turned red when he heard the name HBC and died in the belief that he had been its victim' (Tóth, 2009). However, as stated above, some members of the ISP also belonging to the HBC provided a good pretext for the Communists to eliminate its largest opposition party, which ultimately resulted in 'the first in a series of show trials' (Kenez, 2006: 218), as well as being the beginning of the end for the ISP (Schöpflin, 1977: 100).

Göncz escaped this purge as he was never a member of the HBC and his position within the ISP was a low-ranking one. The excessive nationalism that the HBC advocated was against Göncz's political beliefs, which in turn distanced him from it. Göncz said: 'From the beginning, my opinion was against the Hungarian [chauvinism] that the HBC represented . . . They never asked me to join . . . Perhaps, they sensed my resistance, because every time, I stood against the HBC' (Hegedűs, 1985).

Despite his non-membership however, Göncz was also taken to a military court soon after Kovács's abduction (Papp, 2002). The charge on which Göncz was arrested was not related to the HBC affair but rather an illegal visit to Romania he made at the end of 1946. The available documentation does not allow us to uncover why the ISP entrusted Göncz to visit local Hungarian politicians residing in Romania or the nature of the specific goal to be attained.[28] However, inferring from Göncz's own account, the main objective of his business in Romania seemed to have been of little importance. Göncz argued that, given his low-profile position in the party, he was far from taking on an important role during his visit to Romania. His visit was, instead, aimed at observing the country's situation in transition and presenting a report to the ISP afterward:

Kim: As far as I know, while you worked at the ISP, at the behest of the party, you went to Romania. For what purpose did you visit that country?

Göncz: I just looked around to see what the situation was. In Romania, this was the transitional period [after the war] and it was not possible to tell how the situation would evolve. I talked to some Hungarian politicians residing in Romania and later I gave my report to Béla Kovács.

Kim: Was your visit not concerned with matters of peace between Hungary and Romania?

Göncz: Look, I was not an important person. My position was far from that which would have allowed me to do anything such as concluding a peace treaty. I just looked around Romania, and no more than that. *I was not assigned a seriously important political task . . . Do not assume that I was an important politician at this time.*

(Interview with Göncz, 18 June 2006, my emphasis)

As Göncz suggested, from a political perspective, his visit to Romania may not have carried great significance. However, the Communist authorities who accessed information regarding Göncz's meeting with the Hungarian politicians in Romania, interpreted this as a serious matter, taking him into custody for interrogation as a result. Göncz was detained for three weeks and during this confinement, he underwent harsh interrogation. In his memory, this was a distressing experience:

> It was a cruel place. They made me stand up 36 hours in a row . . . [When I] collapsed, they made me stand up using a rifle butt . . . it was hard to stand up for 36 hours. Next day [after interrogation began], I was already seeing rabbits on the wall. In the morning, [I] was given a black coffee in a mess-tin, but they did not let me go to the toilet. When I was released, they said 'Congratulations, Comrade to be freed from here'. It was an inhumane, strange, and terrible experience.
>
> (Wisinger and László, 2007: 28)

Despite this interrogation, not one useful piece of information that could have been used to charge Göncz regarding his involvement in ISP affairs, particularly in connection with Béla Kovács, was obtained and Göncz was released. By this time, the ISP had lost its key leadership due to their alleged machinations against the Republic, and the Communists were ready to take power. Indeed, this was evidenced by the rise of Communist power led by a quartet of Hungarian Muscovites: Mátyás Rákosi, Ernő Gerő, Mihály Farkas, and József Révai. Hungary was destined to enter one of the murkier periods of her modern history – Communist rule. Unemployed as a consequence of the ISP's dissolution, Göncz took on several part-time skilled manual jobs, including soldering and pipefitting (*The Baltimore Sun*, 24 September 1990). At the same time, he took a distance learning course at Gödöllő Agricultural University, where he specialised in soil erosion and protection (interview with Szunyog, 19 August 2007). Göncz then utilised his knowledge working as an agronomist at the Soil Improvement Firm until the outbreak of the 1956 Revolution.

Summary

This chapter has examined the development of Göncz's political views as they took shape during his adolescence and early adulthood. As a whole, the analysis presented here has led to the conclusion that during the early years of Göncz's life, two elements – liberal and democratic political beliefs and radical peasant populism – were crystallised and entrenched in his ideological trajectory. The genesis of Göncz's liberal and democratic political beliefs lay in the PTWG, where he participated in a series of social seminars of intellectual forum and that later led him to find his role in the student armed resistance movements. The fundamental ideas and values that Göncz espoused and struggled for during the resistance rested in their commitment to the realisation of a free, democratic and socially responsible society. His first-hand experience in the resistance movement served as a catalyst which, in turn, contributed to the development of Göncz's liberal and democratic political beliefs.

Similarly, but more importantly, the idea of peasant populism was embedded in the fabric of Göncz's political beliefs. Göncz's understanding of peasant populism originated from his scouting activity, which served as a basis of raising his social awareness regarding the situation of poor peasantry. Göncz sensed that there was a moral imperative for the radical social and political change, and firmly believed that land reform and the provision of national education to the peasantry would serve as the key means to resolve the social issue of the age. Göncz's first political activity was in the ISP, which embraced the idea of peasant populism and endeavoured to formulate it into actual policy. This leads to the conclusion that at this period in his life peasant populism was the most consistent and pronounced element entrenched in Göncz's political beliefs. Having noted this significance, the following chapter further examines and traces the continuity of the influence of peasant populism on Göncz's political ideas and their coexistence in his thinking with liberal democratic ideas, when he experienced one of the most crucial social and political changes of the age, the 1956 Hungarian Revolution.

2 The 1956 Hungarian Revolution

Introduction

The previous chapter examined the development of Göncz's political views during the early years of his life. It was argued that two elements – the idea of peasant populism and Göncz's first-hand experience in anti-Nazi student resistance movements – were the most important factors contributing to Göncz's democratic political beliefs prior to 1956. With this in mind, the present chapter examines Göncz's subsequent political and intellectual development by exploring his first-hand experience of the 1956 Hungarian Revolution. On 15 June 1995, in a speech delivered at the commemoration of Imre Nagy's execution, Göncz clearly stated what the Revolution meant to him: '1956 was a turning point in my life too. It has determined my personal life to this very day. Without 1956 I would not be standing here in front of you' (Tóth, 1999: 55).

A detailed discussion regarding the events and developments of the 1956 Revolution, however, is not provided in this chapter. As Cox notes, research exploring 'the events, meanings and memories of 1956' are on-going in academia (Cox, 2006: 3) and, as a biographer and a historian looking into the political life and achievement of Árpád Göncz, my research necessarily focuses upon him. Relevant background information will be presented where it is necessary. The chapter is laid out as follows.

The first section examines Göncz's activity in the Petőfi Circle. As will be discussed here, Göncz gave a speech to the Circle which was in fact his only notable political activity before the outbreak of the Revolution. Although this was an isolated action and the implications of this activity are open to question, it is worth examining his speech as it exhibited Göncz's own view regarding Soviet farming models in Hungarian agriculture.

Subsequently, a brief chronology of the key events of the Revolution, and Göncz's role and actions in the resistance of 1956 which followed the suppression of the Revolution are discussed. In particular, Göncz's liaison role in negotiations between István Bibó and India (which took a proactive role in the Hungarian issue) are examined in depth. The chapter will examine what Göncz sought to achieve through these activities.

The remainder of the chapter examines Göncz's life in prison and, ultimately, the chapter will probe in what way Göncz's experience of this pivotal event impacted the shaping of his political beliefs.

In general, Göncz had a fragmented memory regarding the 1956 Revolution. As Göncz acknowledged, he was incapable of reconstructing the development of the Revolution until he gained access to the relevant history book: 'I could hardly recount the moments regarding the Revolution . . . Until I obtained Bill Lomax's book, I could not even arrange my memories chronologically. The entire thing was so blurry' (Hegedűs, 1985).[1] Despite this vagueness, drawing upon the collated information and documentation discovered in Göncz's own essays, his personal Oral History, speeches, interviews and newspaper articles, one can be certain that Göncz did not participate in the armed resistance of the Revolution. Until 10 November 1956, when the Soviet forces finally quelled the armed insurgency of the Hungarian freedom fighters, Göncz's main activity comprised observing and witnessing some memorable events. For example, on 23 October 1956 when thousands of demonstrators gathered in front of Parliament demanding Imre Nagy's presence, Göncz and his daughter were there and experienced the powerful atmosphere. Göncz recounted: 'In front of Parliament when people demanded Imre Nagy, I was there with my little daughter [Kinga] who was on my shoulders. [People] litcrumpled newspapers like torches' (Göncz's interview with Kossuth Radio, 22 October 1990). This activity carried a certain importance as Göncz witnessed and took part in the development of the Revolution. Similarly, Göncz's participation in a meeting where Imre Nagy and young insurgents were present at Nagy's house was a notable political activity. Göncz reminisced about it thus:

> We had a discussion at Imre Nagy's house. Nagy received us saying 'hat 'here it is, the entire resistance movement'. The discussion was interrupted when Nagy's secretary came with a memo. Nagy [who saw the memo] said, 'Gentlemen! From now on, we need to discuss another thing because there is a dangerous possibility of a Third World War' [breaking out]. This was about the Alexandria intervention.
> (Göncz's interview with Kossuth Radio, 22 October 1990).

The memo concerned the Suez Crisis, which took place on 29 October 1956 when Great Britain and France attacked Egypt over access to the Suez Canal. Göncz's account provides an interesting perspective regarding Nagy's perception of the Suez Crisis and his sense of reality. In terms of Göncz's position, however, it is far from clear as a sufficient explanation of his relationship with Nagy and other insurgents who participated in the meeting. How could it be possible for Göncz to attend the meeting? Given Göncz's position and career at this time – that of an agriculturalist – it is unreasonable to suggest that Göncz suddenly took on a position of leadership and was able to discuss affairs of state.[2] In this way, there were a number of similarly interesting moments, pictures and impressions that remained in Göncz's memory, but all of these are fragments of overarching revolutionary developments. As a whole, the lack of relevant material in available documentation prevents us from reconstructing Göncz's political role and actions over this time period. Thus, research must necessarily be focused on those events in which Göncz not only became involved, but which also offered a valid starting point for a discussion of his proactive political activities. This exercise can justifiably be begun with the speech that Göncz delivered to the Petőfi Circle.

2.1. The Petőfi Circle (*Petőfi Kör*)

On 6 November 2001, in a public lecture delivered at Corvinus University of Budapest, Göncz stated that:

> In the preparation for the Revolution, within the framework of social debate, the Petőfi Circle discussed numerous important questions of the age, which also gave rise to the sea-change in theoretical and moral authority [*elméleti és morális tekintélyek pályfordulását*].[3]

The so-called Petőfi Circle, which was named after the heroic poet of the 1848 Revolution, Sándor Petőfi, was a forum where intellectuals and the general public alike participated in social debates. Göncz utilised this forum to offer his critique of the Soviet farming model and its relevance to Hungarian agriculture. Despite the fact that Göncz did not take a leading role in the Circle, it is important to consider the significance of Göncz's involvement in it. As Litván noted, the Circle 'created the opening wedge of future intellectual revolt' (Litván, 1996: 39), leading to the development of the Revolution.

Founded in March 1955, under the auspices of a Party youth organisation– the Union of Working Youth – (Cartledge, 2006: 461; Kovrig, 1984: 93), the Petőfi Circle was initially no more than a loose association of former activists constituted from the League of Hungarian University Students and the National Association of Peoples' College (Litván, 1996: 39).[4] With the dissemination of Khrushchev's 'Secret Speech'[5] to members of the party elites and intellectuals, the Circle was gradually transformed into a forum and platform where reform-minded intellectuals and professionals (Romsics, 1999: 299) and, more importantly, intra-party opposition gathered and debated topical issues. Twelve important agendas, including the need for reform in agriculture, education and the economy, and above all, political renewal were set as the central themes for the debates.[6] The Circle meetings took place throughout the spring and summer of 1956, and attracted an ever growing audience (Hegedű s, 1997: 115–24); in effect the Circle mobilised the hitherto obedient, passive and acquiescent society in the discussion of how to address pressing issues that weighed upon the Hungarian population at the time. In Gyarmati's terms, the Circle functioned as the 'parliament of society', where participants exchanged their opinions and ideas 'with such frankness and willingness that it was as if [meetings] were not taking place in the shadow of monolithic party domination' (Gyarmati, 2005: 586).

As an agronomist Göncz had an opportunity to voice his opinion regarding the adequacy of the Soviet farming model in the Circle. The available

42 The development of Göncz's political views

documentation does not enable us to clarify precisely when and how he became a part of the Circle.[7] According to records and minutes compiled by the former secretary of the Circle András B. Hegedűs, however, on 17 October 1956 at the Kárl Marx Economic University of Budapest, Göncz attended one of the agricultural debates entitled 'Garden Hungary' (*Kert Magyarország*).[8] In this meeting, Göncz contended that the Soviet farming model – 'extensive farming' – which required vast areas of land for large-scale production of wheat and barley – was essentially not favourable to Hungary's agricultural environment.[9] Instead, as a way of enhancing the efficiency of Hungary's agricultural system, Göncz suggested that 'intensive farming', which is advantageous for increasing the yield of crops in smaller land areas, be introduced. Above all, Göncz considered that the extension of agricultural education to the peasants and farmers was required to help equip them with adequate knowledge of agriculture. Göncz stated: 'Education is very important, because two-thirds of the peasants and their children do not have an opportunity to learn how to become a cultivated peasantry' (Hegedűs, 1994: 150). Additionally, Göncz detailed the way, in which intensive farming could be implemented and what short-term effects and consequences could be expected, after its implementation:

> An important precondition of intensive farming is the reduction of the sowing area of bread-grains . . . If the sowing area of wheat is reduced across the country, it is expected that, in a smaller area, for the first year, the average production would not increase significantly. However, a few years after, [owing to the increase of] forage, stock and farm yard manure, favourable green crops would increase to the extent to which the average production could reach the current level of yield. *To be sure, it would be an illusion to believe that all of the economies belonging to the socialist sectors could function [well] and be managed via a large scale mode.*
> (Hegedűs, 1994: 151, my emphasis)

This speech clearly highlights Göncz's dissenting opinion and show his critical thinking that was distinct from the official partyline on agricultural policy. As Romsics noted, if the Communist authorities' strict control over education – including political indoctrination and re-indoctrination courses – meant that pluralistic values were neglected and dissenting opinions and critical voices among people were neutralised (Romsics, 1999: 281–92), the Circle undoubtedly resisted this by demanding reform and revision of state policy. Not surprisingly, the Communist leadership watched the Circle's activities anxiously and finally decided to ban it. However, this decision was reversed with the removal of Hungarian Stalinist Mátyás Rákosi from the party leadership; it had become apparent that it was too late to turn back the tide of the reform movement. Indeed, as the Soviet leadership foresaw, it became a harbinger of the development of the 1956 Revolution: 'the discussion of the Petőfi Circle [is] an ideological Poznan without the gunshots' (Kramer, 1998: 179). Given this historical significance, it is fair to suggest that Göncz's participation in the Circle and his speech regarding the necessity of agricultural reform carried a certain significance, albeit a manifestly symbolic one.

2.2. Chronology of the key events of the 1956 Revolution

On 22 October 1956, the students who believed that more should be done to persuade the Communists to accept their demands gathered at the Budapest Technical University. They formulated a sixteen point agenda outlining the need for fundamental radical reform in education, the economy and politics; among these, the withdrawal of Soviet troops was set as the top priority.[10] The following day, university students took to the streets where they were joined by the general public, and they also insisted that the sixteen point agenda be broadcast on Budapest Radio Station. However, the guards who were defending the Radio Station building shot at protestors and consequently, a peaceful demonstration turned into an armed insurgency. This was the beginning of the 1956 Revolution which lasted for two weeks thereafter.[11]

Between 23 October 1956 and 27 October 1956, freedom fighters and Soviet forces were engaged in armed clashes. The Soviet military intervention which had commenced on 24 October at the request of the general secretary of the Hungarian Workers' and Peoples' Party, Ernő Gerő, met with scattered but strong armed resistance from the Hungarian people. Engagement continued until 28 October when Imre Nagy, who had by then been reinstated as the prime minister, announced his government's willingness to begin negotiations with the freedom fighters, acknowledging that 'the uprising is a national democratic revolution' (Litván, 1996: 184).

Over the following three days, from 28 October 1956 to 30 October 1956, the domestic situation of Hungary was stabilised and democratic political reforms followed. A truce between the freedom fighters and the Soviet forces was called and Nagy announced the dismantling of the one-party system and the establishment of a coalition government. In response, the Soviet leadership displayed leniency towards Nagy's reform plan and backed his government. The Soviet leadership seemed to be willing to negotiate on the withdrawal of troops from Hungary and the 'declaration of mutual respect for the independence of socialist states' was announced (Litván, 1996: 185). In the meantime, on 30 October, Anglo-French forces attacked Egypt over Suez, and Göncz along with his friends were at Nagy's house when they heard the news.

During the next phase, 31 October 1956 to 4 November 1956, the prospect of armed clashes between the freedom fighters and Soviet forces once again loomed. On 31 October, the Soviet leadership changed their lenient position towards the Nagy government and decided upon the re-introduction of a military presence in Hungary (Békés, Byrne and Rainer, 2002: 41). In response, on the following day, Nagy declared Hungary's neutrality and asked for protection from the United Nations. However, no positive response and practical help from the West was forthcoming and, on 4 November, Soviet forces began to crush the armed insurgency. Nagy sought, and was granted, asylum in the Yugoslav Embassy[12] and, on that day, István Bibó (a minister of state in the Nagy government) composed an official letter of protest – the Proclamation entitled 'Hungarians' (*Magyarok*) (Berki, 1992: 514) – against the forced removal of the legitimate Nagy government.[13] Bibó was mistaken for an ordinary clerk and so survived the military crackdown, escaping from Parliament with the proclamation (Falk, 2003: 136; Granville, 2001: 2). This declaration was later widely circulated 'either in part or in whole' in both the Hungarian press and 'the world's major newspapers' (Rainer, 1993: 32) which, in turn, contributed to making the Hungarian situation and Bibó's name known to the public at large. Over the period 5 to 11 November 1956, the armed uprising wound down and the two week long revolution was at an end.

2.3. Rearguard Struggle: Liaison between István Bibó, India and the West

By 11 November 1956 the last of the armed uprising had been quelled by the Soviet army. However, the resistance of democratic forces to the newly established Soviet-sponsored Kádár regime continued for some months thereafter. Workers launched a series of general strikes demanding the withdrawal of Soviet forces and the return of the Nagy government (Cartledge, 2006: 486), and the Revolutionary Council of Hungarian Intellectuals – primarily writers, journalists and student bodies – issued statements of protest against the Soviet invasion and appealed for help and mediation from any quarter in the West (Litván, 1996: 100–22; Romsics, 1999: 316–20). István Bibó, a symbol of democratic intellectual resistance, drafted statements, exposés, and proclamations and offered his own solution to the challenges which arose during and after the suppression of the Revolution. Among Bibó's writings were the Draft Proposal for a Compromise Solution to the Hungarian Questions (hereafter the Draft Proposal) which is particularly worthy of in-depth discussion, as it is this proposal that provided the fundamental basis for the democratic forces to negotiate with the Kádár regime (Granville, 2001: 2; Szilágyi, 1991: 541). Göncz participated in debates on the Draft Proposal and helped Bibó to establish a rapport with Indian government officials who mediated in the conflict between the democratic forces and the Soviet leadership (Litván, 2008: 378). Moreover, Göncz endeavoured to smuggle a manuscript authored by Imre Nagy – 'On Communism in Defence of New Course'– to the West and campaigned for clandestine financial support for the families of imprisoned 1956 revolutionaries.

One of the key aspects requiring examination is the question of how Göncz became acquainted with Bibó and, how he established a collaborative relationship with India concerning the Hungarian situation. The discussion of this issue begins by considering India's attitude towards the 1956 Revolution. Initially, India was 'slow, cautious and hesitant' about becoming involved in the Hungarian Revolution (Kidwai, 1984: 64). The Hungarian Revolution and the Suez Crisis were concurrent and India promptly reacted to the latter by condemning the Anglo-French intervention. The Indian Prime Minister Jawaharlal Nehru stated that: 'In all my experience in foreign affairs I have come across no greater case of naked aggression than what France and England are trying to do' (Stein, 1969: 86). In relation to the former issue, the Indian leadership took an ambivalent stance, expressing sympathy for those anonymous Hungarians who fought for freedom, but the Indians were hesitant about becoming directly involved. On 2 November 1956, in a telegram forwarded to his ambassador, Kumara Pladmanabha Sivasankava Menon (hereafter K. P. S. Menon),[14] Nehru stated that:

> It is difficult for us to intervene in any way but I should like you to let the Soviet authorities know informally that this situation in Hungary is causing people in India much concern and naturally sympathy goes to those who represent the national desire for freedom.
> (Hasan, Prasad and Damodaran, 2005: 453)

More strikingly, when the UN voted for the adoption of a resolution condemning Soviet military aggression, the Indian delegates led by Nehru's confidant, Krishna Menon, abstained from voting (Gopal, 1989: 307). This differentiated approach provoked controversy among the members of the international community and India was essentially criticised for adopting a double standard in its treatment of two apparently separate, but intertwined events (Guha, 2007: 165). As a biographer of Nehru, Judith Brown, has noted, 'the juxtaposition of Suez and the Hungarian uprising placed Nehru in an unenviable position' in terms of defending his non-alignment policy (Brown, 2003: 263).[15]

By the middle of November 1956, signs of the shift in India's position towards Hungary were emerging. In a speech, Nehru called for the swift withdrawal of the Soviet troops from Hungary and expressed solidarity with the Hungarian people who fought for freedom, stating that 'the people of Hungary should be allowed to determine their future according to their wishes' (Nehru, 1961: 555). What led the Indian leadership to reconsider its initial position towards the Hungarian question? International pressure from the members of the UN, advisors within the government and ambassadors' reports, and Nehru's sister's contact, Vijaya Lakshmi Nehru Pandit, (who by then was acting as a High Commissioner in London), all contributed to changing Nehru's stance towards the Hungarian crisis (Brown, 2003: 264–5). According to Göncz, however, an Indian diplomat named Mohamed Attaur Rahman was crucial to the change of India's position. Rahman was the Chargé de Affairs in the Indian Embassy in Budapest (Farkas, 1991). He was assistant to the ambassador K.P.S. Menon. Menon, however, was also accredited to Moscow and had another important diplomatic commitment there; Rahman was *de facto* the only legal representative leading the Embassy. In his personal Oral History, Göncz explained how Rahman might have contributed to altering the Indian leadership's position in dealing with the Hungarian question:

> In Budapest, there was the Chargé de Affairs of the Indian Embassy named Rahman. He changed the attitude of the Indian government towards the Hungarian Revolution. Rahman clearly [saw] the possibility that India's [role in

the Hungarian question] could be [one] of participating in the settlement of an international conflict as a moral authority. In the Indian parliament, Nehru said that 'based on the report given by our official resident in Pest, we should [consider] correcting our previous stance'

(Hegedűs, 1983)

Göncz may have overstated Rahman's role but, as Stein has observed, while 'no senior diplomat was present in Budapest, one member of the Indian Embassy [Rahman] managed to get several well-written and detailed reports out of Hungary via Austria' (Stein, 1969: 90) a fact which demonstrates Rahman's significance for the Hungarian question. Indeed, several telegrams exchanged between Nehru and Rahman indicate that Nehru's changed stance towards Hungary had been informed by Rahman. In the telegram dated 18 November 1956, in response to Rahman's reports, Nehru made his position on events in Hungary and their possible solution very clear:

> We have received your telegrams . . . We welcome this detailed information which enables us to form a clearer picture of events. Our policy is to encourage the speedy withdrawal of Soviet forces from Hungary but that this should be peacefully done. Any violence will not only bring fresh misery but delay such a withdrawal.
>
> (Hasan *et al.*, 2005: 457)

Four days after this correspondence, Nehru began to proactively engage with the Hungarian question. He took the initiative in the formation of a Delegation of UN Observers to be dispatched to Hungary. This action was aimed at providing relief, clarifying the situation that had developed as a result of the Kádár regime's deportation of some Hungarian young people who had participated in the Revolution. On 22 November 1956, Nehru simultaneously sent letters to Marshall Nikolai Alexandrovich Bulganin, János Kádár[16] and Josip Broz Tito, requesting their cooperation in his arbitration on the Hungarian question. The letter forwarded to Tito is worthy of examination, as it conveys Nehru's ideas most explicitly:

> In Hungary there appears to be widespread belief that deportations have taken place and some evidence is also produced to that effect. As you know, [the] resolution sponsored by India, Indonesia and Ceylon was passed by the UN General Assembly last night . . . It would be exceedingly unfortunate if [the] Hungarian Government or [the] Soviet Government refused to allow [the] Secretary General of [the] UN or UN Observers to go to Budapest now . . I have sent a personal message today to Premier Bulganin as well as Premier Kádár of Hungary pointing out to them that our resolution passed by the UN Assembly notes Hungarian denials [of the deportations] and fully recognises [the] sovereignty of Hungary . . . In view of serious allegations and doubts that have arisen in people's minds, it is highly desirable for [the] UN Secretary General and UN Observers to be allowed to go to Budapest for talks with

the Hungarian Government. I am afraid that if this permission is not given, [the] consequences will be disastrous. I would request [that] you also exercise your great influence to get the Hungarian Government to agree to the Secretary General or UN Observers going to Budapest.

(Hasan *et al.*, 2005: 478–9).

As Gopal noted, Nehru's diplomatic endeavour 'marked an emphatic change in his attitude' on the Hungarian event (Gopal, 1989: 309).[17]

The news regarding the change of India's position towards Hungary was circulated among a narrow circle in Hungarian society and, in mid-November 1956, Göncz came across a journalist who provided him with this crucial information:

> Around 10 November 1956, I [Göncz] ran into a newswriter, Pál Magyar. He told me that the Indian officials would undertake arbitration [between the Hungarian democratic forces and the Soviets] if they received a request signed by the Hungarian democratic forces.
>
> (Hegedűs, 1985)

Having been informed of the news, Göncz visited Bibó who was composing the Draft Proposal at this time. According to Göncz (in an interview with Hungarian daily *Magyar Hírlap*), he first:

> got to know Bibó when [Bibó] worked at a university library . . . Bibó drafted a treatise with [Ferenc] Erdei and [Jenő] Matyasovszky. At this time, I worked in a soil improvement firm and Matyasovszkzy was my colleague. *But my really close relationship with Bibó was [formed] around 10 November 1956.*
>
> (Lengyel, 1992, my emphasis)

Thus, according to Göncz's statement, it would appear that the 1956 Revolution provided the momentum required to bring him and Bibó together and a good working relationship between them was developed thereafter. Indeed, Bibó confirmed Göncz's view that the meeting of November 1956 represented the starting point of their working relationship:

> Sometime between 9 and 11 November, Göncz dropped into my flat. I had known him previously but we were not close friends then. However, from that point onwards, we were in constant touch . . . In the middle of November, Göncz showed me something he had written requesting the Indian government's mediation [in the Hungarian question], which I favoured. Later, having collected signatories from other [social] organisations, Göncz handed over [the request] to the Indian Embassy, which he visited constantly during December and informed me of [the situation].
>
> (Litván and Varga, 1995: 495)

Throughout December, Göncz visited the Embassy frequently and one of the notable acts he undertook was that of conveying Bibó's Draft Proposal there. Bibó composed the Proposal after the second Soviet intervention had quelled popular Hungarian armed resistance. In this Draft, as a way of resolving the situation that had developed after the suppression of the Revolution, Bibó proposed the withdrawal of Soviet troops and the convention of a national assembly (Kenedi, 1996: 60–2). First, Bibó saw that from the beginning, Hungary had no intention of breaking away from the socialist order, but the intervention of Soviet forces in the popular uprising was counter-productive to the consolidation of the domestic political situation achieved by the Nagy government. For this reason, Bibó urged the withdrawal of the Soviet army and proposed that foreign policy between Hungary and the Soviet Union be revised in a way that put them on an equal footing (with the eventual conclusion of a bilateral treaty). Second, and more importantly, the manner in which the social democratic order could be re-arranged and re-aligned upon the departure of Soviet troops was detailed. Bibó's concept was that an interim national assembly – made up of the delegates of Workers' Councils and Revolutionary Committees – could play a major role in the political arrangement in terms of the fundamental structure of the state, the constitutional order and the formulation of basic laws. Among the most important issues to be decided in the national assembly were the following:

> According to Article I of the draft law of 1946, the form of the Hungarian state is that of a Republic;
>
> - According to Article III of 1848, the form of the Hungarian government is that of a parliamentary democracy built upon an independent government accountable to the general public;
> - The form of Hungarian society is that of one free of exploitation (socialism), which means the maintenance of the 1945 land reform, and [that] of nationalised mines, banks and heavy industry; the provision of opportunity for the free undertaking of individual and cooperative business with a guarantee of the prohibition of exploitation.
>
> (Kenedi, 1996: 61–2)

This proposal was discussed and signed by the leaders of parties, workers' councils and revolutionary committees that had emerged or been reconstructed during the short-lived Nagy government (Litván, 1996: 116; Wisinger and László, 2007: 37). Bibó and Ferenc Farkas signed on behalf of the Peasants' Party, and on behalf of the Smallholders, Göncz's friend József Antall Jr. and Zoltán Tildy appended their signatures. Göncz himself, as a member of the Peasant Alliance, signed the Proposal (Litván and Varga, 1995: 496), and delivered a copy to Rahman. Bibó confirmed this act, noting that: 'On 14 December, at the draft editors' behest [Ferenc Farkas and I] Göncz took copies of the Proposals – one in English and two in Russian – to the Indian Embassy' (Litván and Varga, 1995: 497). Within a week, feedback regarding the Draft Proposal came from the Indian side. Rahman informed Göncz of the Ambassdor K.P.S. Menon's visit to Pest for the business of discussing the Proposal. On several occasions, between 16 December and 8 January 1957, meetings between Bibó, Göncz and Menon took place at the Indian Embassy and the Margit Hotel (Tóth, 2009). Menon confirmed his willingness to undertake shuttle diplomacy between Hungary and the Soviet Union, and agreed to convey the Proposal to the Soviet leadership. It was ultimately handed over to Bulganin (Lendvai, 2008: 156), but no positive response was forthcoming from the Soviet side (Falk, 2003: 136; Göncz, 1991: 282). In his personal Oral History, Göncz clearly remembered the result of India's mission:

> István Bibó and Ferenc Farkas composed the proposal . . . We [Bibó and I] handed it over to Menon . . . Menon said that it was delivered to [Bulganin][18] but he did not receive feedback. He said [Bulganin] did not refuse to accept it but made no comments on it either.
>
> (Hegedűs, 1985)

Another important activity undertaken by Göncz was smuggling Nagy's manuscript on Communism in Defence of the New Course to the West (Cservenka, 2000; Kőrösi and Molnár, 2003: 159; Kozák, 1991: 115; Petri, 2002). The manuscript was originally written by Imre Nagy after he was ousted from the premiership. In this manuscript, Nagy defended the New Course,[19] the main aim of which was easing the problems caused by 'forced collectivisation and industrialisation' and 'mitigating the repressive and arbitrary features of the totalitarian system' (Kovrig, 1984: 92). One copy of the script was kept by László Kardos, who was not a member of the Nagy Group but who sympathised with the New Course.[20] Göncz had become acquainted with Kardos when he joined student armed resistance movements during the German occupation of Budapest. Kardos was active as one of the leaders of the Freedom Front of Hungarian Students at this time.[21] Around March 1957, Kardos and Göncz collaborated with one another in the smuggling of Nagy's manuscript to the West (Cservenka, 2000; Litván, 2008: 326). This operation was made possible through the assistance of Nagy Regéczy-László, a former military officer, and a chauffeur to the first secretary of the British Legation, Christopher Lee Cope (Kőrösi, 1991: 217). Regéczy-László, a distant relative of Göncz, acted as an intermediary between Cope and Göncz and arranged a series of secret meetings. In his Oral History, Göncz explained why it was necessary to take the manuscript out of the country:

> Kardos said there was some material written by Imre Nagy that had to be sent abroad. If Nagy was tried, it would be possible to prove he was a Communist after all. I looked for my old friend Regéczy-Nagy . . . and at his flat I met Cope.
>
> (Tóth, 2009)

Göncz and Kardos expected that if the manuscript was successfully smuggled to the West, it might have helped to rescue Nagy from execution after his forthcoming trial. It would provide important counter-evidence to the official propaganda and disinformation disseminated by the Kádár regime to the effect that Nagy had sought 'a counter-revolution in a socialist system' (Gough, 2006: 110) and attempted to restore a capitalist order.[22]

Cope agreed to become involved in this mission and established the precise manner in which the manuscript could be smuggled out of the country. An exact time and venue were arranged in advance and in the early spring of 1957 Göncz met Cope. The moment when the manuscript was handed over is vividly described by Göncz:

> On 14 March [1957] I was at the Miniatür coffee-shop to receive the file from Kardos . . . He brought a briefcase [with Nagy's script inside], and put it on the ground, then left the scene with my bag . . . I stayed there to hand over the briefcase to a passing car . . . [Cope's] car appeared and the manuscript was taken. It went to the [British] Legation.
>
> (Hegedűs, 1985)

The joint operation was successful and the manuscript was ultimately delivered by the British Legation to the Émigré Revolutionary Committee based in Strasbourg (Rainer, 2002b: 307). In an enclosed letter forwarded to one of the leaders of the Strasbourg Revolutionary Committee, Sándor Kiss, Göncz urged the publication of Nagy's manuscript and detailed the situation of Nagy, who was awaiting trial at this time. Göncz wrote:

> It appears that Imre Nagy's trial is imminent. Before this trial, I saw the publication of the enclosed piece of work was necessary, even if you [may] not agree with all aspects of Nagy's political views. I guarantee the authenticity of it . . . The condition of publication is that only the Hungarian Revolutionary Committee must act as publisher – other publishers cannot take this role. The entire text must be published . . . The publication of the work is urgent. I trust your judgement [regarding whether the work needs to be] distributed via radio or the press . . . I consider the translation of the work into English, French, Italian, German and any other languages spoken in Democratic People's Republics is necessary.
>
> (Kiss, Kőszeg and Solt, 1992: 889)

Indeed, Nagy's work was translated and published in several countries, including France, Germany, Italy and the UK (Rainer, 2002b: 291), and news regarding the publication of Nagy's essay was broadcast by the BBC in London and Radio Free Europe (Kiss *et al.*, 1992: 889). As former British Ambassador to Hungary, Peter Unwin noted, the essay 'created a stir' among its Western readership and offered a unique insight and valuable revelations regarding 'the closed world of the Communist leadership' (Unwin, 1991: 112). However, as Bibó's Draft Proposal could not change the direction of the Soviet leadership's foreign policy towards Hungary, the essay – other than drawing Western interest and sympathy for Nagy and his reform policy – failed to give support and practical assistance to Nagy at his trial; Nagy and his associates were destined for execution.

The last activity carried out by Göncz before he was arrested was campaigning for the Hungarian Aid (HA – *Magyar Segély*) movement. Originally, the HA was a world-wide solidarity movement led by Western governments and civil organisations. Sympathising with the Hungarian population, it had drawn on individuals and organisations across Europe to provide moral and material support to the freedom fighters during the Revolution (Kőrösi and Molnár, 2003: 73).[23] Göncz, one of the 1956 revolutionaries who committed himself to rearguard actions, knew, directly and indirectly, the families who were in desperate need of moral and material support and thus decided to act for them. In particular Göncz endeavoured to win émigré support for families and friends in need. In a letter forwarded to Sándor Kiss, Göncz appealed for material assistance for the dependent families of the revolutionaries who had already been arrested:

> At home, another wave of new arrests has hit and as a consequence, László Kardos and others among my acquaintances have been arrested. More and more, the families who were arrested are finding themselves in a difficult situation . . . Please offer financial support to those people listed in the enclosed letter . . . [24] Probably, in one or two weeks, Bibó and I will be taken into custody. In this case, please take care of our families.
> (Kiss *et al.*, 1992: 889).

Shortly after this correspondence, Göncz's clandestine activity was uncovered by the Communist authorities and on 28 May 1957 Bibó and Göncz were both arrested and their rearguard actions ceased. Despite their arrest, the solidarity of Hungarian society demonstrated during the Revolution continued, though fewer people were willing to take part in resistance as Kádár's power was gradually consolidated. As Göncz's wife Zsuzsánna Göntér neatly asserted, this sense of social solidarity shared by anonymous Hungarians served as an impetus for the families in need, enabling them to cope with the difficult circumstances:

> Everyone who shared a sense of solidarity with the 1956 revolutionaries took risks . . . I received money from Göncz's Boy Scout friends and his paediatrician friends who collected money for us in the hospital. Although I was unable to make a decent living with my pay, our family had no problem with finance. I really don't know where and how many times we received support. They just left money next to the window or left an envelope at the door without a name on it. Our circle of friends was fantastic.
> (Interview with Göncz and Göntér, 10 January 2008)

2.4. Trial, imprisonment, hunger strike and the translation bureau

At midnight on 28 May 1957, two weeks before Nagy's trial and his subsequent execution, Göncz was arrested by secret police at his flat on suspicion of

52 The development of Göncz's political views

complicity in overthrowing the state order of the People's Republic of Hungary (*Beszélő*, 1990; Mátraházi, 1989; Pál, 1991; Petri, 2002). Göncz was taken to the head office of the police and justice department where the Investigation Division of the Budapest Police Department, Capital Military Court, Capital Military Attorney's Office and Psychiatric Examination Institute were located.[25] According to Litván, this place was hidden from the world, and in it secret trials were prepared, which then proceeded under a shroud of secrecy. Imre Nagy's trial on 15 June 1957 was at this venue. Litván noted:

> The police and justice system operated in secrecy so that they [the Communist authorities] could conceal the truth that the Imre Nagy group was not in Romania but at home [*Gyorskocsi* Street] in preparation for the trial. The trial proceeded [as planned] but the news became known to the public only after Nagy's execution.
>
> (Interview with Litván, 22 July 2006)

By the end of Nagy's trial, Göncz, together with Bibó and Regéczy-Nagy, had been detained for 14 months and during this time they were primarily interrogated in connection with their actions pertaining to India and the West. Each of the accused was questioned individually thus preventing any meetings between Bibó, Göncz and Regéczy-Nagy during the interrogation. Nevertheless, before the trial, they once had an opportunity to see each other. In that meeting, Bibó and Göncz behaved altruistically to save Regéczy-Nagy by taking all the responsibility for their collaborative actions. Regéczy-Nagy reminisced about the manner in which questioning proceeded and how Bibó and Göncz acted at the time:

> They [the investigators] wrote down our personal records. Bibó was interrogated alone then Göncz followed . . . When it was [my turn], both of them sat down . . . Bibó wanted to save us, and Göncz wanted to save me . . . The interrogators said if they could hang anyone twice, they would hang Bibó and Göncz twice. They were angry on account of Bibó and Göncz's [attitudes].
>
> (Interview with Regéczy-Nagy, 5 October 2007)

The extract above implies that the spirit of solidarity that Göncz, Bibó and Regéczy-Nagy had shared and demonstrated in the course of resistance activities was kept alive during their internment. The quote does not furnish us with a sufficient explanation regarding the circumstances under which interrogations were held. However, given the precedent of Nagy's trial, of which 'preparation, inquiry and [interrogation] were carried out in absolute secrecy' at this place (Lendvai, 2008: 221), it is almost certain that Bibó, Göncz and Regéczy-Nagy were also placed at a similar disadvantage in terms of defending themselves in their forthcoming trial. Indeed, in his Oral History, Göncz confirmed that during the questioning, defence lawyers appointed to him and Regéczy-Nagy *de facto* were unwilling to represent them in trial, and instead provided impractical counselling. Göncz noted that:

> I realised my lawyer could not defend me in practice . . . The only defence [suggested] to me was to say that Bibó was accountable for [everything] and forced me to join in . . . Regéczy-Nagy's lawyer did the same thing, saying that Göncz was responsible for [everything].
>
> (Hegedűs, 1985)

While Göncz and his associates did not receive any useful legal advice and counselling from their lawyers, there were people who offered moral support and help to them. In Göncz's case, these people included his wife and, interestingly, his prosecutor János Kovács. During the interrogation period, Göncz was banned from receiving any visitors, but occasional exchanges of letters were permitted under strict conditions, and this correspondence encouraged Göncz to endure hardship and adversity during his internment; it became the source of the maintenance of 'a strong spiritual link' between him and his family. Göncz recounted how letters from his wife served to sustain his mental strength:

> I was allowed to receive letters from my wife at times, but no names and numbers could appear. Once they [the censors] rejected her letter because there were too many names in it. It was useless to explain to them I had four children . . . I am very proud of my wife who did a good job [in delivering messages to me]. Once when she sent in a package of [clothing], she wrote a letter in dark blue ink on a dark blue scarf. The guard did not recognise it . . . We had a very close spiritual link.
>
> (Hegedűs, 1985)

In addition to his wife's support, the prosecutor Kovács played an important role in defending Göncz at trial. Given that some questioning conducted before the trial was arranged in preparation for imposing a severe sentence on Göncz, he anticipated the verdict that would be handed down. Göncz recounted:

> I realised it was a hanging matter when the psychiatric examination was done . . . When I returned to the jail from [the examination], the guard told me that it wouldn't be painful to be hanged. It wouldn't be worse than having teeth out.
>
> (Tóth, 2009)

Yet, in this unfavourable situation, Kovács helped Göncz by informing him before the trial of the legal rights he retained for example, the right to remain silent and more importantly, by his action during the trial in declining to ask for capital punishment (Papp, 2002; Petri, 2002). It is not known why Kovács tried to defend Göncz during the proceedings, but the unusual character of this situation was demonstrated by the reaction of the embarrassed judge who had expected the prosecutor to ask for capital punishment. Göncz vividly remembered the dramatic moment of the day of trial, thus:

When the prosecutor did not ask for the death penalty, the judge leapt up in anger. 'Now, please give us the sentence you demand'. The prosecutor said 'I request the second heaviest sentence'. In response, the judge once again said 'give us the sentence you demand'. The prosecutor said, as I already mentioned, 'I request the second heaviest sentence'.

(Hegedűs, 1985)

Whether or not the prosecutor's request was considered in the verdict for Göncz's trial is unknown, though the judges did decide not to hang Göncz (Göncz's interview with Bartok Radio, 12 July 2002). It is not clear what circumstantial factors could have affected the change of verdict at the last moment, but according to Göncz, the India government was behind the commutation of the death sentence. In numerous interviews, Göncz underscored the significance of the Indian government's role. For example in an interview with a Hungarian political and cultural monthly, Göncz commented that, 'According to legend – I cannot confirm the truth – Nehru saved us [Bibó and Göncz] from hanging' (*Beszélő*, 1990: 6–7). Similarly, Göncz once again highlighted the role of Nehru stating that 'Miraculously, they did not hang us [Bibó and Göncz]. Probably, there was an intervention from Nehru, but I cannot confirm this'.[26]

Since this remained an unconfirmed story as far as Göncz was concerned, I endeavoured to locate evidence to shed light on Nehru's role in the proceedings of Bibó's trial. Nehru's autobiographies, biographies of his life and K. P. S. Menon's diaries and other available documentation were scrutinised.[27] Although no compelling evidence demonstrating Nehru's direct intervention in Bibó's trial was discovered, there is an indication that Nehru was consistently exerting pressure on the Soviet leadership and the Kádár regime to stop the reprisals against those who fought for freedom and were later imprisoned for their involvements in the Revolution. For example, according to one of Nehru's notes dated 6 September 1957 recalls:

I met the Soviet Chargé d'Affaires this afternoon and spoke to him about Hungary. . . . I was worried . . . about reports of present happenings in Hungary. We were informed that large numbers of arrests and convictions were still taking place and that the secret police which has ceased to function in the Soviet Union and Poland and other countries was still very much in evidence in Hungary. Our own Ambassador [K.P.S. Menon], who had recently visited Budapest, also reported to us that while there had been some improvement in some [aspects of] the situation, it was regrettable that so many political arrests were being made . . . I mentioned to [the Soviet Chargé d'Affairs] also that I had received a telegram from some International Association of Jurists saying that trials in Hungary did not allow adequate facilities for defence . . . I added that I hoped that the Soviet Government would exercise their influence in this matter in creating normal conditions in Hungary. The Soviet Chargé d'Affairs said that he would communicate what I said to his government.

(Hasan *et al.*, 2007: 663–4)

Nehru's conscience was evidently disturbed by the developments that followed the suppression of the 1956 Revolution. He was clearly of the view that a series of reprisals and political trials taking place in Hungary were counter-productive to the restoration of social order and normality. Thus, he urged the Soviet leadership to influence the Kádár regime to change or at least ease their retributive actions against the Hungarian people. Moreover, according to a journal article containing the testimony of Mohamed Attaur Rahman, the Indian chargé d'affaires, the Indian leadership's diplomatic effort did effect a change in the sentence imposed on Bibó and Göncz. Rahman recounted:

> The interesting point for us is that the coroner is likely to have had enough evidence against the two freedom fighters [Bibó and Göncz] to have sentenced both to death by hanging. [But this did not happen] I must therefore assume that our intervention has saved them from that.
>
> (Bonn, 1991: 46–7)

Similarly, and more explicitly, in an interview with the Hungarian socialist daily *Népszabadság*, Rahman once again highlighted the fact that diplomatic efforts made by Indian officials were crucial to the alteration of a decision made at Bibó's and his associates' trials. This was realised through an Indian military attaché who established warm and amicable relations with a high-ranking official of the Soviet military leadership – the former chief of the State Security Agency, Ivan Aleksandrovich Serov. Rahman reminisced about how diplomatic action might have acted in saving Göncz's life:

> When their [Bibó's and Göncz's] trial was under way, an [Indian] military attaché who was accredited to Hungary and had a good relationship with the Soviet military leadership came over from Moscow to Budapest. I asked him to try to intervene in the trial, because the charge [against Göncz] – collaboration with a foreign force – seriously threatened to [result in] a death sentence. On 1 April [1958], among guests, as his old friend, the attaché thanked Serov for [his presence] in the military parade . . . and he later discussed [the matter] with him for a long time. *This [may have] had an impact on [the trial] or it may have been Nehru's personal intervention* . . . Today it is difficult to clarify [which affected the trial]. In any case, among the convicts of the Bibó trial, our friend . . . *had a narrow escape* . . . Today, [his identity] no longer needs to be concealed. His name was Árpád Göncz.
>
> (Farkas, 1990, my emphasis)

This still does not tell us whether it was the Indian attaché's influence or Nehru's personal mediation that was responsible for the change of the verdict given to Göncz. However, it is certain that the influence exerted by the Indian leadership ultimately prevented Göncz from being hanged. This relief effort fell short of stopping Kádár's extensive reprisals taken against those anonymous Hungarians who were incarcerated for their actions during the Revolution.[28] Nevertheless, in doing this, India demonstrated a good example of solidarity in action and of the values they upheld. In an interview with a Hungarian political weekly *168 Óra*, Rahman made clear that the values embraced by the Indian leadership was their understanding of and appreciation for the will of Hungarians' yearning for freedom and truth, which came from peoples' hearts and minds:

Newspaper interviewer: What was your motivation in deciding to stand on the side of revolutionaries in the Hungarian Revolution?

Rahman: I had to stand by the truth. From the very beginning of the Revolution, even a blind man could have seen that the entire [city] of Budapest was in a fever of freedom. Above all, we heard [this] – 'finally we are free'. 'We are not afraid of fighting for freedom'. In these circumstances, I would have been very cynical if I had not resolved to [do something].

(*168 Óra*, 23 April 1991)

With the end of trial in August 1958, Bibó and Göncz began their imprisonment at the Gyűjtő jail (*Gyűjtő fogház*), which had also been the venue[29] for the execution of Imre Nagy and his associates.[30] Within the Gyűjtő, they were confined to the specially designated cell, the so-called *Kis fogház*, where a group of political prisoners who received heavy penalties for their involvement in the Revolution served their sentences. According to Litván and Varga, between March 1958 and December 1961, around 411 political prisoners were in custody.[31] Among them were high profile figures – whose registration numbers began with the prefix 476 – László Kardos, Gábor Tánczos (secretary of the Petőfi Circle), Tibor Déry (an eminent writer), Zoltán Tildy (secretary of state during the Nagy government), Miklós Vásárhelyi (chief press secretary of the Nagy government), György Litván (a historian), and Bibó and Göncz. The authorities could have mixed '476-ers' together with common criminals as a deliberate attempt to further humiliate and brutalise them. According to Bibó, however, the 476-ers were separated from common criminals. Bibó noted:

The 476-ers exclusively occupied here [*Kis Fogház*]. This meant the prisoners with registration numbers beginning 476 were there. This [the 476-ers] was a kind of society, [. . .] a leadership whose names were known well [to the people].

(Litván and Varga, 1995: 470)

Isolation from the outside world and separation from friends made it difficult for the 476-ers to serve their long sentences and endure the extremely restricted conditions and circumstances surrounding them. According to a former convict and 1956 veteran, Imre Mécs, the restricted conditions included regulation of visits, letters and parcels. At the *Kis fogház*, visitors were permitted for ten minutes every six months and correspondence was allowed every three months (Wisinger and

László, 2007: 85). All of this meant that the prisoners were very disconnected from the outside world. The greatest anguish the 476-ers had to bear was that of witnessing the final moments of the prisoners who were to be executed. Göncz recalled the crushing effect that witnessing the final day prior to execution of his friends had on him and his fellow convicts:

> At the *Kis fogház*, every other second or third day, two or three prisoners, shouting –'Dear fellows! Don't forget us'– were taken out for execution. I didn't know anyone who had to be brought under the gallows . . . There were two girls who were to be executed – Mari Wittner and Kati Sticker. Perhaps they were taken out to be hanged because we – who were on the first floor – heard their screaming. 'Murderers!' and then the voices of [the guards retorting]. 'You are the murders!' . . . Next day, we were taken out for exercise and heard one girl crying . . . The girl cowering was Mari and when she recognised me, she told me: 'Boys, forgive me! I was not executed, only Kati'.[32]

Prisoners who had to spend time at the *Kis fogház* would have shared similar experiences and these remained painful events in their lives. However, prison life was not always so testing; there were moments of relief and solace which helped the jailed revolutionaries to endure. Some such moments were provided by the translation bureau located at the Vác prison where intellectuals met and could discuss the issues of the day.

The Vác prison, nicknamed the 'House of Lords' held some good memories for the 476-ers.[33] Unlike the *Kis fogház*, prisoners were not executed there (Wisinger and László, 2007: 83) and, more importantly, the prisoners were able to work and see one another at the translation bureau. It is not known precisely when the translation bureau was set up within the Vác jail. According to Litván, however, it was established in order to meet the demand from high ranking functionaries within the Communist party for information and intelligence deriving from Western literature. These bureaucrats lacked a good command of foreign languages so the 476-ers were put to the task of translation. Litván explained what type of literature the intellectuals were able to access and in what way translation work brought benefits to them:

> We translated the memoirs of Churchill and De Gaulle, literature relating to military [history] and so on. These had to be translated, because the Communists did not know foreign languages . . . Later, some of these [works] were published [in numbered editions] by the party publisher. Copies were numbered, because they were not legally allowed to be read outside [the upper echelons of the Communist hierarchy] . . . Bibó, Göncz and other intellectuals worked there for several months. We were able to meet regularly . . . This was the best workplace in the prison.
>
> (Interview with Litván, 22 July 2006)

In order to better understand the reasons why reading this particular type of literature was prohibited outside the prison, it is worth briefly looking into a cultural policy adopted by the Kádár regime. In essence, the main framework of the Kádár regime's cultural policy consisted of the so-called three Ts: 'Support (*Támogatás*) Toleration (*Tűrés)*and Ban (*Tiltás*)' (Cartledge, 2006: 506; Kontler, 2002: 445 Romsics, 1999: 389). Literary works that fell within the first category were non-political and pro-government in character, whereas any works containing an element of criticism or voicing defiance of the regime were denied distribution to a wider readership. Of these three criteria, toleration was the most tactful and crafty self-censorship measure. As long as the message that authors tried to convey to their readers did not overtly challenge the regime, publication was permitted, and thus a little freedom was granted. The goal that Kádár sought to achieve through using the three Ts system was clear: the neutralisation of the criticism from the intelligentsia and silencing the voice of dissent. In this light, it is hardly surprising that the Western literature the 1956 intellectuals gained accessed to at the Vác prison was forbidden material for Hungarian society. Göncz neatly captured how this cultural policy actually affected writers and their readers, and more importantly what consequences it had for the 476-ers themselves:

> Writers were classified into three groups: the sponsored, the tolerated and the blacklisted. Those in the first group had prostituted themselves for everyone to see. The third group was equally cut off from living literature. The tolerated writer was in the hardest, but professionally healthiest, situation. He became tough like a hunted fox, his work was sometimes published . . . by writing coded messages between the lines he took a risk . . . But his honour remained intact, he had not prostituted himself and he was still a writer.
> (Tóth 1999: 224–5)

The translation work that the 1956 intellectuals were compelled to do at the Vác seemed bearable, even enjoyable.

First, translation work laid the foundation for Göncz's later literary career. As Litván explained, Göncz, along with other 1956 revolutionaries, was able to access various works of Western literature primarily concerned with the Cold War and military history. In addition, Göncz gained access to some classical western literature and *belles-lettres*; for instance, Galsworthy's *Forsyte Saga*, which he managed to read through, translating it into Hungarian (Barabás, 1989). This work was ultimately smuggled out of the prison by his associate, György Litván, and the translation work later served a basis in Göncz's pursuit of a career as a literary translator and writer. In an interview, Göncz explained what translation work meant to him personally:

> In the prison, for three years, I worked as a translator at the translation bureau which meant I was given [a chance] to prepare for my later career. For the first attempt, I managed to complete translating the *Forsyte Saga* and Litván smuggled it out to my wife for our wedding anniversary. When I was

released from prison, this brought me a job, as I found employment in [literary translation].³⁴

Second, and more importantly, translation work contributed to the development of Göncz's intellectual life. Reading and translating various pieces of work not only helped Göncz to widen his scope of knowledge in the related field, but the translation bureau itself also provided the main impetus for Göncz to engage in discussions and debates with other imprisoned intellectuals. When Göncz was interned at *Kis fogház*, he was separated from his associates and placed in solitary confinement. This effectively disconnected Göncz from communication and connection with his friends. The translation bureau, however, provided an opportunity for the re-establishment of contact and engagement between them. For example, of the well-known 1956 revolutionaries, Göncz was reunited with Imre Mécs, György Litván and István Bibó at this translation bureau (Hegedűs, 1985). The lack of relevant material in available documentation prevents us from reconstructing the content of the discussions that went on. Nevertheless, inferring from Mécs's account, during their discussions, a wide range of topical issues including politics were covered. Mécs recounted:

> Physically we [may] have been confined in the prison but, in spirit, we freed ourselves. We were able to debate and discuss politics and social issues. We did not [feel] we were losers . . . We were on an island, the island of 1956, where dissidents could preserve the picture of Hungary breaking out [from the prison].
>
> (Wisinger and László, 2007: 90)

Mécs's statement demonstrates that the intellectual engagement the 1956-ers shared at the prison provided an important impetus to sustain their mental strength. The prison might have restricted and deprived the 1956-ers from their individual liberty but they were able to maintain an intellectual capability through discussions. Mécs's account implies that intellectual engagement served as a vital means of resisting the sense of being vanquished that some of the 1956 revolutionaries might have felt in the prison. Furthermore, it was the main channel through which the 1956 intellectuals were able to overcome the physical limitations and constraints imposed upon them. It should be noted that while they were working at the translation bureau, the prison guards were not present; this in turn encouraged an atmosphere in which the 1956 intellectuals freely discussed and exchanged their ideas. Göncz noted: 'We were very pleased to have translation work. The guards were not allowed to enter the cells when the prisoners were doing translation work. This was an interesting [phenomenon] of the Communist system' (interview with Göncz, 18 June 2006). In this respect, it is also fair to suggest that emotional attachments or bonds of friendship among the 1956 revolutionaries deepened to the extent to which they became their *raison d'être* during imprisonment. Göncz reminisced about the Revolution and assessed the effect that it had on him in terms of the development of human relationships:

I considered my time in prison to be useful . . . Two weeks' revolution remained superficial [in my memory], but before my arrest, I made durable friendship [with the 1956-ers]. Later, this friendship was deepened to the extent [that] it signified a reason for being to me . . . If people spent more than a year in prison, [feelings of] hatred could develop but fortunately, I did not come to have such feelings.

(Hegedűs, 1985)

Göncz, together with other 1956 intellectuals, undertook translation work until Easter 1960 when they began a hunger strike.

In April 1960, a hunger strike of convicts began at the Vác prison (Kőrösi and Molnár, 2003: 159). The direct cause of the strike was indignation over the 'double standards' applied by the Kádár regime (Lendvai, 2008: 219). Initially, the prisoners were informed that they would be granted an amnesty and released by autumn of the same year (Révész, 2000: 175); this was confirmed by Kádár's speech delivered at the General Assembly of the UN. In this speech, Kádár announced that the vast majority of political prisoners who had been sentenced for their involvement in the 1956 Revolution had been or would be released from prison. Kádár claimed:

More than three-quarters of the people called to account for their acts in connection with the 1956 counter-revolution have already been released by general amnesty and returned to their daily lives. Today in our country, fewer people are in prison than at any time in the existence of Hungary as an established state.

(Romsics, 2000: 241)

In reality, only partial pardons were decreed to a certain group of high-ranking party functionaries; 'the generals, the leaders of the Communist Party, writers and politicians were released, whereas students, ordinary soldiers and members of the small local committees were excluded from the amnesty and stayed in jail' (Litván and Varga, 1995: 475); among the well-known figures freed by this amnesty were a former minister of defence Mihály Farkas and the head of the State Security Authority Gábor Péter (Kurcz, 2010; Lendvai, 2008: 219).

Discontented with and infuriated by official propaganda and lies, the prisoners launched a hunger strike. It is not known who made the first move, but Göncz and Bibó joined the strike. Unsurprisingly, the action was received with hostility by the prison guards, who considered the strike as a serious challenge to order. The wardens attempted to use the incident to make prison sentences more stringent under the pretext of prison riot or disobedience.[35] This, however, came to nought and instead the authorities decided to separate the group of prisoners by transferring them to different branches of the prison service. Consequently, Göncz and Bibó were transferred to Márianosztra – an infamous prison where the so-called 'Class Enemies' (*idegen osztály*) served their sentences,[36] whereas other figures from the 1956 revolutionaries such as György Litván and Sándor Fekete were relocated to Gyűjtő.[37] Litván remembered how the action of the hunger strike could have changed the sentence of prisoners:

> They [guards] recorded how many times the prisoners refused to eat meals. I think Göncz refused to eat lunch once, but he was also categorised as a striker ... The prisoners were transferred to other jails according to the record. The vast majority of prisoners were transferred to Sátoraljaúhely ... while the prisoners who committed serious crimes were taken to Márianosztra. At the time, Göncz and Bibó were taken to Márianosztra ... The guards wanted to initiate new trials against them [Göncz and those who joined strike] as they [in the guards' view] had committed another crime. The charge against Göncz and Bibó could have meant their sentences being changed from life sentences to the maximum penalty. However, this did not happen.
> (Interview with Litván, 22 July 2006)

As Göncz eloquently asserted, the hunger strike which took place at the Vác was 'a manifestation of solidarity in action among the prisoners' (interview with Göncz, 18 June 2006) who were outraged by the official propaganda and the double standard applied by the Kádár regime.

In March 1963, a general amnesty was granted to all political prisoners who had been prosecuted for their involvement in the Revolution and who had been excluded from the partial amnesty issued previously (Ekiert, 1996: 98; Swain and Swain, 2003: 162). This action was due to Kádár's agreement with the United States (later consented to by the UN) that a compromise would be made, and once the 1956 prisoners were freed, the question of Hungary would be removed from the UN agenda (Romsics, 1999: 332).[38] Kádár, who had already gained 'approval for an amnesty from Khrushchev' (Gough, 2006: 143) used it as a bargaining chip to reinstate Hungary's legal status within the UN[39] and ultimately win international recognition for the legitimacy of his regime (Kontler, 2002: 437). A former co-convict from Bibó's trial, Regéczy-Nagy, explained the core of the issue:

> After the 1956 Revolution, with an absolute majority, the General Assembly of the UN [agreed] that the Soviets must leave Hungary, free elections were to be held, and amnesty granted. [But] with the passage of time, it became clear that the Soviet forces would not withdraw [from Hungary] ... U Thant [the secretary general of the UN] said 'the question of Hungary is protracted'. 'At least the issue of an amnesty for political prisoners [needs resolution], then, Hungary could retrieve the right of attending the General Assembly of the UN'. This was the [essence] of the matter.
> (Interview with Regéczy-Nagy, 5 October 2007)

As a result of the amnesty, four thousand people were released from prison, including Bibó (Gough, 2006: 143), but his co-convicts –Göncz and Regéczy-Nagy – did not benefit from the amnesty (Cservenka, 2000). The precise reason for their further stay in prison remains unclear to this day but, according to an official account given by the authorities at the time, Göncz and Regéczy-Nagy were excluded from release because they did not fall within the limits of the cut-off date set for the amnesty. In the event that political prisoners committed a crime after 1 May 1957, they would be excluded from the amnesty (Hegedűs, 1985). However, the given explanation is contradictory as Bibó – who had acted with Göncz – was freed at this time, whereas Göncz and Regéczy-Nagy remained in jail. Bibó's high-profile – he was the minister of state of the Nagy government and several of his works had become known to the West – may have drawn international attention and pressure from the international community resulting in his release. As Göncz noted,

> Bibó had to be released as the eyes of the world's press were on him . . . Probably Regéczy and I stayed in jail because little attention was paid to us and we were less important and not internationally recognised figures . . . [But this] remains an enigma.
>
> (Hegedűs, 1985)

Three months after Bibó's release, in July 1963,[40] Göncz and Regéczy-Nagy were granted individual pardons and released (Kőrösi and Molnár, 2003: 159, 173; Petri, 2002; Szálé, 2006). Following his release from prison, Göncz attempted to resume his agricultural study which had been interrupted by the outbreak of the Revolution. However, he was unable to complete his study due to his involvement in the Revolution. Göncz recalled:

> The head of department told me that I was not allowed to change the world and at the same time finish university [. . .]. He banned me from completing my agricultural studies at any of the universities in Hungary.
>
> (Göncz, 1991: 296)

Having been thwarted in this regard, Göncz took up writing professionally. Firstly he worked as a part time translator for the Veszprém Chemical Heavy Industry Research Institute. Thereafter, he continued utilising his English language skills to build up a professional career as an English-American literary translator and writer (*Esti Hírlap*, 20 June 1995). This literary life was interrupted in the second half of the 1980s when the time came for demanding reform and political change once again. Göncz, alongside his friends who had shared his fate during prior attempts at anti-Soviet resistance, was ready to act and take the leadership of the revived dissident movement. This intention was realised when the taboo topic of the rehabilitation of Imre Nagy and his associates was raised and the Committee for Historical Justice was founded. This will be discussed in detail in the next chapter. Before embarking on this task, the chapter concludes by exploring the reasons for Göncz's participation in the resistance of 1956 and what his aims were. Finally, I will examine in what ways, if any, his first hand experience in the 1956 Hungarian Revolution contributed to the shaping of his liberal and democratic political beliefs.

One possible explanation for Göncz's determination to participate in the resistance of 1956 may have been his sympathy with Nagy's political vision. As has been discussed in Section 2.3 of the chapter, Göncz demonstrated his political stance in favour of Nagy's position. The following two comments are of particular relevance here. First, in 1953 when Nagy delivered a radio speech regarding the introduction of the New Course, Göncz was surprised but showed his appreciation of it. Göncz noted:

> We listened to the [speech], Zsuzsa and I looked at each other, agreeing that some kind of new world was upon us because he spoke in Hungarian and told the truth for the first time in several years. It was impossible not to see the importance of the thing.
>
> (Tóth, 2009)

Similarly, but more strikingly, in an interview with Hegedűs, Göncz asserted that during the development of the Revolution, he not only saw that the future of Hungary lay in the Hungarian Socialist Workers' Party (HSWP) led by Nagy,[41] but he could also have joined it:

Göncz: I could have joined the HSWP led by Nagy. I believed that a way out from the given socialist [order] was necessary. This was not only my opinion but was also shared by others, because [people's] loss of belief in the programme and its morality became apparent.
Hegedűs: Whose loss of beliefs in what are you talking about?
Göncz: [What I mean is] the loss of belief in socialism itself or in that of the Communist Party. A Communist party led by Nagy could have started from scratch.

(Hegedűs, 1985)

It appears from this statement that Göncz wished to suggest that a new world breaking with the past could have been opened up to the Hungarian population and that Nagy was a central figure bringing this fundamental change. On the one hand, Göncz saw that the root of the problem weighing upon Hungarian society lay in people's distrust of the ruling Communist party. Lies, propaganda and promises pledged but unfulfilled by the Communist party had distanced the Hungarian population from the party, and this in turn led to the moral crisis of the existing socialist order.[42] On the other hand, Nagy's radio speech provided a realistic assessment regarding the country's situation and gave hope and vision to the Hungarian people. Göncz, along with the Hungarian population shared this view and considered Nagy's programme as a blueprint for a remedy to help extricate the country from its predicament. For this reason, Göncz thought that, if necessary, he would have joined the party led by Nagy, playing his own part within it.

However, it should not be concluded from the above discussion that Göncz's support for Nagy's political vision means Göncz was a Communist who attached himself to the Maxist-Leninist idea and dedicated his life to its realisation. On the contrary, Göncz had pursued his political path in the ISP, an anti-Communist party that existed between 1945 and 1948 (Section 1.5 of Chapter 1). This therefore suggests to us that there would be other reasons as to why Göncz saw the future of Hungary in Imre Nagy. According to Péter Kende – Göncz's life-long friend, who lived through the Communist era – for Göncz, and in fact to the Hungarian population in general, the name of Nagy signified the feasibility of democratic change *within* the existing socialist order. This idea of so-called 'democratic socialism' was a prevalent phenomenon of the age and Göncz believed that Nagy was foremost in embodying and representing the Hungarian variant of this idea. In response to my question,[43] Kende succinctly stated:

> Like Bibó, Göncz thought that social justice could be achieved through economic improvement and that the equal distribution of [income] was a means to this end. In this respect, Göncz, along with Bibó, was a socialist but not in the sense that the Maxist-Leninists [conceived]. In 1953 or 1956 Göncz sympathised with Nagy because he saw that he could link socialism with democracy through Nagy. The [foundations] and potential of this democratic socialism were formed in the middle of the twentieth century but by the end of the century, when the world economy became globalised, [this] idea became [obsolete] as people no longer considered it [to be realistic]. But in 1956, many people considered it as a possible form of socialism. Today, it remains a principle or a concept.
> (Interview with Kende, 5 October 2007).

Regéczy-Nagy reaffirmed Kende's views, stating that the idea of Nagy's socialism was sufficiently visionary so that he was also under its influence; not least because it was seen by him as the only alternative form of socialism. Regéczy-Nagy noted:

> I accepted the idea of socialism, because there was no other alternative. In the presence of Soviet troops, the maximum extent of reform Nagy could have [implemented] was the easing of political pressure and terror . . . But the Soviets never understood this and were not interested either.
> (Interview with Regéczy-Nagy, 5 October 2007)

In view of these statements, it is safe to suggest that Göncz's comments regarding his willingness to join the Nagy-led HSWP were an expression of his sympathy and respect for Nagy's political vision, and not a sign that Göncz could indeed have pursued his political career as a Communist.

A second and more plausible account lies in Göncz's support for the popular will and values proclaimed by the Hungarian population during the Revolution. Initially, Göncz was hesitant and unsure about whether the event was simply a protest to serve the interests of a particular group or an uprising that arose from the aspirations of the Hungarian population. Having realised that it was a genuine manifestation of popular will (the will of those anonymous Hungarians who wished to construct a society different from the previous regime), Göncz decided to join the event. In an interview with *168 Óra*, Göncz clearly stated:

> When the revolution broke out, I had to ask myself whether the event was simply [led by] the reform Communists (by the Imre Nagy group) or whether this was also my revolution. When one or two days passed, while people were making up their minds, [I was able to make my decision] that this was a *popular* revolution so *it also belonged to me*.
>
> (*168 Óra*, 27 October 1992, my emphasis)

This lends weight to the claim that Göncz's sympathy with and, appreciation of, the will of the Hungarian population led him to join the Revolution. Although this does not provide us with a solid context regarding the demands and goals the Hungarian people sought to achieve, Göncz implied that the spirit of unity or solidarity was embodied in the 1956 Revolution. In his memory, the event remained a symbolic flame of the popular uprising that belonged to everyone; it could not be appropriated by a person, an interest group or a political party. In fact, when one examines Göncz's own assessment regarding the significance of the 1956 Revolution, it becomes evident that unity of the nation was the most essential value for Göncz. In a parliamentary speech delivered for the 34th anniversary of the 1956 Revolution, Göncz defined the practical meaning of unity and what it meant to him personally:

> We went on defending the memory of unity, the shared emotion: 'we are one'. It meant more than just the undisputed common goal we had proclaimed together during the Revolution: national independence, neutrality, justice, the creation of a communal society thought to be socialist, non-exploitative and cleansed from every stain.
>
> (Tóth, 1999: 64)

The above extract suggests that – for Göncz – the significance of unity was more than an emotional attachment to the people he interacted with during and after the Revolution. Göncz implied that under this slogan –'we are one' – people took an oath of their commitment to the common goals they sought to achieve. Above all, the restoration of an independent nationhood, the right to self-determination and the creation of a socially equal society, all of which would lead to the democratic transformation of the country, were set as the main objectives to be attained. This was also engraved in Göncz's mind and consciousness, which in turn led him to participate in the Revolution. In an interview with the *168 Óra*, Göncz once again highlighted the assertion that the unity of the nation culminated symbolically in the events of 1956 and that this was a moment of the truth demonstrating the will of Hungarian nation:

> In modern Hungarian history, 1956 was the moment of grace and truth that unequivocally [manifested] the [will] of national unity . . . The revolution so

united [people] as it began from a *tabula rasa* [*tiszta lappal*] . . . [In 1956] there was nothing other than tackling the dismantling [*kitakarítás*] of the Stalinist dictatorship and the restoration of the country's independence. The goal set for the revolution was so clear.

(*168 Óra*, 22 October 1991)

Judging by the above excerpt, it is clear that, in Göncz's historical consciousness, 1956 remained a juncture epitomising the unity of the nation in Hungarian history. Göncz implied that people's long-cherished desire to break with the practices of the previous regime – or its social order–led the Hungarian population to take to the streets. The abandonment of Stalinist dogmatism and its ritual practices and the reinstatement of national sovereignty were demanded and set as the key issues to be addressed. Göncz supported this idea and believed that the realisation of these goals would contribute to opening up a new beginning of the country's history. As Rainer noted, if 'the ideas and experiences of the revolution influenced the life and thinking of all of Hungarian society' (Rainer, 2002a: 7), Göncz was also influenced by the Revolution and imbued with this idea. It can thus be assuredly stated that Göncz's willingness to take a role in the resistance of 1956 signified his support and respect for the ideas that the Hungarian population aspired to achieve.

In terms of the development of Göncz's political views, what impact did his first-hand experience of the 1956 Revolution have on him? As noted in Chapter 1, it was established that during Göncz's adolescence, the idea of radical peasant populism and his experience in student armed resistance movements were the most important contributory factors in the shaping of his political views. In the former idea, land reform and the provision of education to the poor peasantry were considered as the main issues to be tackled. In the latter, Hungary's extrication from the Second World War and the restoration of the country's independence, democracy and social justice were set as principal goals by the student resistance. While Göncz interacted with and was influenced by both ideas, peasant populism was the more pronounced factor in shaping Göncz's political beliefs at this time of his life. If one traces the continuity and discontinuity of peasant populism and its impact on Göncz's political ideas, it becomes evident that the significance of this factor was receding into the background during and after the Revolution. Instead, there was a shift in his political orientations towards liberal and democratic values. Despite the fact that Göncz's pursuit of the idea of peasant populism was evidenced in the speech delivered at the Petőfi Circle and in his attempt to complete his agricultural studies, all of which were prevented (or interrupted) by the development of the Revolution. Göncz was still under the influence of peasant populism, but the will of Hungarian population epitomised under the banner of the creation of a free, self-determined and socially responsible society more convincingly imbued him with liberal and democratic beliefs. Such a sign was evidenced through Göncz's commitment to resistance which he firmly believed would contribute to informing the outside world of the truth and ethos of the Revolution. Even during his imprisonment, Göncz along with his friends ruminated on the significance of the Revolution that they witnessed and experienced.

The 1956 Hungarian Revolution 67

Thus, the events of 1956 had a reinforcing effect on the development of Göncz's liberal and democratic ideas which had been shaped through his proactive role in the student resistance movements. The common denominators that bound Göncz with the 1956 Revolution and the student resistance movements lay in his aspiration for and commitment to the realisation of a free, democratic and socially responsible society. Having noted this importance entrenched in the fabric of Göncz's political beliefs, the following chapter further examines and traces the significance of democratic and liberal values when he witnessed and underwent another dramatic change of the Hungarian society in the late 1980s. The chapter will probe the process by which Göncz's political views were developing and crystallised into a cogent, more or less definite liberal and democratic ideological trajectory. It is appropriate to conclude this exploration of Göncz's political and intellectual development with his own thoughts and views regarding his experience in the student resistance movements and the 1956 Revolution:

> I am not a saint. When I was conscripted into the [Hungarian] army, I deserted with arms, I fought against the Nazis . . . If once one gave one's life for democracy, there is little doubt that one would give one's life again. The Revolution ended my [agricultural] studies. On this occasion, I was lucky again because I witnessed a great deal of inhumanity. After the defeat of the Revolution, with my friends, I did not want to [choose] something like a political way out or a compromise, a *modus vivendi* with [an order established by] the Soviet Union. [We] did not [want to] repeat the eight terrible years of the past. [But] our attempt was not successful . . . In a closed and secret trial, with summary proceedings, without any possibility of appeal, I was convicted to life in prison on a charge of conspiracy and treason . . . In the prison, I taught myself English and today I feel that it was worth being imprisoned for this reason alone.
>
> (Göncz, 1991: 8–9)

3 Dissidence in the 1980s

Introduction

The previous chapter examined the development of the 1956 Hungarian Revolution and its impact on the shaping of Göncz's political beliefs. As has been argued, Göncz's first-hand experience of the Revolution had a significant impact on his political development. Despite the fact that the activities which Göncz undertook following the suppression of the Revolution failed to influence the Soviet leadership's intentions for Hungary, Göncz succeeded in making a clear demonstration of his own political stance. The basic but fundamental elements of democracy – the realisation of a free, self-determined and socially responsible society – were Göncz's ultimate goal and it was to the achievement of this aim that he committed himself wholeheartedly.

It was also noted that Göncz's subsequent imprisonment contributed to his intellectual and political development. For Göncz, incarceration did not mean the cessation of his intellectual and political activities. On the contrary, the existence of a translation bureau within the prison meant that Göncz was able to access valuable Western literature which was largely beyond the reach of the general public. The intellectuals alongside whom Göncz served his sentence proved able and vigorous debating partners. They, along with Göncz, envisaged the future of Hungary and waited for the appropriate circumstances in which they might realise their ideals. Such an opportunity first appeared for Göncz early in 1988 when he began to engage in political activities, founding the so-called Committee for Historical Justice (CHJ). In his personal Oral History, Göncz reminisced about this moment:

> Early in 1988, there were three great things in the making . . . I remember at least [among 1956-ers there were] three preliminary agreements on the need for the Commitee for Historical Justice. We felt a moral obligation to [form the organisation] and we felt the time [for action] was ripe.
>
> (Tóth, 2009)

This chapter continues the exploration of Göncz's political development in the late 1980s. The first section of the chapter briefly examines the main features of the social and political change in Hungary during the second half of the 1980s. The main focus of the remainder of the chapter is then devoted to examining the role and the activities that Göncz was engaged in while associated with these opposition movements. Finally, the chapter explores what Göncz sought to achieve by undertaking these actions and explains their significance in terms of the development of his liberal and democratic beliefs as well as his political career at this time.

3.1. Political and social changes in the second half of the 1980s

In the literature on Hungary it is generally accepted that the late 1980s was an epoch marked by the regime's deepening crisis. Although the then leaders had held power for the three decades since Revolution, their grip was no longer as assured as it had once been (Barany, 1999; 113–25; Bayer, 2005; 130–5; Kontler, 2002: 458–68; Körösényi, 1992: 1–10; O'Neil, 1998; 579–603; Pittaway, 2003: 57–61; Romsics, 1999: 412–23, 2007: 13–139; Rothschild and Wingfield, 2000: 239–43; Schöpflin, 1991: 60–3; Swain, 1993: 66–70). The domestic situation was described as 'Gulash Communism', a system based on an 'unsigned informal tacit social contract' between the Kádár regime and Hungarian society (Hankiss, 1990: 35), the essential conditions of which were the provision of relative material affluence by East European standards, in return for the relinquishment of the right to public participation in politics. However, by the late 1980s this arrangement was losing what little attraction it had held. In the Kremlin, Mikhail Gorbachev – an advocate of the fundamental, far-reaching reform of state socialism under the banner of *Perestroika* (restructuring) and *Glasnost* (openness) – came to power. Gorbachev's significance is nicely captured by Whitehead: 'The most crucial shift in the international context [was] Moscow's decision to lift its military veto over the unfolding of indigenous political processes . . . The linchpin that upheld the entire regional system was removed' (Whitehead, 1994: 41, 47). In turn, the consequence of this internal and external change strengthened dissident voices and increased the level of social dissatisfaction with regard to the decline of living standards[1] and the gerontocracy, led by Kádár, which was too slow to react to the rapidly changing circumstances.[2]

Although the core of the party-state institutions remained intact, Kádár's grip on power was at stake and the pendulum of public opinion swung decisively towards the politics of change.[3] As a result, in June 1987, a new Social Contract (*Társadalmi Szerződés*) was formulated by the democratic opposition made up of the urban intelligentsia who had appeared in the late 1970s as a response to the formation of Czech Charter 77.[4] They concluded that 'Kádár must go' (Kiss and Vida, 2005: 47–8). Similarly, in September 1987, another major strand of the opposition – the populist intellectuals who primarily came from writers' backgrounds and had a politically nationalist outlook – gathered at Lakitelek and established the Hungarian Democratic Forum. In its founding statement, the populists declared what they sought to achieve: 'The Hungarian people have been swept into one of the gravest crises of [their] history . . . This forum would be suitable for discussing our serious problems, analysing certain topics, and preparing proposals of alternative solutions' (Romsics, 2007: 372–3). Inspired by the formation of a populist front, the democratic opposition, who were by then mainly concerned with the formulation of reform programmes and the circulation of underground publication, chiefly *Samidzat*, also decided to found their own forum, creating the Network of Free Initiatives, which later became the Alliance of Free Democrats. This followed the establishment of an alternative non-Communist youth league, the Alliance of Young Democrats (AYD).[5] All of this was indicative of an emerging political plurality, as Bayer notes, this political pluralism was one of the distinctive characteristics of the Hungarian process of political transformation in the 1980s (Bayer, 2005: 133).

At this historically dynamic juncture, Göncz, as a member of the older generation who had experienced the Second World War and the 1956 Revolution, engaged in the emerging social movements and played a part in the development of political change. Imre Mécs noted: 'It was in the Committee for Historical Justice and the Network of Free Initiatives that Göncz's political activities began in the 1980s' (Papp, 2002). Göncz's dissident activities contributed to increasing his moral authority which, in turn, led him to be nominated for the post-Communist Presidency. The following sections of the chapter explore Göncz's participation in these pivotal social and political movements.

3.2. The Network of Free Initiatives and the Alliance of Free Democrats

The Network of Free Initiatives (NFI), a loose alliance of various independent civic groups, clubs and organisations, was founded on 1 May 1988 (Bozóki and Karácsony, 2002: 87; Jenkins, 1995: 185). In its founding statement the NFI urged Hungarian society to break its silence and to confront the need for the creation of a societal forum where intellectuals and the general public could hold a dialogue to confront the deepening political and socio-economic crisis:

> The economic and political crisis of our country is rapidly deepening. Society no longer believes that the regime is capable of preventing the decay [of the system] . . . Social groups must be organised and [articulate] their demands . . . But this movement must reach a higher level to break the fatalism [prevalent] in public opinion so that society itself becomes political force. We consider it to be important for the newly organising groups to preserve their independence and diversity [and that this] develop[s] into pluralism . . . Ultimately, we believe that such a body which is capable of assessing the situation and stating its position regarding important national issues, must be established.
>
> The current initiators[6] – members of different groups and those outside the groups who agree with us – suggest that the Network of Free Initiatives be created.
>
> (Miszlivetz, 1995: 229–31)

As individuals and representatives of autonomous groups that were critical of the regime's policies joined the NFI,[7] it attempted to operate as a single umbrella organisation integrating existing democratic forces (Kontler, 2002: 464; Romsics, 1999: 420, 2007: 101). In fact, according to a Hungarian political scientist, Ervin Csizmadia, the founding of the NFI was partially attributed to cross-national influence emanating from Poland. The parallel lesson that campaigners drew from the Polish Solidarity movement was that Hungary needed to create a similar pressure group which would represent a unified societal stance, as this would create the conditions in which a political space for public participation could evolve. Csizmadia noted 'Society is also accountable for its own situation. The [current] crisis would last long[er], the longer the different groups of society [took to press their] demands' (Csizmadia, 1995: 435). The NFI was expected to fill this gap, and it aspired to function as a viable alternative political force. With its basis in grassroot initiatives and, having underscored the significance of pluralism, the NFI did not represent a single political line or platform and the structure of the association was naturally horizontal. The Provisional Coordination Committee of the NFI did not give specific direction but rather acted as a channel through which members of various groups were able to communicate and update information regarding its recent activities.[8] With the exchange of information, opinions, and the sharing of experience among its supporters, the NFI was intent on drawing a social consensus and stating its position with regard to critical issues of the age. For example, on 1 May 1988 when the NFI adopted the draft of its operating principle, it also unveiled a visionary concept regarding political reform. The document – entitled 'There Is a Way Out' – contained a fundamental political framework including demands for the formulation of a new constitution, the establishment of a new parliament and the guarantee of civic rights.[9]

By the end of summer of 1988, it had become evident that the NFI's strength – the representation of pluralism and civic initiatives – had turned into its weakness. In the absence of coherent leadership, the NFI attempted to encompass different ideas and varied values but, 'this participative way of functioning based on wide-ranging negotiations among the member organisations was too slow and time-consuming' (Bozóki and Karácsony, 2002: 88), and resulted in operative weakness. Furthermore, the ruling Communist leadership announced that they were only willing to discuss state affairs with those opposition groups that 'had [their own] programme and formal membership that could be considered as a party' (Miszlivetz, 1995: 122); the NFI faced a dilemma – the Network had to decide whether it should continue to function as a front for the existing democratic forces or to transform itself into a party with individual membership. One of the advocates of the second option, Bálint Magyar, reasoned that without organising the NFI into a properly coherent framework, its political role would become marginalised in the process of political transition (Bozóki and Karácsony, 2002: 90).[10] In contrast, Ferenc Miszlivetz preferred the first choice as he was of the opinion that the maintenance of the NFI might become the platform for the creation of a robust civil society in Hungary. Miszlivetz argued:

72 *The development of Göncz's political views*

> They [those who supported changing the Network into a party] told me: let's close off the regular meetings. 'We neither need many people nor have time to listen to the opinion of all taxi drivers . . . We are the vanguard and elites'. I did not like this . . . I think it was a mistake to close off the Network at such an early [stage]. We should have sought compromise and cooperation [among various groups]. We should have created a strong civil society. At least, it should have [functioned] for another six months in order to become a political force.
>
> (Interview with Miszlivetz, 16 July 2007)

This incongruence in opinions was brought to an end on 13 November 1988 at the Jurta Threatre, where the future of the NFI was ultimately decided through a vote. The vast majority of participants supported the second option and agreed to establish a proto-party[11] named as the Alliance of Free Democrats (AFD) (*Magyar Hírlap*, 14 November 1988; *Magyar Nemzet*, 14 November 1988; *Népszabadság*, 14 November 1988).

From the outset, Göncz undertook a proactive role in the founding of the NFI and also participated in the composition of the founding statement.[12] It is not clear who first took the step towards establishing the NFI but, according to Göncz, 'I have to say that this thought was already in the air. It just had to be initiated by someone. I was also one of the initiators' (Wisinger and László, 2007: 59). As an observer, Göncz, along with other 1956 veterans, took part in discussion and debate at the NFI meetings; Göncz saw the sharing of his experience and knowledge with people as one of his most important tasks. According to Miszlivetz, it was at an NFI meeting that Göncz first encountered the future leader of the country, Viktor Orbán, who took the leading role in the founding of the AYD at the time. Miszlivetz noted:

> I am not saying that Göncz was too active in the NFI. He did not speak out much but he was there and at times expressed his opinion. He was rather an observer. Göncz wished to share his experience with the younger generation and, precisely with Orbán's circle. He said that 'he would be happy to talk with the students'. But the Orbán circle never came to Göncz.
>
> (Interview with Miszlivetz, 16 July 2007)

It is not known why Orbán and his associates distanced themselves from Göncz, but in Göncz's explanation Orbán's decisive and independent personality appears to be one of the factors. In his Oral History, Göncz remembered Orbán as an attentive participant but one who was cautious about committing himself to anything specific:

> Göncz: I got to know Orbán and László Kövér at the NFI meetings . . . Normally, they listened to [other people] and, if necessary, expressed their opinion. They remained [both] within and simultaneously outside the NFI. They had not decided yet where they [should] belong to . . . I

once spoke to Orbán saying 'come to see me' . . . Orbán said, 'I will tell them [members of the AYD] about your offer'. But, up to today, they have never done so . . .

Hegedűs: I think they might have been afraid of your influence.

Göncz: Yes, perhaps. Unfortunately, this [fear] was decisive in their attitude . . . I was sad to see this situation.

(Hegedűs, 1990)

This still does not sufficiently account for the question of why, and for what ends, Göncz was willing to meet with Orbán and his camp. Given the role of the NFI as a social forum for all, Göncz may have thought that this would be a good opportunity to share his experience with an energetic but still inexperienced younger generation. Moreover, NFI members may have been keen to foster the pluralism they were advocating for wider Hungarian society within the alliance itself.

Inferring from an interview Göncz gave to Hegedűs, it is possible to establish that ideas of political pluralism were of utmost importance for Göncz. In the interview Göncz presented his own definition and the concept of democracy:

I think we must support initiatives which came from grass-roots, because they expand the [scope] of democracy. My views on democracy have never changed. Perhaps, the only difference was that in 1956, I didn't feel pluralism [as] a timely [demand] . . . Democracy is not a matter of goodwill, an idyll, but the question of an institutional system. And, of a precisely circumscribed sphere of influence where stronger interest groups come to the fore in free contest. But we must also listen to the opinion of the minority because it could become a majority view tomorrow. So the basic requirement of democracy is pluralism, a democratic institutional system which [allows for] free enterprise to release human energies and an increase in the number of independent personal and economic units. Since I was [active] in the Pál Teleki Work Group, I felt this way and my views [on democracy] basically have not been changed.

(Hegedűs, 1985)

Evidently, the significance of pluralism was underscored by Göncz.[13] On the one hand, he acknowledged the importance of free competition and thought that those interest groups which exerted stronger influence with articulate demands would be the major players in democratic politics. On the other hand, Göncz took the minority view into consideration, implying that the ideal democracy he envisioned was an established political system which could reconcile differing interests and varied values and, if possible, strike a balance. As discussed in Section 1.2 of Chapter 1, this political vision had already taken some shape when he was active as a member of the Pál Teleki Work Group (PTWG) and was maintained over the course of his life.

In terms of the development of Göncz's democratic ideas with particular reference to his view on pluralism, there was a continuity between the PTWG and the NFI, and this had consistently remained in his political consciousness. By the time that Göncz gave an interview to Hegedűs, his views on democracy and pluralism had crystallised and been firmly established in the fabric of his political beliefs. The quotation above does not tell us specifically whether Göncz's attachment to the significance of pluralism was a factor which led him to become a part of the NFI. However, given the paramount significance of pluralism in his political beliefs which was the common denominator between the PTWG and the NFI, it can be argued that Göncz's involvement in the NFI was related to his liberal and democratic political ideas.

There is another reason why Göncz's liberal and democratic idea was primarily responsible for his decision to become a part of the AFD. While Göncz was active in the NFI and later the AFD, he also demonstrated an interest in the re-organised ISP party. With József Antall, with whom he had collaborated during the 1956 Revolution, Göncz attended a preliminary meeting of the ISP that took place on 18 November 1988 at the Pilvax Coffee House (Révész, 1995: 30). According to Göncz's account, however, it is clear that the ISP was no longer attractive to him. In response to my question on the subject,[14] Zsuzsánna Göntér stated:

> The prominent Smallholders known to Göncz were not in [Hungary]. Béla Kovács was taken to the Soviet Union and other Smallholders fled the country in 1949 [when the Communist came to power]. In reality, the real Smallholders' who [led the party] after World War II did not exist at home. Instead, a position hunting, [i.e. ambitious] József Torgyán – with whom Göncz had nothing to do – was there [in the party]. *In a word, for Göncz, the Smallholders was defunct in [1949].*
> (Interview with Göncz and Göntér, 10 January 2008, my emphasis)

Thus, for Göncz, the ISP was the party which existed during the short-lived democratic period in Hungary (1945–1948). As a one time ISP party member, Göncz might have entertained the idea of reinvigorating peasant populism along with his friends. However, having recognised the infeasibility of re-establishing the ideal of the post-war ISP, Göncz decided not to become a part of it. It should be noted that those close friends with whom Göncz had worked in the ISP, had sought asylum in the US[15] when the Communists purged the ISP leadership for their involvement in an alleged conspiracy against the Republic (see Section 1.5). In terms of Göncz's position, then, even if the re-organised ISP was operating under the same name, it was not the same party that Göncz had known. Instead, Göncz came to realise that those 1956 veterans who shared a common fate during the resistance that followed the defeat of the 1956 Revolution had found places in the AFD and Göncz also decided to attach himself to it. In this way, the practical reason for Göncz's membership of the AFD was informed by his friends' choice of joining the same party. In response to my question,[16] Hungarian political scientist, András Körösényi reaffirmed the reasoning:

> Perhaps one reason may be found in his personal relationship with people, amongst the AFD, the 1956 veterans, such as Miklós Vásárhelyi . . . Göncz

maintained contact with them in the 1980s and these people rather went in the AFD direction. I think, *Göncz's personal relationships were decisive in leading him to join the AFD*.

(Interview with Körösényi, 11 July 2007, my emphasis)

János Rainer also upheld the view:

> One of the reasons lies in Göncz's personal relationship with the 1956 veterans. For example, György Litván joined the AFD and this influenced him. At the initial stage of [systemic change], *personal ties were very influential for one's political orientation. This must not be forgotten.*
>
> (Interview with Rainer, 22 August 2007, my emphasis)

From the discussion above, however, one should not assume that Göncz always followed his friends' political path or that he did not have his own views and principles. Even if his friends' influence was an important contributing factor leading him to find his role within the AFD, Göncz would not have joined had he not also embraced the values represented by the AFD. Indeed, in an essay that he authored, Göncz indicated that there were other reasons for his determination to become a member of the AFD. These were grounded in his own belief that the idea of peasant populism was no longer applicable to Hungary's changed agricultural society. Göncz stated:

> The populist opposition [*népi ellenzék*] came from the populist writers, those who had been influential for me during my adolescence. I was also attached to the idea of the significance of rural Hungary. [But] I thought that, in wider societal terms [*társadalmilag már*], the legacy of radical peasantism had lost its significance, although I still felt it was important. With [the implementation] of land reform and the termination of large estate land-ownership, the village had been transformed, albeit forcibly [. . .].
>
> (Wisinger and László, 2007: 59)

This highlights the fact that Göncz had the intellectual capacity to judge the existing circumstances independently of the influence of his 1956 veteran friends. According to Göncz, it is clear that with the transformation of Hungary's society, the significance of peasant populism was receding; *emotionally*, Göncz still attached himself to the idea of peasant populism, but certainly it lost its contemporary relevance in his political beliefs. Instead, liberal and democratic ideology – the significance of which had come to the fore for Göncz through his first hand experience in fighting against the oppression of Nazis and the dictatorial rule of Communist regime – had a stronger influence on his political direction. It is important to remember that during his adult life, the importance of peasant populism diminished whereas Göncz's political orientation shifted towards liberal and democratic values (see the conclusion of Chapter 2). By the time the ISP was re-organised, Göncz had realised that his political ideal was rather close to those incorporated into the programme of the AFD. Göncz stated:

76 *The development of Göncz's political views*

Göncz: Look, this is not about against the Smallholders' Party. I have never denied my relationship with the Smallholders, especially my relation with Béla Kovács. But the liberal thinking of the AFD was much more closely in line with my own [. . .].

Kim: Are you saying that you were attracted by the liberal and democratic ideology of the AFD?

Göncz: Yes . . . It was self-evident that [my own] way of thinking was being changed.

(Interview with Göncz, 18 June 2006)

In view of this statement, it can be argued that Göncz's activities in the ISP and the AFD in the late 1980s were an attempt to find a role and to pursue his political ideals and, whereby his pursuit of peasant populism ultimately moved into his firmly established liberal and democratic ideological trajectory.

3.3. The Committee for Historical Justice

The Committee for Historical Justice (CHJ) was officially founded on 5 June 1988 eleven days before the 30th anniversary of the execution of Imre Nagy and his associates (*Élet és Irodalom*, 13 June 2008; Komor, 1989). Göncz with thirty six protagonists– primarily composed of the families of the executed, the 1956 veterans and writers[17]–signed the Committee's founding statement.[18] Revealing the truth which had been concealed by the Kádár regime for three decades, the CHJ drew Hungarian society's attention to the iniquity of the system and appealed for public support and mobilisation:

> Proclamation to the Hungarian people
>
> Thirty years [have passed] since 16 June 1958, the day when the prime minister of the 1956 Hungarian Revolution, Imre Nagy and his two associates, the Minister of Defence Pál Maléter and journalist Miklós Gimes were executed. Another prisoner in their trial, József Szilárgyi had already been hanged in March [1958] . . . the Minister of State Géza Losonczy was [killed] in prison in December 1957 before the last act of this legal farce. [For] three decades, many hundreds of people fell victim to the neo-Stalinist vengeance that followed 4 November 1956. [Their bodies] had been hidden in the bushes in the remote Lot 301 of the Rákoskeresztúr Cemetery . . . It is the [request] of their families and friends that we, the comrades of the martyrs, wanted to give voice to. We turn to the public of the country, to Hungarian society: Help us! [We want] our dead comrades and martyrs to be honoured. For the sake of justice!
>
> (*Irodalmi Újság*, 1988)

The CHJ's main goals were to right past wrongs by uncovering the remains of the executed and giving them a decent burial, and providing legal rehabilitation for the victims of post-Revolutionary repression, both dead and alive. Additionally, the CHJ demanded the opening of legal cases and secret files containing information on the show trials and miscarriages of justice that had occurred since 1945 and the implementation of a full-scale investigation into the circumstances surrounding these events. The official discourse concerning the events of 1956 (which considered that the Revolution had been a counter-revolutionary attempt to restore a capitalist order),[19] did not allow for dissenting views or judgements which deviated from the party's; the CHJ demanded the opening of political trials and independent investigations. It is important to remember that research and publications on the subject of Nagy and the Revolution had been banned over the course of the Kádár regime (see Chapter 2). In fact, according to Gyula Kozák – the former Director of the Oral History Archive at the 1956 Institute – a series of illegal roundtable talks that took place between December 1981 and summer 1982 at András B. Hegedűs's house[20] were instigated as an attempt to overcome the restriction imposed on independent research at the time. These secret meetings were led by nine 1956 veterans including Göncz.[21] The recounting of memories from 1956 and the creation of an alternative reliable source of non-regime sanctioned information were the main goals of this assembly. Kozák recalled:

Kozák: 1981 was the 25th anniversary of the Revolution. Commemoration of the event of 1956 was shown on television, radio and in the press, which portrayed the Revolution as a terrible counter-revolution . . . All real, reliable materials which were held in the archives were inaccessible to [researchers] . . . [In this situation], the prominent 1956 veterans who represented different groups gathered and sat at table. Miklós Vásárhelyi and Ferenc Donáth represented the Nagy Group and Imre Mécs represented the [view] of university students [. . .].
Kim: What was the main aim of the meeting?
Kozák: [It was aimed at] refreshing the memories of 1956. Every participant recounted their own 1956 . . . This led to the formation of a mosaic and a new picture of the Revolution.
(Interview with Kozák, 19 September 2007)

In short, as Rainer notes, critical reflection and impartial assessment regarding the events of 1956 was not practicable 'as long as [the] conditions prevailing at the time of the formation of the Kádár regime continued to exist' (Rainer, 2002b: 292); the CHJ demanded the cessation of the political manipulation of the country's history and pushed for a change.

Another issue that the CHJ wished to address was the end of direct and indirect harassment by the authorities and the discrimination that was suffered by the families of those who had been executed and of the 1956 veterans. By 1962, the Kádár regime had consolidated of its grip on political power (Ekiert, 1996: 107). To realise this level of supremacy, coercion and brutal repression had been employed in an attempt to crush the resistance to the regime within Hungarian society. The execution of Imre Nagy was a good example of how the regime approached the achievement of its aim. From 1962 onwards, however, the regime's political tactics had gradually altered. The level of coercion was eased as evidenced by the reduction of political terror and the issuing of an amnesty to political prisoners (Rothschild and Wingfield, 2000: 204). Instead, softer tactics of manipulation were employed in order to control the dissenting voices of those political prisoners who had been released from jail. One of the methods used by the regime was that of discrimination against, and stigmatisation of, the prisoners and their families. Children whose fathers were imprisoned due to their activities in the Revolution were taught by teachers that their parents received due punishment as they had acted to harm society. In contrast, at home, mothers told their children that their fathers were innocent men who had acted heroically and in defence of the nation. This contradiction between the interpretation established by the regime and that of the families meant that the children concerned had to confront the question of 'who was right?'. If the children upheld the view of the regime, the past of their fathers remained a stigma and a disgrace to the family. If, however, the children concluded that their fathers had acted correctly, they were nonetheless faced with an irreconcilable question: why were their right-thinking fathers being punished? In Kőrösi's and Molnár's terms, this 'irreconcilable contradiction between the values represented by society and those represented by the family' led to 'a double system of values' when assessing the Revolution (Kőrösi and Molnár, 2003: 91).

Similarly, various discriminatory acts were undertaken against the families of the political prisoners. For example, Judit Gyenes – the widow of the former defence minister of the Nagy government Pál Maléter – was unjustly treated in employment and housing as a consequence of Maléter's involvement in the Revolution. In my interview, Gyenes said that she was evicted from her house and forcibly relocated to a commune where she had to live with another family. Moreover, she was deprived of an opportunity to be employed as a full time worker, instead she had to make her living by taking on several part time manual jobs. Gyenes recounted:

> In May 1957, I received an order from the local military authorities telling me that I had to leave my house within 24 hours. I protested against it, asking on what grounds I had to leave . . . But it was not possible to negotiate with them . . . I was put into a commune where a family of six members already lived. One room for this family and another was for me, but there was no bathroom. I washed myself in the kitchen . . . An instruction came from the Ministry [of Labour] [instructing my employer] to dismiss me from my work place . . . [From that point on] I took on baby-sitting, gardening work, cleaning and I [even] dug graves in the cemetery. I did not rely on anyone and I am proud of myself [for having survived through during this difficult time].
> (Interview with Gyenes, 23 August 2007)

Thus the CHJ considered the issue of discrimination and stigmatisation as one of the major areas of social inequity which had to be properly addressed. Not surprisingly, the ruling Communist leadership regarded the demands of the CHJ as too radical but displayed signs of leniency with regard to the remembrance of the events of 1956. On 14 June 1988, the Political Committee of the Hungarian Socialist Workers' Party (HSWP) brought a resolution that they would tolerate the holding of a memorial service commemorating Nagy's death and those of his associates. This tolerance was extended on the understanding that the service was not used as a platform for displays of discontent against the regime (Ripp, 2006: 171). Members of the CHJ, dissident intellectuals and the 1956 veterans visited Lot 301 of the Rákoskeresztúr Cemetery where victims of the post-Revolutionary crackdown had been buried in unmarked graves. In a solemn and quiet atmosphere, a memorial service took place; a poem was recited and a eulogy delivered (Molnár, 2009: 49–53;Ripp, 2006: 172). In central Budapest by contrast, peaceful rallies organised by the members of the democratic opposition were brutally dispersed by the riot police (Hegedűs, 1998; *Népszava*, 16 June 2009;Papp, 2002), however, the authorities presented a false report to media. In an interview with members of the foreign press, Károly Grósz – János Kádár's successor as the general secretary of the HSWP – claimed that police intervention at the event did not constitute excessive use of force, not least because the demonstration that had taken place did so in breach of public order bylaws and had instigated violence.[22] Grósz claimed: 'We do not like it when our police are beaten up but we have evidence that this happened . . . The protest that occurred on 16 June was stirred up by fascist propaganda, chauvinism and irredentism' (*Népszabadság*, 12 July 1988).

Having disagreed with and been infuriated by Grósz's false statement, Göncz, as a vice-president of the CHJ, wrote a letter of protest to him. In this letter, Göncz expressed his deep regret at the way in which the authorities handled the events at the demonstration:

> Dear Prime Minister,
>
> I am a witness, an observer, and a partial participant and victim of the incident of 16 June . . . and this compelled me to write a letter to you [. . .].
> You are one of the party leaders who supported the memoriali[sation] of the dead. . . . For this reason, I feel extremely sad to [see] that on 16 June, the batons of [the riot police] and all those endlessly bitter acts [perpetrated in the regime's name] such as the removal of banners from the wreath and the confiscation of the memorial pole, [but these acts] have not silenced the voices of the dead [Imre Nagy and his associates] but [instead] made them louder [. . .].[23]

Göncz protested against the regime's use of violence as he viewed that coercion applied by the Grósz regime as contradictory to the General Secretary's promise to allow people to pay tribute to the fallen. Although Göncz did not mention the name of Grósz's predecessor or the policies Kádár was known to employ, he implied that there was no difference between the manner in which the Grósz regime dealt with the past and its remembrance and the attitude of previous party leaders. For this reason, Göncz considered that the question of coming to terms with the past could no longer be discounted, and proposed his own solution to deal with the past appropriately, he appealed to Grósz:

> If you wish to complete your historical task and renew the party [image], you must clearly dissociate yourself [from the party-line] not only through your [words], but also through your deeds . . . I know this may be against the interests of some and might seem detrimental to you as well. But it would serve the interests of society, the credibility of your words and your domestic and foreign policy. In this respect, dealing with the past cannot be avoided . . . I believe the vast majority of Hungarian people would be pleased, if you committed yourself to reckoning the past before [them] . . . I firmly believe that [the holding of] a dialogue is the basic moral condition and, the key to the future of this country . . . Without this, neither the shattered belief of the Party's politics nor [wider] social supports can be restored [. . .].[24]

This once again highlights Göncz's earlier point. In Göncz's view, there was a discordance between Grósz's word and his actions. This still does not present us with the full context regarding Grósz's pledge to Hungarian society, but Göncz clearly implies that the Grósz regime had failed to renew the image of the party and to restore public confidence. Above all, settling accounts with the past was seen as a long-pending issue which contributed to disharmony between the regime and the Hungarian society. For this reason, Göncz urged the regime to face the past honestly as, in his view, this was a pre-requisite to societal reconciliation. It should be noted that Grósz could have acted coercively in an attempt to silence Göncz and Göncz's letter of protest carried a certain importance, albeit a manifestly symbolic one.

In response to Göncz's letter, Grósz sent a reply a week later. In his letter, Grósz essentially refused to accept Göncz's proposition, and adhered to his previous stance. With regard to the actions of the police, Grósz defended his earlier position, reasoning that the conduct of police was correct as it served the maintenance of public order. Grósz claimed:

> On 12 June, I had already made clear to the protest organisers that [people must] refrain from violating public order . . . There is no political system [in the world which would] tolerate [a situation where] their police are kicked [by people]; this is never going to happen.[25]

Secondly, Grósz stated that the question of dealing with the past in the manner that Göncz had suggested would not be possible, because this would serve to undermine the fundamental political pillars which supported the regime. Grósz stated:

> You suggested securing my moral authority with relentless reckoning of the past. Unfortunately, I cannot accept this. Before the world, I pledged that I am not willing to reckon a past which lasted 42 years, but only its crimi[nal elements], distortions and errors [committed by] the rightists and leftists.[26]

Thus, Grósz firmly believed that political reform, including dealing with the past would not be necessary for securing the interests of the established order and of

Hungarian society; by the end of 1988, no positive sign regarding re-evaluation of the past had emerged.

At the end of January 1989, the momentum which broke the stalemate originated from within the ruling party leadership. In a radio interview, a leading reform Communist, Imre Pozsgay, made the startling announcement that the events of 1956 were not a 'counter-revolution', but a 'popular uprising' (Bayer, 2005: 134; Cartledge, 2006: 518; O'Neil, 1998: 100). Opinions regarding Pozsgay's statement may be differently perceived and assessed by the Hungarian population, but a general consensus established in the academic literature suggested that its effect was unequivocal and far-reaching: the re-evaluation of 1956 undercut the regime's legitimate political principles 'to their very foundation' (Ekiert, 1996: 119; Lewis, 1994: 244; Linz and Stepan, 1996: 305; Rainer, 2002b: 298; Tőkés, 1996: 299). While Pozsay did not mention that the reassessment of 1956 included Nagy's rehabilitation, the redefinition of 1956 opened up just this possibility, a fact that was indeed demonstrably evidenced by the change in the regime's attitude towards its historical consciousness. On 14 February 1989, the regime assented to the CHJ's demand that Nagy and his associates be reburied, albeit in a private family ceremony (Ripp, 2006: 348; Unwin, 1991: 221).[27] With the CHJ and the families of the deceased having agreed with the government's proposition, Nagy's exhumation and those of his associates followed (28 March–1 April 1989). The concession that the regime made to society thus far was, that Nagy's reburial could be dealt with as a family matter, excluding any possibility of public involvement in it.

The change of status quo was, however, once again initiated by the regime. On 19 April 1989, newly appointed Prime Minister Miklós Németh announced that Nagy's reburial 'could be no longer considered as a private matter', reasoning that 'it required the government's cooperation' (Ripp, 2006: 349). Moreover, Németh stated that Nagy's trial was unlawful, indicating that the legal redress – in due course – Nagy's exoneration would be inevitable. Evidently, Németh's actions suggest that there was a rift within the regime and that such a cleavage became increasingly apparent after Pozsgay's public statement. Indeed, Bruszt and Stark note that in an evening news programme, Németh made such a gesture by 'publicly repudiating one of [Grósz]'s speeches and distanc[ing] himself from the party hierarchy' (Bruszt and Stark, 1991: 225–6); which is highly indicative of the fact that the separation of government and party was already occurring within the regime.

Once the Németh government acknowledged that Nagy's re-interment would be treated as a public funeral, the main issue for the CHJ to address were those of venue and time. This was negotiated between Göncz and his associates and the Németh government. The result of negotiations showed that on 16 June 1989 the following government representatives – the Premier Miklós Németh, Deputy Prime Minister Péter Medgyessy, Secretary of State Imre Pozsgay and Speaker of Parliament Mátyás Szűrös – were allowed to pay tribute to the deceased at Heroes' Square.[28] At Göncz's suggestion, both parties also agreed that, along with five coffins for Nagy and his co-defendants, an empty casket would be included as a representation of the Unknown Insurgents who shed their blood during the Revolution (Bozóki, 2003: 90). On 1 June 1989, the result of agreements was announced by communiqué of the Central Committee of the HSWP, stating that June 16 would be a day of national mourning to the deceased and one which would also symbolise 'national reconciliation' (*Népszabadság*, 1 June 1989). The regime expected that allowing Nagy's reburial and the presence of some government members at the funeral might be helpful for the cause of redeeming the past.

However, Nagy's reburial turned out to be a symbolic day, epitomising the beginning of the end of Communism and catalysed Hungary's democratic transformation. It was not simply the day of Nagy's ceremonial re-interment but that of the entombing the old system itself. In the presence of a quarter of a million of the Hungarian population, it became a public political demonstration, one which de-legitimised the Kádár era.[29] Those people who had made a pledge to the Kádár regime were now put in a position of historical paradox. 'Kádár was Macbeth' whereas 'Banquo's ghost [Nagy] was lying in state on Heroes' Square' (Ash, 1990: 48–53). Just as Nagy had claimed during his final statement at his trial, his prophecy had finally been realised. Nagy stated:

> If my life is needed to prove that not all Communists are enemies of the people, I gladly make the sacrifice. I know one day there will be another Nagy trial that will rehabilitate me. I also know I will have a reburial. I only fear the funeral oration will be delivered by those who betrayed me.
> (*The New York Times*, 16 June 1989)

Therefore, for those anonymous Hungarians who fought for freedom alongside Nagy, this was 'the day of resurrection of the fallen and their crushed ideal[s] and [their] revolution' (Litván, 2008: 288).

Göncz did not give a memorial speech on this historical day but, from the beginning he, alongside a small group of 1956 veterans, had prepared for this moment. It was Göncz, who opened the funeral proceedings (*Magyar Hírlap*, 17 June 1989) stating 'Fellow Hungarians let us pay our *kegyelet* [tribute], let us remember' (Benziger, 2008: 22). Göncz vividly remembered the event and noted its significance both for him and for Hungarian history:

> I had no idea of the power of the spoken word [until then]. I saw several hundred thousand faceless people in front of me. When the list of those executed was read out, every name was like a hammer stroke on one's heart and on history. It was stupefying. I had never felt such psychological pressure or such a responsibility. I felt as if everything had slipped out of my hands and everything was in God's hands, myself included. I felt something enormously importance was taking place, as if this really was the final cathartic moment in Hungarian political development. This was the breakthrough in its [society's] silent force and amazing discipline.
> (Tóth, 2009)

Indeed, after the end of the funeral, root-to-branch political change ensued. On 24 June 1989, Grósz's sole leadership was replaced by the presidium of four: Rezső Nyers, Miklós Németh, Imre Pozsgay and Grósz himself (Izsák, 2001: 391), thus Grósz was marginalised within the party (Ash, 1990: 56). Two weeks later, on 6 July, the very day when the Supreme Court overturned the case against Imre Nagy and his fallen associates, János Kádár, who had reigned over the country for three decades died (Gough, 2006: 256; Rainer, 2002b: 303). Over the summer of 1989, the democratic opposition entered negotiations with the new leadership of the HSWP over the matter of arranging free elections and changing the Constitution. On 11 September 1989, Hungary opened its border with Austria to allow the East German asylum seekers to flee to West Germany; this act denoted the symbolic collapse of Communism (Lendvai, 2008: 239).[30]

At this juncture, Göncz was active as a member of the AFD and simultaneously assumed the brief chairmanship of the Hungarian Writers' Association (HWA) until May 1990. On 26 November 1989, at the annual meeting of the HWA, Göncz had been elected to the post. Initially, Göncz had received the same number of votes as a leading representative of populist writers Sándor Csoóri (Tóth, 1990: 66), but with Csoóri's voluntary relinquishment of his candidacy Göncz became the chairman of the HWA without runoff election. According to Göncz, winning the presidential post of the HWA was somehow related to his early political activities in the peasant populist movements.

Newspaper interviewer: It was said that you were elected to the president of the HWA, because you had the least number of enemies within it . . .

Göncz: Perhaps, it was something like that. [Those belonging to] the populist camp thought I am the 'solution' [to their problems]. My political school is back in the March Front. The way of thinking of the populist writers deeply influenced me, because they [dealt with] the crucial question of our lives: what the [future] of the peasantry and land reform would be. To this end, we stood against the Horthy system. Even today, I feel the original tradition of the Hungarian Democratic Forum is back to the [era] of the peasant populis[m] and came close to me.[31]

Göncz was able to attract support from both populist and liberal wings of the HWA (although these camps were traditionally loathed to co-operate). Thus Göncz's integrative personality contributed to his selection for the position of the first post-Communist president which, in turn, meant that he had reached the zenith of his political career. The details of Göncz's tenure in the post will be thoroughly examined in the next chapter in which I analyse the actual process and political negotiation required in order to institutionalise the presidency in

84 *The development of Göncz's political views*

the post-Communist era and Göncz's selection to the post. This chapter concludes by exploring the significance of Göncz's activism in the CHJ for his political development.

First, Göncz's role in the CHJ contributed to strengthening his liberal and democratic values. As has been discussed in Section 3.2 of this chapter, Göncz's determination to join the NFI rested with his appreciation of the significance of pluralism inherent in the NFI. Having noted this, his actions in the CHJ also showed that seeking societal reconciliation was of equal importance to the democratic values that Göncz upheld. Above all, Göncz, along with the CHJ members, considered that three issues – the rehabilitation of Imre Nagy and his associates, the opening of secret files to independent research and the cessation of police harassment – ought to be addressed as a matter of urgency. They believed that meeting these demands would not only serve to clarify a past that had been overshadowed by the oligarchic rule of the Communist regime, but would also lead towards societal concilation. Göncz, as the vice-president of the CHJ, urged the regime to change its conventional tactics with regard to dealing with the past and its remembrance; prior concealment of the truth and the use of coercion underscored the importance of an open approach. In particular, Göncz stressed the holding of a social dialogue as a key means of breaking down the wall between the regime and society. Despite the fact that the regime ultimately refused to accept Göncz's proposition, this act clearly illustrated the democratic values that Göncz had committed himself to.

Secondly, Göncz's activity in the CHJ contributed to the strengthening of his moral authority. As has been examined in Chapters 1 and 2, the origin of this is seen in a number of his proactive, political acts: beginning with his participation in student armed resistance movements against Nazi Germany, continuing through his important actions that followed after the defeat of the 1956 Revolution and his subsequent imprisonment to the founding of the CHJ, all of which laid the foundation of his moral authority. While Göncz was not able to achieve all of the objectives that he set himself, he nonetheless clearly demonstrated the values which he embraced. The common denominator that bound Göncz with those who fought together in these democratic movements was their commitment to the realisation of a free, democratic and socially responsible society. As Holmes notes, Göncz's democratic activities for which he spent a considerable time in jail 'under the old regime symbolises the courage and decency of anti-Communist dissidents' (Holmes, 1993), and displayed untainted moral authority to the public at large. It is appropriate to conclude this exploration of Göncz's political development with Göncz's thoughts and views regarding his democratic activities and their implications:

> It was not all that surprising that I was nominated to be president of the Republic by the [Alliance] of Free Democrats, which, as a liberal movement and later political party, was the direct successor of the democratic opposition. The grand old men of Hungarian politics – who had languished in limbo for years, who led every democratic initiative since 1941, resistance to the

Nazis and before that the March Front, the peasant-radical writers' movement for national unity, 1956, the movements for a peaceful transformation in the late 1980s – did not live to see the changes that they should have represented and symbolised. All this left just me, a writer with three politically colour[ful] chapters in my life.

(Tóth, 1999: 232)

Part II
The post-Communist presidency

4 Development of the post-Communist presidency in Hungary

Introduction

This chapter examines Göncz's political career after his election as Hungary's first post-Communist president (3 August 1990). An exploration of the factors which contributed to his accession to the presidential post is the main focus of the chapter, but in order to examine Göncz's political development in a wider context of Hungary's political history, the chapter is laid out as follows.

The first section of this chapter briefly examines the National Roundtable Negotiations and its significance, as it was in this forum that the fundamental framework of governance for the country was decided by participants, and the form and structure of the presidency was included. The next section critically reviews and re-examines the actual process of institutionalising the presidency. This includes the analysis of accounts offered by those of my interviewees who actually participated in the Roundtable Talks and subsequent political negotiations.

The remainder of the chapter is devoted to analysing the constitutional powers granted to the Hungarian president. The chapter asks what the main characteristics of the Hungarian presidency are and identifies their significance and their implications for Göncz's exercise of powers during the term of his presidency.

4.1. The National Roundtable Negotiations, the beginning of a new 'political game in town'

On 23 October 1989, the People's Republic of Hungary which had lasted for more than four decades, was proclaimed the Republic of Hungary. The date is significant as it was the anniversary of the day that the Hungarian people rose against Communist rule and proclaimed their will to struggle for freedom and national independence in 1956.[1] The new rules for the governance of the country had been established in the national Round Table Negotiations (RTN) between the ruling Communist party and the Opposition Roundtable (OR).[2] The OR – a *tentative* alliance of the eight democratic forces[3] – was founded on 22 March 1989 with the aim of coordinating oppositionist actions more effectively and, above all, of forming a united front against the ruling Communist party (Hungarian Socialist and Workers' Party, hereafter HSWP). The RTN lasted from 13 June 1989 until 18

September of that year,[4] during this period both parties held a series of intensive negotiations to discuss the six items on the agenda: the Draft Bill on the Electoral Law; the Draft Bill on the Amendment of the Criminal Code and Proceedings; the Draft Bill on the Media and Publicity; the Draft Bill on the Amendment of the Constitution, including the Bill on the Establishment of the Constitutional Court and the Presidency; the Draft Bill on Political Parties and Party Finance; and Guarantees of a Peaceful Transition (which concerned the dismantling of the Communist paramilitary unit: the workers' militia) (Bozóki, 2003: 95).

The result was mixed (*Népszabadság*, 19 September 1989a, 1989b). Both the HSWP and the OR managed to agree on the first four issues, at least in principle,[5] whereas they failed to reach a consensus over the last two questions. In particular, divergent opinions among the political elite centred on the establishment of the Office of the President and in particular on the method of presidential election (by popular vote or indirectly elected by Parliament), the timing of the election (before or after the founding parliamentary election) and the range of the president's constitutional powers (Elster, 1993: 96, 1996: 14). The HSWP leadership demanded that the timing and method of the presidential election be decided *before* the parliamentary election and by a popular vote. In contrast, the OR insisted that the creation of the presidency be dealt with only *after* the first parliamentary election. Ultimately, the only element agreed upon during the RTN was the establishment of the presidency itself. As Péter Tölgyessy – a key delegate of the OR and former leader of the Alliance of Free Democrats – noted, it was the presidency that invoked the most contentious debate among the Hungarian political elite during the RTN (Tölgyessy, 1999a). The following section of the chapter probes what was behind this political intransigence.

4.2. Designing an institutional system: the presidency

4.2.1. Bargaining over the presidency

As stated above, an agreement over the establishment of the presidency was reached between the HSWP and the OR during the RTN. The actualisation of this agreement, however, was far from easy and did not proceed without incident; above all, the legal procedure had to be settled upon advance. In practical terms, this meant that the previous Communist Constitution promulgated by Act XX of 1949,[6] had to be revised so that new political institutions could be introduced. Interestingly, the proposal for the amendment of the Constitution was first offered by the HSWP and this occurred even before the first rounds of RTN talks (Stanger, 2004: 7). According to constitutional expert, István Somogyvári, in March 1989 the legal experts, Géza Kilényi, Kálmán Kulcsár, Somogyvári himself and others, were assigned the task of composing a constitutional draft for the amendment of the Constitution. Somogyvári observed:

> We received an instruction to immediately draft a set of rules required for the creation of the presidential office . . . Since the presidential office could only

be created after the amendment of the Constitution, I composed a draft of the constitutional revision.

(Interview with Somogyvári, 22 May 2007)

In addition to the presidency, relevant provisions for the establishment of the Constitutional Court and the Office of Audit were also subsequently prepared; in April 1989, a draft Constitution formulated by these legal experts was approved by the politburo of the HSWP (Schiemann, 2005: 86).

The essence of the draft changes to the Constitution was that the post-Communist presidency should be built upon the model provided by the French Fifth Republic (Tölgyessy, 1999a, 1999b), which is, a 'semi-presidential' or 'premier-presidential system'.[7] According to this draft, the Hungarian president was to exercise wide 'legislative' and 'executive' powers, taking on an important role in the separation of powers (Kukorelli, 1995: 195). For example, the president was to be able to dissolve Parliament and declare war, although the exercise of the latter power could only occur under circumstances where Parliament could not be convened (Schiemann, 2005: 86). Furthermore, the president was to be directly elected by the population, and the presidential election was due to be held before the first parliamentary election. The OR were strongly against the HSWP proposal, arguing that the institutionalisation of the presidency ought be dealt with by the first democratically elected Parliament. The OR reasoned that since neither the Parliament elected in 1985 nor the HSWP had legitimacy to introduce a new political institution, little reason remained for further discussion (Bozóki, 1992a: 65). Instead, the OR focused on ensuring that the basic institutional conditions be met (for example, the enactment of a new electoral law), in preparation for the first free parliamentary election. At the initial stages, therefore, the OR took a resolute and intransigent stance against the HSWP proposal; a clear, bi-polar cleavage between the HSWP and the OR was established.

By the end of the summer of 1989, however, a conciliatory political stance was slowly taking shape on the OR side. According to Tölgyessy, a number of world leaders who visited Hungary in the summer of that year advised OR members not to 'take on a radical solution' (interview with Tölgyessy, 15 October 2007). The practical meaning of this message was that the political transformation of Hungary should be made democratically, but at the same time *peacefully*. The leaders who advanced this idea did not directly mention that a compromise should be sought to ensure a peaceful transition to democracy. Nevertheless, as Tölgyessy pointed out, 'in reality the West allowed the Communists to retain some prerogatives' (interview with Tölgyessy, 15 October 2007), indicating that compromise should be key to the process of Hungary's transition to democracy. The West's view along with the prevailing domestic political situation assessed by political elites (for which the withdrawal of the Soviet army from Hungary was a top priority) meant that the intransigence of the OR began to shift. On 6 July 1989, the conservative members of the OR, the Christian Democratic Peoples' Party and the Hungarian Peoples' Party gradually moved toward the HSWP's position, showing a willingness to accept the HSWP proposal (O'Neil, 1997: 204; Schiemann, 2005:

89).⁸ In contrast, the other members of the OR, particularly the Alliance of Young Democrats (AYD) and the AFD which took a radical anti-Communist stance at this time, persistently refused to accept the HSWP proposal.

Thus, by the summer of 1989, the political cleavage that existed between the HSWP and the OR further developed a more complicated form. Tensions now existed among the members of the OR *and* between the OR and the HSWP. Consequently, negotiations concerning the establishment of the Office of President ended in a stalemate. According to the historian, Zoltán Ripp, throughout the summer bargaining over the presidency was at a standstill until a representative of the HDF, József Antall, proposed a solution. With the approval of the HDF Presidium, on 17 August, Antall proposed a package deal, arguably an ambiguous, compromise-seeking solution which was neither entirely representative of HSWP nor OR preferences. The important point of the proposition was as follows:

> The presidential election can be held after the parliamentary election or simultaneously. Until then, the Speaker of the House will be the interim President. For the first occasion, the President of the Republic shall be directly elected for five years.
>
> (Ripp, 2006: 443)

The only clear element of Antall's proposition was that a one-off direct presidential election could be held, if the Communist and OR members agreed on his proposal. The timing of the holding of a presidential election, however, remained unclear. On 29 August 1989, Antall made another proposal. This time, he suggested that with the restoration of Act I of the 1946 Constitution, legal disputes over the institutionalisation of the presidency can be settled. Reasoning that, according to Act I of the 1946 Constitution, the president is elected by Parliament, Antall suggested that the presidency be built on this historic model (Ripp, 2006: 447). However, he insisted that a one-off direct presidential election be further considered. Thus, although Antall made two different proposals, they had one element in common: the holding of a one-off direct presidential election. In practical terms, this meant that the initial intransigence displayed by the HDF was now developing into leniency towards the HSWP, if the Communists would accept the condition: the presidency should be based upon Act I of the 1946 Constitution but, on one occasion, direct presidential elections could be held.⁹ As Swain notes, the populist camp led by the HDF 'changed their opinion over the issue of the Presidency and came to support the your president and our prime minister solution, with Pozsgay the favoured candidate for a directly elected Presidency' (Swain, 2006: 150).

Indeed, according to O'Neil, apart from the AYD, the AFD and the Democratic League of Independent Trade Unions, in September 1989, all other members of the OR accepted Antall's proposal, signing a 'preliminary agreement' between the HSWP and the OR (O'Neil, 1993: 187, 1997: 205). According to this agreement, on only one occasion, the direct presidential election would be held on 28 November 1989. Frustrated with this agreement, the AYD and the AFD refused to sign the final RTN agreement as an expression of protest, although they did not challenge the act of signing the agreement (Ripp, 2006: 456). Instead, these two rebellious groups decided to collect signatories in order to push for a referendum. In November 1989, their efforts came to fruition when the so-called 'Four Yes-es' referendum was held. Göncz recounted how this historical political process took place during the initial transitional period of Hungary's democracy.

Newspaper interviewer: You were not at the centre of this talk [RTN] but you firstly [proposed] a solution that if an agreement was reached that the AFD found unacceptable, they should neither sign nor veto it. Is that correct?

Göncz: Yes, as far as I know, I was the first to say this. At least, according to my memory, it was me although it is possible that there were others too . . . Antall saw – and for a while myself [I was in agreement] – that the future of the [country] could be only imagined as a cooperation between the main forces of the HSWP [or its successor] and the opposition. But in September 1989, the AFD thought that for the transition to [democracy] the HSWP's participation was not [required]. The [root] of this [thinking] lay in whether the presidential election should be held before or after the parliamentary election, and Imre Pozsgay was not necessarily [the preferred presidential candidate] for the AFD. [Refusing to] sign [the agreement] overturned Antall's carefully thought through strategy, as he saw the alliance with Pozsgay as indispensable. The HDF or Pozsgay would never forgive me or the AFD for this.[10]

4.2.2. *'Four Yes-es' (Négy Igen-es) referendum*

With the adoption of the agreement between the HSWP and the OR, disputes over the establishment of the presidency seemed to have ended. According to this agreement, the presidential election was due to be held before the end of the year. However, this was not realised as a result of subsequent joint political action taken by the AYD and the AFD (the liberals). Having disagreed over the outcome of the RTN, particularly concerning the timing and method of the presidential election, the liberals collected signatories to launch a referendum. The ultimate goal of this campaign was to retract the decision to hold a one-off direct presidential election. In addition to this, members of the dissenting groups sought to settle other issues which had not been resolved during the RTN. These included whether the Communists should retain their long-held privileges and, on 26 November 1989, the Hungarian population were asked the following questions:

1. Should the HSWP ['s party activity] in work places be banned?
2. Should the workers' militia be dissolved?

3. Should the HSWP's party property be liquidated?
4. Should the presidential election be held after the parliamentary election?

(Bozóki, 2003: 104)

In this referendum, the Hungarian Socialist Party (HSP)[11] campaigned for three yes-es and one no (on the last issue), whereas the liberals appealed to the population to vote for four yes-es. The HDF, however, initially boycotted the referendum (O'Neil, 1997: 206; Pittaway, 2003: 62), yet interestingly they later went on to nominate their own presidential candidate, Lajos Für (*Népszava*, 23 October 1989). Given that the HDF *de facto* supported the HSP's presidential candidate, Imre Pozsgay during the RTN – one of the most popular reform Communists (see Section 3.3) – there was a question mark over Für's nomination for presidency.[12] According to Ripp, Für's nomination was an *ad hoc* tactical solution taken by the HDF leadership to neutralise criticism raised by the AFD. Ripp asserted that before the referendum, the HDF was heavily criticised by the AFD and labelled as 'Communists' friends' or 'collaborators' (Ripp, 2006: 496). Having faced fierce criticism, the HDF leadership sought to find a way to neutralise these allegations, but without damaging the relationship with the HSP. The solution was the nomination of an independent presidential candidate from within the HDF, in the expectation that this would help the AFD to vindicate themselves in light of the allegations that had been made. In hindsight, however, Für's nomination for the presidency was merely window dressing. Given that the HDF's real stance towards the HSP was questionable, the HDF had to exhibit an image to the public through which it could dissociate itself from the HSP. A former factional leader of the HDF, Ferenc Kulin, noted:

> The AFD launched a campaign against the HDF . . . They said the HDF wanted to collaborate with the Communists . . . [In response] we had to demonstrate that we had our own independent candidate . . . For this reason, we put Lajos Für forward as the presidential candidate.
> (Interview with Kulin, 14 November 2007)

In terms of the HDF's position, Für's nomination did not militate against Pozsgay, but rather, aided his position (Ripp, 2006: 496).

The referendum was held and its result supported the liberal's position over the HSP by a margin of only 0.2 percent (Dezső and Bragyova, 2007: 91–2). According to the result, the timing of the presidential election was now rescheduled so as to take place after the parliamentary election. With hindsight, this referendum was not about the scheduling of the presidential election, but was a question of accepting Pozsgay as the first post-Communist president (Elster, Offe and Preuss, 1998: 66). Given that no other candidates from the liberals group 'could run for the presidency [against Imre Pozsgay and have] any realistic chance of winning' (Pokol, 2003) by deliberately deferring the presidential election, the liberals prevented the HSP from reconsolidating their powers within the Office of President. In his memoir, Pozsgay expressed his devastation at the impact of the referendum on the defeat of his political ambition thus:

After the blows [rained upon] me, I concluded that I had been defeated in a venture of high stakes but,[that I] had not failed . . . It was as if I had been kicked in the stomach. I would be a Pharisee and a hypocrite if I denied [this].

(Izsák, 2001: 401)

The disputes over the issue of a direct presidential election appeared to have ended. However, in 1990, the HSP found another way to recast their powers in the presidential office. This time by launching another plebiscite along with the independent parliamentarian, Zoltán Király,[13] the HSP asked the population about the form of the presidential election itself. However, this attempt to reignite the discussion on the presidential election was not realised as a result of an extremely low turnout of only 14 percent (*Népszabadság*, 30 July 1990). Given this political history, it is thus clear that the HSP persistently attempted to reconsolidate their power through the presidency, but its plan was largely thwarted by the joint action of the uncompromising and intransigent members of the OR – the AFD and the AYD. In terms of the position of the AFD and the AYD, the success of the referendum would have contributed to an increase in their recognition factor with the general public and this would have been beneficial for gaining more seats than might have been expected in the forthcoming parliamentary elections. However, as will be discussed in the following section, the actual result of the general election did not come about in this manner, and required a new configuration of power-sharing between the electoral victor and the largest opposition.

4.2.3. The pact

The first free and competitive general election in Hungary was held in the spring of 1990. The HDF, whose founding ideology was rooted in populist-nationalism (*népi és nemzeti*), won the first general election (Körösényi, 1999: 35–6). Securing 42.75 percent (164 out of 386 seats) of the vote, the HDF defeated their counterparts, but their number of seats in Parliament fell short of an outright government parliamentary majority.

To overcome this, the HDF sought a coalition agreement with two ideologically close conservative parties, the Independent Smallholders' Party (ISP) and

Table 4.1 The outcome of the 1990 parliamentary election.

Parties	1990
HDF	164 (42.75%)
AFD	92 (23.83%)
ISP	44 (11.14%)
HSP	33 (8.55%)
AYD	21 (5.44%)
CDPP	21 (5.44%)

Source: Adapted from *Népszabadság* (10 April 1990).

the CDPP (Christian Democratic People's Party), which together secured a sufficiently large number of seats (229/386) to form a majority. Subsequently, on 23 May 1990, the president of the HDF, József Antall, was sworn in as premier.

Having secured a qualified majority of parliamentary seats, Antall's decision to make a pact with the leading opposition party – the AFD – is questionable. There are various accounts explaining his decision, but a general consensus offered by academics suggests that the decision was informed by new legislation, which required a majority vote of two-thirds among the Members of Parliament (MPs) (Bihari, 2005: 395–6; Debreczeni, 2003: 298; Lomax, 1993: 87; Romsics, 1999: 440; Sajó, 1996: 89).[14] Despite the fact that Antall formed a conservative coalition government, the coalition's total of parliamentary seats was insufficiently high to ensure the passage of legislation, which required a minimum of 256 votes from MPs. The Antall government, for instance, could not even pass the law on the state budget without the receipt of votes from the opposition. A former factional leader of the HDF, Imre Kónya, noted:

> When the HDF won the general election, it became clear that with selected coalition partners, we comprised more than 50 percent of [parliamentary seats]. In a normal country where a normal parliamentary system is functioning, it would have been possible to govern the country thus. But, according to the Constitution at the time, for the passage of almost all bills, such as the bill of the state budget, a two-thirds majority vote was required. With the AFD we met this [quorum].
> (Interview with Kónya, 11 December 2007)

The AFD, which had ninety two seats (23.8 percent) in Parliament at the time, was selected as a potential ally for the conclusion of a stability pact. Subsequently, between 27 and 29 April 1990, after two days of intensive talks, Antall concluded a pact with the AFD (Kis, 1990). The essence of this political bargaining was that the HDF secured the support of the AFD in the passing of the laws which required a two-thirds majority vote, conceding the presidency to them in return (Debreczeni, 2003: 298; Kis, 1990; Szegő, 2010).

The puzzle of the AFD

Antall was able to secure a stable basis for the governance of the country through the conclusion of the pact with the AFD. In terms of the AFD's position, however, there is a question mark as they simply accepted Antall's proposition. If these issues had been differently resolved, the HDF–AFD coalition government could have met the requirement of a two-thirds majority quorum with ease. Alternatively, by forming a grand coalition with the AFD and the AYD, the Antall government could have benefited from a wider legitimacy within Hungary's new democracy. In fact, before the conclusion of the pact, Antall made a gesture of cooperation with the AYD (Tölgyessy, 1993) and the AFD had already signalled to the HDF that they were willing to enter a coalition government (Debreczeni, 2003: 81).[15]

The president of the AYD Viktor Orbán noted: 'Everyone knew that the situation needed something like an agreement among political forces. We would have been pleased if the HDF had invited several parties to make a [coalition] agreement' (Papp, 2002). It is thus interesting to ask why the formation of a coalition government was discarded as an option at a very early stage.

There is no clear explanation in the available documentation as to why the coalition government failed to come to fruition. As Tökés notes, this question remains 'one of the great still-unresolved puzzles of the Hungarian transition' (Tőkés, 1996: 397). However, according to my email exchange with the former chairman of the AFD and one of the key participants in the pact-making process –one possible explanation lies in the objection of the HDF founders to form a coalition with the AFD. The ex-chairman of the AFD suggested that although Antall might have considered the formation of a coalition with the AFD, 'the Lakitelek founding members of the HDF vehemently opposed it'(emails with a former president of the AFD, 4 and 10 August 2010). Given their contrasting political orientations and differing political backgrounds rooted in rural and urban politics respectively – the AFD was largely a left-liberal party whereas the HDF was at the right-conservative end of the political spectrum – this oppositional political position made it difficult for the HDF founders to accept the idea of sharing power. For example, if as a part of the fulfilment of a coalition agreement, key ministerial posts were distributed to the AFD and a conflict was to arise between the AFD affiliated ministers and the HDF premier, an impasse could result. It is important to remember that the political split between the HDF and the AFD had begun in 1987 when the populists founded the HDF at Lakitelek, and their united position ultimately broke down in the aftermath of the Four Yes-es referendum.

Moreover, in terms of Antall's position, making a pact with the AFD would be more advantageous for the consolidation of his position within the HDF. At this time Antall was not yet strong enough to lead the HDF outright. He was not a founding member of the party and he came to a leading position only after an authority in the populist camp, Sándor Csoóri, helped him find a role within the party. Political commentator, László Lengyel stated:

> Csoóri was a spiritual leader for the HDF. He suggested to the HDF that they accept Antall as party president. Aside from Csoóri, Antall did not know anyone within the HDF. Neither had he known István Csurka nor Zoltán Bíró. Csoóri was the only figure Antall had known.
> (Interview with Lengyel, 13 September 2007)

Thus, given Antall's reliance on the support of the HDF founders, he could not challenge their opinion which in turn, meant that he needed to find an alternative solution to the question of power sharing. In effect, Antall decided to make a *secret* pact with the AFD without the approval of the HDF's founders. Zoltán Bíró – a key founding member and the first president of the HDF – recounted the process of Antall's rise and the process of pact-making:

> I was the first president of the HDF. When the first general election began I resigned my post, because the AFD at the time criticised us claiming that we are anti-Semite and had made a pact with the HSP. I thought Lajos Für would be an eligible figure for the post [of president] . . . but at the request of Csoóri, we accepted Antall . . . He made the pact with the AFD but he did not even ask the opinion of the Presidium. He made the pact with the HDF's opponent in secret.
>
> (Interview with Bíró, 10 December 2007)

Indeed, Csoóri convened the meeting of the HDF founders at Selyemgombolyító to discuss the developing situation and, accordingly, to find a solution (Révész, 1995: 85). However, it was too late to thwart Antall's move, whereby the HDF founders had been marginalised within the party and moved to the periphery of politics as a whole (Tőkés, 1996: 398). Similarly, Antall's success in concluding the pact with the AFD meant that the largest of the opposition's forces and the one which could potentially have obstructed the passage of new legislation had been neutralised. In effect, Antall seemed to have 'killed two birds with one stone', but in terms of the AFD's position, it is still not clear why they were willing to accept Antall's proposal.

The pact: a power-sharing scheme or the origin of confrontation?

With the agreement of the AFD, Antall was able to secure a necessary quorum required in order to adopt new legislation and to govern the country. To this end, Antall offered the presidential post to the AFD which, in turn, strengthened the AFD's position in the decision-making process – this would also ensure that the AFD had more influence than would have been the case if the party had merely remained a member of the opposition. *Apparently* this political bargaining was advantageous to both parties. However, if one looks into the details of the pact, it suggests an alternative perspective in which the pact was not merely a power sharing scheme but that the potential for confrontation was built into its fabric. This section examines the significance of this bargaining process through analysis of the content of the pact as it was negotiated.

On 29 April 1990, the HDF and the AFD agreed on the following points of the pact. The salient parts of the agreement for the argument presented here were as follows:

> The Hungarian Democratic Forum and the Alliance of Free Democrats agree that both the parties of the government and the parties of the opposition have a special responsibility before the nation for the consolidation of the new democratic institutions and for the governability [*kormányozhatóság*] of the country . . . For this reason, the following is agreed:
>
> - The original status of the President of the Republic should be restored according to Act I of 1946 Constitution;

- ... The president of the Republic appoints ministers according to the suggestion of the prime minister;
- In the interests of the governability of the country, the presidential right to dissolve Parliament can be conditionally expanded, if necessary;[16]
- The election of the prime minister requires an absolute majority; and a motion of no confidence against the prime minister also requires an absolute majority;
- ... The institution of the motion of no confidence shall not apply against individual ministers, but only against the prime minister. The motion of no confidence will take the form of a constructive vote of no confidence;

<Supplement number III>
The parties also agree that ... in the presidential election, the HDF supports Árpád Göncz, and upon this, the Speaker of the House will be György Szabad;
<Supplement number IV>
The national television [and] radio [stations] and the Hungarian News Agency should be free from party political interference. For this reason, [both parties agree] that according to the suggestion of the prime minister, the president ... appoints the president and two vice-presidents of the national television and radio [stations].

(Izsák and Nagy, 2004: 555–60)

Both parties concluded that, in order to lay a stable basis for the governance of the country in the future, the amendment of the Constitution that had been concluded during the RTN was essential (Körösényi, Tóth and Török, 2007: 35; Ripp, 2006: 543). To this end, both sides agreed that the introduction of several institutional guarantees was required; among these, agreement would have to be reached regarding the institutionalisation of the presidency. The HDF and the AFD concluded that the post-Communist presidency be built upon the reinstatement of Act I of the 1946 Constitution.[17] According to this Act, the president was to be elected by Parliament for a term of four years, and the exercise of power was significantly circumscribed by a counter-signatory system. For example, concerning the issue of personnel management, the president was required to have the prime minister to act as a co-signatory. Similarly, the president was capable of dissolving Parliament only if such a proposition was put forward by the premier or by at least two-fifths of MPs.

In terms of the president's position, thus, Act I of the 1946 Constitution essentially established weak presidential powers which, in turn, established the prime minister as the locus of executive power in Hungary's political system. This was, indeed, evidenced in the strengthening of the position of premier. With the introduction of a constructive vote of no confidence, akin to the German chancellery system (Baylis, 1996: 300; Szoboszlai, 1996: 126), the removal of the prime minister from power could be practicable only if an equivalent candidate was simultaneously nominated by Parliament. Likewise, placing the cabinet under the control of the premier contributed to the expansion of the jurisdiction of the Executive over the Legislature. Together, it appears that the competences of the Antall government were enhanced regarding the extent to which they could govern the country with their own programmes.

However, the pact also contained provisions which could potentially turn into sources of conflict. This was particularly the case when Antall agreed that the HDF would support Göncz's election to the presidency. Considering Göncz's political affiliation, if the presidential post were to be used by the AFD as such an attempt to expand their influence in the decision-making process, this agreement would be counter-productive for the Antall government. For instance, Supplement IV of the pact specified that the appointment of the presidents and vice-presidents of the broadcasting media would be made possible through a two-step process: according to the suggestion of the prime minister, the president would appoint them. In the event that the president disagreed with the premier's proposal, a tug-of-war between them and their camps seemed to be inevitable. Indeed, one of the most controversial issues in which Göncz became involved during the first term of his presidency (1990–1995) concerned the issue of control over the broadcast media and, this conflict occurred during the Antall government (will be discussed in detail in the next chapter). In Viktor Orbán's terms, the pact may have been a clumsy political attempt to 'create a friendship between a cat and a dog' (Papp, 2002).

Göncz's selection for the presidency

If the presidential post was a bargaining chip in the process of creating a stable power base for Antall, why did he single out Göncz for the presidency? In principle, Antall could have opted for other figures from within the AFD. According to my interviews and, articles found in the Hungarian literature, there are three primary explanations for his appointment.

Firstly, it has been suggested that Antall's decision to nominate Göncz stemmed from pre-existing personal ties (Lengyel, 2000) or a mutual trust between them (Buják, 2000; Somos, 1997a). In order to understand better how their relationship was built, it is worth revisiting the relevant points of the previous chapters. In Section 2.3, it was noted that it was the ISP that brought Göncz and Antall together. During the time when Göncz worked for the general secretary of the ISP, Béla Kovács he also became acquainted with József Antall Sr., the minister of reconstruction of the ISP. Through his father, Göncz became known to József Antall Jr., a secondary school student at the time. Thereafter, in 1956, particularly in the struggle that followed the suppression of the Revolution, Göncz and József Antall Jr. appended their signatures to the Draft Proposal composed by István Bibó. Considering the political activity in which Göncz participated in the ISP and their collaboration in the resistance of 1956, Antall may have had reason to find common ground between them. It should be noted that on 18 November 1988 Antall and Göncz once again participated in the meeting to reconstruct the ISP, which is highly indicative of the fact that in terms of their joint past activities, they had a

Development of the post-Communist presidency 101

good reason to trust one another (see Section 3.2). In practice, this meant that after the change of regime and, even though they represented different parties, in the eyes of Antall, Göncz may not have appeared entirely as a member of the AFD. As László Lengyel notes, Göncz's political orientation was relatively unknown when compared to those of other potential presidential candidates, and this also contributed to his selection for the presidency:

> People did not know which political camp Göncz belonged in. For example, people knew the political camp into which Miklós Vásárhelyi fell, and the populists in [the HDF] did not want to accept him. It could have been a big struggle for Antall if he had tried to have Vásárhelyi accepted. György Konrád[18] might have been possible but he also had enemies. He was a well known writer. [Compared to them], Göncz was much less well-known to people . . . When [the decision was made] that Göncz would be president, politicians asked each other, 'who is Göncz?' . . . I am saying this because obscurity [*ismeretlenség*] also helped Göncz in his selection for the presidency.
> (Interview with Lengyel, 13 September 2007)

The second explanation lies in Göncz's distinguished moral authority (interviews with Horkay-Hörcher and Kende). Central to this argument is whether Göncz was able to represent the idea of democracy when its legitimacy was essentially underpinned by the process of breaking with the Communist past. As we have seen in Lengyel's account, there were several potential presidential candidates with dissident backgrounds and democratic credentials within the AFD. Among those, MiklósVásárhelyi, Press Secretary of the Imre Nagy government and a spiritual leader of the democratic opposition, was once considered as one of the presidential candidates within the party. However, this possibility was not realised, as Vásárhelyi's political disposition was unacceptable to Antall and his political camp. Tölgyessy explained how this actually worked for Göncz, but against Vásárhelyi:

> A significant part of the 1956-ers was constituted from Communists who had once been enthusiastic about [the idea] of Communism but later came to realise it was a bad system . . . Vásárhelyi was once a real Communist . . . Antall could have considered Vásárhelyi as a partner but had never accepted him as a suitable candidate . . . Göncz's secret was while he was also a 1956-er, he was not a Communist at all and this was acceptable for Antall.
> (Interview with Tölgyessy, 15 October 2007)

As one of the leading Hungarian political scientists pointed out, the proactive role Göncz undertook in 1956 imbued him with moral authority, leading Antall to choose him for the presidency:

> During the 1956 Revolution, Göncz played an important role and because of that he was imprisoned. His legitimacy originated from this . . . On the

one hand, moral [authority] and on the other hand, very strong political legitimacy was given to him, as he stood against the totalitarian Kádár system and stood with freedom . . . This explains why Göncz was acceptable to Antall.

(Interview with one of the leading Hungarian political scientists, 16 November 2007)

The final explanation lies in Antall's political calculation. It was possible that Antall considered the presidential post to be another locus of power which the HDF members could potentially misuse to challenge his authority (O'Neil, 1997: 214). The formal or *de jure* powers of the president were codified in the Constitution. Yet 'the separation of powers between the head of state and the head of government remained unclear' (O'Neil, 1997: 210); the presidency could be tested as a power-base. Indeed, according to a former president of the AFD, Antall's concern about this was demonstrated when he tactfully dealt with a potential presidential candidate within the HDF, Sándor Csoóri:[19]

If the HDF [had] appointed their own presidential [candidate], Sándor Csoóri [could have been chosen] for the presidency. But Antall did not want Csoóri to become the president . . . Antall thought he should satisfy Csoóri by offering him the chairman of the World Hungarian Association . . . This office did not have any real power and influence.

(Interview with a former chairman of the AFD, 27 September 2007)

It is therefore possible to argue that Antall may have expected Göncz to fill the presidential post, satisfying the requirements of parliamentarian democracy while leaving the '*real*' state of affairs to the Antall government. However, as numerous instances during the first term of his presidency demonstrated (details of which will be examined in–depth in Chapter 5), Göncz did not interpret the role of the president in the manner that Antall had expected. As an MP of the AFD, Imre Mécs, neatly summarised:

Antall's idea appeared to be genius, because a kind, warm-hearted, gentle looking [man] like [Göncz] was acceptable even to the conservative side. A 1956 veteran, a writer rather than a politician, would not intervene in [state] affairs and would sign everything. In a word, [Antall thought] he gave his friend to us to ensure governability with constitutional amendment . . . But it soon turned out Göncz had a very resolute and clear idea when it came to [dealing with] the most important questions.

(Wisinger and László, 2007: 96)

Hitherto, this chapter has examined the actual process of institutionalising the post-Communist presidency and multiple explanatory factors involved in Göncz's selection for the post. Having noted that bargaining over the presidency in which the political elite engaged was, *de facto,* a key to shaping the institution; ultimately, this resulted in a major amendment of the Communist Constitution, the following section of the chapter is devoted to analysing the presidential competences (formal powers) through investigation of the revised Constitution itself. The scope of this examination encompasses the constitutional amendments with respect to any change of presidential powers that have been made from 1989 up to 2011. The comprehensive investigation of these aspects lays an essential foundation for, and background to, an understanding of the president's position in *Real politik,* the context in which Göncz interpreted and exercised his vested constitutional powers during his presidency.

4.3. The constitutional powers of the Hungarian president

> Hungary's head of state is the president of the Republic who represents the unity of the nation, and monitors the democratic operation of the State; The president of the Republic is the commander-in-chief of the Hungarian Armed Forces.[20]

These are the principal roles of the president of the Republic of Hungary as defined in the current Constitution. As these clauses indicate, the main tasks of the head of state can be largely divided into three functions: assuming representative, ceremonial or symbolic roles; overseeing the democratic functioning of state institutions involved; and acting as the commander-in-chief. While the practical meanings of performing these functions are open to debates, according to the legal status of the president, the head of state appears to have some executive authority. For example, leading the Hungarian army implies that the president may be able to decide over the mobilisation and de-mobilisation of armed forces. However, if one examines the other constitutional powers vested in the president, particularly in relation to the president's power over the government, it becomes evident that the head of state exercises only nominal or minimal powers. The main constitutional powers granted to the president are as follows:

- Accredit and receive ambassadors and envoys;
- Grant individual pardons;
- Conclude international treaties in the name of the Republic of Hungary; if the subject of the treaty falls within its legislative competence, prior ratification by the Parliament is necessary for the conclusion of the treaty;
- Confer titles, orders, awards and decorations specified by law;
- Appoint and dismiss state secretaries in accordance with regulations specified in a separate law;
- Appoint and dismiss the president and vice-presidents of the National Bank of Hungary . . . and university rectors . . . upon the recommendation of persons or organisations specified in a separate law;
- By the suggestion of the prime minister (after listening to the open hearing of the Parliament's Cultural and Press Affairs Committee), the president of the Republic appoints and dismisses the presidents and vice-presidents of

Hungarian radio and television, as well as the director of the Hungarian News Agency;
- In order to exercise the [above] right, the President is required to have a counter-signature from the Prime Minister.

(Adapted from Ács (2000: 57); Sükösd (1996: 361); 'The Law No. LVII of 1990 on the Appointment Procedure of the Heads of the Public Media'[21])

The first two rights noted above apparently suggest that they are realms of the president's independent authority, whereas the remainder refers to circumscribed presidential powers. Evidence demonstrating the limitation of presidential powers is found in stipulations where the president is required to consider separate or specific laws for the exercise of each legal power. For example, the right to nominate to state apparatus and the conclusion of international agreements indicate that the president is obliged to have prior approval from the branch of powers responsible for that area of governance. In contrast, there are no additional conditions restricting the president's rights to receive ambassadors and issue individual pardons. However, it should be noted that all of the legal powers stated above must be approved by the counter-signatures of the prime minister or responsible ministers. As McGregor notes, the system of co-signature of the prime minister or ministers is one of 'the sources of presidential weakness' (McGregor, 1994: 30). The only exceptional case which may not need co-signatories from other political organs is in an extraordinary situation where the president is required to activate his or her 'reserve' (*tartalék*) function (this refers to additional powers afforded to the president in a state of emergency).[22] However, given that the president's extraordinary powers are even shared by others – the prime minister, the Speaker of the House and the president of the Constitutional Court – the extent to which the president is able to make an independent decision without seeking a consensus is unclear (Körösényi *et al.*, 2003: 560), which is highly indicative of the fact that the presidential powers over government are minimal. In practice, this means that the president does have some *de jure* powers, but he or she cannot take independent action without the endorsement of the government (Halmai, 1991).

Concerning subsequent constitutional amendments, particularly with respect to the presidential powers listed above, until the present day there have been changes on two occasions. According to Law XXXI of 1989, the president was initially able to appoint and dismiss state secretaries upon the suggestion of the prime minister, but Act XL of 1990 brought about a change in the stipulation, as stated above.[23] In terms of the range of presidential powers, however, this change of wording does not make any difference, as the president is still unable to decide without reference to the premier or Parliament. Thereafter, Act LIV of 2006, once again altered the relevant stipulation, yet this amendment did not lead to any change of presidential powers either, because it remains undecided as a gap in the Constitution.[24] Therefore, despite several attempts to alter the scope of constitutional powers, the weakness of the presidency has remained, as the president is still obliged to have a co-signature to validate his or her actions.

This raises important questions. Why does the Constitution grant such limited power to the president? It is also questionable whether the Constitution does grant discretionary power to the president in any capacity. According to Hungarian legal experts, the president's lack of political responsibility is primarily responsible for the weakness of the presidency (Ács, 2000: 61; Báldy, 2003: 391; Sükösd, 1996: 354–5). According to Article 31/A which specified the president's legal status in terms of potential prosecution, the head of state is not held accountable for his political actions, not least because his jurisdictional independence is guaranteed (*Magyar Hírlap*, 25 May 1992; Petrétei, 2001: 90). The only exception is applicable to a case where the president has consciously violated the Constitution or other laws (Ács, 2000: 61; Báldy, 2003: 391; Petrétei, 2001a: 100). In reality, however, calling the president to account is very challenging, due to legal requirements which demand the overriding of the rule of party discipline. According to Article 31/A, in order to launch impeachment proceedings, a two-thirds majority vote by MPs is required. If the vast majority of MPs (including those who come from the same party as the president) voted against the president, the case would be forwarded to the Constitutional Court to decide whether the president has violated the Constitution. Yet, in the event that MPs from the president's party vote according to their party line, the chance of meeting the necessary quorum is slim indeed. As will be discussed in detail in the next chapter, Göncz served out his term largely due to this complex procedure, even though he took very controversial political decisions and may have overstepped the limits of his constitutional role.

Concerning the discretionary powers of the president, despite the fact that the president's room for manoeuvre is significantly circumscribed by the cross-signatory system, the Constitution does grant some flexibility nonetheless:

- The right to participate and speak in the plenary session of Parliament;
- The right to announce parliamentary and municipal elections and mayoral elections as well as the dates of the European Parliamentary elections and national referenda;[25]
- The right to propose bills to Parliament;
- The right to veto legislation proposed by Parliament;
- The right to make a political statement.

(Adapted from: Ács (2000: 54–6); Körösényi *et al.* (2003: 561); Sükösd (1996: 356–60))

In general, the president's power over Parliament is relatively more wide-ranging and flexible than his or her power over the government. In order to exercise the above rights, the president is *not* required to have a counter-signature from any other political organ. For example, the right to propose a bill suggests that not only the Legislature, but the president him- or herself is entitled to act as an initiator of legislation. Furthermore, the right of veto underscores the fact that the Constitution does vest the president with some discretionary powers. The activation of these powers is possible through the 'constitutional or political veto',[26] even though both types of veto cannot be exercised by the president at one and the same time. The former is exercised by the president when he or she has a reservation regarding the constitutionality of a given piece of legislation (Article 26. §4). If the president's concerns about legislation are legally grounded, he or she refers it to the Constitutional Court for judicial review. In the event that the Court finds the legislation is unconstitutional, the president returns it to Parliament. In the opposite case – if the Court upholds the legality of legislation – the president must sign the contested legislation into law and promulgate it within five days (Körösényi et al., 2003: 561). In the strictest sense, however, the constitutional veto cannot be understood as a powerful political tool for the exercise of presidential influence, as the final decision falls under the jurisdiction of the Constitutional Court. As Petréti notes, use of the constitutional veto means that the president acts as an *initiator* to facilitate the creation of laws, which conform to the principle of constitutionality (Petréti, 2005: 134).

The political veto is exercised by the president when he or she disagrees on adopted legislation or any part of it, prior to its promulgation to the public (Article 26. §2). In this case, as an expression of disagreement, with or without comments, the president returns the law to Parliament for reconsideration. Since the president's reservation with regard to signing the law is not legally grounded (but instead based on any other reasons), this may be interpreted as an influential political tool at the president's disposal. However, the use of a political veto only has a restricted impact in terms of changing the adopted legislation. Parliament does not need to follow the president's instruction, this is due no small part to the simple procedure by which the political veto can be overridden; in reality, the president's influence on politics through the political veto channel is marginal. As one of the former judges of the Constitutional Court argues, a simple majority vote is sufficient to void the political veto:

> Ferenc Mádl [Göncz's successor] returned an adopted bill to [Parliament] for reconsideration. On the same day, the same number of MPs once again voted for the bill. But Mádl was not called into Parliament. Some MPs did not even know that the extraordinary parliamentary session was held at 9 pm in the evening ... They were in Brussels at the time ... The rank of the president's veto should be raised to the extent that MPs are not allowed to override it with a simple majority.
>
> (Interview with a former senior judge of the Constitutional Court, 9 May 2007)

Ultimately, this means that if Parliament once again votes to the challenged legislation with the majority votes that MPs have cast, the president must sign the law that has been returned (Rose-Ackerman, 2005: 63). The only impact that the president could have on politics through the political veto over Parliament is the deferment of the promulgation of the law for the period of time that it takes for Parliament to decide to amend or re-adopt the challenged legislation (because of this effect, the political veto is also called as the 'suspensory veto'). In this regard, if one strictly judges the scope of the president's discretionary powers, the political veto cannot be interpreted as a genuinely powerful tool of presidential authority. Thus, the president's power under Hungary's parliamentarianism is minimal; weakness persists as the defining feature of the institution of the presidency.

This, however, does not suggest that the president always follows the will of Parliament or moves within narrowly defined constitutional boundaries. 'Institutions do matter' as 'they create incentives and disincentives for political actors . . . establish the context in which policy-making occurs, and help or hinder in the construction of democratic regimes' (Ishiyama and Velten, 1998: 217). However, as Ishiyama and Velten point out, political actors do not all respond and act in the same way according to the given 'institutional incentives' (Ishiyama and Velten, 1998: 231); it cannot simply be said that institutions themselves determine the strength of presidencies. For example, other than constitutionally defined formal powers, there are numerous informal sources or channels which the president is capable of translating into an expansion of actual influence. Holmes aptly maintains that:

> It is perfectly normal, too, that informal resources help determine the real powers of a sitting president: a well-organised staff, a strategic use of appointment powers to build up a dense network of collaborators, sheer popularity and access to the media, agility at playing off some parties against the others, personal involvement in negotiating cabinet coalitions, and the ability to bully Parliament by threatening convincingly to appeal to the street . . . Where legislatures are fragmented, coalition cabinets are unstable, and courts are inexperienced, even a modestly powerful president can wield decisive influence.
>
> (Holmes, 1993: 36)

In inexperienced democracies, therefore, there is considerable leeway for even constitutionally weak presidents to convert these informal resources into their real powers. The characteristics of the presidency would be, then, shaped by and reflected through the presidential actions, such as how they interpret the scope of presidential powers and interact with other political players. Some ambitious presidents may capitalise on vaguely defined constitutional powers and also use informal resources to maximise political influences for the purpose of achieving the goals that they set themselves. The question of this will be addressed in the next chapter, in which the main characteristics of Göncz's presidency are examined in-depth. The most important instances and examples of Göncz's proactive engagement in politics will be placed under scrutiny. In particular, the chapter will ask how Göncz's own liberal and democratic political values were reflected through and embodied in his engagement with important transitional political and socio-economic issues. Ultimately, I will ask what Göncz sought to achieve in pursuing his liberal and democratic ideas during the term of his presidency.

5 The first presidency (1990–1995)

Introduction

This chapter examines the main characteristics of the first term of Göncz's presidency (1990–1995) and assesses his presidential role and decisions. In Chapters 1, 2 and 3, it was established that liberal and democratic ideas were the most consistently pronounced elements which Göncz developed throughout life and which became entrenched in his political beliefs. With this in mind, the present chapter examines how Göncz's liberal values were embodied in his presidency. This examination includes an in-depth discussion of Göncz's interpretation of his constitutional powers in dealing with important transitional issues emerging over the course of Hungary's post-Communist history.

It is generally established in the Hungarian literature that the presidential role Göncz undertook during the first term of his presidency was proactive, controversial (Buják, 2000; Szomszéd, 2005) and was marked by conflict between the president and the first democratically elected Antall government (Bakony, 2005; Somos, 1997a; Varró, 2000). The literature highlighted particular aspects of Göncz's relationship with the Antall government; the president, it was proposed, had sought a counter-balancing role to the Antall government (Babus, 2000; Kontler, 2002: 476–77; Körösényi, 1999: 280) and this political activism had been counter-productive to the development of democracy, for he failed to act for the unity of the nation as a non-partisan figurehead (Debreczeni, 2003: 298–311; Varga, 1995). Göncz's political origins in the AFD (a liberal left-wing party) were proof – critics claimed – that Göncz was acting in the vested interests of his party (Fricz, 2010; Lovas, 2002) and, against the Antall government (whose political orientation conservative and right-wing).

However, as will be discussed in the next chapter, Göncz's partisanship does not explain his acquiescence during the last two years of the second term of his presidency (1998–2000), at which time another conservative, right-wing government – the Orbán government – was in power. Given that the AFD was once again on the opposition side at this time, had Göncz determined to act in favour of the party, he would have taken a balancing role against the Orbán government. As the Hungarian political scientist András Lánczi noted:

This [the Orbán government] was again in the situation where the head of government was strong and the head of state was weak. *Politically* it may have been possible for Göncz to be more active than [he showed himself to be], this is not how it turned out.

(Interview with Lánczi, 12 July 2007)

Therefore, in addition to political affiliation, there would have been other factors responsible for Göncz's role as counter-weight to the Antall government. In particular, the chapter addresses this gap in the literature by exploring other factors. The first gap concerns, how, after the collapse of Communism, in a context where there was no preceding example to follow and little experience of democratic governance had been gained, political actors interpreted their formally granted constitutional powers and interacted with one another. This includes Göncz's perception of the role of president and how it affected the shaping of this newly established political institution. The second gap which must be addressed concerns that of a plausible explanation for Göncz's controversial role – opposing the Antall government – which may be that his actions were guided by his democratic and liberal beliefs rather than any partisanship on behalf of the AFD. Thus, the chapter seeks to examine Göncz's actions in the presidential role in the context of the time at which they were undertaken and, to critically assess them with respect to his partisanship and his liberal and democratic values.

The chapter is structured as follows. The first section of the chapter briefly discusses the main features of the Antall government's policies and political orientations. This is done in order to provide the contextual background which is essential for gaining an understanding of the Antall government's politics. The remainder of the chapter is devoted to examining – on a case-by-case basis – instances in which Göncz was proactively engaged during the first term of his presidency.

5.1. The Antall government

On 25 January 2001, in an interview with Wisinger, Göncz stated that:

The [level] of blood pressure and diabetes of the President depends on the Prime Minister. Likewise, the level of blood pressure and diabetes of the Prime Minister depends on the President or the President's personality.

(Wisinger and László, 2007: 329)

On 22 May 1990, a week after the formation of the new cabinet, the Prime Minister, József Antall, gave his first high-profile speech on the government programme. Various issues and goals that his government sought to achieve were outlined, but the fundamental principle that they were to adopt would be that of a 'government of freedom'. The practical significance of this can be interpreted in various ways; Antall's suggestion was that the government of freedom embraced basic democratic values such as freedom of the press, freedom of expression, and equality before the law (*Népszabadság*, 23 May 1990). In established democracies these freedoms are perhaps taken as essential elements of the political system. However, at this juncture of Hungary's political history – the Antall government marked the new beginning of post-Communist politics – the premier's reference to freedom was significant, even if only symbolically so. The significance of freedom was also emphasised by Antall in the realm of economic transformation. The reasoning was that if, in the past, free entrepreneurialism had largely been oppressed then, this government would reshape the economic order to follow the 'principles of market, competition and risk' (Romsics, 2007: 296). Indeed, having aspired to attain these goals, over the summer of 1990, the Antall government had worked intensively to build a fundamental framework for governance through the passage of new bills (Romsics, 2007: 302). As Rothschild and Wingfield argue, Antall 'employed his formidable political skills' to realise government programmes in the interest of laying 'the foundations for parliamentary democracy and market economy' (Rothschild and Wingfield, 2000: 278).

However, considering the policies that Antall actually pursued – demonstrating a preference for strong state intervention and state control – it appears that there was a discrepancy between the premier's legitimising principles and the reality of the government actions undertaken during Antall's tenure in office. Privatisation, for example, was to be governed by the principle of the market economy and free competition, albeit at a gradual pace.[1] However, the mode of economic transformation employed by the Antall government brought the whole process of privatisation 'under strict state control, attracting accusations of effecting a renationalisation of property' (Cox and Furlong, 1994: 4). Despite the fact that, by 1993, a substantial portion (55 percent) of Gross Domestic Product stemmed from the private economic sector (Ágh, 2000: 157), the transfer of the State Property Agency from parliamentary control to that of the government demonstrated the manner in which the government approached the problem.[2] As Stark has asserted, this government-controlled privatisation method led to a blurred or quasi privatisation, in which the transformation of property ownership could not be categorically divided into public and private spheres (Stark, 1996: 998–1001). Thus, the conservatism of the Antall government was 'interventionist and in the economic sphere it has favoured state control rather than direction' (Swain, 1993: 78). The Law of Arable Land (discussed in Section 5.2.4) is a good example of how the concept of control was interpreted and applied by the Antall government in the form of economic protection. Similarly, and more strikingly, the significance of state control appears to have negated the stated desire for media freedom (as will be discussed in depth in Section 5.2.5). The placement of the media under state control was one of the most controversial moves that the Antall government undertook.

Thus, it is important to explore the relationship formed when the conservative Antall government, (which embraced strong state control) encountered a president for who liberal democratic values were of crucial importance. In such a situation one can justifiably ask whether the president ought to seek to become involved in those events and issues with which the government was concerned. On the basis of their differing political outlooks, one might expect conflict to arise between them. Conversely, if the president were to take a passive and neutral stance on state affairs, the appearance of liberalism given by the president could be regarded as a mask, hiding basic agreement between nominally opposed government and presidential camps from public view. The following section of this chapter addresses these questions exploring those important issues and events in which Antall and Göncz became engaged, and interacted with other political players.

5.2. Göncz's first presidential term: liberal and democratic values vs. partisanship

5.2.1. The taxi-drivers' strike

In autumn 1990, less than four months after the Antall government took office, the Hungarian socialist daily, *Népszabadság*, ran the news of the development of a spontaneous public protest, the so-called 'Taxi Blockade' or taxi-drivers strike, under the following headline: 'The president of the Republic is against the [application of public force]' (*Népszabadság*, 27 October 1990b).The sudden announcement of a sharp increase in the price of oil – 'With effect from midnight, oil prices will increase by 65 percent' (*Népszabadság*, 26 October 1990)–prompted taxi and lorry drivers to take to the streets in protest. The government explained that the rise in the price of petrol was unavoidable due to the sharp increase in the price of crude oil on the international market (Romsics, 2007: 328).[3] However, this account was far from satisfactory to the lorry and taxi drivers who saw the action as a direct threat to their livelihoods (O'Neil, 1993: 192). They blockaded major bridges, demanding that the increase in the price of petrol be suspended. The obstruction of critical points on main roads meant that their protests soon paralysed the transportation networks of Central Budapest. Consequently, their demonstrations brought about immediate reactions from both the government and opposition, and also from Göncz. Minister of the Interior, Balázs Horváth[4] announced that there would be no concession or compromise, stating that 'the government would not rescind the decision and would restore order employing all available legal measures' (*Népszabadság*, 27 October 1990b). In response, the chairman of the AFD, János Kis, expressed the AFD's solidarity with the protestors, stating that with the statement of such a threatening message, the government had committed a crime (*Népszabadság*, 27 October 1990a).

No specific details concerning what measures the government was proposing to take were forthcoming. Thus, in the uncertainty of the situation, a rumour was circulated that the government might use the forces of public order to deal with the crisis (Gyarmati, 2005: 623). However, this never came to pass due to Göncz's intervention. In a letter sent to the minister of interior, Göncz made his position clear, stating that, as the commander-in-chief, he would not allow the forces of public order to be employed in order to tackle the crisis (Debreczeni, 2003: 160–1). Additionally, on the same day, in a televised public statement, he called on the government to enter into negotiations with the protestors (*Magyar Hírlap*, 27 October 1990). Facing mounting pressure and criticism over the development of the crisis and their attitudes towards it, the government changed its original decision. At the National Interest Reconciliation Council, in which the delegates of government and those of the employers and the employees participated,[5] a compromise was reached by lowering the petrol price increase by 20 percent (*Népszabadság*, 29 October 1990), putting an end to the four-day strike.

The first sizeable public protest of the post-Communist era ended peacefully at the negotiating table. During the development of the crisis, Göncz acted as a mediator between the government and the protestors. However, his intervention prompted considerable controversy among the political elite and the issues of whether his intervention was ever in fact necessary and, what led him to make such a statement, were particular points of contention.

Göncz explained that intervention was prompted by the information available to him at the time. Heavy military vehicles had been dispatched to the capital to clear the blockade (*Magyar Hírlap*, 24 October 2000; Mester, 2000; *Népszabadság*, 24 October 2000; Veress, 2010) which Göncz interpreted as meaning that the government might act coercively. In contrast, the government strongly denied that such an order had ever been issued. In addition, they emphasised that Göncz had overreacted to, or misjudged, the given situation. For example, even a decade after the occurrence of the strike, when a public debate was broadcast on an RTL television programme, the former minister without portfolio in Secret Services, Péter Boross, responded to Göncz's comments:

Newspaper interviewer: Recently, Göncz stated that as the commander-in-chief, he stopped a military intervention and by so doing, prevented bloodshed . . . Were you aware of this operation?
Boross: I am concerned about Göncz's statements and afraid to say that the previous period begins again [meaning a confrontational relationship between the president and the government]. On several occasions, the president confronted the government [. . .].
Newspaper interviewer: Are you saying that the government did not plan armed intervention or did not want to dispatch military vehicle to the taxi drivers?
Boross: I was present at government meetings, but this kind of [plan] was out of the question [. . .].
Newspaper interviewer: At the time, Minister of the Interior Balázs Horváth made a statement saying that he would restore order, whatever it may take.
Boross: He did not say that [he would restore order] even by resorting to illegal [actions]. The Hungarian army did not have a public order remit, so this kind of question cannot even be raised [. . .].

(Stefka, 2000)

The first presidency (1990–1995) 113

Since the official documents that would enable us to substantiate this order remain inaccessible for the purpose of research (*Népszabadság*, 24 October 2000), there is no hard evidence proving the order had ever been given.[6] Nevertheless, inferring from accounts offered by an eyewitness and government members, it is very probable that military vehicles had indeed been dispatched to the scene. A former judge of the Constitutional Court stated:

> Around half past eight in the morning, four huge trucks showed up on the Árpád Bridge. Soliders were [on board these trucks]. They were not armed, but they wore military uniforms. I felt terrible, because [apparently] the government was using military [force] against unarmed people . . . [The government] claimed the [use] of the army was out of the question, but I witnessed it with my own eyes.
> (Interview with a former senior judge of the Constitutional Court, 9 May 2007)

Similar views were held by government members, although the emphasis of their statements differed from that of the former judge's. The first president of the HDF, Zoltán Bíró, claimed that:

> The minister of interior, Balázs Horváth and the minister of defence, Lajos Für agreed that a temporary military bridge should be built. They did not want to [act coercively], but [help people] to cross bridges blocked by strikers.
> (Interview with Bíró, 10 December 2007)

Similarly, a former factional leader of the HDF, Imre Kónya, maintained that:

> No! It is out of question! This was about asking the Hungarian army to borrow towers, or cranes to [help remove] taxis from bridges. The Hungarian army had this [equipment]. So, [the government] did not want to introduce the Hungarian army [itself].
> (Interview with Kónya, 11 December 2007)

In light of these statements, Göncz appears to have misjudged the existing situation, and this, unsurprisingly, prompted sharp criticism from members of the government. In essence, the government claimed that Göncz's actions were an attempt to expand his authority beyond his constitutional remit (*Magyar Nemzet*, 29 October 1990). In response to my question 'How do you evaluate Göncz's actions in the event of the taxi-drivers' strike?' the former factional leader of the HDF, László Salamon, claimed:

> During the blockade, Göncz made a statement that he would not allow the introduction of the army into the situation. This was pointless, because nobody wanted to introduce the army. He also made a mistake because he did not even have such jurisdiction.
> (Interview with Salamon, 24 October 2007)

114   The post-Communist presidency

It is not a coincidence that six months after the blockade, when a jurisdictional dispute arose between the Defence Minister Lajos Für and President Göncz over the right to be the commander-in-chief (*Népszabadság*, 3 April 1991), Für turned to the Constitutional Court. In its ruling, the Court concluded that 'the President of Hungary is *outside* of the [power] of the commander-in-chief' (Sólyom and Holló, 1992: 190), suggesting that this right is only a title. Thus, in terms of the government's position, the pursuit of power or seeking personal gain was the principal reason behind Göncz's intervention in the situation.

However, Göncz's televised public statement suggests that there was in fact an important reason for his intervention. On 26 October 1990, Göncz, who had anxiously followed the development of events at the presidential office, [7] made the following statement:

1. I propose that the government suspend the increase of oil prices.
2. I request that the government, the assigned [officials] and the taxi drivers [hold] negotiations in line with the taxi drivers [proposal and] in a way that makes it possible to [reach] mutual agreement.
3. On the announcement of the suspension of [petrol prices], provisionally, I ask the lorry drivers to go home and [clear] the road blocks.
4. I propose that on Monday, the Parliament convene an extraordinary session to discuss the situation.

I ask the country's population, during the negotiations, to refrain from such acts which make it difficult to [seek] a solution.
Above all, I ask the country's population to maintain normality, allowing the delivery of daily goods and medical [services] to continue.
(*Magyar Hírlap*, 27 October 1990)

Thus, Göncz was very involved in mediation between the government and the protestors. In order to reconcile conflicting interests, he was of the opinion that the government ought to concede its position or step down. Göncz was certain that this concession could be realised through negotiations, over the course of which the government should reconsider its decision. Thus, Göncz clearly recognised the legitimacy of the demonstration and acted in favour of the protestors. Given Göncz's stance, it is hardly surprising that his act displeased those in government who may have thought that Göncz had interfered in the government's business without having a right to do so. They may have thought that, on the pretext of seeking a consensual solution, Göncz capitalised on the public media to propagate his opinion. A former MP of the HDF, József Debreczeni, recalled thus:

During the blockade, the role undertaken by Göncz was the first sign of anxie[ty] . . . The most obvious mistake was [with] his presidential statement: he [acted] in such a way as to facilitate the reaching of an agreement, but in practice he ordered the government to accept the demands of the [protestors].
(Kovács, 1993: 46)

Given the position and political allegiance of the commentator, however, this criticism is not unexpected. For example, when one looks at other aspects of the above statement, a different perspective is revealed: the restoration of public order and securing peace was behind Göncz's determination to intervene in the event. That is, even if Göncz sympathised with the protestors and this act was considered a sign of his interference in a governmental matter, the principles on display in Göncz's statement emphasised a peaceful and non-coercive solution. It is important to remember that doubt over whether the government might have used force to disperse the protestors was eliminated only *after* Göncz made this public statement. As Kis aptly observed, where democracy, by all accounts, was in jeopardy, Göncz stepped into the situation. Kis noted: '[If] the government [had] prove[d] capable of breaking the mass movements or they [the protestors] had prove[d their ability] topple the government, democracy [would have been] in danger' (Kis, 1991: 6). Thus, considering the critical situation in which Hungary's nascent democracy faced its first crisis, it is possible to argue that this predicament could 'only [be] retrieved by the statesmanlike action of President Göncz who adopted a relatively even-handed approach towards the protestors and the government' (Lewis, 1994: 284). As the Hungarian political scientist, Gabriella Ilonszki, asserted, Göncz's intervention in the impasse amply demonstrated where his political values lay:

> The question is not one of whether there was a plan to disperse the demonstrators [with the use] of military or police force, but that there was a head of state who said that under no circumstances would he accept such a [coercive] solution in a democratic state . . . Ultimately, in the creation of democracy and democratic order, Göncz played his role.
> (Interview with Ilonszki, 16 October 2007).

In this light, it is fair to suggest that coping with the first public protest (a context in which a crisis-management mechanism was not well-established in Hungary's inexperienced democracy), Göncz pursued his own democratic and liberal ideas and this contributed to resolving the crisis peacefully.

In terms of the subsequent impacts that Göncz had on Hungarian politics, however, the event of the taxi-drivers' strike was only a catalyst contributing to the beginning of a political separation between the HDF and the AFD, including Göncz and Antall. András Lánczi neatly captured the implication of the strike for Hungarian politics thus:

> The taxi-drivers' blockade was the critical juncture when it became clear that the AFD was the party which had turned against the HDF . . . Before the taxi-drivers' blockade, the Four Yes-es referendum was an important event for [the split between these two] . . . But the blockade was the point of [complete] political separation.
> (Interview with Lánczi, 12 July 2007)

5.2.2. The Visegrád Summit

If the blockade catalysed the disintegration of cooperation between the Antall government and the opposition, as Lánczi contended, the Visegrád Summit demonstrated how significant cooperation between the head of state and the head of government can be. Despite the fact that neither public mobilisation nor confrontation between the governing party and opposition emerged as a result of the Summit, this event clearly illustrates how the relationship between Göncz and Antall moved into conflict. The Summit took place in early spring 1991, when the presidents of Czechoslovakia and Poland – Vaclav Havel and Lech Walesa – and their delegates gathered in the historic Hungarian city.

The central aim of this regional group meeting was to lay a cooperative framework for joining Western European institutions (Farkas, 1991; Weydenthal, 1991: 28). Economic and political issues, along with future relations with the Soviet Union, were discussed; in signing a 'General Declaration', this regional meeting concluded successfully. Before holding the Summit, however, Göncz and Antall clashed over the right of international representation in foreign countries. Having been informed that the delegations of Hungary's counterparts were to be led by their presidents, Göncz insisted on participating in the Summit. However, Antall opposed this, arguing he himself directed foreign policy. Ultimately, after a debate, both parties agreed that they would jointly attend the Summit on the condition that Hungarian delegates would be led by the prime minister (Vajda, 1991).

Central to the dispute at the Visegrád Summit was the question of what the presidential foreign policy rights meant in reality. More specifically, the president's constitutional tasks and role in foreign policy should have been succinctly defined in relation to, and contrast with, those of the prime minister. Surprisingly, however, considering the relevant stipulations embodied in the Hungarian Constitution, vagueness appears to have provoked a jurisdictional debate between Göncz and Antall. Relevant clauses in use at the time were as follows:

Article 30/A
The President of Hungary represents the State of Hungary;

The President of Hungary concludes international agreements in the name of the Republic of Hungary, if the subject of the treaty falls within its legislative competences, prior ratification by the parliament is necessary for the conclusion of the treaty.

Article 35
The Council of Ministers (Government) cooperates in the decision making process concerning foreign policy issues;

The Government concludes international agreements in the name of the Government of the Republic of Hungary.[8]

(My emphasis)

Since the Constitution vested the head of state and the head of government with almost the same authority, it was unclear who actually had the final say in the conclusion of international agreements. The only difference was found in the conditional stipulation on the president's side, stating that the president was required to have a prior approval from Parliament, if his or her signing international agreements fell within the jurisdiction of the legislature. However, the clause in question does not tell us whether Göncz was obliged to have Parliament's approval for attending the Summit. If one compares these stipulations with the revised version, it becomes evident that the ambiguity of the Constitution was not clarified even after its subsequent amendments.

(The Constitution in use after amendment in 2002)

Article 30/A
The President of Hungary represents the State of Hungary; concludes international treaties in the name of the Republic of Hungary; if the subject of the treaty falls within its legislative competences, prior ratification by the parliament is necessary for the conclusion of the treaty.

Article 35
The Government participates in the development of foreign policy; conclude international treaties in the name of the Government of the Republic of Hungary.

Article 35/1
The Government represents the Republic of Hungary in the institutions of the European Union that require government participation.[9]

The difference between the 1989 version and its subsequent amendment is found only on the part of the government, which made subtle changes to parts of Article 35 and 35/1. The wording of the stipulation has been slightly altered in Article 35, and it is now clear that it was within the jurisdiction of the government to represent Hungary in the European Union. Nonetheless, this still does not provide an answer to the original question – should the president or the premier have represented Hungary at the Visegrád Summit? The answer could have clarified whether the Summit required the president to have Parliament's approval for his participation. The main problem was, however, that the president's constitutional competencies regarding international representation were not clarified during the Summit. Under these circumstances, Göncz, who may have interpreted his presidential scope broadly, argued that he was entitled to participate in the meeting. Göncz may have thought that he was authorised to exercise similar powers, to the extent to which his counterparts Havel and Walesa could.[10] In contrast, the premier, Antall, interpreted the scope of the president's authority more narrowly than Göncz had expected.

Hence, the Visegrád Summit demonstrated how ambiguity within the Constitution contributed to jurisdictional dispute over the president's role in foreign policy. In fact, issues of constitutional obscurity resurfaced when Göncz and Antall clashed over control of the broadcast media. Although the causes of their conflict and Göncz's determination for involvement, differed from issues surrounding foreign policy, this also demonstrated how ambiguity in the Constitution was leading to different interpretations of the document. Before examining this issue, the following section of the chapter explores how Göncz coped with one of the most crucial transitional issues that the new Hungarian democracy had to face: the question of coming to terms with the Communist past.

5.2.3. Dealing with the Communist past

With Communism's collapse, perhaps the most common transitional task that the first post-Communist governments in Central and Eastern Europe (CEE) had to address was a question of settling accounts in some way or other. Across the region, while each government had different ideas and conceptions of its past, it was generally recognised that without settling this issue appropriately, social consensus could not be created. As Elster noted, 'the return to democracy [was] accompanied by a desire to see transitional justice done in an orderly manner' (Elster, 2006: 3). Different approaches were conceived and adopted so that a variety of models to deal with the Communist past were created by the governments concerned. Despite these variations, a striking similarity in pattern can also be noted. For example, according to Offe, different models adopted by Eastern European governments can be broadly classified into five typologies: monetary compensation, legal rehabilitation, the revelation of perpetrators' name, the launch of trials and the formation of truth-telling committees (Offe, 1992, in Calhoun, 2004: 7–9). The first two indicate an approach to dealing with the victims of previous regimes, whereas the remainder refer to a way of dealing with those wrongdoers unpunished during the previous regimes' tenure. Across the CEE, these approaches took various forms and were given different names but, under the banner of 'de-Communisation', they were largely formulated into anti-Communist legislation or its related programmes. Hungary was no exception to this process and, indeed, the Antall government adopted the Laws of Compensation and Justice at an early stage.

Despite the fact that the main impact these laws had on Hungarian society differed, the overall outcome of the Hungarian approach to the de-Communisation process suggested that it was conducted at a largely symbolic level (Enriquez, 1998: 277; Welsh, 1996: 415). In practical terms, this meant Hungary avoided taking the path of intense restitution and retribution, adopting the view that 'the best way to deal with the past is to do better now' and emphasising the attitude that 'living well is the best revenge' (Halmai and Scheppele, 1997: 156). As will be discussed later, Göncz also made a significant contribution to this process, particularly by bringing the issue into conformity with the principle of the rule of law. In effect, his intervention led the government to reconsider the way to deal with the past. The following section of this chapter examines the main developments of the post-transitional justice issue and Göncz's role in it, after which comes an examination of factors that may have led Göncz to become involved in this question.

5.2.3.1. The Law of Compensation

On 24 April 1991, the Hungarian Parliament passed the Law on Compensation (Okolicsanyi, 1991a: 10). Aiming to right past wrongs by providing a symbolic level of financial aid to victims of Communist rule (Okolicsanyi, 1991b: 22, 1993: 49), the Antall government adopted 'Law No. XXV of 1991 on Partial Compensation for Damages Unlawfully Caused by the State to Properties Owned by Citizens in the Interest of Settling Ownership Relations'(hereafter the Law on Compensation).[11] According to this law, in principle, victims and heirs whose property had been illegally confiscated by the previous regime were given an historic opportunity to retrieve their losses. In reality, however, the Law on Compensation was far from meeting expectations. The value of vouchers or bonds distributed to victims of Communist rule fell far short of restoring their lost property, because the extent of compensation was calculated against the original value of expropriated property with no allowance for inflation being made. For example, according to criteria set by the government, the level of material damage up to £1000 was fully compensated by this scheme, whereas the rest of the case was partially compensated according to a significantly declining scale (Fleming, 1995: 72–4).[12] Additionally and more importantly, the Compensation Law had a serious legal drawback. According to Act XXV of 1991, for example, *not* everyone was granted an opportunity to claim compensation, and arguably this meant that citizens eligible for compensation were also discriminated against. In particular, only those who lost property after 8 June 1949[13] were entitled under the government scheme (Okolicsanyi, 1993: 49). Furthermore, politically persecuted victims who lost lives and freedom under the previous regime were essentially excluded (Mihály, 1997: 9, 2004: 10).[14] Consequently, as Okolicsanyi has noted, Act XXV of 1991 neither covered property and personal losses incurred before June 8 1949, nor paid for claims lodged by Jews and other foreigners who had lost their property primarily before and during the Second World War (Okolicsanyi, 1991a: 8).

Consequently, legal disputes over the Law on Compensation did not only arise among parliamentary parties, but also among the public at large. As a whole, a division of opinion emerged between the Antall-led coalition government and the opposition, as well as within the coalition itself, with the point of contention centring on differing conceptions of the law. For instance, within the coalition the HDF and the CDPP both supported the partial compensation scheme, whereas the ISP demanded the implementation of 'reprivatisation' which meant the return of assets to original ownership (Comisso, 1995: 210–11; Fahidi, 1994: 55; 218–19; Paczolay, 1992: 811). As for the opposition, the AYD and the HSP refused even to adopt the Compensation Law (Romsics, 2001: 420), while the AFD claimed that an equal amount of monetary compensation should be allocated to all Hungarian citizens.[15] Public opinion was also divided, showing an almost equal percentage

(48 percent to 46 percent) of respondents for and against any type of compensation (Lázár, 1992: 575–6).

On 14 May 1991, Göncz, who had shown reservations about signing the Compensation Law, turned to the Constitutional Court (Bodnár, 1991). Raising four questions (of which details are discussed below), he asked for a judicial review on the issue of whether the law could be upheld in its constitutionality (*Magyar Dokumentáció*, May 1991). In response to Göncz's questions, the Court ruled that the Law on Compensation was unconstitutional in several respects (Sólyom and Holló, 1992: 80–1). Above all, the cut-off date of 8 June 1948 was found to be unconstitutional, because it was arbitrarily set (*Magyar Nemzet*, 30 May 1991). The Court also decided that discrimination made between land and other types of property was against basic law (*Magyar Dokumentáció*, May 1991), as it contravened the principle of equality. However, the Court found that the state had a 'moral obligation to compensate the former owners' (Paczolay, 1992: 824), underlining the idea that the Law on Compensation could enter into force if discriminatory elements within the law were removed. Accordingly, in spring 1992, the law was revised several times so that contentious legal debates appeared to have been brought to an end.[16] However, on 16 April 1993, Göncz once again referred the amended version – Law No. I of 1993 Compensation – to the Constitutional Court (Sólyom and Holló, 1994: 221),[17] and controversies over this law continued throughout the Antall government.

Given that the implementation of the Compensation Law was conditional upon the amendment of the law, it is possible to question Göncz's intentions for forwarding it to the Constitutional Court. Göncz himself was a political victim of Communist rule, a person who was unjustly imprisoned and the introduction of the Compensation Law may have benefitted him financially. This might explain Göncz's reluctance to sign the law. An interview Göncz gave to Kossuth Radio implies that one of the primary reasons for his reluctance lay in his anxiety about the lack of social consensus prevalent in Hungarian society at the time:

> Countless requests were [sent] to me. These came from both sides. On the one hand, it was suggested that the implementation of the law be accelerated ... On the other hand, there were appeals about how the law violated [various] interests. Public opinion was also divided by age and social [background]. In these circumstances, naturally, I [had] doubts about the law. I felt that it was my duty to [address this doubt] by raising questions and receiving answers.
> (Wisinger and László, 1994: 161–2)

Having faced this dilemma, which made it difficult for Göncz to reconcile conflicting interests, he may have thought that the law should be more carefully drafted prior to its introduction. According to Göncz's account, it would appear that he did not object to the *idea* of compensation *per se*. However, any doubt over legal deficiencies inherent in the law was required to be resolved, because this was seen by Göncz as the main cause of controversy among people, something which in turn contributed to social division. For example, according to an historian of the State Security Archive, László Varga, the Compensation Law had numerous inherent problems which violated the right of ownership and people's interests. Varga noted that:

> The biggest problem of monetary compensation is the question of ownership. Let's say in 1938, land belonged to a Jew. [During the Second World War] the Arrow Cross expropriated this land and in 1945, the [new government] took it away from the Arrow Cross and someone bought it. But if this land was again taken away from the third owner as a consequence of collectivisation, in principle, the government would have to compensate for land owners three times. In practice, of course, this rarely happened.
> (Interview with Varga, 27 August 2007)

In these circumstances, Göncz naturally had reason to doubt the legality of law. Indeed, an attempt to remove the doubt was evidenced by the letter he sent to the Constitutional Court in which he raised these questions:

1. Does it correspond to the spirit of the Constitution that compensation is not complete [in scope], but only partial [indicating moral obligation]?
2. Does it correspond to the spirit of the Constitution that much of the legislation concerning compensation is deferred until a later date? This applies to the [nationalisation] which took place before 8 June 1949, and also applies to the Church and other bodies.
3. Does it correspond to the spirit of the Constitution that discrimination between citizens is based on the nature of nationalised property?
4. Does it correspond to the spirit of the Constitution that compensation will be made at the expense of local authorities and cooperatives?[18]

(*Magyar Hírlap*, 14 May 1991)

In essence, Göncz questioned whether the Law on Compensation violated the principle of equality by discriminating against the dispossessed based on the expropriation date and the type of once-nationalised property. In particular, the cut-off date for one specific criterion set by the Antall government was questioned by Göncz, as this decided whether people were eligible for demanding any compensation for material damages. Similarly, Göncz wondered why certain types of lost property could be retrieved, while others could not. According to the Compensation Law, partial compensation would be provided only to those who had forcibly lost their lands and some buildings, but excluded any possibility of being recompensated for material losses of their goods and chattels. Thus, the law had intrinsic legal defects as it treated land restituants preferentially, a fact which is indicative of the contravention of the principle of equality.

Considering the specific questions formulated by Göncz and their implications, it is fair to suggest that Göncz dealt with one of the most controversial transitional laws in light of his own liberal and democratic values. The significance of the principle of equality was demonstrably highlighted in this instance. Göncz clearly sensed that the main cause of social division over the Compensation Law lay in possible discriminatory measures within it, which he interpreted to mean that the issue should be addressed through the constitutional review process. Moreover, given his intellectual and dissident background in the struggle for the realisation of justice, it is likely that Göncz would have had his own ideas or suggestions when dealing with the compensation issue. Indeed, the inference to be drawn from an interview Göncz gave to Kossuth Radio supports the reasoning that Göncz had his own opinion regarding the Compensation Law. In essence, Göncz argued that the Law on Compensation should have been more thoroughly examined in the context of the holistic view of Hungary's entire socio-economic transformation process. Göncz stated:

> I would be very pleased, if they [MPs] evaluated the social consequences and side-effects of the law in the course of parliamentary debates . . . For example, how those people who bear financial burdens would react to the [compensation] law; what long-term impacts the law may have . . . how the law affects next year's budget . . . Not only from [the point of view of] inflation, the financial market, and economic processes, but also from the viewpoint of the [overall] general conditions of the social transformation process, [the law should have been more comprehensively investigated].
>
> (Wisinger and László, 2007: 185)

With this in mind, it can be fair to say that along with the deficiency of the principle of equality within the Compensation Law, the short-sighted economic policy that the Antall government proposed cannot be ruled out as a factor which influenced Göncz's determination to intervene in the issue.

5.2.3.2. The Law on Justice

On 4 November 1991, less than six months after the Compensation Law was challenged by the Constitutional Court, the Hungarian Parliament passed the 'Law of Zétényi-Takács', named after its initiators, Zsolt Zétényi and Péter Takács:

> §(1) On 2 May 1990, the statue of limitations on certain crimes committed between 21 December 1944 and 2 May 1990 begins. According to the 1978 [Criminal Law] which was in effect at the time, perpetrators committed the following crimes: treason as defined in 144.§(2) paragraph, premeditated murder as described in 166. §(1) and (2), and manslaughter as dictated in 170.§(5). The start point of the statue of limitations is [reset] if the perpetrators of a crime [originally escaped] punishment for political reasons.
>
> (Hack, 2007: 544)

Designed to reset statutory limitations for certain crimes – 'premeditated murder, treason and aggravated assault' – committed between 21 December 1944 and 2 May 1990 (Pataki, 1992a: 21; Welsh, 1996: 416),[19] the primary goal of the

Zétényi-Takács Law lay in calling Communists to account (Huyse, 1995: 69). According to this law, the renewal of the statute of limitations meant that those perpetrators who had not been punished for political reasons during the previous regime could now be brought to justice. Not surprisingly, in the course of legislation, controversy arose, with legal disputes centring on the issues of whether retroactive law could be implemented in the name of justice. The governing coalition (comprising the HDF, ISP and CDPP) supported the law (Hámor and Bártfai, 1991), reasoning that the state had a moral responsibility to undo past injustices. A CDPP MP Miklós Hasznos argued that:

> The question of justice is not a simple legal question but a much more complex [issue], because it [requires] the realisation of moral justice . . . People demanded and always demand that time does not give a free pass to those offenders who acted against their own people.
> (Kurtán, Sándor and Vass, 1992a: 549)

In contrast, the opposition – the AFD and AYD – were against the law, raising concerns about its possible social consequences (*Magyar Dokumentáció*, October 1991). For example, an AFD MP, Imre Mécs, said that he would oppose the law, as he believed that its enactment might stir up a sense of fear and hatred among the population and, could also be misused to launch political trials or witch-hunts (*Népszabadság*, 18 November 1991).

Having become aware of the lack of social consensus on this issue, Göncz referred the law to the Constitutional Court on 18 November 1991 (Fekete, 1991; *Népszava*, 19 November 1991). With an emphasis on the fact that the calling of perpetrators to account ought to be done strictly within the framework of a state built upon the rule of law (*Magyar Dokumentáció*, November 1991), Göncz asked the Court whether the adopted law contravened democratic principles. Sensing the significance of the issue, he also visited the Court personally (Sereg, 1991). Göncz acted in this way having seen that social division over the Justice Law had raised concern about potential consequences (details are discussed below).

Upon Göncz's request, the Constitutional Court issued its ruling on 3 March 1992. Eight points of constitutional violation were raised by the Court (Sólyom and Holló, 1993: 77–8), the essence of the verdict was the Zétényi-Takács Law was against the Constitution, because it violated the principle of legal security, whereby 'the citizen can count on the law to protect him and the law cannot be [distorted] by the state' (Oltay, 1993a: 6). In practice, this meant that once the statute of limitations had expired, those criminals who had not been punished in the past were also entitled to benefit from legal immunity. Various reactions soon followed the Court's ruling, but division between the government and opposition once again manifested itself. The AFD and the AYD welcomed the Court's ruling, but the HDF governing party found the decision surprising (*Magyar Nemzet*, 4 March 1992). Göncz stated that 'no one can appeal or reverse the ruling' (*Magyar Dokumentáció*, March 1992), adding that he himself would respect the Court's decision.

However, Göncz stressed that people had a right to know about their own history and past (Kovács, 1992); the pursuit of the truth had to go on. To this end, Göncz offered his own proposal to Parliament, suggesting that a Special Commission for Historical Investigation, a body whose main task was to elicit confessions from those criminals who were responsible for past misconducts, be set up in Parliament (Göncz, 1993: 1–5). The results of these investigations, such as the names of those accountable for crimes, were also to be made available to the public (details are discussed below).

Meanwhile, in February 1993, almost a year after the Zétényi-Takács Law was overturned by the Court's ruling, the Hungarian Parliament passed two new laws dealing with Communist crimes (Oltay, 1993a: 7). One was concerned with the procedure relating to crimes committed during the 1956 Revolution. Another was a version of the Zétényi-Takács Law but this time amended 'the Criminal Procedure Act of 1973 to make it obligatory for public prosecutors to level accusations in certain cases' (Halmai and Scheppele, 1997: 165). In practice, there was no fundamental difference between the Zétényi-Takács Law and its revised version. However, in the case of the law dealing with crimes committed during the 1956 Revolution, the government introduced two new elements – war crimes and crimes against humanity – to bring the Communists to account. The government explained that during the 1956 Revolution, Hungary was in a state of war, and the crimes committed during this war did not fall under the jurisdiction of statutory limitations (Oltay, 1993a: 7). They claimed that perpetrators belonging to this category should be tried as war criminals.

While the constitutionality of these two laws was in question, on 8 March 1993, Göncz again called on the Constitutional Court to review them. Three months later, the Court ruled that the amended Zéteny-Takács Law was unconstitutional.[20] Referring to the same rationale which had previously been made in the case of the first draft of the Zétényi-Takács Law, the Court concluded that the revised law still contravened the principle of legal security. On 12 October 1993, the Court also ruled that the law which dealt with crimes committed immediately after the 1956 Revolution was unconstitutional. According to the original Bill, crimes committed after the 1956 Revolution should be considered as war crimes. However, the Court ruled that crimes committed during the 1956 Revolution did not fall within the category of war crimes by the definition of international agreements (Halmai, 2004: 57). The Court nonetheless found that, according to the Geneva Convention of 1949 and the New York Convention of 1968 (which Hungary had also signed),[21] crimes committed after the 1956 Revolution belonged in the category of crimes against humanity, highlighting that the criminals could now be brought to justice without reference to the statute of limitations. Subsequently, on 22 October 1993, in consideration of the Court's ruling, the Hungarian Parliament adopted Law No. XC of 1993 on the Procedure related to Crimes committed during the 1956 Revolution and Struggle for Freedom.[22] The constitutionality of the law having been upheld by the Court's ruling, Göncz finally signed it (*Népszabadság*, 25 October 1993).

This issue clearly demonstrates the dilemma of transitional justice that the post-Communist Hungarian government had to tackle. On the one hand, it was recognised that 'no deed deserving punishment' should remain unpunished (Kis, 2003: 274), as this was deemed to be morally reprehensible. On the other hand, it was agreed that, in a constitutional state, justice is workable only if it is sought within the framework of the principle of the rule of law. The main problem was that taking legal action against the wrongdoers was not possible, as the time limit for prosecution had already expired. Thus, a clash between the concept of moral justice and the new government's commitment to the principle of the rule of law emerged. This was recognised by the political elite, legal experts and the general public alike but they could not reach an agreement over the best way to deal with the past. More precisely, they were not certain that on moral grounds, justice could be enacted retrospectively. In this uncertain situation, Göncz, who had once strongly urged the redress of past injustices through the establishment of the Committee for Historical Justice (see Section 3.3), now firmly stood with the rigorous application of the principle of the rule of law. Thus, it is necessary to question what it was that led him to deal with this delicate issue in this manner.

According to my interviews and articles found in the academic literature, three factors are primarily responsible for Göncz's stance. Firstly, it has been suggested that the consensus-based democracy underpinning Göncz's political beliefs or philosophy influenced him in challenging the Zétényi-Takács Law (interview with Babus, 19 May 2007). As the main concern about the Compensation Law for Göncz was the issue of social division over the possible discriminatory elements within it, the Zétényi-Takács Law also contributed to the polarisation of Hungarian society so was equally inadmissible to him.[23] The significance of social consensus embedded in Göncz's political beliefs was displayed when he personally visited the Constitutional Court. Göncz stated:

I came to this Court for the following reasons:

- During the parliamentary debate about the proposed [the Zétényi-Takács Law], there were several concerns about its [constitutionality].
- The petitions handed over to me have proved that the position of the law enforcers is divided. There are judges who find it irreconcilable with their conscience to cooperate in the law enforcement of the legislation.
- According to several scientific conferences, the position of the law on these issues is divided in Hungary as well as abroad.
- The foreign reactions to this law are rather unfavourable and numerous press publications have questioned the constitutionality of our country.

(Kurtan *et al.*, 1992b: 563).

Certainly, the law not only divided general public opinion, but also legal experts at home and abroad. In this polarised situation, Göncz naturally questioned the constitutionality of the law, not to mention that the legislation conflicted with his political beliefs about consensus-based democracy. A former chairman of the AFD explained how Göncz's commitment to the idea of a consensus-based democracy could have affected Göncz's action of vetoing the law:

The constitutional democracy Göncz and other Free Democrats understood was not a system in which the majority in Parliament decides everything. There are civic rights must be protected even against the majority's will. The branches of power are duly separate and complement each other. Within Parliament, the opposition has certain rights to exercise and [this means] the majority is not in a position to decide everything. Göncz made serious efforts towards the realisation of a real constitutional democracy.
(Interview with a former chairman of the AFD, 27 September 2007)

Given this statement, democracy was workable for Göncz, if there was consensus in decision-making or if the problematic law itself was changed in a way that meant that dissenting opinions could be minimised. However, at the time, the Zétényi-Takács Law was not unproblematic and neither did Hungarian society show consensus, in conflict with Göncz's political beliefs. In this regard, the Court's involvement seemed to be indispensable and, given that the major issue for Göncz was to find a way to bring about demands for political justice in a reassuring and democratic manner, it was perhaps unavoidable. It should be noted that, even if this act were only symbolic, in the annual New Year's Greetings speeches Göncz gave to the general public; the significance of seeking *social consensus and solidarity* were the words most consistently emphasised throughout his presidency.[24]

A second plausible account for Göncz's refusal to sign the retroactive legislation lies in his future-orientated or prospective political values. A great number of Hungarian academics have suggested that Göncz was one of the advocates for a peaceful transformation to democracy (interviews with Babus, Hegedűs, Kende, Rainer and Varga). This concept can be variously interpreted according to the context. According to Babus and Rainer, however, the rationale behind the peaceful democratic change was that it drew a thick line between past and future. Thus, if the Communists were to be punished for their past misconducts through the application of retroactive justice, this would contradict the fundaments underpinning the legitimacy of a new democracy. The chief political editor of the economic weekly, *Heti Világgazdaság*, Endre Babus, maintained that:

> The basic notion of Hungary's systemic change was that it must be orientated to the future ... Without violence, the Communists handed over their power to the [opposition] ... The new political elite did not wish to seek revenge on the old political elite ... I think *Göncz also attached [himself] to this notion and seriously tried to [keep to] it all the time.*
> (Interview with Babus, 19 May 2007, my emphasis)

Similarly, János Rainer expressed this view:

> My impression is that *peaceful transformation for Göncz meant tabula rasa in the sense of [granting] an amnesty ... He thought* that if [that] was the price for the peaceful transformation to democracy, it was worth not seeking political reckoning [...].
> (Interview with Rainer, 22 August 2007, my emphasis)

The consistent emphasis above underscores the fact that Göncz also shared the basic notion of a peaceful transformation. A peaceful transition to democracy could be seen by Göncz as the turning point of a new beginning for Hungarian history and retroactive justice would not be harmonious with the fundamental concept of peaceful democratic change. In fact, in an interview with the Hungarian daily, *Népszava*, Göncz reaffirmed the assertion, stating that:

> The political transformation to democracy for me [meant] that a line [between the past and present] must be drawn or [we must] stop [showing] hatred to the institution [which had dominated] for the last four decades. The law on Justice was not compatible with the ideal of the transformation and the requirement of a new beginning [of Hungary's history].
>
> (Bíró, 2000)

The final explanation lies in Göncz's liberal democratic ideology or values. Firstly, the concept of liberal democracy, in particular concerned with justice, should be defined. According to Calhoun, liberal democratic ideology is in harmony with three elements: 'social contract, the rule of law, openness and an inclusive approach' (Calhoun, 2004: 29–44). Explaining that before making a social contract, individuals live in 'a state of nature' (a concept introduced by Thomas Hobbes), Calhoun argues that a social contract establishes a society in which the principle of the rule of law applies. Also, reasoning that the past is the time *before* the-rule-of-law based society existed, Calhoun contends that these two elements essentially refer to a forward-looking value system. The final explanation offered by Calhoun is that liberal democracy guarantees that all people are equally treated before the law, and opportunity is open to everyone. According to this rationale, the rule of law, equality and perhaps the guarantee of basic human rights are the ultimate goals that liberal democracy pursues. Furthermore, as these democratic elements are intrinsically intertwined with future-orientated values, retroactive justice is precluded from the idea of liberal democracy. If Göncz also held this view then, it is highly probable that he would refuse to accept any type of retroactive justice.

As has been discussed above, Göncz constantly rejected the retroactive law based on his commitment to future-orientated values. It is possible to argue that liberal and democratic ideology was behind his determination not to sign the law. Moreover, in view of a speech that Göncz delivered on the occasion of the International Colloquium on the European Agreement on Human and Cultural Rights, it would appear that his commitment to the guarantee of human rights had also informed his decision to veto the retroactive legislation. Göncz explained what human rights meant for him:

> Human rights, for me, . . . are a never-ending struggle for human dignity . . . a political struggle concerned with curbing the powers that the state may exercise against the individual . . . We cannot make concessions where others who need protection from persecution or discrimination, or who suffer violation

of their human rights [are concerned]. When the dignity of human beings is violated, we must protest as hard as we can. We cannot tolerate the loss of other people's dignity.

(Tóth, 1999: 46)

Göncz acknowledged that the human rights issue was the most challenging to him, but he made clear that he could not and – would not – concede his position on this issue. He stressed that in a democratic state, where human rights were guaranteed, perpetrators who committed crimes ought also to be equally treated before the law. Although this does not tell us whether Göncz had considered the human rights' issue when dealing with the Communist past, this factor cannot be excluded entirely given its significance to his political beliefs. Indeed, a letter Göncz wrote to the Constitutional Court highlights the fact that Göncz did consider the human rights' issue when dealing with the retroactive legislation. In his letter of 18 November 1991, one of the questions raised was as follows: 'Does this law not undermine the principle of law *nullum crimen sine lege*[25] which has become the principle of human rights supported by historical practice and international agreement?'[26] Thus, it is fair to suggest that in so far as the question of settling accounts with the past is concerned, Göncz sought to address the issue within a framework guided by the principle of the liberal-democratic equality before the law.

Göncz's democratic stance, however, was not favourably viewed by all Hungarian citizens. For instance, in response to my question,[27] Szilvia Varró, political editor of the Hungarian internet daily, *Hírszerző*, expressed her regret at Göncz's role:

> It would have been good if Göncz had stood by justice . . . As a 1956 veteran and a [member] of the democratic opposition, he should have played a more active role in [dealing with] the Communist past. As the president, he should have demanded the enactment of laws [rendering justice]. I think it was his job to lead Hungary to face the past [honestly], which has remained undone to the present day . . . He did nothing to help the [creation] of social peace. I regret to say that he could have done many [more] things for justice.
>
> (Interview with Varró, 15 August 2007)

For Varró it was deplorable to see that Göncz had not only failed to take a proactive role in the question of settling accounts with the past but, had actively prevented it. Varró believed that Hungary had not dealt with the past, and this remained a deficiency within Hungarian democracy. Göncz was responsible, because he was perceived to have done nothing to assist the process of coming to terms with the past. Thus, Varró implies that Göncz failed to fulfil his one of primary presidential duties – the representation of the unity of the nation – as his neglect of the past contributed to national discord which might have arisen due to the lack of clarity in attitudes toward the Communist era.

However, one should bear in mind that Göncz did offer his own solution to deal with the past. After the Court overturned the Zétényi-Takács Law, Göncz proposed a Bill for establishing a Special Commission for Historical Investigation.[28] Reasoning that the preclusion of culpability decided by the Court did not mean that the state should avoid its obligation to examine important past events, Göncz urged that 'the state must co-operate [in the process of] look[ing] into the truth and reveal the names of perpetrators' (*Magyar Nemzet*, 4 March 1992). Göncz stated that:

> I asked [for] Parliament [to] . . . establish a Commission for Historical Investigation to Research (CHIR) . . . The Commission would be charged to [name] those responsible for violations and for acts committed against individual human lives . . . A complete disclosure of events and naming of persons responsible for the violation of law might help familiarise us with the nation's tragic recent past . . . [but] without infringing the Constitution and existing legal principles . . . [The CHIR] is to [help] ease the tension prevailing in our society because of our lack of clarity about the past [. . .]
>
> (Göncz, 1993: 4–5)

The extract above suggests that dealing with the past for Göncz does not mean the purge of wrongdoers, but a path of historical process for societal reconciliation. Göncz viewed that a key condition for this process – that of allowing people to exercise their legitimate right to knowledge about the past – should be met first. Göncz stressed that, without meeting this basic requirement, Hungarian society would not be able to reconcile itself with those perpetrators who had violated society's democratic rights. For this reason, Göncz proposed the founding of the CHIR in the expectation that this body would help people face the country's past honestly and their individual records that they had been sealed for decades. It should be noted that, when Göncz was active as a member of the Committee for Historical Justice, a full-scale independent investigation regarding show trials and legal cases that had been enforced since 1945 was considered as the key issue to be addressed (see Section 3.3). In this respect, Göncz seemed to have made a clear distinction between the right to know about the past and, the issue of calling the Communists to account. In Kiss's terms, Göncz may have been one of the advocates of the virtues of 'reckoning with the past in order to ensure openness and to give everyone a chance for an honest confrontation with past behaviour' (Kiss, 2006: 926). Indeed, Péter Kende confirmed that Göncz's determination for establishing the CHIR originated in the concept of allowing people to judge their past records for themselves. Kende noted thus:

> Göncz clearly saw that Hungarian society could not stand on its own without closing off the Communist past. At least, it must be closed symbolically . . . It required a body which had a moral authority, which could say to the public 'Dear Hungarians and Fellow Citizens! We live in a new era, which came into being after the systemic change. We live in a society built on legal continuity which cannot bring retroactive laws. But we can bring our verdict on some [important] matters which occurred during the Communist era' . . . [Where] it

required a moral initiative, [Göncz realised this with his Bill]. [But] he could not find any partners for this.

(Interview with Kende, 5 October 2007)

The genesis of this moral initiative lay in Göncz's understanding and the lessons that he gained from his first hand experience of the hardship caused by miscarriages of justice. As Göncz stated:

> Reckoning is necessary. In my personal opinion, it should be made strictly within the framework of a state built on the rule of law. In a closed trial, I was sentenced to life imprisonment. It was not possible to appeal. I strongly feel that no procedure should be repeated that could be found illegal in retrospect.
> (*Magyar Dokumentáció*, November 1991)

In view of this, it is fair to say that, when assessing the question of coming to terms with the past, Göncz sought to address the issue within a framework guided by the liberal-democratic principle that everyone ought to be treated equally before the law.

5.2.4. The Law on Arable Land (Termőföldről szóló törvény)

On 6 April 1994, the Parliament in Hungary adopted 'No. LV Law of 1994 on Arable Land'(hereafter the Law on Arable Land) for the following reason:

> On the basis of transforming ownership, in order to convert agriculture into a market economy built on private ownership; to help the trade of arable land and the use of land to obtain credit so that this facilitates the efficient functioning of new[ly] operating firms; to facilitate the establishment of landownership that is capable of pursuing competitive agricultural produce [. . .].[29]

Central to the debate over the Law on Arable Land was whether placing limitations on the purchase of land was necessary for the transformation of land ownership in Hungarian agriculture. The relative weakness of Hungary's agricultural competitiveness on the international market was the official reason given for the adoption of this law (Halmai, 2004: 349); its aim was clear – the protection of Hungary's land market from foreign purchase. Several stipulations were included in the law, of which the point of contention centred on the regulation of who would be entitled to purchase land. Three categories – an individual Hungarian citizen; a domestic body or organisation; and a foreign individual or body – were identified to decide whether claimants were eligible for buying land (*Heti Világgazdaság*, 16 April 1994; Izsák and Nagy, 2004: 592). Those who fell within the first category could buy land, albeit with limited scope,[30] whereas those in either of the other two were essentially excluded from undertaking land purchase transactions. There were some exceptions in this law, but both domestic and foreign *private* organisations were ruled out for the purchase of land. For instance, among the exceptions, local government, public foundations, the Church and the state itself were granted a legal right to buy arable land with unlimited scope (Félix, 1994; *Népszabadság*, 30 April 1994). In contrast, other bodies such as the National Association of Agricultural Cooperatives and Producers were excluded. Consequently, the legality of the law was questioned, particularly with respect to whether it discriminated against potential buyers, who were foreigners or public bodies and private associations located at home and abroad. While the constitutionality of the law was in doubt, on 29 April 1994, Göncz, who had a reservation about signing the law, turned to the Constitutional Court, requesting a judicial review (of which details are discussed below). Two months later, the Court ruled that the Law of Arable Land was not unconstitutional (Sólyom and Holló, 1995: 197).

Given that the Law of Arable Land may have included discriminatory elements, the question arises as to the grounds on which the Court justified that it conformed to the Constitution. When Göncz forwarded the law to the Court, he referred to the following clauses, asking whether the law was in harmony with these principles:

Article 70/A: The Republic of Hungary shall respect the human rights and civil rights of all persons in the country without discrimination on the basis of race, colour, gender, religion, national or social origin [. . .];

Article 56: In the Republic of Hungary, everyone is legally capable;

Article 9 (1): The economy of Hungary is a market economy, in which public and private property shall receive equal consideration and protection under the law.

(Halmai, 2004: 347)

In essence, Göncz questioned whether distinctions being made between individual Hungarian citizens and foreigners, public bodies and private businesses at home and abroad upheld the principle of equality. Göncz wondered whether the law might have undermined the egalitarian principle which related to the human and civil rights elements of the Constitution and the right to enterprise and market economy. In response to Göncz's questions, the Court ruled that the entitlement to ownership was not a part of the fundamental rights that were defined in the Constitution; it could, the Court ruled, be restricted if reasonable grounds were given for the imposition of the limitation (Halmai, 2004: 348). Additionally, the Court ruled that it was rare to contravene the principle of the market economy, and the Law on Arable Land did not fall into this legal realm. The Court's final justification was the exclusion of domestic and foreign bodies from the subject of land ownership was required, *since allowing foreigners and certain domestic potential purchasers to buy land would give them leeway to use the law* (Halmai, 2004: 349). This meant that since establishing companies or private bodies could be considered the easiest way to bypass the law, for example, avoiding the legal limit on the acreage of land that could be bought, private businesses and bodies should be banned altogether from land ownership. In arriving at this conclusion, the Court's deci-

132 The post-Communist presidency

sion seems to have considered the relative strength of purchasing power vested in legal bodies compared to that of an individual Hungarian citizen. Following the rationale of the Court's decision, it is likely that without this protective measure, only those individuals and commercial bodies that possessed considerable financial resources would be capable of purchasing land.

In this ruling, however, there was an element of ambiguity. Even if discriminatory measures were necessary for the protection of Hungary's farmers and of its vulnerable land market from relatively richer foreign buyers, the law still seems to have compromised the principle of equality. Since none of the clauses within the Constitution detailed the circumstances under which land purchase would be restricted from domestic and foreign legal bodies, this legal lacuna itself suggested that the principle of equality was contravened. It should be noted that the arbitrariness of the Court's decision was questioned by a dissenting judge of the Court, Géza Kilényi (Sólyom and Holló, 1995: 210), whose view was later supported by the European Court of Justice (ECJ). The ECJ ruled that the Hungarian Law of Arable Land violated the European Community Law, which required non-discrimination in the free movement of capital, goods, persons and services (Majoros, 2000: 5–6).[31]

Göncz may have recognised this legal deficiency, and his anxiety may have been expressed in the form of a constitutional veto. He may have known that in the short term, the imposition of protective measures on agricultural landownership might benefit those farmers who were unable to compete with their counterparts possessed of greater financial resources. However, in his decision-making process, Göncz may have considered that in the long term, protective measures would not be advantageous for the modernisation of Hungary's economy, particularly in relation to Hungary's integration into Europe. It should be noted that at this time, Hungary had already applied for membership of the European Union,[32] and the accession was considered as a principal way of modernising the transitional Hungarian economy. A speech delivered by Göncz at the twenty-fifth anniversary of the Club of Rome[33] demonstrated how he understood 'integration' with respect to economic transformation:

> Integration – by which we mean the European Union – is a framework and a means to help the two halves of the continent adjust to each other and to the global environment . . . The Central and Eastern European economies will have to modernise to achieve growth. For this modernisation, capital is required. It must come from exports [to] more accessible markets, particularly in Western Europe, from direct foreign investments and loans. We also need more advanced technology and better skills. Much of this will have to come from external sources, first of all from Western Europe, which has a direct and unequivocal interest in the rise of the other half.
>
> (Tóth, 1999: 150–1)

The extract above underscores the fact that for the modernisation of the Hungarian economy, an influx of foreign capital was essential. While this does not tell us how Göncz related the modernisation issue of Hungary's agriculture to the whole economic transitional process, it is certain that economic transformation could not be achieved without opening Hungary's market to Western Europe. Göncz had a holistic way of thinking and a good understanding of the complexity of contemporary transitional problems and integration was seen as the key means for addressing the existing issues. In this respect, precluding foreign investors from land ownership would be counter-productive to Hungary's integration process into Europe. In fact, the significance of integration as a way to modernise Hungary's economy was again underlined by Göncz. At a Think Tank Network meeting, [34] Göncz defined what integration meant to Central and Eastern Europe:

> On the Central and East European side, the *pros* of integration, especially pan-European integration, are obvious:
>
> Politically, it can provide the security that many of these countries lack.
> Economically, it can increase the modernisation process in Central and Eastern Europe and greatly facilitate our access to outside markets.
> Socially, it can help us establish the standards and systems appropriate to a modern society.
>
> (Göncz, 1992: 207–8)

This once more highlights the main contention that Hungary's socio-economic and political transformation to democracy could not be attained without its integration into Europe. In a wider context and long-term perspective, Hungary's accession to various international organisations was required as, not only would this bring about prosperity, but also social security, as well as democratic norms established in developed states. Mapping out Hungary's position within Europe, Göncz may have thought that foreign access to the Hungarian land market would outweigh the benefits which a short-term protective measure might have brought to the modernisation of the Hungarian economy. As an agronomist who had gained first-hand knowledge and experience in the field (see Chapter 1 and 2), Göncz would have fully realised the inherent weakness of Hungary's agriculture. However, this issue suggests to us that in the situation of a dilemma where nationalist or protectionist ideas and liberal or cosmopolitan ideas clashed, Göncz ultimately opted for the latter. Behind this decision, his commitment to the principle of equality was clearly highlighted in this economic transitional issue. Having noted the importance of the egalitarian principle for Göncz's political beliefs, it is now necessary to trace the continuity and discontinuity of these values in other areas of economic interest – the Law on Privatisation (which will be examined in Chapter 6). Before embarking on this task, the following section of the chapter examines one of the most controversial issues in which Göncz became involved: control over the broadcast media.

5.2.5. *Control over the broadcast media*

As in other Eastern European states during the Communist era, the media in Hungary was placed under the control of the Communist party (Milton, 2000: 76). The 1974 Decree which justified the placing of the media under the control of the Council of Ministers (Arato, 1996: 226; Milton, 2000: 129) provides a good example of Hungary's media situation. The end of Communism, however, opened a new era and offered an opportunity to transform this system of control. This was raised as a key topic for the agenda of the RTN (see Section 4.1) and 'in 1990 immediately after the political change in Hungary', there was a desire among new political elites to legislate a new media law (Pataki, 1992b, 1994: 30, 43). This plan, however, had never been realised during the Antall government and the issue of controlling the media demonstrated how difficult the birth of this basic condition of democracy was. In the beginning, conflict over controlling the media was considered only as a matter for the heads of broadcast media and the Antall government. It developed into a serious political issue when Göncz stepped into the debate. In effect, his involvement not only brought about a series of sharp confrontations with the Antall government, but also contributed to political polarisation. This was evident in a series of pro-government versus anti-government public demonstrations, with the latter culminating in the formation of the Democratic Charter.[35] The following section examines this historically important event regarding the issue of media control and explores the background to this controversy.

In July 1990, with the agreement of six parliamentary parties, two prominent sociologists, Elemér Hankiss and Csaba Gombár, were chosen as the new heads of the Hungarian national television and radio (Mézes, 1992: 61; Milton, 2000: 130; Pataki, 1994: 40). It was intended that these nominees could – until the passage of a new media law – lead the broadcast media in an impartial manner, free from political interference (Hankiss, 1996: 246, 1999: 276). After six months, however, the first sign of a breach in this initial agreement became apparent when the Antall government began to put increasing pressure on national radio, in an attempt to place it under their control. The former chairman of the national radio, Gombár, said:

> At the time, there were no commercial radio stations and this [the public radio] was the only radio station we had. In this situation, political parties naturally wanted to influence the programming of radio and television. I tried to resist this, to ensure that public radio be neutral and beyond government influence.
>
> (Interview with Gombár, 1 October 2007)

Thus, in the beginning of a struggle for control over the broadcast media, conflict was primarily centred on tensions between these two heads of the broadcast media and the head of government; polemical confrontations between Antall and Göncz were not yet crystallised in comparable political tensions.

In the summer of 1991, when Antall submitted new nominees for the vice-presidencies of the state media to Göncz, conflict between premier and president began. The nominations were aimed at placing pro-government figures in important positions, in the expectation that they might provide a counterbalance to Hankiss and Gombár (Sükösd, 1992, 2000: 154). Objecting to Antall's suggestion, however, Göncz did not sign the submission on the nominations, reasoning that 'his conscience would not allow him to agree with the nomination'(*Magyar Hírlap*, 13 July 1991; *Népszabadság*, 13 July 1991). Göncz's comment prompted Antall to ask him to reconsider his decision, arguing that the president did not have the real right to refuse the prime minister's suggestion. Despite this, Göncz did not yield, so Antall forwarded the issue of the president's right of nomination to the Constitutional Court. On 23 September 1991, the Court ruled that the president must not oppose the nomination of state officials proposed by the government, unless those appointments endangered the democratic functioning of state institutions involved.[36] Despite this decision, Göncz did not change his position, citing that 'the danger of government control over broadcasting as the reasons for his refusal' (Oltay, 1992: 42).

In January 1992, having faced an intransigent president, Antall again turned to the Court, asking whether there was a deadline for the president's signing of the nomination of state officials proposed by the premier. On 28 January 1992, the Court ruled that the president should give his signature *in due course* (Sólyom and Holló, 1993: 51). Additionally, the Court adjudicated that failing to meet a deadline would be against the law. Missing a deadline was considered to be unconstitutional, with the result that after a month, Göncz signed the nomination (*Magyar Hírlap*, 3 March 1992) and the conflict with Antall appeared to have come to an end.

In the late spring of 1992, however, their confrontation resurfaced over the decision to dismiss the head of national radio. In May 1992, Antall asked Göncz to sign his endorsement of Gombár's dismissal, reasoning that Gombár had failed to fulfil his duties. However, Göncz did not accept Antall's request and Antall again turned to the Constitutional Court. At this time, Antall raised four questions (discussed below), which included asking whether the president could refuse to endorse the removal of state officials suggested by the prime minister. On 8 June 1992, the Court replied, concluding that 'the president should not withhold his signature from the appointments and dismissals of leaders of state institutions requested by the prime minister, unless those suggestions endangered the democratic functioning of the state institutions' (Sólyom and Holló, 1993: 207–8).

On 22 June 1992, two weeks after the Court's final ruling, Antall asked Göncz to agree to Gombár's dismissal, along with that of the head of national television, Elémer Hankiss. However, Göncz opposed Antall's request, reasoning that he would delay his signature until the passage of a new media law. At the end of the year, a new draft media law was eventually put to the vote, but the bill was killed off due to the abstention of the AFD (discussed below). Consequently, by the end of 1992, the issue of media control was not resolved, either by the decision of the Constitutional Court, or by the agreement of the Members of Parliament.

The following year, on 6 January 1993, Hankiss and Gombár, who had been prominently involved in the media issue, asked Göncz to release them from office, claiming that:

> It would have been nonsensical and cruel if each of our several thousand colleagues, managers, producers, cameramen, editors, security guards, cleaning women and others had been forced to decide day-by-day whom to obey: us, or the new men delegated by the Government. We did not want to involve our innocent colleagues in this ordeal and we did not want to get entangled in a hopelessly vicious and degrading squabble with the Government's men.
> (Hankiss, 1996: 253–4)

With their resignation, the protracted media issue appeared to have ended. The former head of the Hungarian Journalists' Association, István Wisinger, remembered the consequence of the removal of the heads of public media thus: 'Immediately after Hankiss and Gombár's dismissal, a house-keeping took place in the Hungarian state television and radio . . . 129 employees were dismissed from the radio station [alone]. [Luckily] I kept my job but in return, I was silenced' (interview with Wisinger, 7 June 2007).

The dismissal of Hankiss and Gombár, however, did not end the issue of controlling the media. A petition of journalists for the removal of the new Vice-Presidencies submitted to Göncz (*Magyar Hírlap*, 2 November 1993) suggested that he was still in a position to assume a proactive role against the Antall government's media policy. Indeed, as the subsequent issues of the Law of Radio Frequency and the *La Stampa* affair demonstrated (details are discussed in Sections 5.2.6 and 5.2.7), the question of the control of the public media continued until the end of the Antall government.

Despite the fact that the issue of media control was a matter of contention for the political elite, it is unclear whether the severity of the crisis was simply attributable to tension between Göncz and Antall or whether it was a political battle compounded by the vested interests of various political forces. The present section examines possible factors which may have contributed to the development of the media issue, and explores the ways in which this relates to Göncz's political values.

In effect, the issue of control over the broadcast media was aggravated by Göncz's persistent refusal to comply with Antall's plan of restructuring the personnel and programming of public television and radio. Since the Court ruled that Göncz should conform to the premier's request, his constant refusal certainly increased the tension between these two figures and their political camps. It should be noted that Göncz's intransigence not only incurred sharp criticism from members of the government, but also became a source of contentious legal dispute as to whether he had overstepped his constitutional authority. In response to such questions,[37] Hungarian political scientist, András Körösényi, explained how he observed the issue of media control with particular respect to its effect on the alteration of presidential power:

It was possible to debate what the scope of power was. This had to be [clarified] in the course of the political process . . . Ultimately, the Court curtailed and narrowed down the scope of presidential powers. As a result, in this constitutional debate, Göncz was defeated. Nevertheless, in my opinion, at the time, it was possible to interpret the Constitution in various ways. Göncz acted according to his beliefs, but he interpreted the scope of his power too broadly and went beyond it.

(Interview with Körösényi, 11 July 2007)

Similarly, but with a different emphasis, a former Counsellor of the Constitutional Court, Gábor Halmai, stated that:

Sólyom [the president of the Constitutional Court] always thought that Göncz overstepped his constitutional authority . . . He did not say this in public, but once he said something like 'if one read these decisions, it is clear who was in possession of the truth, either the prime minister or the president . . . Following the ruling, one can clearly see who did not perform his constitutional duty'. He did not say this was Göncz . . . but he thought Göncz had to sign those appointments.

(Interview with Halmai, 15 November 2007)

Therefore, the question arises as to why Göncz constantly refused to accept Antall's proposal, despite being aware of mounting criticism against him and the possible consequences for his political career. One may assume that personal emotion, such as animosity between Antall and Göncz, could have been responsible for Göncz's controversial stance. Despite the fact that their personal relationship had been gradually eroded through their clashes in a series of events, it is unlikely that personal hostility was the principal reason for the severity of the standoff that developed over the issue of control of the broadcast media. In response to a television reporter's question – 'Mr President, how would you describe your relationship with the prime minister [József Antall]?'– Göncz stated that:

The father of the prime minister was [seen] as a prominent politician by me. This was at the time [when] I [worked] in the Smallholders' Party. In 1956, we [Göncz and Antall] collaborated closely with one another . . . I considered him a friend. . . . The current conflict between us is not a personal clash.

('TV 2 Interview' in *Magyar Hírlap Observer*, 2 July 1992)

One may interpret this as empty political rhetoric which helped to dissociate Göncz from any claimed accusations regarding his uneasy relationship with Antall. However, if, as Göncz argued, a sense of hostility between himself and Antall was not responsible for the impasse in this media control situation, one must look elsewhere for the origin of their conflict and the worsening of the crisis.

One possible explanation may lie in the misconceptions of the Hungarian political elite about the overall role of the media in public and political life. According to Oltay, the Antall government and the opposition had differing perceptions of the function of the media (Oltay, 1993b: 41). Whereas both parties supported the independence of the media in principle, in practice they both expected the media to provide flattering coverage of their political positions. As far as the governing party was concerned, they claimed that they were entitled to have more favourable coverage in programming, as their seats in Parliament represented more constituencies than the opposition. Accordingly, the airtime of programming should be proportionally allocated according to seats in Parliament (Oltay, 1993b: 41; Sükösd, 1992). In contrast, the opposition argued that one of the key roles of the media was to present a critique to the audience, often accompanied by commentary or pre-judged opinions in favour of the opposition, regarding the performance of the government (Oltay, 1993b: 41).

Hence, while both sides interpreted the role of the media differently, their failure to understand the concept of independent or objective broadcasting left them struggling for control over the media. Furthermore, in terms of the position of the governing party, since the majority of the Hungarian press was politically inclined towards the left (Mézes, 1992: 63; Oltay, 1992: 42),[38] they were desperate to keep the broadcast media under their control. As media expert, Áron Monori, asserted, supervising the broadcast media became an increasingly important issue to the governing party (whose popularity had fallen dramatically following the taxi-drivers' strike) for the propagation of their own political views (Monori, 2005: 265).

The second explanation may lie in the Pact made between the HDF and the AFD. As has been examined in the Section 4.2.3, the nomination procedure of the heads of public media was agreed in the Pact, and was fully formalised as follows:

> §(i) By the suggestion of the prime minister (after listening to the open hearing of the Parliament's Cultural and Press Affairs Committee), the president of the Republic appoints and dismisses the presidents and vice-presidents of the Hungarian radio and television, as well as the director of the Hungarian News Agency.
>
> (ii) In order to exercise the right specified in Provision (i), the president is required to have a counter-signature from the prime minister.[39]

Clause (i) defines the role-sharing regarding the appointment and dismissal of the heads of broadcast media. The premier acts an initiator who recommends eligible candidates for the posts of media heads, and the president decides whether the heads of media remain in office or not. According to this procedure, the president is *apparently* granted some discretionary power regarding the right of implementing personnel management. The next clause, however, confuses the picture. The president's right of decision is significantly constrained, as he or she cannot exercise this right without co-signature by the prime minister. According to Clause (ii), the premier who initially recommends the potential candidates for

The first presidency (1990–1995) 139

media headships, now has the right to decide on the matter him- or herself. This is known as the counter-signatory system, where the premier may disagree with the president by refusing to give his or her signature. However, the counter-signatory system could be utilised against the prime minister as well, as the president may object to the premier's proposition. This means that the actions of the heads of both state and government will only become effective if they reach a consensus about the appointment and dismissal of media heads.

The main problem in this procedure, however, was that it failed to spell out a concrete stipulation as to what the president's appointment right meant in practice. According to the rule above, it is not clear whether the president is granted a *real* right to refuse to sign the premier's decision. Should it be an operative power, as far as the right to implement personnel management is concerned, the president has a certain jurisdiction and, within its scope, he or she could act as a part of the Executive alongside the premier. However, given Hungary's parliamentarianism, vesting the president with certain executive powers is contradictory to the fundamental form of government. It should be noted that in Hungary's history, throughout the period from 1848 until the present, the prime minister, who is politically accountable to Parliament, has governed the country (Bölöny and Hubai, 2004; Szoboszlai, 1996: 122). The Pact also reaffirmed this principle as the basis of governance (see Section 4.2.3); thus it is illogical to suggest that the president is placed outside of the Executive branch, but has jurisdiction only in the appointment of state officials. If such were the case, there would be an explanation for this exception. Conversely, if the president's right of appointment is in name only, the president is not authorised to oppose the premier's decision. However, the appointment procedure specified in the Pact does not provide such detail, which leaves considerable room for various interpretations. For example, László Salamon understood that the president's right of appointment was only titular. Salamon argued thus:

> In a parliamentary system, the president does not have a discretionary power to decide. *The right to make a decision is for only a formality* . . . Not only does this apply to the president's right of appointment of [media heads], but it is also concerned with the right to make all other appointments (generals, ambassadors, university professors and rectors); he does not have the right of deliberation. But, Göncz thought he did have this right. . . . As a result, in the media war, he acted wrongly.
>
> (Interview with Salamon, 24 October 2007, my emphasis)

In contrast, a former chairman of the AFD who personally participated in drawing up the Pact asserted that, with the HDF leadership agreeing that the president be given an important role in the appointment of state officials, this agreement itself suggests the imposition of self-constraint on the premier's power:

> The aim of role-sharing lay in the securing of an impartial public media service. *Clearly, the intention of the legislators was that the president should play*

a real role so that impartiality is better secured. This is [possible] because the prime minister and the president must agree with one another.

(Interview with a former chairman of the AFD, 27 September 2007, my emphasis)

In short, as Milton notes, the obscure rule of sharing authority built into the appointment procedure 'generates opportunity as much as constraint, actors see different prospects and options that they can each justify as being within the rules' (Milton, 2001: 513).

A third key factor which contributed to the stalemate was the ambiguous ruling issued by the Constitutional Court and its subsequent interpretations by Göncz and Antall. As stated above, during the development of the media issue, the Court brought in three rulings regarding the president's right of appointment of state officials. However, these decisions were not completely clear and further contributed to a protracted media issue. For example, on 25 May 1992 when Antall turned to the Court, he asked what the president's right of appointment and dismissal meant in practice. The questions raised can be summarised as follows:

1. Whether the dismissal of the heads of public media put forward by the Prime Minister could violate the freedom of the press.
2. Whether the president has a right of accepting [or refusing] a law related to the appointment and dismissal of [state officials].
3. Whether the president can exercise his deliberation right to dismiss [state officials].
4. Whether the president needs to justify his decision if he refuses to dismiss state officials (what are the grounds on which the president can refuse to dismiss state officials?).

(*Magyar Dokumentáció*, June 1992a)

In essence, Antall wished to know whether Göncz had a constitutional right to oppose his decision on the removal of the heads of the broadcast media, and whether his proposal would undermine the fundamental democratic principles of freedom of expression and freedom of the press. Upon Antall's request, the Constitutional Court made a decision, but it was far from unequivocal. In its ruling, the Court replied that the head of state could only object to the nominees of the broadcast media suggested by the head of government, *if such nominations endangered the democratic functioning of the state institutions involved* (*Magyar Dokumentáció*, June 1992b). The practical meaning of the last phrase was open to debate and this ambiguity contributed to further disputes between Göncz and Antall (and even among the judges themselves). For instance, having dissented from the ruling, one of the judges of the Constitutional Court held a different opinion. He argued that since the Constitution does not specify the context of the legal grounds on which the president may disagree with the government's decision, the Court cannot provide its decision:

In Europe, there is no single Constitution with a text, [specifying] the grounds on which the president can refuse to give his signature. If he is not pleased with [those suggestions], he can refuse to sign the law in question.
(Interview with a former judge of the Constitutional Court, 9 May 2007)

According to this statement, the Court appears to have taken too active a role, because making a new law or clause does not fall within the Court's jurisdiction but belongs in the Legislature.[40] In Arato's terms, 'the Court itself has acquired quasi-[constitutional] power' by making a new provision (Arato, 1995: 48); and this activism leads us to wonder whether the Court in fact overstepped its constitutional boundary.

According to Kovács, the Court brought this ruling to demarcate the boundaries of the president's discretionary power (Kovács, 2006: 20). This means that, other than in those exceptional instances where democracy is gravely at risk, the president is not authorised to make an autonomous decision. In the remaining cases, the president is obliged to secure agreement either from Parliament or the government. This legal requirement, however, does not mark the boundary of the president's discretionary powers, but rather leaves leeway for various interpretations. When the president activates this right, the only legal condition that he or she needs to meet is *always considering the situation within the entire context of democratic institutions involved* (Ács, 2000: 53; Petrétei, 2001a: 89). Having said that, neither the practical meaning of this nor that 'of democracy being in danger' is defined in the Constitution; this legal lacuna once more gave rise to ambiguity. The only clear issue is that the Court did not entirely remove the right of deliberation from the president. As long as the president refers to this provision (that democracy is in danger) as a solid grounding for his decision, in principle he or she can object to any governmental decision. As Arato notes, the president's ability to resist to the governmental decision 'would survive unless the ruling coalition had the necessary two-thirds [majority] vote to impeach the president' (Arato, 1996: 228). Indeed, even after the Court's ruling, Göncz refused to countersign citing that 'the danger of government control over broadcasting as the reasons for his refusal' (Oltay, 1992: 42).

Thus, it is important to ask why the Constitutional Court was unable to make an unequivocal decision regarding jurisdictional disputes occurring in political institutions. While there may be various explanations for this,[41] one possible account offered by Halmai and Ilonszki suggests that *indirect* political influences which built into the procedure of appointing judges were responsible for informing the decision. Gábor Halmai explained how political parties appointed Court justices who were politically close to their own ideological spectrums: 'The HDF [chose] László Sólyom; the Socialist or Liberal party [chose] Péter Schmidt, Imre Vörös, Antal Adám and Géza Kilényi' (interview with Halmai, 15 November 2007).

Similarly but more explicitly, Gabriella Ilonszki accounted for the consequence of the judges' appointment procedure on their decision, asserting that:

In principle, the Constitutional Court is the most independent organ. But what is our [real] situation? Parties nominate constitutional judges and decide who will be the judges . . . If the candidates are intelligent enough to think of their future, we can imagine that they will [make a point of] joining whichever party will be beneficial to them to get a seat in the Court. The dominance of parties [túlpártosodás] is the most serious problem of Hungarian politics . . . This is the weakness of Hungarian democracy.

(Interview with Ilonszki, 16 October 2007)

Despite the fact that the independence of the Constitutional Court was guaranteed on paper, in reality, the Court cannot be entirely free from political intervention without changing the appointment procedure currently in use. This by no means suggests that all Constitutional judges related their rulings to their previous political affiliations. It would rather depend on the matter of judgement whether justices were true to their judicial oaths or consciences. Nevertheless, given the political character of the Court and its highly politicised role, it is fair to suggest that the Court is another important decision-maker in the political process. As András Körösényi eloquently asserted:

The Court's broad powers and activism, and the judges' philosophy of judgement and their understanding of their role, according to which they may go beyond the text of the Constitution, all show that the Constitution and Constitutional review do not involve some form of objective, neutral systems of norms that exists above politics, but are instead themselves a part of the political process.

(Körösényi, 1999: 272–3)

The final, and perhaps most important, factor that led to the exacerbation of this crisis was the absence of new media legislation. Without this basic legal framework, the 1974 Decree was still effective which, in practice, meant that the Antall government had the legal authority to interfere in the programming of the state media. Under these circumstances, the broadcast media was naturally susceptible to political pressure and influence. It should be noted that the 1974 Decree was found to be unconstitutional (Lánczi and O'Neil, 1996: 92) and the government was instructed by the Court to legislate a new media law (*Népszabadság*, 9 June 1992a). The way in which the passage of the media law might provide a possible solution for the stalemate was discussed by a great number of media and legal experts. Among them, commentaries offered by Sükösd and Halmai are of particular relevance. Sükösd asserted that: 'The cause of the media war was there is no media law in Hungary . . . In my opinion, a [new] media law will give a guarantee that [will] reduce the intensity of the media war' (Monori, 2005: 275). Similarly, Halmai upheld the view that:

The media war demonstrated that in the absence of legal guarantee, it [will] not be possible to eliminate the problem that politics would directly intervene in the functioning of the electronic press . . . The adoption of a media law will not only bring a cease-fire, but also a sustainable real peace [into politics].

(Monori, 2005: 275)

Having noted that the media situation of Hungary was at an impasse because of the absence of a new media law, one must ask why the passage of a new media law was so difficult. Was this simply attributable to different viewpoints of the government and the opposition in their perceptions of the role of the media? Conflicting opinions on media function may have been one important contributing factor to the stalemate, but it is arguable that this is too simplistic an account. Perhaps, a more plausible explanation lies in the reluctance of the Hungarian political elite to relinquish control over the media. This attitude was exemplified in December 1992 a few days before the voting of the draft of a new media law. The wording of the draft content was somewhat amended by the Parliamentary Constitutional Committee in favour of the Antall government. Having noted that the draft had been arbitrarily altered, the AFD refused to take part in the vote, obstructing the passage of the new media law (Pataki, 1993: 19). This one example does not mean that the Hungarian media was always manipulated by political elites. However, given the situation of the time and the continuing practice evident even after the adoption of a new media law, it is certain that political control over public media remained an issue.[42] Áron Monori captured this well:

> Although the 2002 socialist–liberal democratic government's interventions in the media and the press reached neither the level[s] of the period of the previous media war, nor did the psychosis which had characterised that period, this government also showed that after the systemic change, political elites in Hungary were [still] incapable of relinquishing their influence over the press and the media.
>
> (Monori, 2005: 287)

Thus, it can be argued that the birth of a new media law was indeed hindered by the negative attitude of the Hungarian political elite.

Having examined the various factors which may have contributed to this issue, it is necessary to ascertain why Göncz persistently held fast to his view. Was Göncz's persistence primarily related to his political attachment to the opposition, especially to the AFD, as members of the Antall government claimed? Given that the issue of media control was further protracted by the clashes between the vested interests of the Antall government and the opposition, if Göncz was subject to the influence of the opposition, it is likely that he acted favourably towards them. An article published in one of the official dailies of the HDF, *Magyar Forum*, highlights this point, claiming that: 'During the four years of the HDF government, Göncz, [sought] an anti-democratic, counter-balancing role and actions against the will of electorate, and in any case his refusal to sign [the premier's proposal] represented the [interest] of the AFD' (Varga, 1995). In contrast, judging from Göncz's own explanation, his political affiliation with the opposition appears not to have been the principal reason for his objection to accepting the premier's decision. In an interview with a weekly political magazine, Göncz argued that he had his own principles for making a decision independently of party influences. Göncz said: 'To be honest, it never occurred to me that party leadership tied me. I am a free man [and I am free to] have my own opinions which are not influenced by party membership. Rather I identify with the party which is closest to my own [beliefs]' (Rádai, 1990). Similarly, in another interview, Göncz reaffirmed the position, arguing that: 'Unless the president wants to commit political suicide, he is not allowed to attach himself to a party. The president's main task is to ensure that daily political skirmishes do not influence the decisions [which] may affect the entire society' (Wisinger and László 2007: 330).

Perhaps, given the positions of their different political orientations, one can expect that the governing party and Göncz would hold opposing stances. In the normal practice of politicians, Göncz's account may be just empty political rhetoric. However, the independent critical thinking which was evident in numerous documents suggests that a plausible explanation of Göncz's controversial role in the media issue could be found in his liberal and democratic political beliefs.[43] Göncz made numerous statements on what he thought about the role of the media in a democratic state, but a letter he wrote to Antall is of particular relevance. On 6 November 1992, Göncz wrote:

Dear Prime Minister,

In March 1994, there will be an election in Hungary. Among several things, it is necessary to [ensure] that radio and television fully and genuinely mirror the opinions of society and impartially give information on the events and facts in the public interest. Public service radio and television belongs to neither the coalition government nor the opposition, but to the people [. . .]

(Kurtán *et al.*, 1993: 200)

This lends weight to the claim that Göncz was a free statesman capable of judging the media situation according to his political beliefs. Although Göncz did not state his position regarding the government's media policy, he was clearly of the view that, without the guarantee of press freedom, the Hungarian population would be incapable of forming their views and judgements on important matters. Göncz above all stressed that public media ought to be free from any political interference and be placed under the control of society. In an interview with Kossuth Radio, Göncz reaffirmed this position, stating that:

Television and radio is a commonly-owned, national treasure. It belongs to the nation. As the Hungarian army is a national institution, as the Court is a national institution which must be independent, the state media should be controlled by society, not by other political forces. These institutions must be protected from daily political skirmishes.

(Wisinger and László, 1994: 192)

The extract above again highlights the fact that the significance of press freedom was entrenched in the fabric of Göncz's political beliefs. As he had emphasised in a letter sent to Antall, Göncz consistently maintained that under no circumstances should the independence of public media be violated by any political influences. This still does not tell us what precisely the media situation of the time was. However, it is clear that Göncz had his own idea on the role of media that it ought to be placed under civilian control to present the general public of impartial information. Thus, Göncz's determination to resist the government's decision should be interpreted as stemming from his political beliefs, or conscience rather than his partisan role, as members of the Antall government had claimed. In response to my question – 'In circumstances in which you were not certain of whether your decision was right, on what grounds you did make a decision?' – Göncz reaffirmed this reasoning, stating that:

Göncz: Not only myself, but also everyone in power was put in [the difficult situation] of avoiding advisors. There was the endless wave of advice. Advice also came from each opposing side . . .
Kim: If the advice was conflicting, how did you make a decision?
Göncz: It may sound very strange to you, but people have their [own] instincts.
Göntér: Göncz often said that he could feel [where] the truth was.
Kim: How? According to his political instinct?
Göntér: Yes, instinct!
Göncz: This was my political instinct!
Göntér: This instinct came from his 70 years of experience. This was his subconscious [developed through his life], of what he had lived through, [important moments] which he decided and experienced and the essence of all of these [. . .].
Kim: Was that his instinct and conscience?
Göntér: His conscience and instinct! There was no doubt that Göncz always stood with poor and [socially] disadvantaged people. In a word, he never sought power.
                              (Interview with Göncz and Göntér, 10 January 2008)

In terms of the impact Göncz had on Hungarian politics, his proactive role in this issue was not always desirable. In a situation of political division where the Antall government and the opposition clashed through a series of transitional issues – as evidenced by the taxi-drivers' strike, the issue of the protection of Hungarian agriculture from foreign ownership and the question of settling accounts with the Communist past – the media issue certainly contributed to the widening of a political polarisation. In this process, Göncz, rather than remaining the passive figurehead that his ceremonial and nominal role might have suggested, intervened in the events, stating his position based on his own agenda. As has been argued in this chapter, Göncz acted according to his political beliefs, but the members of the government considered his presidential conduct as that of a party politician who had failed to position himself above party factionalism or who preferred to meddle in the government's business. Thus, the leadership of the Antall government concluded that Göncz was not eligible for the presidency and attempted to adopt a draft parliamentary resolution to impeach him (*Magyar Hírlap*, 26 May 1992).

András Körösényi captured this historic process well, particularly with respect to what long-term impact Göncz's proactive presidential role had on the shaping of power relations in Hungarian politics:

> Well, in the light of Göncz's view, these issues – the laws on compensation and on justice and the appointment of the heads of public radio and television – were crucial to him. They were the issues which he and Antall came into conflict about, and this [further] exacerbated the clash between the HDF and the AFD . . . They were the key events of political polarisation . . . In the development of Hungarian politics, from the 1990s until now, these issues determined the formation of the left-wing and right-wing blocs or at least affected the move in this direction . . . Göncz played a significant role in this political process.
>
> (Interview with Körösényi, 11 July 2007)

Thus, had Göncz not stepped into the government's business, a different image could have been formed of Hungary's party system and its politics. Perhaps, the escalation of conflict and political division between the HDF and the AFD could have been less severe than it was. However, this does not necessarily mean that Göncz should have remained silent in these critical transitional issues. As the Constitution dictates, in monitoring the democratic functioning of state institutions involved, the president is given another important task to fulfil. As already discussed above, this was a legitimate constitutional right of the president and the question of activating this power depended on the president's understanding of the existing situation, and whether he or she regarded it as a sign of threat to democracy. In the event that Göncz felt obliged to invoke this right in dealing with the issue of controlling the media, this suggests that Göncz in fact committed himself to his constitutional duties. Indeed, in a public statement, Göncz indicated that his decision not to sign Antall's proposal was grounded in his understanding of the existing situation of the media and its possible consequences on democracy. Göncz stated that:

> I am pleased to hear that, above all, the Constitutional Court stated that the freedom to express an opinion and, the concept of press freedom, are organically intertwined with the independence of information free from the state, the government, the parties and any other political forces. By taking this [view], the Court made clear that in the absence of this [the independence of information], democracy is in grave danger which one must protect it. *My decisions were led by this awareness* [. . .].
>
> The [government] attempted to dismiss this personnel [media heads] without putting equivalent [figures] in place, and [this] would have endangered the conditions for providing entire, balanced and factual information, and *thus directly would have brought about the serious disruption of democratic order.* For this reason, I did not dismiss the head of radio [. . .]
>
> (*Népszabadság*, 9 June 1992b, my emphasis)

It is therefore arguable that conviction originating from his liberal and democratic views was the principal reason for Göncz's objection to accepting Antall's decision concerning the dismissal of the heads of the broadcast media. In the absence of a new media law, Göncz may have regarded the removal of the heads of the broadcast media as an infraction of both freedom of information and freedom of the press, which could in turn jeopardise Hungary's transformation into a democracy. It is appropriate to conclude this exploration of controlling broadcast media and Göncz's controversial proactive role with Hankiss's views regarding the nature of Hungary's democracy and its implications:

> After 1989 we had to learn that democracy cannot be imported, it cannot be bought 'off the peg'. And, it is not brought about and established overnight by a first and single free election. It may be generated only in the course of a long and tedious learning process in which everybody has to take part and has to take up his or her responsibilities . . . The Media War may have shown many that there is no democracy without citizens acting with responsibility and, if necessary, civi[c] courage . . . The fact that two fragile public institutions [radio and television], which could rely only on the letter and spirit of the law, were able to protect their newly-won autonomy against extremely strong pressures and attacks coming from the side of the Government and the governing parties, proves that all the main political actors observed, at least until the last act, the rule of law and accepted the basic rules of the democratic game, including one of the most important rules or principles that, in a democracy, interests can be achieved only within the framework of laws and rules that have been accepted by the community.
>
> (Hankiss, 1996: 256–7)

5.2.6. *The Law on Radio Frequency Management*

The next issue in which Göncz became involved concerned the 'No. LXII Law of 1993 on Radio Frequency Management' (hereafter, the Law of Radio Frequency). There was not an immediately apparent link between the adoption of this law and the protracted issue of control over the broadcast media. However, considering the timing of the passage of the law – it was adopted a couple of months after the heads of broadcast media resigned – it is unlikely that the Antall government enacted the Law on Radio Frequency without considering the stalemate media issue. If a connection between these two issues did exist, the government's intransigence over placing the public media in independent hands would have been displayed in this case, too. Similarly, in terms of Göncz's position, he would have tackled the law in the same way he had the issue of control over the broadcast media. Thus, over time, Göncz would sustain his consistent liberal and democratic position in so far as media freedom was concerned. The present section examines the key aspects of the law and asks how it related to Göncz's political values, it is argued that Göncz is indeed committed to a consistent liberal and democratic stance which is evident in all his dealings on issues of media freedom.

On 27 April 1993, the Hungarian Parliament adopted the Law of Radio Frequency noting that:

> 3.§b) The government's task is to set the objective of long-term radio frequency management and supervise the process [. . .].
>
> c) The government's task is to harmonise the distribution of [public] radio frequencies [. . .].
>
> 24. § In a state of emergency, under martial law and [in the event] of a natural disaster, with the authorisation of Parliament, the minister concerned can temporarily limit or suspend the use of radio[frequencies] for its own [benefit] [. . .].[44]

Central to the Law of Radio Frequency was the question of whether the extraordinary situation could be justified as a legitimate reason for the temporary restriction of radio frequencies. 'The management of radio frequencies is a state affair' was the official reason given by the government; however, Göncz, who questioned the constitutionality of the law, turned to the Constitutional Court (*Magyar Nemzet*, 26 May 1993; *Népszabadság*, 26 May 1993;Szerető, 1993), for the following reasons:

> The president expressed his concern about the law in relation to [two issues]: whether the law contains a basic guarantee to [uphold] the [principle] of the freedom of press and opinion; whether it contains [a stipulation] to prevent [a government] monopoly on information.[45]

In addition, Göncz asked the Court whether the Law on Radio Frequency should be considered as a 'separate or special law', which required a two-thirds majority vote from MPs. Referring to Article 19/D of the Constitution, which specified that a two-thirds majority vote of MPs was required to declare a state of emergency, Göncz questioned whether the law fell within this special category (Halmai, 2004: 199–200). In response, on 29 July 1993, the Constitutional Court ruled that the Radio Frequency Law was not unconstitutional.[46]

However, the grounds on which the Court ruled that the law was constitutional are open to question. In response to Göncz's questions, the Court presented a somewhat ambiguous and contradictory ruling. For instance, in responding to the possibility of violation to the principle of media freedom, the Court ruled that public radio and television frequencies could be limited because both media present a *special case* in relation to the principles of press freedom and freedom of expression (Halmai, 2004: 200). However, this definition as a special case contradicted the Court's second reasoning, which stated that the Law of Radio Frequency was not a special law, thus it did not require a two-thirds majority vote from MPs.[47] In its first legal interpretation, the *special character or peculiarity* (*sajátosság*) which public radio and television may have had was the legitimate reason for the possible limitation of the use of radio frequencies. Thus, it is possible to question the reason for the Radio Frequency Law, which also dealt with a *special situation*, not being approached in the same way. In principle, the same rationale – of significance or peculiarity – should have been applied to the Law on Radio Frequency.[48]

In view of this, it is perhaps not surprising that Göncz had doubts about the constitutionality of the law. In the absence of a new comprehensive media law[49] and more importantly, on the basis of his political beliefs he may have wished to clarify whether the adopted legislation could be harmonised with the Constitution. Göncz may not have objected to the enactment of the law itself, but before its introduction, he preferred to clear up any doubts about the law. Indeed, in one Hungarian daily, Göncz stated his opinion that the law (which could have had a far-reaching impact for other issues) ought to be thoroughly examined before its implementation. Göncz maintained that:

> [In terms of] economic, infrastructural development, broadcasting, national defence and security policy, it is an extremely important law. Special [attention] should be paid to this: during the enforcement of the law, such constitutional anxiety that could be addressed before its enforcement, should not be [raised] and, [yet] the law shall take effect as soon as possible.
> (*Magyar Nemzet*, 26 May 1993)

Göncz clearly identified the main problem with the law: according to its current legislative form, there was not only a legal deficiency but also a critical time issue. Thus, in the form of his constitutional veto, Göncz expressed his view that a cautious approach would be appropriate and preferable to 'shutting the stable door after the horse has bolted'. In fact, in an interview with Kossuth Radio, Göncz further detailed his thought on the way in which radio frequencies could be regulated. In essence, he argued that the law should have been examined in a framework which took account of the country's transitional situation, lest other important issues and democratic principles be undermined:

> After all, due to the absence of a media law, the issue of uncertainty occurred . . . This law is interconnected with economic, military and human rights. For instance, the law limits the functioning of [radio] frequencies in circumstances [under] which the lives of citizens and property security are endangered and under martial law or in a state of emergency. These are all delicate legal regulations which are also connected with other laws. I felt that, before its introduction, it would be much better to thoroughly examine the law which may have had complicated and far reaching [consequences for other issues]. If I do not ask for norm[ative] control [from the Court], [I] have accepted the law which my conscience allows me to sign.
> (Wisinger and László, 2007: 283–4)

Thus it can be argued that Göncz's use of the constitutional veto on the Radio Frequency Law was not an act intended to oppose the law itself but, an attempt to clarify the obscurity within it. Through the veto, Göncz sought to address the question of whether extraordinary situations could be used as legitimate grounds for the temporary suspension of radio frequencies. Though Göncz's view was not supported by the Court's ruling, this issue clearly highlights the consistent point that Göncz made a decision according to his own democratic principles. Moreover, given the way in which he dealt with the Law on Radio Frequency, it is fair to suggest that this issue was not isolated in time, but in fact it was a continuation of the issue of control over the media. This was not, however, the end of the issue of control over media, as it resurfaced in autumn 1993 in dealing with the foreign press, namely *La Stampa*.

5.2.7. The La Stampa *affair*

The event took place in November 1993 when Göncz held an informal discussion with foreign correspondents, from Reuters, the *Financial Times* and elsewhere (Wisinger and László, 2007: 308). Among them, the Italian newspaper, *La Stampa* wrote that the public media in Hungary had been placed in a serious situation, since the press was again subject to government censorship (*Népszabadság*, 22 November 1993; *Új Magyarország*, 25 November 1993). In an article entitled – '[Dealing with] the media issue, the president asks for international help!'(*Pesti Hírlap*, 22 November 1993) – Tito Sansa reported that the freedom of Hungary's public media was overshadowed by the right-wing government's policies (*Magyar Hírlap*, 26 November 1993). The article infuriated the government and, in refuting the reporter's allegations, the factional leaders of the governing party called for an explanation from Göncz (*Magyar Hírlap*, 23 November 1993). In a written response Göncz explained that the analysis presented in the *La Stampa* article was the journalist's interpretation, albeit one partially based on his comments (*Magyar Nemzet*, 24 November 1993; *Népszabadság*, 24 November 1993; *Népszava*, 24 November 1993). As it left room for various interpretations, Göncz's explanation did not satisfy the conservative wing of the government members, among whom members of the extreme right wing party the Hungarian Justice and Life Party (HJLP) attempted to set up an examination committee in Parliament (*Népszabadság*, 24 November 1993). The HJLP reasoned that the establishment of an examination committee was required, since the president had denigrated the country's image by representing foreign interests (*Népszabadság*, 24 November 1993). On 6 December 1993, voting took place but, the HJLP's proposal was rejected (*Magyar Hírlap*, 7 December 1993) with an absolute majority (48 yes, 159 no and 26 abstention).

The key to comprehension of the *La Stampa* issue lay in whether Göncz's comments reflected the true situation of Hungary's public media. Under the circumstances where the issue of the control of the broadcast media was a point of ongoing contention, publication of Göncz's comments on Hungary's media situation in the foreign press was seen as significant. The main problem was, however, that in dealing with the foreign press, Göncz had once again clashed with the government. In a letter, the factional leader of the HDF, Imre Kónya, denounced the comments published in *La Stampa* which, he claimed, presented a false and distorted image which disparaged Hungary's prestige (*Magyar Hírlap*, 23 November 1993). Moreover, having strongly disagreed with the subtitle of the *La Stampa* piece – 'The president is also against the right-wing government: Europe helps us!'– Kónya asked for an explanation from Göncz. In response, Göncz stated that, although he did not agree with the given title, the article showed an aspect of the true situation of Hungary's public media:

My Dear Friends!

The article in *La Stampa* was partial[ly] an interpretation [by] the journalist based on his assessment of the situation and partially [based on] my comments. The news writer has the right to choose the title of an article independently of whether or not I agree with his summarised judgements [. . .].

Cause and effect are not same, but they are interrelated. In my opinion, the article in *La Stampa* and any other similar foreign [publications] do not hurt the interest of the Hungarian government [any] more than those political processes [control over the public media], which have given risen to the opportunity to write this article.

(*Népszava*, 24 November 1993)

Göncz stressed that addressing the issue behind the *La Stampa* scandal was more important than entering into an attempt to clarify whether or not he had ever made such a provocative statement regarding the country's media situation. Göncz's reply (especially in terms of its consequence for his relationship with the Antall government) certainly would not have alleviated any of the existing tension between him and the government. Having disagreed with the title of article, Göncz could have asked for its correction, which in turn would have helped him dissociate himself from the piece and thus, to avoid some of his critics' most pointed accusations and allegations.

Members of the HJLP have argued that Göncz's allegiance to the AFD and the HSP was primarily responsible for his controversial stance on this issue (*Magyar Hírlap*, 7 December 1993). They claimed that, in dealing with the media issue, Göncz constantly represented the interests of the opposition who disagreed with the government's position on media freedom and, that this case was not exceptional. However, according to a political commentator, László Kéri, the *La Stampa* issue rather appeared to be a politically exaggerated scandal, which was not uncommon in the routine of Hungarian politics at the time:

In Hungary, the government in power is always wary of what [the international press] such as *Le Monde*, *The Times* and the *International Herald Tribune* write . . . This is a common [phenomenon] . . . Generally, politicians ask reporters in advance what the headline will be, and sometimes such comments which were not made during the interview are highlighted [such as the headline] . . . I do not think Göncz asked the journalist what the headline would be. But the governing party unreasonably overreacted to this. It was ridiculous.

(Interview with Kéri, 12 June 2007)

Given that the issue of media control was ongoing, it may also have spilled over into the *La Stampa* affairs; it is thus probable that the governing party reacted disproportionately. Otherwise, as Kéri proposes, some excerpts of the article were not derived from the interview upon which the piece was supposedly based. Göncz, however, did not take any action with regard to requesting clarification from Sansa or *La Stampa*. In response to a reporter's question – 'On the basis of interview given to the Italian newspaper, [criticism] is again mounting against you. What is your opinion on this matter?' – Göncz stated:

It would be a lie if I say that I was pleased with [this scandal] . . . In the case of the *La Stampa* article, it's a [matter] of interpretation . . . The journalist mention[ed] an event about which he had never spoken [during our talk]. But, how he interprets my words, this [depends on] what one's impression is . . . There is nothing more ridiculous than asking for redress, only because someone has a different impression. If fact is written incorrectly, it may be possible to request redress. But, this is not the practice of international press either . . . Because of [different] impressions and evaluations, asking for redress is almost inconceivable in the [maintenance] of international relations. I kept the transcript of the talk and the tapes, but I consider that using these would be entirely useless. This is not my issue, but *La Stampa*'s.

(Wisinger and László, 2007: 307–8)

The extract above underscores a consistent aspect of Göncz's political beliefs; that media should be free from any political and personal interference. According to Göncz, all influences should be minimised in the interests of freedom of expression and of the press. Göncz clearly understood international practice and norms as well as written or unwritten rules regarding journalism. Following this line of thought, Göncz certainly made a decision based on his own judgement, even if he did not agree with the entire reportage. Göncz stressed that in a democracy, the value of pluralism, including the rights to express opinions and to make arguments and counter-arguments, ought to be guaranteed, even if such views could be reflected differently from an individual's standpoint. Thus, it is fair to suggest that Göncz dealt with the *La Stampa* affair, as he had previously tackled the issues of the media – the control of the broadcast media and the Law of Radio Frequency. As Göncz publicly made clear, he may indeed have endeavoured to keep his presidential oath as prescribed by the Constitution or stood by his own democratic principles. Göncz stated:

Concerning the [role] of the president, the Constitution dictates that the head of state [shall] express the unity of the nation and safeguard the democratic

The first presidency (1990–1995) 153

functioning of state institutions. This means that the head of state neither represents [the interests] of the opposition nor [those] of the coalition government, but the common interest . . . Among the rights of freedom, the freedom of expression is given particular prominence, [as] the Constitution states that the Republic of Hungary acknowledges and protects the freedom of the press [. . .].

At present, radio, television and electronic news agencies belong exclusively to the state; it is extremely important to [ensure] that the Hungarian population is informed of objective and multi-faceted opinions and counter-opinions. It is important to ensure that people themselves establish facts and different views and form their own political opinions. Without this [the freedom of the press], free elections with different political forces and the smooth functioning of the democratic order is inconceivable. Without this, citizens cannot be informed of contradictory statements and would not have a chance to discover the standpoints of various parties, interest groups and any other political [forces] in state affairs.

(*Magyar Nemzet*, 2 July 1992)

In light of this statement, it can be conclusively argued that when dealing with the issue of the media, Göncz pursued his democratic and liberal principle that freedom of the press and the freedom of expression must be firmly guaranteed, independently of political and personal influence. In Göncz's terms, among the presidential tasks to be fulfilled, he may have considered that 'freedom of the press to be of the utmost significance' (*Magyar Hírlap*, 2 November 1993). However, the proactive presidential role he undertook on this issue and that of dealing with the Communist past was not favourably received by the government and this prompted the occurrence of a major political scandal on the 36th anniversary of the 1956 Hungarian Revolution.

5.2.8. Göncz's interrupted speech

On 23 October 1992, Göncz was to deliver his annual memorial speech at Kossuth Square. However, Göncz received a frosty reception from a dozen of young extremists wearing Hungarian Nazi uniforms and demanding Göncz's resignation (Miszlivetz, 1995: 115) and was unexpectedly heckled by a group of the 1956 veterans; as a result, Göncz left the podium without saying a word (*Magyar Nemzet*, 4 August 2000). The group of 1956 veterans hissed and booed Göncz, because they disapproved of his decision not to sign some of the proposed laws dealing with the Communist past (Debreczeni, 2003: 308).[50] However, a difference of opinions existed as to whether the young extremists had been brought to the national ceremony in the expectation that they might stir up a negative atmosphere. The opposition suspected the incident was organised, whereas the government saw it as a spontaneous event. The minister of the interior, Péter Boross, who was in charge of security at the time, claimed that Göncz made a mistake, because if he had commenced his speech, the heckling might have ceased (Papp, 2002; Stefka,

2000). He also claimed that the police did not intervene in the incident because there were no signs of a threat to the president's security (*Beszélő*, 3 July 1993; *168 Óra*, 6 July 1993). In contrast, the opposition considered the incident as a serious security breach (Dornbach, 1992), questioning whether Boross had received prior warning of the incident. Ultimately, in an attempt to clarify the confused situation, the opposition suggested that a special examination committee be set up at parliamentary level (*Magyar Hírlap*, 29 October 1992; *Népszabadság*, 26 October 1992). However, the proposal was challenged by the Antall government who considered that the case should be closed off with an amendment of the criminal law dealing with the symbols of autocracy (Fowkes, 1999: 28; *Magyar Hírlap*, 27 October 1992). With no agreement reached, half of the examination committee (whose membership was primarily composed of opposition and independent MPs) was established (Somos, 1994; *168 Óra*, 6 July 1993). The Committee's report suggested that this issue has not yet been clarified and was unresolved.

In the plenum, the Prime Minister, József Antall, stated that he regretted the occurrence of the incident, yet he strongly denied any allegations of the government's involvement (*Magyar Dokumentáció*, October 1992; *Magyar Hírlap*, 27 October 1992; *Magyar Nemzet*, 26, 27 October 1992). This contradicted the opposition, who felt that the possibility of the government's direct and indirect support for the incident could not be excluded. In response to Antall's comments, the president of the AFD, Péter Tölgyessy, questioned whether the police and other responsible security agencies had dealt with the security issue appropriately. Referring to a previous incident which had occurred to the prime minister as an example – on 15 March 1990, Antall's speech was interrupted by crowds of young people but police acted promptly to remove them – Tölgyessy was suspicious of the fact that similar action had not been taken to protect the president (*Magyar Hírlap*, 27 October 1992). For the opposition the *inconsistent* security approach towards the prime minister and the president may have led them to question whether political pressure had affected the case. For the government, however, the matter may have been deemed as one for the minister of interior to resolve.

While both accounts sound convincing, evidence discovered in the Hungarian press highlights the fact that the police knew about the extremist rally in advance. According to this information, the police waited for the extremists, who travelled to Budapest from the countryside, at the Eastern Railway Station.[51] On arrival, the police confiscated their weapons and escorted them to the head office of the Association of the Hungarian Political Prisoners, and later to Kossuth Square (*Beszélő*, 3 July 1993; *Népszabadság*, 30 October 1992; *168 Óra*, 6 July 1993). However, this does not prove that their aim was to hinder the president's speech. Under police supervision, the extremists could have marched as they had planned. Since the Law of Assembly in effect at the time did not specify any provisions for the exclusion of simultaneity (Kilényi and Lamm, 1990: 60–2),[52] in principle, two different programmes could take place together. In view of this, there seemed to be no direct connection indicating that the event was organised by the government. Rather, it is more likely that the incident was an accident. The report of the chief prosecutor nonetheless suggests that

The first presidency (1990–1995) 155

a connection between the government's instruction and the actions of the police cannot be ruled out entirely:

> There was a [scenario] whereby the police would hold back the skinheads who were arriving at the Eastern Railway Station until 9 [pm]. But the police did not find a legitimate reason to detain them . . . The fact is that János Bodrácska [the Chief of Budapest Police] ordered that the police stop the skinheads from [marching] to Kossuth Square, [but] the execution [of this order] was unsuccessful.
>
> (Tódor, 1997)

According to this report, Bodrácska's decision appears to have been superseded by an order which may have come from his superior. Otherwise, miscommunication between police units may be responsible for the incident. Since the full report of the chief prosecutor is not accessible to research (Tódor, 1997),[53] a conclusion cannot be drawn. It is only clear that this incident further escalated tension between Antall and Göncz and their political camps. As Mécs contended, due to the embittered relationship between them, it is possible that 'the government may have wished to [teach] a lesson to the intractable president' (Wisinger and László, 2007: 100) who refused to play a rubber-stamping role in dealing with state affairs. On the other hand, it could have been only a simple incident which was then politically exaggerated. As László Kéri asserted:

> I do not think the event was organised by Boross. It was an exaggeration of the HSP and the AFD claiming that Boross organised the entire thing. This is not true . . . Perhaps, Boross knew this would become a scandal but he didn't want to prevent it . . . It would not be a big problem even if there was a small scandal . . . The government's position at the time was Göncz got what he deserved. The opposition's position was Göncz was a victim of the government's conspiracy.
>
> (Interview with Kéri, 12 June 2007)

Whether the incident was organised or not, the question arises as to why Göncz did not give his speech. According to the official account offered by the president's office, Göncz was incapable of commencing his speech, due to the loud noise from the crowds (*Népszabadság*, 28 October 1992). This, however, does not mean that Göncz was placed in a situation in which he should give up on his speech altogether. As other instances had shown, in even more hostile circumstances, politicians had been able to make speeches. For example, the former president of the Czech Republic, Vaclav Havel, completed a speech even when faced with an egg-throwing reception by nationalist students (*Népszabadság*, 27 October 1992). Following Havel's example, Göncz could have begun his speech, although one cannot assume that they would have behaved in the same way under the same context. Therefore, it is necessary to look into other possible explanatory factors that might have contributed to Göncz's decision not to give a speech.

An article published in one Hungarian daily indicated that the psychological effect of heckling may have been one factor in Göncz's failure to even begin his speech. Göncz was expected to attend an evening programme after delivering the memorial speech at Kossuth Square (*Pesti Hírlap*, 26 October 1992). For a state ceremony, along with the prime minister and the Speaker of the House, Göncz should have appeared at the National Opera House. The fact is, however, that despite the request of the prime minister (*Pesti Hírlap*, 26 October 1992), Göncz did not attend the evening programme, which is indicative of the fact that the incident that took place at Kossuth Square had affected him. Having encountered an unsympathetic reception from the crowds he was somehow *emotionally* offended, and this may have led him not to participate in the evening programme. His feeling of frustration or anger may have been expressed in the form of protest by his absence from the Opera House. Gabriella Ilonszki aptly captured the way in which Göncz's character had been put on view:

> I think this was exemplary, demonstrating Göncz's faith in the role of the president. In my opinion, Göncz was basically a civil democrat who did not let himself drift into the defenceless position that political opponents or the extreme right-wing groups had envisaged, nor did he play fast and loose with them. He showed an example of civil courage of how he would behave towards, and treat, such people whom he didn't consider as political partners.
>
> (Interview with Ilonszki, 16 October 2007)

Göncz may have understood that in a democracy, everyone has the right to express their opinion. However, in a circumstance where he did not approve of the disorderly behaviour of some extremists, he may have wished to send a message about his disturbed feeling. As conventional wisdom teaches, 'silence can speak volumes'.

6 The second presidency (1995–2000)

Introduction

This chapter examines the main characteristics of Göncz's second presidency (1995–2000). In the previous chapter, it was established that the decisions and actions that Göncz took during his first presidency were far from uncontroversial, but in fact his presidential style was proactive and contributed significantly to the development of Hungary's post-Communist democracy. With this in mind, the present chapter further assesses Göncz's actions and the role he played for the consolidation of post-Communist democracy during his second presidential term.

Some of the existing Hungarian literature suggests that compared to the proactive and controversial style that Göncz exhibited during the first term of his presidency, during his second presidential term he was, in contrast, largely passive and insignificant (analysis is presented in detail in Section 6.1). Moreover, it has been suggested that one of the main reasons for this changed presidential style lay in the specific political context in which Göncz and his party – the AFD – were positioned. During Göncz's first presidency, the AFD was an opposition party and, as such, Göncz's political attachment to the party meant that he fulfilled the role of counter-balance to the Antall government. In contrast, during Göncz's second presidency, the AFD was a member of the coalition government; Göncz's oppositional role was reduced accordingly. This account is, however, limited as a justification for the evident transformation in Göncz's role and influence. As has been argued in the previous chapter, Göncz's proactive presidential role was not an outcome which had been shaped according to adherence to a particular party's influence but rather lay in Göncz's pursuit of liberal and democratic political beliefs. Furthermore, as will be discussed in Section 6.1, Göncz's political affiliation does not explain his passive presidential style as evidenced during the final two years of his presidency. This was the time when the conservative Orbán government was in power and the AFD was in opposition. Had Göncz sought to give expression to his partisanship, he should have taken a position which counterbalanced the Orbán government and their political agenda.

This chapter therefore addresses a gap in the literature on Göncz's political style and motivations by exploring the other factors which informed his political evolution. It is posited that the deterioration of Göncz's mental and physical strength, the changing role of the Constitutional Court and the nature of Hungary's democracy are all contributory factors which must duly be considered if the last years of Göncz's presidency are to be understood fully.

The first section of the chapter presents an overview of the main features and style of each encumbent government along with their relationship with Göncz. This lays the essential foundation for understanding the president's relationship with the government of the time. The next section examines a set of issues and events in which Göncz became involved during his second presidential term. This section will question whether Göncz sought to pursue his liberal principled line, independently of governmental change.

The remainder of the chapter is devoted to an examination of the factors which contributed to Göncz's diminished political activities. This follows Göncz's own views, thoughts regarding and reflections on his experience of serving as the first post-Communist president of Hungary and concludes the chapter.

6.1. Government in transition: The Horn and Orbán governments

The parliamentary elections of 1994 and 1998 resulted in the establishment of two ideologically contrasting governments: the socialists (HSP) led by Gyula Horn, and the conservatives (AYD) led by Viktor Orbán. In 1994 the HSP secured a large majority in Parliament (209/386 seats, 54.1 percent) and could have formed its own government. Despite this advantage, it has been suggested that the socialists preferred to introduce 'consensual elements' into the decision-making processes (Ágh, 2001c: 480). This was evidenced, above all, by the formation of a coalition government with the former anti-Communist party, the AFD (Morlang, 2003: 75). During negotiations, a rift within the AFD's party leadership led to the departure of the party's former chairman, Péter Tölgyessy (Romsics, 2007: 436) however, the power-sharing scheme eventually came to fruition.[1] Similarly, the Horn government widened channels through which the opposition could participate in the decision-making process. In the composition of a draft of new Constitution, for example, a two-thirds majority vote which the HSP–AFD coalition government secured was sufficient to pass it. But the coalition government voluntarily increased the quorum from a two-thirds to a four-fifths majority (Halmai, 1998: 195), which is highly indicative of the fact that there was an attempt to create the conditions in which a wider consensus among the opposition parties could be reached. Additionally, and perhaps more importantly, the socialist leadership made a conciliatory or consensus-seeking gesture towards the president. As has been examined in Chapter 5, the president's relationship with the Antall government was characterised by conflicts. In this hostile political atmosphere, consensus-based decision making between the prime minister and the president was hardly sought, not to mention that informal meetings which might have helped to alleviate these tension never took place.[2] In contrast, during the Horn government, Monday breakfast meetings were arranged on a regular basis between the Speaker of the House and the prime minister and the president (Babus, 2000; *Népszava*, 29 June 2010). Thus, there was a substantial change in the style of governance. Endre Babus recalled that:

> The socialist-liberal government was committed to the idea of a consensus-based democracy. They commanded a 71 percent majority [of seats] in Parliament. They could have adopted the new Constitution by themselves. But, they voluntarily constrained their power. They made and kept a promise that they would adopt a new Constitution with at least a five party consensus out of six parliamentary parties.
> (Interview with Babus, 19 May 2007)

Thus, had the socialist-liberal government sought to maximise their majoritarian rule in the decision-making process,[3] this could have led to a so-called 'constitutional dictatorship' (Arato, 1994: 7). However, the actual style of governance that they chose demonstrated that, at least, they made a consensus-seeking gesture toward the opposition and the president.

In contrast, the Orbán government established a stronger, power-concentrated institutional structure. At the centre, the Office of Prime Minister (OPM) became the key institution, which not only operated as an assistant body to the prime minister, but also had a strong decision-making function. For instance, during the Antall and Horn governments, cabinet meetings were convened as a forum where ministers were able to express their opinions and offer solutions to various matters. The cabinet's political significance was diminished, since these meetings became a forum for the formalisation of decisions which had already been taken in the OPM (Körösényi, 2006: 30). In some respects, the opposition's exclusion from the decision-making process is hardly surprising; a simple majority was primarily sought for the passage of new legislation.[4] Indeed, according to Fricz, the government preferred to 'limit negotiati[ons] with opposition parties [on] questions in need of consensus' (Fricz, 2001: 543), even though some cases required a two-thirds majority. This tendency was evident in the passage of the Law on Organised Crime, the so-called 'Anti-Mafia Package' (which will be discussed in Section 6.2.5) and, more strikingly, in the introduction of new rules for the House (Bozóki, 2008: 215). Hitherto, a plenum had been held on a weekly basis. According to the new rules introduced in February 1999, the plenum in Parliament was to be held once every three weeks (Csuhaj and Kéri, 1998). As Körösényi and Kiss have noted, the plenum was a forum for open criticism of government policy by the opposition, and a chance for non-governing parties to offer their own alternatives (Kiss, 2002: 746; Körösényi, 1999: 236); a reduction in the frequency of plenary sessions demonstrates the manner in which the Orbán government approached the opposition at the time. Indeed, having grown discontent with this approach, the opposition turned to the Constitutional Court, asking whether the changes made to the Rule of the House contravened the Constitution (East European Constitutional Review, 1999, hereafter EECR). In response, the Court ruled that the Rules of the House 'did not provide adequate guidance for the planning of regular parliamentary sessions' (EECR, 1999 Summer), since the legislature had failed to include relevant regulations in the guideline. Thus, the Court instructed Parliament to pass new rules no later than 15 December 1999 but the Orbán government proceeded as planned, claiming that the new rule of plenum 'had not been changed but simply re-interpreted' (Ágh, 2001a: 103).

Thus, as Ágh contended, the structure of power concentration embedded in the decision-making process and 'exclusive' approach towards the opposition and other political forces adopted by the Orbán government established a Hungarian style of 'quasi-majoritarian democracy' (Ágh, 2001a: 105; 2001b: 170–3) or the beginning of 'presidentialisation' of Hungary's parliamentarianism (Körösényi, 2006: 31).[5]

In terms of both governments' relationship with the president, the different styles of governance pursued by Horn and Orbán raise the following questions: how did these specific governing styles affect the character of Göncz's second presidency? Is there any causal relationship between the change of government and of Göncz's presidential style? During the first term of his presidency, Göncz's desire for democratic, consensus-based decision making was clearly evidenced in his approach towards the question of the Communist past and the taxi-drivers' strike. With this in mind, one would expect the Horn government, with its desire for consensus-based decision-making, to find a natural ally in Göncz. In contrast, the governing style of the Orbán government might have been expected to come into conflict with Göncz's political beliefs. Thus, one might expect that Göncz's presidential style would be marked by an adaptive or harmonious relationship with the Horn government, and conflict with its successor. Indeed, having noted the difference in Göncz's approach towards these successive governments, critics argued that there was a link between governmental change and Göncz's presidential style. The political editor of the Hungarian political weekly, *Élet és Irodalom*, Eszter Rádai noted:

> It is true that during the first term of his presidency, Göncz took an oppositional role [to] the Antall government. [In contrast], during his second presidential term, Göncz visibly adapted himself to the Horn government. He did not do anything which went against the government.
> (Interview with Rádai, 11 October 2007)

Similarly, Szilvia Varró stated that:

> In the beginning, [perhaps] from the taxi-drivers' strike onwards, Göncz was full of character. During the Antall government, he was very active ... But in my memory, there was no single issue on which he stood against Gyula Horn. At least, it looked like this in public. Göncz liked Horn and he tended towards the left liberal [camp] during his second presidency.
> (Interview with Varró, 15 August 2007)

Both commentators emphasised that there was a difference between Göncz's presidential style in the first and second terms of his presidency; in contrast to his first presidency, Göncz's generated a less active – or more passive style – during

The second presidency (1995–2000)   161

the latter term, and his leniency towards the Horn government was very apparent. Moreover, according to these opinions, the main reason for this change of presidential style lay in Göncz's political attachment to the socialist-liberal camp. Other relevant academic literature explaining Göncz's presidential style has been cross-checked with these commentators' accounts. According to quantitative evidence and qualitative assessments presented by some political scientists (Körösényi, Tóth and Török), when compared to his first five years in office, the activities that Göncz undertook and style that he preferred during his second presidential term were more passive or weaker than those which characterised his first term.

Table 6.1 illustrates that the amount of political activity Göncz undertook during the governments which followed the Antall government reduced considerably. Foreign policy was the only exception to this pattern, where Göncz's representative and ceremonial role increased. Generally, however, his activities on the domestic political side diminished noticeably. It might also suggest that Göncz's presidency can be largely divided into two contrasting presidential terms: a proactive and relatively strong presidency during the Antall government; and a less active, acquiescent and weaker presidency during the other governments. Indeed, in their qualitative assessment, Körösényi, Tóth and Török came to this conclusion with regard to Göncz's presidential style.

Table 6.1 Göncz's political activities between 1990 and 2000.

Göncz's activities / Governments in power	1990–1994 Conservative coalition government led by Antall	1994–1998 Socialist–liberal coalition government led by Horn	1998–2000 Conservative government led by Orbán*
Speeches in parliament	22	4	2
Representing Hungary abroad (the number of State visits/days spent abroad)	49 (215)	79 (273)	35 (119)
Concluding international treaties	1	—	—
Initiating referenda	—	—	—
Proposing independent legislation	5	—	—
Initiating an extraordinary parliamentary session	—	—	—
Participating in parliamentary sessions	71	15	12
Veto of legislation on constitutional grounds	7	—	1
Veto of legislation on political grounds	—	2	—

Source: Körösényi *et al.*, (2003: 569)

Note: * The Orbán government lasted from 1998 to 2002. However, since Göncz's presidential term came to an end in August 2000, the table has been adapted to his presidential term.

Inferring from the Table 6.2, if one can divide Göncz's presidential style according to two contrasting sets of criteria – proactive and strong versus passive and weak presidencies – what explains Göncz's changed perception of the presidential role? In their conclusion, Körösényi, Tóth and Török suggest that one of the key factors of Göncz's altered presidential style could be found in the particular political structure, from which the president originated. Given Göncz's political origins from within the AFD – the largest opposition party during the Antall government – they argued that his political affiliation to the party led him to undertake an oppositional role during his first presidency (Körösényi *et al.*, 2003: 565). In contrast, during the Horn government where his party was a coalition member, Göncz would not and did not undertake a counter-balancing role. This account, however, has limited justification. Given that during the Orbán government, the AFD was once again positioned on the opposition side, in principle, Göncz should have undertaken a counter-weight role. Yet, as Table 6.2 demonstrates, Göncz did not seek an oppositional role to the Orbán government and instead maintained a symbolic and conflict-averse presidential style.

Indeed, opinions offered by my interviewees highlight the fact that Göncz did not come into confrontation with the Orbán government. László Kéri characterised Göncz's relationship with the Orbán government thus:

Table 6.2 Government in transition and Göncz's political role.

	1990–1994 The Antall government	1994–1998 The Horn government	1998–2000 The Orbán government
Parliamentary parties which voted for the president	AFD (HDF)	HSP, AFD	HSP, AFD
The political orientation of the parliamentary majority	Right-wing (HDF–ISP–CDPP)	Left-wing (HSP–AFD)	Right-wing (AYD–ISP–HDF)
The relationship between the president and the parliamentary majority (in terms of political orientation)	Oppositional or contrasting	Harmonious	Oppositional or contrasting
The president's perception of his role	Counter-balance	Symbolic or supportive	Symbolic
Political conflicts between the president and government	Frequent	Minimal	Rare
The president's political activities, his intervention in day-to-day politics	Significant	Diminished	Diminished
The political weight of the president	Intermediate–Strong	Weak	Weak

Source: Adapted from Körösényi *et al.*, (2003: 571)

Orbán knew where the threshold of constitutional power was. He always went to the boundary, but he did not do things which could have offered Göncz any opportunity to protest. . . . He left Göncz in peace and did not seek to enter into conflicts with him.

(Interview with Kéri, 12 June 2007)

With a different focus, but a similar view, a former advisor to Orbán and the minister of the OPM, István Stumpf, held the opinion that:

Orbán did not come into conflict with Göncz. I do not remember concrete examples which could have aggravated their relationship. Politically, they had different priorities [with regard] to representation. Göncz was a popular and liberal figurehead who preferred to bring his presidency close to the people. He wanted to speak to people directly with openness. Orbán had a different perception of the roles of the president and the premier, [a perception] which was much closer to a traditional concept. The head of state should not condescend to people but show a vision of the future and the direction of the country . . . Orbán had a different vision of what the president should be . . . But Göncz was not in conflict with him.

(Interview with Stumpf, 3 July 2007)

In view of these statements, it is certain that Göncz's political attachment to the AFD alone does not sufficiently explain the evident transformation in his presidential style. Moreover, it can be fairly suggested that there were other important factors responsible for Göncz's changed conception of the presidential role. Detailed analysis of this is presented in Section 6.3 of the chapter but, before embarking on this task, the following section of the chapter examines a set of events and issues in which Göncz became involved during the second term of his presidency. The section will question the consistency of Göncz's actions with reference to understandings of Göncz's democratic and liberal views that have been set out in the framework of this book.

6.2. The pursuit of democratic values: the principle of equality and consensus-based decision making

The Hungarian Constitution does not specify any clause for the president's role with regard to economic policy. More precisely, economic policy does not fall within presidential competences. Despite the absence of this constitutional right, members of the opposition to the Horn government – the AYD, CDPP and HDF – urged Göncz's intervention on economic issues. Their request, however, was rejected and subsequently Göncz's acquiescence on the matter became a political scandal. This issue is not directly related to that of Göncz's liberal and democratic ideas. Nevertheless, it is worth examining as it demonstrates well how Göncz's sense of social consciousness was reflected in his presidential activities.

6.2.1. Dealing with the economic stabilisation programme

A month after the adoption of the economic stabilisation programme, Göncz stated his position: 'Let's put an end to misery and create social security so that everyone knows what is going to happen tomorrow. [People] in the country wish to live without shock' (*Magyar Nemzet*, 3 April 1995).

On 12 March 1995, the Horn government made a sudden announcement that they would adopt an economic austerity programme, the so-called 'Bokros Package' (named after the minister of finance, Lajos Bokros) (Bak, 1995; *Népszabadság*, 13 March 1995). Horn argued that, without such drastic action, the country's economy would soon become unmanageable (*Magyar Nemzet*, 13 March 1995), the government claimed this package was the only way to resolve Hungary's economic crisis (Andor, 1998). Horn said: 'This country faces state bankruptcy with a 20 billion dollar foreign debt. It needs foreign resources to pay its debts, boost growth and catch up. These foreign resources can be obtained if our affairs are put in order' (Fowkes, 1999: 156).

Aiming to restore financial equilibrium to the prevailing situation and to the state budget (Adam, 1999: 61–4; Morlang, 2003: 78), specific approaches were formulated within this stringent programme. Among these, the most controversial measure directly affecting the general public was the radical retrenchment of state expenditure on social support and welfare benefits (EECR, 1995 Spring). In accordance with this package, for example, the government's budgetary outlay for child-care and family benefits was to be suspended (*Népszabadság*, 13 March 1995), along with the introduction of tuition fees in higher education (*Magyar Hírlap*, 13 March 1995).

Not surprisingly, this drastic action prompted an immediate reaction from not only parliamentary parties, but also the general public and, Göncz himself. The general public, infuriated by the government's announcement, took to the street to protest against the austerity programme and Lajos Bokros (*Magyar Hírlap*, 23 March 1995; *Népszava*, 14 June 1995). Having faced such strong resistance, debate over the implementation of the programme continued in Parliament; among the opposition members, the AYD and the HDF asked Göncz not to commit his signature to the programme (*Magyar Hírlap*, 1 June 1995; *Magyar Nemzet*, 3 June 1995; *Népszava*, 3 June 1995). However, on 13 June 1995, Göncz signed the Bokros package into law (*Magyar Hírlap*, 14 June 1995), reasoning that 'the question of economic policy did not belong to his competences' (Varró, 2000). Frustrated, the dissenting members of Parliament, the AYD, HDF and other social organisations turned to the Constitutional Court (*Magyar Nemzet*, 14 June 1995a), asking for a ruling on whether the package violated the Constitution. The Court ruled that in several areas the package was unconstitutional and would have to be amended accordingly.[6] Despite the constitutional amendment which restricted the programme's scope, public discontent grew. In the face of severe criticism, Lajos Bokros resigned in the early spring of 1996 and was replaced by Péter Medgyessy (Adam, 1999: 63). The new finance minister, however, continued the implementation of the stabilisation programme, and from the second half of 1996, the financial disequilibrium of Hungary's economy was turned around and an economic recovery began (Bozóki, 2003: 428; Marer, 1999: 185).[7]

The opposition's main criticism of Göncz's role in dealing with the Bokros package was that he put his own self-interest above important socio-economic issues (*Magyar Nemzet*, 1 June 1995). Reasoning that Göncz's re-election (which was due at the end of June in the same year) would depend on the votes of the socialist-liberal coalition government, which comprised an absolute majority in Parliament at the time (71 percent), the opposition claimed that Göncz's signing of the Bokros package was directly related to his hope for victory in the presidential election.[8] For example, in response to Göncz's signing the package, an MP of the AYD, Lajos Kosa, claimed:

> In a difficult situation, Göncz had to decide [whether he would sign the package or not] because, the next Monday, the presidential election was to be held in Parliament. Since the coalition government has an absolute majority, obviously Göncz had to weight up the pros and cons.
> (*Magyar Nemzet*, 14 June 1995b)

However, if re-election was the sole reason for Göncz's signature on the package, it is unreasonable to suggest that Göncz (who had pledged his commitment to the protection of people in need) was willing to accept such harsh economic measures without any hesitation whatsoever. In his inauguration speech, Göncz pledged that:

> I have had the good fortune to share in the real lives of workers, peasants and of the free intelligentsia. I am therefore not the man to hammer away at narrow class interests. If I want to serve a particular group, it must be those who are not served by anyone: the unprotected, the defenceless ... and those unable to compete in a competitive society, those who lack the means to protect themselves and who are therefore most in need of protection.
> (Tóth, 1999: 21)

As has been examined in Chapter 1, Göncz had first-hand experience working as a skilled manual labourer which, in turn, contributed to the enrichment of his understanding of ordinary people's lives. Göncz recounted that:

> All [my experience] [brought about] a schooling [effect] on my presidency. If I had not known the lives of industrial workers, prison life and the internal structure of Communism within the prison, agriculture in which one third of the population was engaged, I could not have performed my presidential duty.
> (Papp, 2002)

Hence, it can be argued that, had Göncz appreciated the concerns and needs that Hungarian population had to tackle on a daily basis, the austerity package would have disturbed his sense of social consciousness. But if the lack of presidential competences in economic policy put him in a position where he was obliged to sign the package, Göncz might perhaps find an alternative way to help the needy. Indeed, according to Göncz's former social policy advisor, Sára Elias, he was not only conscious of social problems, but also tried to tackle them *informally*. This informal help was offered through various channels and in different ways, such as 'financing poor families, and feeding the children in need' (interview with Elias, 6 December 2007); the most important task Göncz and his wife committed themselves to was the establishment of the Special Care Foundation (*Fogyatékos Alapítvány*).This was founded in 1993 by a mutual initiative of civil society alongside the First Lady, Zsuzsánna Göntér and named the Special Education of Children with Learning Disabilities. According to Göntér, during state visits to foreign countries, she and Göncz raised this issue with their counterparts and managed to establish partnerships. Göntér recalled:

> We established the Foundation with 2000 Forints. After that George Soros donated 3 million Forints and when we visited foreign states, we also managed to get some financial support. For instance, it came from the Great Nobles' Party of Luxemburg and the wife of the Dutch prime minister . . . They were also interested in [the provision] of Special Care. We received a series of donations from the Dutch government and civil organisations. For three or four years, we cooperated with the leading Dutch Special Care civil organisations. We launched a movement of building houses for children who need special care . . . Across the country, we built 35 houses for children with disabilities.
> (Joint interview with Göncz and Göntér, 10 January 2008)

In consideration of this activity, it is unfair to suggest that Göncz's pledge to represent the under-represented remained scant political rhetoric or that he put his self-interest before his commitment to the presidential oath. On the contrary, these actions substantiate the claim that Göncz possessed a well-developed social consciousness. Moreover, it is highly probable that the harsh economic measures called for in the Bokros package would conflict with Göncz's social awareness. Therefore, the discrepancy between Göncz's social consciousness and his decision not to challenge the austerity programme suggests that there were other important contributory factors leading him to sign the stabilisation programme. One of the contributory factors can be found in his appreciation of the general consensus – the introduction of the austerity programme was necessary for stabilising Hungary's economy – that was shared by Hungarian intellectuals at the time.

There was some disagreement over the necessity for the introduction of the package,[9] and some criticism of the way in which the government handled the crisis. For example, a former president of the Hungarian National Bank, Ákos Péter Bod, contended that had the Horn government taken more timely action, the introduction of radical economic actions could have been prevented:

The second presidency (1995–2000) 167

On 8 May 1994, there was a general election . . . The socialist party won the election by a big margin . . . The Bokros package was adopted in March 1995 . . . So there was a period, almost one year in which the government did nothing, but [instead] just let the country's economy drift . . . For me, the package was not a problem, but the eight [wasted] months; this infuriated me.

(Interview with Bod, 8 November 2007)

Despite this dissenting opinion, a great number of Hungarian academics suggested that, given the country's poor economic performance, the austerity programme was an indispensable part of the process necessary to settle Hungary's financial crisis at the time (interviews with Ágh, Csaba, Hegedűs, Ilonszki, Kéri and Lengyel). The former government economic policy advisor, László Csaba, asserted that:

The Bokros package was a necessary measure taken very late . . . The country struggled with a [budgetary deficit] which cannot be sustained especially after the crisis in Mexico . . .[10] [There was a] 10 percent shortage in the balance of payments from the 1994 state budget . . . Neither the European Union nor the US were willing to intervene in this crisis . . . We had to do something. We had to act promptly.

(Interview with Csaba, 5 July 2007)

Similarly, László Kéri expressed the view that:

From the outside, it was possible to know something must be done, because financial collapse [could have occurred] within two months . . . I was in London in February 1995. I spoke to Miklós Németh, the vice-president of the European Development and Investment Bank. He told me that bankers in London said 'the Hungarian economy would collapse by the end of May'. And, 'no one would finance Hungary'.

(Interview with Kéri, 12 June 2007)

It can be seen that the Horn government had seemingly been put in a situation where it was no longer possible to rely on external sources or to balance the state budget. In these circumstances, tightening the budgetary outlay was perhaps the only viable option. It should be noted that the maintenance of the welfare-orientated economic system that was dependent on foreign capital and borrowing as had been established by the Kádár regime was only discontinued *after* the introduction of the Bokros package (Kornai, 1996: 946–9), which is highly indicative of the fact that macro-economic reform and fundamental restructuring of Hungary's economy was long overdue.

Göncz also seemed to be aware of the seriousness of the situation, primarily through regular consultation with the president of Hungarian National Bank, György Surányi. According to Surányi, when the stabilisation programme was almost ready for implementation, Göncz neither supported nor opposed it:

Göncz always asked me when poor and outcast people would be able to live in more humane and acceptable lives in this society ... In February 1995 ... although the package programme was not yet entirely prepared, I outlined it to Göncz [as to] how painful the measure looked from the country's [point of view]. The president neither accepted the package nor objected to it. He took the necessity [of the measure] into account, but understandably his social conscience was disturbed ... Göncz always judged socio-economic questions in light of his plebeian mentality [*plebejus szellemben*] ... On countless occasions, he said that 'his task was to represent the [interests] of the neediest and the poorest, because the others can stand on their own two feet' ... Göncz consistently showed an interest in economic policy, but government [members] and the Prime Ministers hardly knew about this.

(Surányi, 2000: 112–18)

The extract above underscores the fact that accepting the stabilisation programme would have been irreconcilable with Göncz's social conscience, but he showed an appreciation for, and understanding of, the prevailing situation. According to Surányi's testimony, Göncz's silence does not mean he was indifferent towards these economic issues and the possible consequences of the austerity programmes. Rather, it suggests that Göncz unwillingly accepted the package as the situation was such that stringent economic measures were required. Indeed, in an interview with a Hungarian daily, *Népszava*, in response to the reporter's question – 'Why did you not say a word when the Bokros package brought about unendurable burdens to the people?' – Göncz explained the reason behind his silence, stating that: 'I know that the Bokros package had a significant adverse impact on the poor, but [this] was the only way to prevent economic collapse [...]' (Bíró, 2000).

This substantiates the view that Göncz was indeed aware of the possible consequences of the retrenchment action, especially for destitute people. Having expected the negative effects of the measures, he could have opposed them; however, it was Göncz's appreciation of the urgent need to solve the country's economic predicament. According to Göncz's account, he reluctantly acceded to radical economic action and perhaps may have wished that the subsequent consequences would not be long lasting. Indeed, in 1997 when the first signs of economic recovery became apparent, Göncz was quick to emphasise that the most difficult period of readjustment had passed:

Twenty months ago, the government was faced with the direct threat of economic collapse ... The prevention of the crisis required forceful [and] crude actions. Above all, those people who live on benefits and pensioners paid the price for ... We got over the crisis. We cut out the roots of the [crisis], although the defenceless people still do not feel it at this moment ... We can say that the first period of transformation has ended.[11]

In light of these comments, it can be argued that Göncz's acquiescence did not mean that socio-economic issues were outside of the realm of his interests or that he supported the government's economic policy in order to secure his re-election to the presidency.

6.2.2. The Law of Incompatibility (Összeférhetetlenségi törvény)

On 17 December 1996 the Hungarian Parliament adopted 'Law No. V of 1997 on the Amendment of the Legal Status of Members of Parliament' (hereafter, the Law on Incompatibility).[12] The law was aimed at preventing MPs from exercising their political interests on the process of privatisation, the Incompatibility Law was to provide a basic legal framework for the separation of the economy from the political sphere.[13] According to the law, MPs could not, for example, assume leading positions in public economic associations, while simultaneously acting as parliamentarians. The amendment process, however, was far from smooth and the legislation process was hampered by political divisions between the socialists and the right wing opposition, as well as within the socialist-liberal coalition. In general, all agreed that the Incompatibility Law was necessary for the creation of a transparent public space (Stépan, 1997). However, consensus diverged on the matter of deciding the time of the law's enforcement and delineating the limits of the legality. The socialist leadership claimed that the law should only apply to those MPs who could secure their seats in the next Parliament, reasoning that the application of a retroactive rule contravened the principle of legal security (*Magyar Nemzet*, 17 June 1996). In contrast, the AFD and the opposition, especially AYD and the ISP insisted that sitting parliamentarians also be included as subjects in the application of the law (György, 1997; *Magyar Nemzet*, 17 June 1996). The result was a compromise within the socialist–liberal coalition in which it was agreed that MPs could keep their dual positions if their post in business was acquired *before* they were elected to Parliament (EECR, 1997 Winter).

Two weeks later, however, Göncz, who once supported the incompatibility legislation enactment refused to sign the law, instead returning it to Parliament for reconsideration (*Népszabadság*, 3 January 1997; *Új Magyarország*, 3 January 1997). Göncz gave specific reasons for his refusal (discussed below), but immediate reactions followed from parliamentary parties. As a whole, the opposition welcomed Göncz's decision, whereas the socialist–liberal coalition expressed surprise (*Magyar Nemzet*, 3 January 1997). While debates over the Incompatibility Law continued in Parliament, the Speaker of the House, Zoltán Gál, made an important announcement – he would *not* call for the holding of an extraordinary parliamentary session (*Magyar Hírlap*, 7 January 1997; *Magyar Nemzet*, 7 January 1997; *Népszabadság*, 7 January 1997) – which, in practice, meant that the revision of the original legislation would not be considered (*Népszava*, 9 January 1997). Subsequently, on 25 February 1997, Parliament overrode Göncz's decision by re-adopting the law in its original form (*Magyar Nemzet*, 26 February 1997; *Népszabadság*, 26 February 1997a).

Göncz raised ten points of contention regarding the Law on Incompatibility, of which the following three were the most important elements: the principle of equality; the guarantee of free economic competition; and the protection of personal data and privacy.

First, Göncz questioned whether the Law of Incompatibility contravened the principle of equality (*Magyar Hírlap*, 7 January 1997; *Magyar Nemzet*, 7 January 1997; *Népszabadság*, 3 January 1997; *Új Magyarország*, 7 January 1997). In particular, the distinction which depended on the timing of the acquisition of seats in Parliament was seen as a major problem, given that this clause decided whether MPs were permitted to retain a dual position. According to the amended incompatibility law, if a post in business had been obtained before MPs were elected to Parliament, they were allowed to take on a dual position. In a situation where a post in business was obtained after one had been elected to Parliament, the parliamentarian had to choose between positions (staying as an MP or becoming a businessman). For instance, it could bring about a contradictory situation (see Table 6.3).

This contradiction not only undermined the principle of equality, but could also have far-reaching consequences. Since the party illustrated in Case B was still allowed to assume a dual position, if this firm was due to be privatised from state ownership, it is very probable that Ákos could exercise his political interest in the privatisation process. Göncz may have recognised this legal drawback. It should be noted that 52 MPs who shared Göncz's view turned to the Constitutional Court, asking whether this distinction contravened the Constitution (the Court ruled that it was against the principle of equality).[14]

Second, Göncz suspected that the distinction made between public and private business violated the principles of free economic competition and of equality (Kéri and Zsoldos, 1997; *Magyar Nemzet*, 7 January 1997; *Új Magyarország*, 7 January 1997). The law prevented MPs from engaging in public business, whereas seeking private business was permitted. The reason for the latter regulation was that some leeway should remain for MPs to enact private business because they may need an additional income source. However, even if this flexibility was necessary, the discriminatory measure itself was seen as a problem. Referring to Article 9 prescribed in the Constitution –Hungary has a market economy in which public and private property are to receive equal consideration and protection under the law – Göncz wondered why this principle was not applied to the Incompatibility Law.

The final issue raised by Göncz was whether the Law of Incompatibility guaranteed the protection of personal data and privacy (*Magyar Hírlap*, 7 January

Table 6.3 The Law of Incompatibility.

Case A: In April, Ákos became an MP in the Parliament. In June, Ákos joined the board of directors in a state-owned firm.
(Incompatible or not permissible)

Case B: In April, Ákos was the director of a firm. In June, Ákos became an MP in the Parliament but still runs the firm.
(Compatible or permissible)

Note: The name Ákos does not refer to a real member of the Hungarian Parliament.

1997; *Magyar Nemzet*, 7 January 1997; *Új Magyarország*, 7 January 1997). The Incompatibility Law obliged MPs to declare the status of their property holdings at the beginning and end of their mandates, stating that: 'Upon the acquisition and termination of mandates, within 30 days, MPs shall be obliged to declare the [status] of their property to the Speaker of Parliament'.[15] However, Göncz questioned whether this requirement violated Article 59 of the Constitution which prescribed the protection of personal details and secrets (EECR, 1997 Winter).

On the whole, Göncz interpreted the Law of Incompatibility through the lens of his liberal democratic views. Above all, he asked for Parliament to legislate for a more effective and judicious law which was in harmony with the Constitution (*Népszabadság*, 7 January 1997). Göncz stressed that ill-conceived clauses within the law be redefined prior to its enforcement. In terms of Göncz's objections, however, there was a question mark over his decision to employ his political veto. Should Göncz have found a legal deficiency, he could, in principle, have sent the legislation to the Constitutional Court for judicial review. According to my interviewees and the Hungarian literature, three factors are primarily responsible for Göncz's decision to use his political veto.

The first official explanation offered by Göncz's Spokesman, András Faragó, was that Göncz did not refer the law to the Constitutional Court, because 'it was only concerned with MPs' (György, 1997; *Népszabadság*, 7 January 1997). As the official title of the Incompatibility Law – The Legal Status of MPs – indicated, Göncz may have thought that problems concerning MPs should be tackled at their discretion. According to this account, Göncz appears to have given some leeway to MPs rather than calling on a third party to address the legal deficiency within the law. This explanation, however, is too simplistic and Faragó's comment on the Law of Incompatibility was far from sufficient.

Second, it has been argued that there was a possible link between Göncz's political veto and the concept of a new Constitution (interview with Babus, 19 May 2007). Over the course of the Horn government, there was an attempt to adopt the new Constitution. Despite the fact that this new Constitution was eventually defeated, Babus argued that the concept of a new Constitution which would have resulted in the weakening of the president's position had an impact on Göncz's decision (Babus, 1996a, 1996b, 1996c, 1997). Reasoning that the passage of the new Constitution could have further curtailed the president's authority, Babus questioned whether Göncz's discontent, or his understanding of the existing situation, was expressed in his use of the political veto. For example, among the president's competences affected by the concept of a new Constitution, Babus argued that the following presidential powers could all have been eliminated:

> It appeared that there was a draft Constitution on a desk in Parliament, from which the president's powers were to be significantly curtailed. The rights of the commander-in-chief, to propose bills and initiate national referenda could have been removed.
>
> (Interview with Babus, 19 May 2007)

According to Babus, Göncz's apparent resistance to the new amendment of the Hungarian Constitution (particularly with respect to the reduction of presidential powers) was expressed in the form of the use of his political veto.

However, counter-opinions offered by a great number of legal experts and politicians who actually participated in the enactment of a draft Constitution (interviews with Hack, Somogyvári, a former judge of the Constitutional Court and a former chairman of the AFD) suggest that a connection between these two factors does not exist. A former chairman of the AFD stated: 'Concerning the [scope] of the president's [power], the status quo remained in essence ... There was nothing to curb [presidential power]' (interview with a former chairman of the AFD, 27 September 2007).

Similarly, Somogyvári held the view that:

> No! It was not true ... There were ideas to strengthen the president's position ... For instance, the law professor, Tamás Sárközy suggested that the president have some executive powers ... So, it was not about the curtailment of the president's rights, but the increase ... But this was not realised.
> (Interview with Somogyvári, 22 May 2007)

Both agreed that the proposed amendments to the Hungarian Constitution did not ultimately result in a change of presidential competences, even though there were some disputes over the reshaping of the president's power. Given this counter-evidence, the reliability of Babus' argument is questionable. Having noted this explanatory deficit in the literature, the actual contents of a new draft Constitution were examined. In particular, the relevant areas of presidential power that were to be subject to change were investigated. According to Babus, the rights associated with the role of commander-in-chief and presidential power to initiate national referenda should have been curtailed. However, the results of my analysis suggest that the president's competences essentially remained intact, but for a slight modification in proposition rights (*Magyar Hírlap*, 2 June 1995).[16] Thus, it is unfair to suggest that Göncz's political vetoing of the Incompatibility Law was an act of protest against the curtailment of presidential powers within the new conceptual framework of the Constitution.

Finally, it was claimed that Göncz's veto of the Law on Incompatibility may have been connected to the maintenance of his own popularity (Babus, 1997). Public confidence in the Horn government remained consistently low, chiefly owing to government involvement in corruption scandals.[17] Göncz would also have been wary of the erosion of his own popularity, he may have used the issue of the Law on Incompatibility to dissociate himself from the Horn government. According to this analysis of the situation, self-interest was the principal reason behind the usage of his veto. However, this seems to be limited as a justification. If Göncz sought primarily to protect his own interests, this suggests that he was thinking and acting as a professional party politician. Yet the significance of Göncz's professional political attitude was ultimately set aside, even by those critics who once proposed that a connection between Göncz's political calculation and his veto might have existed. In response to my question,[18] Babus altered the position that he had outlined in his previous statement:

> I am not saying that Göncz could have been driven by his self-interests . . . At the time, I did not find such a contradiction in the draft law which could have explained his vetoing the law . . . For this reason, I began to find other motives in the background [of the constitutional situation which had arisen].
> (Interview with Babus, 19 May 2007)

Moreover, in an interview with Kossuth Radio, Göncz himself refuted the general assumption that he acted as a professional party politician, asserting that:

> I have never been a politician. It was true that I often fulfilled political roles in the course of my previous political activities. The activities undertaken during the resistance movement, during the 1956 Revolution and after the collapse of the old system they were all quintessentially political. However, by nature, I did not behave in a way that people [might have] expected from a politician. Political careerism and ambition were absent in my case . . . I entered politics from the outside.
> (Wisinger and László, 2007: 343)

This stance could be interpreted as mere political rhetoric or gesture. In the routine of daily politics, as politicians normally deal with the press and public inquiry in a way that evades the point in question or justifies their actions, Göncz could have made this comment in an attempt to ward off criticism regarding his presidential role or style. However, even if this was the case, Göncz's political calculation was not, it seemed, the principal reason for his refusal to sign the Incompatibility Law. As has been argued in the previous chapter, over the course of his presidency, Göncz had consistently sought to express his liberal and democratic values. For example, the main reason for Göncz's veto of the Law of Arable Land lay in his concern over potential discrimination against those wishing to purchase land (see Section 5.2.4); dealing with the Incompatibility Law, Göncz once again raised the principle issue of equality as the grounds for his refusal to sign the legislation. It is then unfair to suggest that Göncz put his self interest before democratic principles which he held to be important.

Thus, there are various analyses which go some way to explain Göncz's decision to veto the Incompatibility Law, but none of these furnishes us with a finite explicit explanation. It can be clearly seen that Göncz called on Parliament to reconsider the law due to his reservations about the legal deficiencies evident within its formulation. As these concerns were legally grounded, the reason why Göncz did not use his constitutional veto is still unclear; perhaps, the truth lay in the official explanation as it was presented by his Spokesman. Alternatively, as the political commentator, Orsolya Szomszéd, contended, this issue was exaggerated by those people who assumed that Göncz would sign the law without any hesitation. Szomszed explained the context, stating that:

174 *The post-Communist presidency*

> Perhaps, this was so disputed [among analysts] – including the author you mentioned [Babus] spelled out his assumption regarding Göncz's decision – because Göncz had not used his veto for a long time [since 1993]. Göncz was not in conflict with the Horn government, so this issue attracted a lot of interest. The president's action came as a surprise and caused such a debate.
>
> (Interview with Szomszéd, 14 June 2007)

The day following Göncz's exercise of the veto on the Incompatibility Law, controversy over his veto once again arose when he challenged the revised version of the Law on Privatisation.

6.2.3. The Law on Privatisation

On 19 December 1996, the Horn government passed the amended draft of the Law on Privatisation. This amendment was made based on the previous legal framework ('Law XXXIX of 1995 on the Sale of State-Owned Entrepreneurial Assets', hereafter the Law on Privatisation) with the aim of accelerating the privatisation process. The legislative process was, however, far from smooth and controversy resurfaced between parliamentary parties. In particular, MPs disagreed as to whether local governments and co-operatives should be given preferential treatment in the course of the privatisation process. The point of disagreement was as follows: In extraordinary circumstance, would the State Privatisation and Property Management Corporation (SPPMC) be authorised to transfer state properties to local governments and cooperatives without restriction? (*Népszabadság*, 21, 30 December 1996; Szily, 1997).[19]

Members of the socialist leadership reasoned that, since local government and agricultural cooperatives were assigned important social tasks to perform for the common good, the free handover of state property ought to be supported (Pogány, 1997). László Csaba explained the context and actual manner in which state properties were transferred to local governments in the early stage of the economic transformation:

> The time of free transfer of state property was approximately 1989–1992. This was the first period of transformation and the free transfer of state property was lawful at this time . . . Our constitution [states that] we give an important role to the local government. Property must be given to this local government because without it, local government cannot perform its function . . . [The solution] was basically allowing property to be transferred to [local governments] free of charge.[20]
>
> (Interview with Csaba, 5 July 2007)

It is not clear whether by the amendment of the Privatisation Law the socialists intended to extend the previous business practice to the case of co-operatives. However, the coalition's junior partner (the AFD) and the right wing opposition parties (AYD, HDF and ISP) opposed the adoption of the law, reasoning that the complimentary transfer of state property to local authorities and co-operatives would result in a corruption problem because this would favour those associations closely linked to the governing party (*Népszabadság*, 30 December 1996). Given that no agreement was possible, on 19 December 1996, the socialists passed the revised law without the support of their coalition partner and the opposition (*Magyar Nemzet*, 4 January 1997).

Two weeks later, however, Göncz challenged the law. As with the Law on Incompatibility, Göncz returned the Privatisation Law to Parliament for reconsideration (*Magyar Nemzet*, 4 January 1997; *Népszabadság*, 4 January 1997). His actions were met with a mixed response from parliamentary parties. The opposition welcomed Göncz's decision, whereas the socialist governing party took the same position that they had occupied during the dispute over the Law on Incompatibility; as the socialists viewed it, an extraordinary parliamentary session would not be necessary (*Magyar Hirlap*, 7 January 1997; *Népszabadság*, 7 January 1997). While parliamentary debates over the law continued, the coalition government and the opposition reached an agreement. The result was a compromise, whereby local governments but not agricultural cooperatives would benefit from the free transfer of state property (*Magyar Nemzet*, 26 February 1997; *Népszabadság*, 26 February 1997b).

The Hungarian socialist daily, *Népszabadság*, outlined Göncz's main reservations about the law lay:

> According to the head of state, the law makes a groundless distinction between [various] economic organisations [. . .].
>
> The head of state also agreed with the concerns [shared by] six parliamentary parties; that the amended law violates equality of opportunity in the form of ownership and, in the sphere of [economic] competition and, makes a groundless distinction among the [cited] economic organisations. Co-operatives [are] not subject to any [special] conditions for the free transfer of [state] property [to take place].
>
> (*Népszabadság,* 4 January 1997)

Göncz questioned whether co-operatives should benefit from positive discrimination in the course of privatisation. According to Göncz, discriminatory measures within the legislation contravened the principle of equality across economic units. For this reason, he called on the Parliament to reconsider the point in question whether co-operatives should be regarded as a special case in relation to the privatisation process. Although Göncz did not directly mention that the relevant clauses within the Constitution should be consulted in the enactment of the legislative process, it is clear that the legislation adopted was irreconcilable with the egalitarian principle Göncz held to be of great importance. In fact, an article published in *Magyar Nemzet*, highlights the fact that Göncz further detailed his thoughts regarding what issues should be considered in the establishment of the law:

The president suggested that, before the final vote, the Speaker of the House [should bring] the law to Parliament for reconsideration. [This rethink] should take paragraphs 9 (1) and 12 of the Constitution into account in the composition of the law.

(*Magyar Nemzet*, 7 January 1997)

Article 9 (1) of the Constitution defines the principle of equality under conditions of economic transformation, dictating that 'Hungary is a market economy, in which public and private property shall receive equal treatment'.[21] In pinpointing this stipulation – in the same way that he had dealt with the Laws on Incompatibility and Arable Land – Göncz questioned whether discrimination was ever necessary for the course of the privatisation process. As stated above, the significance of performing social tasks for the common good was the official reason given by the socialists for their support of the Privatisation Law, and they attempted to authorise the SPPMC to transfer certain state properties to co-operatives without restriction. Göncz understood, however, that this allowance might contravene Clause 9 (1) of the Constitution and, urged MPs to consider this in the legislative process. Similarly, Göncz sought to clarify the circumstances around the issue of what support the state was obliged to offer in the case of co-operatives. This question was raised with reference to Clause 12 of the Constitution which dictated the state's duty to support co-operatives: 'The State shall support a co-operative based on voluntary association and shall recognise the autonomy of such a co-operative'.[22] Thus, the main reason for Göncz's quarrel with the adopted legislation lay in an unclarified stipulation within the proposed law, where he highlighted that the principle of equality should be duly considered in the enactment of the Privatisation Law.

In terms of the usage of his political veto, however, there was an element of ambiguity. Just as with the Law on Incompatibility, the main point raised by Göncz was one of legality, he could have turned to the Constitutional Court and requested a judicial review. According to the official explanation offered by Göncz's Spokesman András Faragó, Göncz returned the Privatisation Law to Parliament, 'because of the simplicity of the anomalies in the law' (EECR, 1997 Winter). The practical meaning of this was not detailed in the literature; I asked Faragó to address this gap.

According to Faragó, the president's questions were related to technical problems within the Privatisation Law, and Göncz used a political veto to address them (emails with Faragó, 21 and 25 August 2008). Faragó explained that the country had long awaited a new privatisation programme and the amended Law on Privatisation was expected to meet this need.[23] Above all, a prompt promulgation of the law was required, but the existing problem – whether co-operatives should be considered as a beneficiary for the free transfer of state property – had to be resolved. The issue then lay in choosing between the political and constitutional veto and how to proceed to find which was more advantageous to save time and resolve the problem. According to Faragó, in practice, the former required less time than the latter. Had Göncz used his constitutional veto to deal with the Law on Privatisation, the promulgation of the law could have been further delayed and, comparably, any possible delay brought about by the usage of his political veto would be significantly less lengthy. The causal relationship between veto type and potential legislative delay are summarised in Figure 6.1.

It can be seen that in Scenario II the legal procedure is relatively more streamlined and less complex than in Scenario I, requiring less time for the passage of law. In this respect, if 'technicality' was the point at issue, the political veto would be advantageous when compared to the constitutional veto. It should be noted that in Hungary, any individuals and groups have the right to initiate constitutional review proceedings; arguably this is indicative of the fact that the Constitutional Court's caseload must be considered as a factor which may prevent the speedy resolution of veto requests.[24] Legal expert Herman Schwartz noted: 'one very great problem that the Hungarian court faces is caseload. Because anyone can go to the court with a challenge to an enactment, it has been swamped with petitions' (Schwartz, 1993: 31). In contrast, discussing a bill returned to Parliament would require relatively less time, as the Speaker of the House adds it to the agenda for a regular or extraordinary parliamentary session.

Furthermore, in terms of Göncz's desire to promote consensus-based decision making – a key principle of democracy in his view – the political veto might be seen as the reasonable solution for him to help MPs address the existing problem by themselves. Upon the submission of the Law on Privatisation, there was much disagreement both within the governing party and the opposition as well as between the Parliamentary Constitutional Committee (PCC) and the government

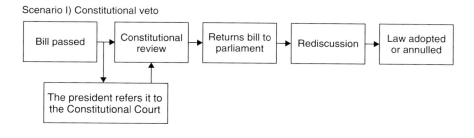

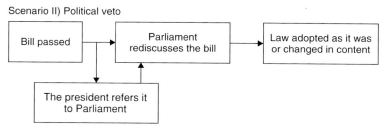

Figure 6.1

(Pogány, 1997). The PCC proposed that the controversial aspects of the legislation (authorisation of the SPPMC to transfer state property to co-operatives without restriction) be reconsidered (Szily,1997), as they found the legislation to be seriously flawed. However, the governing party voted this proposal down and this unilateral decision resulted in the failure to reach consensus over the existing legal problem. Judit Csiha – the minister of privatisation without portfolio – stated: '[It was] regrettable to see that insufficient time was given over to helping two [political] camps reach a consensus or seek a compromise. For this reason, the president returned the law to Parliament' (Pogány, 1997).

As Csiha asserted, had Göncz decided that the lack of consensus between MPs and legal experts had been prompted by insufficient discussion of the law, his attempts to resolve the obstruction would be more effectively served by intervention on the platform of the political veto rather than the constitutional. As discussed in the Section 4.3, once the president invokes the political veto, MPs are obliged to discuss a bill which has been returned to Parliament. Until such time, the law is to, all intents and purposes, suspended (thus, the political veto is also known as the suspensory veto) in such circumstances the president acts as a facilitator for the re-ignition of parliamentary debates concerning the law in question. The available documentation does not allow confirmation of whether Göncz's decision to veto the Privatisation Law was grounded in his desire to forge a consensus among MPs. However, given the significance of consensus for Göncz's political beliefs, such a factor cannot be easily discounted when assessing his decision-making capacity.

Thus, whether Göncz's decision to return the Privatisation Law was driven by his understanding of its technicality or his commitment to a consensus-based decision making, his actions in this case lead to the conclusion that, in so far as his liberal and democratic views are concerned, there is an element of consistency: the pursuit of the principle of equality. Although legislation was dealt with by Göncz at different times, he constantly emphasised that this basic democratic principle ought to be considered in the legislative process. Above all, he urged Parliament to pen a law which conformed to the principle of equality. The significance of this basic but fundamental democratic principle arose once more in connection with the issue of the granting a pardon, in the so-called of Péter Kunos case.

6.3.4. Dealing with the case of Péter Kunos

In an interview with Wisinger, Göncz stated his position with regard to the issuing of presidential pardons: 'In general, a pardon is about making a decision in a situation of dilemma; where cold reason and warm heart clash' (Wisinger and László, 2007: 174).

In the Hungarian legal context, issuing an individual pardon falls within the counter-signatory system, which in practice means that the president is required to have the co-signature of a responsible minister or, the prime minister (see Section 4.3). The following case demonstrates the way in which the president and the minister of justice approached this obligation differently in the matter concerning the release of an imprisoned former banking manager.

In November 1994, the chairman of the Agricultural Bank, Péter Kunos, was arrested by police (Csák, Dániel and Zsubori, 2007). Initially, he was accused of financial corruption in banking, but in the first trial, heard at the Budapest District Court in July 1997, he was found innocent and acquitted (*Napi Magyarország*, 10 November 1998). On 30 April 1998, however, in a second trial resulting from appeal proceedings held at the request of the prosecutor, the Supreme Court overruled the previous decision, sentencing Kunos to two years' imprisonment (*Magyar Távirat Iroda*, 26 September 2001). The court convicted him of financial corruption, reasoning that his misdeeds had compromised the transparency of Hungary's economic society and public confidence in state officials (Csák*et al.*, 2007; *Hetek*, 24 April 1999). Having been denied the right to appeal (Fahidi, 1999; Halmai, 1999), Kunos was due to begin his custodial sentence. However, citing health problems (claims supported by his doctor), Kunos petitioned for the provisional suspension of the sentence; a request that was accepted (*Népszava*, 10 November 1998). Meanwhile, he also pleaded for a presidential pardon.

On 6 October 1998, once Kunos' medical report had been considered, the deputy secretary of state in the Ministry of Justice (MOJ) approved a temporary suspension of the prison sentence (*Magyar Narancs*, 19 November 1998). However, two days later, the decision was overruled by the Minister of Justice Ibolya Dávid who reasoned that the banker had not attached a proper medical report detailing his ill health to the suspension request (*Népszava*, 10 November 1998). Additionally, Dávid stated that she did not wish to overrule the decision of the Supreme Court by signing Kunos' release (*Népszabadság*, 11 November 1998).

The petition was refused and, on 29 October 1998, Kunos began his imprisonment (*Magyar Nemzet*, 10 November 1998). Surprisingly, however, on 9 November 1998, Göncz issued a presidential pardon (*Magyar Nemzet*, 10 November 1998; *Népszabadság*, 10 November 1998) and public attention was focused on whether the justice minister would sign Kunos's release papers and it was far from certain that the minister's signature would be forthcoming. Indeed, on the following day, the minister refused Kunos' release, on the grounds that a medical report provided by the authorities – a MOJ doctor – proved that Kunos's ill health was not serious enough to merit his release (*Népszabadság*, 11 November 1998).

Dávid explained that as Kunos' appeal on poor health grounds was not convincing, the grounds on which Göncz wished to acquit him by pardon were unclear. Was it simply attributable to a difference of opinion regarding the medical report of the banker's health status? Or was it a jurisdictional dispute between the president and the justice minister? According to articles uncovered in the Hungarian literature and my interviewees' testimonies, three explanations were potentially responsible for the conflict between minister and president.

First, differing interpretations of the information given in Kunos' medical reports may account for the divergent conclusions reached regarding his eligibility for release. Göncz issued a pardon for Kunos on compassionate grounds. Having been informed of Kunos' ill health (*Népszabadság*, 11 November 1998), Göncz granted a pardon to suspend his imprisonment for three years (*Napi*

Magyarország, 10 November 1998; *Népszava*, 10 November 1998). Dávid, however, questioned the authenticity of the report prepared by Kunos' doctor and, referring to the opinion offered by the authorities, refused to release Kunos. With hindsight, there was another factor influencing Dávid's and Göncz's decisions. Given that Dávid's party, the HDF, was a coalition partner of the Orbán government which objected to Kunos' release, Dávid would have to represent the position of the government. László Salamon explained the political context in which Dávid's decision may have been made: 'The AYD's stance was the same as Dávid's. Ibolya Dávid was a member of the government led by Viktor Orbán. She was the minister of justice and the chairman of the HDF' (interview with Salamon, 24 October 2007).

Similarly, István Stumpf – who personally participated in the governmental meeting at which the issue was debated – reaffirmed the view that:

> Orbán [was] opposed to the pardon. His standpoint was the same as Dávid's. This issue was raised [during the meeting] of the cabinet. I do not remember precisely when and in what circumstances this issue was raised, but the government unanimously supported the justice minister.
> (Interview with Stumpf, 3 July 2007)

Thus, political circumstances influenced Dávid's decision not to release Kunos. Having considered the political context from the minister of justice's viewpoint, the circumstances surrounding Göncz's decision-making process were also examined. According to Stumpf, Göncz's decision to release Kunos seemed to have been informed by the AFD, which had a close link to the Agricultural Bank (AB) at the time. Stumpf claimed:

> The president represented the interests of the liberal intellectuals. It appeared that it was not the president's idea to release Kunos but [the result] of lobbying [activities] of the AB. They [the AFD] received a great deal of money and support from the AB, and felt that, at least, they needed to try to persuade the president on the issue of a pardon for Kunos.
> (Interview with Stumpf, 3 July 2007)

This account is convincing up to a point as Stumpf may have had an opportunity to observe the situation closely while he worked as a minister in the OPM. However, hard evidence in the form of documentation to substantiate the claim has remained either inaccessible or is non-existent. Thus, it is unfair to suggest that Göncz's decision to pardon Kunos was an act which resulted from party instructions. In response to my question,[25] Gabriella Ilonszki confirmed this: 'I cannot check the truth. Only those who had full access to the decision-making process could know about it. It would not be possible to find any hard evidence. This remains only a speculation' (interview with Ilonszki, 16 October 2007).

Another possible reason for the conflict between president and justice minister lies in their different understandings of the general public's perception of justice at the time. It was not absolutely clear what the public felt about the Kunos issue. However, it is possible to say with some certainty that the majority thought Kunos should remain in jail (*Budapest Sun*, 19 November 1998). One of the leading Hungarian political scientists observed: 'Hungarian public opinion always [held the view] that the small fish are convicted, whereas the big fish and the leaders are always released . . . People always want to see leaders should be also called to account' (interview with a leading Hungarian political scientists, 16 November 2007). Had Dávid released Kunos, it would have infuriated the general public and could have damaged her political future significantly. István Stumpf believed that Dávid took advantage of the existing situation for her own future political career thus:

> In this conflict, her popularity significantly increased . . . She thought she could muster political capital [by] engaging in a [conflict] with the president . . . The public atmosphere – which Dávid sensed – was that if this convicted criminal was released, it would send the wrong message to society: Justice does not extend to people of high position . . . In taking the attitude that she did, Dávid accurately reflected public opinion . . . and profited by [her choice to do so].
>
> (Interview with Stumpf, 3 July 2007)

In the eyes of the Hungarian population, Dávid could be seen as the justice minister who stood by the strict application of the rule of law, in return for which her political position would be consolidated.

Göncz was also aware of the public's sense of justice but according to his own explanation, Göncz viewed it differently from Dávid. In essence, Göncz thought that issuing a pardon and public opinion were separate matters. Göncz recalled:

> I was not surprised . . . I was certain that in her [given] situation, for political reasons, [Dávid] would not sign [the pardon]. At the time, it would appear that the lopsided prejudice [of the] public['s] opinion had [meant that] her hands were tied . . . If the court had convicted – for example – Stadler, a banker, to nine years' [imprisonment] and released him from prison, people would wonder why he was released. People would think this is strange. [Dávid] explicitly told me that she would not sign it and I told her I would.
>
> (Wisinger and László, 2007: 334)

Thus it can be argued that Göncz appreciated that, in the minds of the general public, no deed deserving of punishment should remain unpunished. From this viewpoint, Göncz's approval of Kunos' release would run counter to the concept of justice that the Hungarian population had. However, Göncz implied that despite the possible social consequences that his decision might have contributed to, there was another important reason to deal with public opinion differently from Dávid's position. Although the quote above does not tell us why Göncz thought the public's sense of justice was irreconcilable with his own understanding of the situation, it is certain that he dissociated his decision making from public opinion.

It is therefore necessary to look elsewhere in order to understand what led him to tackle the Kunos issue in a different manner to the justice minister.

The final and most plausible explanation for Göncz's chosen course of action lies with legal deficiencies within the criminal law, particularly with respect to the right of legal redress. In order to understand better why this problem affected Göncz's decision to pardon Kunos, it is worth briefly examining Hungary's judicial system. In essence, Hungary's justice system consists of four levels: local courts; the county courts and the Municipal Court of Budapest; the Courts of Appeal; and the Supreme Court.[26] Local courts – which deal primarily with civil lawsuits – are placed at the bottom of this structure, whereas it is the Supreme Court which gives a final verdict. The Courts of Appeal, which deal exclusively with cases of appeal, were introduced in 1997 to lessen caseloads lodged at the county courts and the Supreme Courts (EECR, 1998 Fall). This is the fundamental institutional basis on which Hungary's judicial system currently operates,[27] and individual citizens are entitled to take legal proceedings with the right of appeals against rulings previously made.

The main problem, however, was that the implementation of the 1998 Criminal Code (which had replaced the 1978 Criminal Code adopted during the Communist regime) was delayed until 2002 by a decision of the Orbán government.[28] This deferment had far-reaching consequences for the right of legal redress of the Hungarian population. Given that Act No. IV of 1978 the Criminal Code contained no clause for the right of legal remedy,[29] deferring the enforcement of the 1998 Criminal Law placed the Hungarian population in a situation whereby they were still restricted by the inadequacies of the outdated 1978 Criminal Code. It is thus hardly surprising that Kunos was not granted the right to legal redress. Gábor Halmai detailed the way in which the absence of legal redress could have affected Göncz's decision:

> At the first trial, Kunos was [found innocent] and acquitted. At the second trial, he was convicted and received two and a half years' imprisonment. The problem was if a person was found guilty at a second trial, he or she did not have the right to appeal . . . There was no such [guarantee] in Hungarian Criminal Law. After this case, the relevant rule was inserted into [the legislation] . . . Kunos could never have enjoyed the [right] to legal redress . . . I think this was against the Constitution.
> (Interview with Halmai, 15 November 2007)

Having recognised this legal lacuna within the Criminal Code, Göncz may have decided to issue a pardon. He may have thought that Kunos was a victim of the existing faulty legal system. It should be noted that when Kunos' lawyer brought the case to the Strasbourg European Court of Human Rights (*Hetek*, 24 April 1999), he referred to the reasoning that Halmai had raised: the absence of the right to seek legal redress contravenes the basic principle of universal human rights and the Constitution. This explanation is persuasive, and in terms of Göncz's position, the issue of a pardon could be seen as a reasonable solution to the impasse, as

Göncz could have addressed the existing problems simultaneously; that of compensating the victim, but *without altering the legitimate ruling made by the Court*. László Salamon explained what a pardon meant in practice within the Hungarian legal context:

> *If one is granted a pardon, this does not mean that one is morally rehabilitated into society.* There was once a famous archbishop József Mindszenty in Hungary. He was imprisoned and in 1956 released. But, when the Soviet army crushed the Revolution, he sought asylum in the US Embassy. He lived there for 15 years . . . This issue was unpleasant to everyone, [including] the Kádár regime and the US government . . . An idea came that he should be sent abroad. If he [was willing to] go, they [the Kádár authorities] would not arrest him. To this end, the Kádár regime figured out a legal [solution] and [promised] to pardon him. But Mindszenty refused to request a pardon, because he was not guilty. I am saying this, because a *pardon does not mean the declaration of innocence or the absolution of the guilt*.
> (Interview with Salamon, 24 October 2007)

In light of this statement, it is fair to suggest that the pardon Göncz issued to Kunos was *not* in fact aimed at overruling the Supreme Court's decision. Rather it should be interpreted as an act undertaken in order to suspend law enforcement on a provisional basis. Göncz could have considered Kunos' ill health or the absence of the right to appeal in his decision making. However, this account still does not enable us to clarify and reconstruct the precise context in which Göncz's decision was reached. In order to address this explanatory deficit, further evidence demonstrating Göncz's own explanation was probed. While very little documentary evidence is found in the Hungarian literature, some conclusions can be drawn from an interview Göncz gave to Kossuth Radio. This interview suggests that Göncz's decision to release Kunos lay in the lack of consensus among legal experts at the time. Göncz stated:

> At the Ministry [of Justice], there is a division [dealing with] petitions . . . Opinions and proposals are offered here and it is very rare [to see] that [these] differ from the president's opinion.[30] If I did not agree with [those proposals], I made my own comment. In this case, it was inevitable that I would [express my disagreement],because the rulings of the court differed and, simultaneously, my perception of the legality [of the situation dictated] that prevailing public opinion should not influence the [case]. I agreed with Dávid that each of us would decide according to [our] conscience and would not regret our conclusions.
> (Wisinger and László, 2007: 335)

This underscores the fact that in his decisionmaking, Göncz had indeed considered legal disagreements among jurists. Göncz was clearly of the view that, among legal experts, there was a discrepancy in opinions over the Kunos trial and the general public was following the case. While this still does not suggest that the absence of

184 *The post-Communist presidency*

the right to appeal was the main reason for Göncz's pardon, it is certain that Göncz considered the separation of public opinion from his decision making to be significant. In contrast, the justice minister and the Orbán government failed to dissociate the public opinion from their decision-making processes. Eszter Rádai detailed the political context in which the Orbán government's decision was originated:

> After all, this was a show trial . . . The Orbán government wanted to use this case to prove that they are different [in terms of] transparency, saying that 'while they are in the government, they would deal with this kind of matter [suspicious corruption in banking business] in this way' . . . But this was a very strange affair. Kunos just sought to protect the bank's interests . . . He wanted to secure a guarantee from his clients to reimburse money for the loan he gave.[31] This was an absolutely rational decision . . . but the people did not really know about what this trial was about, and the public atmosphere was against the banker.
> (Interview with Rádai, 11 October 2007)

This one opinion does not represent the view of the general public on the way in which the Orbán government dealt with the case. According to Rádai, however, it is clear that the Orbán government capitalised on the Kunos issue to promote their vested interests. In so doing, the government and the justice minister might have benefited from this political tactic to increase the public confidence in them and their popularity. Göncz, however, clearly displayed his position that public opinion was a separate matter. Given this differentiated approach, it is fair to suggest that Göncz's mention of his conscience was not a mere political gesture, but a metaphor for his principled decision making.

In terms of the political beliefs that were important to Göncz (the pursuit of a consensus-based democracy), there is a question mark over his decision: a convicted individual was considered to be more important than the general opinion of Hungarian society. As has been examined in the previous and the present chapter, Göncz's desire for consensus-based decision making was consistently evidenced through a series of issues and events: the taxi-drivers' strike, dealing with the Communist past and the Law of Privatisation. Having said that, had Göncz also sought to pursue a consensus-based decision making on this issue, in principle he should have upheld the position of the general public. Gabriella Ilonszki discussed the contradiction of that was demonstrated in this case:

Ilonszki: I think this was a contradictory decision . . . [When] the protection of democratic values and sympathy for an individual were in conflict, Göncz decided to stand by the individual . . . Is a person worth more than democracy? For him, a person was more important than [democratic] principles. Possibly, [this] was his own value-system and he made his decision accordingly.

Kim: Are you saying that Göncz issued a pardon to Kunos on humane grounds?

Ilonszki: This again touches on our earlier discussion. Göncz was a civic-minded [statesman]. In his mind, a person was more important than the presidential post.

(Interview with Ilonszki, 16 October 2007)

This suggests that in the situation of a dilemma where Göncz was unable to reconcile his political beliefs with his personal value system, he opted for the latter. In light of Göncz's commitment to civic values, he may have decided to stand by Kunos. However, this does not mean that if one has a civic mind or attitude, one tends to judge the situation in favour of the person in trouble. It would be a gross oversimplification to say that the term – civic minded – was necessarily associated with sympathy towards the individual, especially those in trouble. Nevertheless, considering Göncz's down-to-earth attitude towards the Hungarian population (Körösényi *et al.*, 2003: 570; Szász, 2010) and their sympathy towards him,[32] this factor cannot be easily discounted when assessing Göncz's decision-making capacity. Indeed, in an interview with Hegedűs, Göncz commented that, in the circumstance under which he had to choose to either uphold his political beliefs or his personal value system, he would opt for the latter. Göncz stated thus: 'Perhaps, it sounds strange and contradictory, but I have my moral principles which I consider it to be more important than my political beliefs' (Hegedűs, 1985).

In consideration of this, it can be argued that dealing with the Kunos case, Göncz pursued a liberal line guided by his own principles which emphasised that every citizen, including wrongdoers, ought to be treated equally before the law.

6.2.5. *The Law on Organised Crime*

The final issue which Göncz became involved in was the Law on Organised Crime. Aiming to tackle organised crime more efficiently, the Orbán government adopted 'Act LXXV of 1999 on the Combat Against Organised Crime and the Related Phenomena and the Amendment of Related Acts of Parliament' (hereafter the Anti-Mafia Package).[33] Göncz, however, returned the Anti-Mafia Package to the Constitutional Court. The controversy which followed was not as significant as that which occurred after the Kunos case, but this issue clearly demonstrated where Göncz's political values lay.

In its electoral manifesto, the AYD stated their commitment to the enhancement of public security and their intention to tackle crimes more effectively (Kurtán, Sándor and Vass, 1999: 867–8). Having noted that the Horn government had not dealt sufficiently well with crime, public safety was an issue which needed to be addressed (Fricz, 2001: 527), the AYD pledged that they would take these issues more seriously. Subsequently, the Orbán government took office and the parliamentary constitutional committee prepared a draft law which was submitted to Parliament in November 1998 for consideration (*Népszabadság*, 10 November 1998). In effect, the Orbán government tightened the law by making a major amendment, which altered more than 100 clauses in the penal code (*Népszabadság*, 10 November 1998) and other related Acts.[34] According to the modified law,

186 *The post-Communist presidency*

for example, crimes concerned with illegal weapon trades, prostitution, human trafficking, border control, money laundering, child and drug abuse and others were subject to heavy punishment.

The main problem was that, in order to implement this toughened law, the government would have to rely on the support of the opposition, given that the amendment of Acts for the regulation of the Police, Aliens and Asylum seekers belonged in the category of legislation which required a two-thirds majority vote.[35] Despite this legal requirement having to be met, on 21 December 1998, the Orbán government decided that the Anti-Mafia Package could be amended with by a simple majority (*Magyar Dokumentáció*, December 1998; *Népszabadság* 22 December 1998). The government reasoned that a simple majority rule could be applied to altering the penal code, as long as it did not affect the fundamentals of the law (*Napi Magyarország*, 28 December 1998; *Népszabadság*, 9 January 1999). In contrast, the opposition members, the HSP and the AFD, argued that the law which required a 'qualified majority' and could not be amended with a simple majority (*Népszabadság*, 9 January 1999).

Given that no agreement was possible, Prime Minister Viktor Orbán asked Göncz to refer the law to the Constitutional Court. Upon Orbán's request, on 8 January 1999, Göncz called on the Court (*Magyar Nemzet*, 9 January 1999), asking whether the law in question could be amended with a simple majority. On 23 February 1999, the Court ruled that the Acts previously passed by a qualified majority could not be altered with a simple majority (Sereg, 1999).

Central to the division of opinions on the Anti-Mafia Package was the question of how the qualified majority rule should be applied to the alteration of laws. More specifically, the decision-making rule should have succinctly defined whether the following Acts – the Police, Alien and Asylum – could be modified by a simple majority, if amendment did not affect the fundamentals of those laws. Surprisingly, however, the Constitution did not provide a clear path of action and this gap within the basic law contributed to legal disputes among MPs. For example, the Constitution dictated that the adoption of the Police Act required a two-thirds majority vote.[36] This legal statement, however, does not provide the relevant guidelines as to which a decision-making rule applied to the amendment of the Police Act: a two-thirds majority vote or simple majority vote. Thus, this legal lacuna left considerable leeway for various interpretations. For example, should the Orbán government consider that strengthening the police's criminal monitoring powers belonged in the sub-category of the Police Act, they could amend the law with a simple majority.

In contrast, should the opposition regard that altering the surveillance rights of the police was a fundamental change affecting the entire Police Act, they would insist on keeping the qualified majority rule. Therefore, without clarifying the decision-making rule regarding the amendment of legislation, legal disputes among MPs would be likely to occur. It should be noted that in 1999, even when the political row over the amendment of Anti-Mafia Package was ended by the Court's ruling, the issue of interpretation was still raised by a judge of the Constitutional Court, Lábady Tamás. In his dissenting view, Tamás argued that the Court should have 'examined each provision of the Anti-Mafia Package separately to determine which articles required passage by qualified majority' (EECR, 1999 Summer).

Göncz, in using his constitutional veto, seems to have been influenced by the desire to pursue a consensual decision making process within Parliament. This preference has clearly been evident throughout Göncz's presidency which has encompassed three different governments (as exemplified by his actions in the event of the taxi-drivers' strike, the issue of dealing with the Communist past and the Privatisation Law). Having noted this, the way in which the Orbán government dealt with the Anti-Mafia Package – the Orbán government's preference for the expression of majoritarian rule – would have conflicted with Göncz's political beliefs. The question is, then, how would Göncz express his discontent with the government's approach and simultaneously help to end this political row? Göncz seems to have opted for a constitutional solution, given that the cause of the disagreement lay in MPs' differing legal interpretations of the law. It is possible to ask for what reason the opposition did not bring the issue to the Court's attention themselves. However, according to a rule adopted in 1998, after the final voting on any legislation, only the president can ask for a preliminary judicial review (Halmai, 2002: 25; Petrétei, 2001b: 148); without his involvement, the row could not have been resolved.[37]

One may argue that Göncz simply initiated the constitutional review proceedings at Orbán's request. Even if this was the case, Göncz did not have to comply if he did not agree with the necessity for the referral. Indeed, Göncz's comments on the Law on Organised Crime (particularly with reference to the decision-making rule) highlights the fact that he had an opinion on how to resolve the issue of the Anti-Mafia Package. On 29 December 1998, when Göncz wrote a letter to the Constitutional Court, he made the following statement:

> The president of the Republic initiated the review of Sections 12–24, 36–37, Sections 46–49, 50 and 54 of the Act on Organised Crime in respect of whether *they have been adopted in a constitutional procedural way, with the required proportion of votes*, taking into account Article 40/A paras (1) and (2), Article 58 para. (3) and Article 65 para. (2) of the Constitution. [author's emphasis][38]

The relevant clauses within the Constitution pinpointed by Göncz were about the duty of the police and armed forces, fundamental human rights and the detailed regulations of the size of majority over the passage of Asylum Act. According to these specific comments, Göncz clearly had his conception regarding the way in which the Court should examine the law in question during the judicial review process. For example, according to the selected clauses, Göncz seemed not only have sought to address the question of a decision-making rule, but also regarded other issues on which the law might potentially have had an impact. This possibility was evidenced through Göncz's comments on whether the amendment of the Law on Organised Crime could be harmonised with the basic principle of human rights guaranteed by the Constitution. As discussed above, the strengthening of police surveillance power was one of the amendments made in the Anti-Mafia Package. Göncz, however, questioned whether this toughened rule could contravene clause 58(3) of the Constitution which guaranteed the right of freedom of movement and residence. Given these specific points and details spelled out by Göncz, it is unreasonable to suggest that Göncz simply acted in favour of the Orbán government's decision. On the contrary, it can be argued that Göncz's veto of the Anti-Mafia Package was an act guided by the important political principles and values he upheld.

In terms of Göncz's desire to pursue consensual decision making within the Parliament, however, there is still a question mark over his silence on the issue of the new rules of the House. In Section 6.1 it was established that the Orbán government had unilaterally decided to reduce the frequency of plenums in Parliament. This move would have been irreconcilable with Göncz's political beliefs, and arguably, it can be seen as an anti-democratic action. However, Göncz did not intervene in this issue chosing instead to remain silent. Körösényi observed that:

> On the issue of the new rules of the House, Göncz would and perhaps should have stated his position. Even if this [rule] did not contravene the Constitution, it at least damaged the spirit of parliamentarism. But to my memory, Göncz did not state his position. This indicates that he [was in the process of] withdrawing from politics . . . At the end of his term, he was very passive.
>
> (Interview with Körösényi, 11 July 2007)

According to Körösényi, Göncz's inactivity was not only evident with regard to the issue of the new parliamentary rule, but it also informed his latter presidential term. In fact, as has already been examined in Section 6.1, this diminished political activism was the general characteristic of Göncz's second presidency and is well-documented in the literature. What, then, explains his changed presidential style? The following section of the chapter probes and addresses this important question by examining three explanatory factors.

6.3. Explanation for Göncz's diminished political activism

According to articles discovered in the Hungarian literature and accounts offered by my interviewees, there are three primary factors responsible for Göncz's diminished political activities. First, the decline of Göncz's mental and physical strengths and capacities may have contributed to the reduction of his activities. Despite the fact that Göncz was in good general health, former chief secretary of the presidential office, Mária Tóth, noted: 'It is possible to assume that Göncz felt more tired during the second term of his presidency . . . albeit he had no serious illness [at any time] during the term of his presidency' (interview with Tóth, 4 September 2007). Tóth would have had an opportunity to observe the president's physical condition on an almost daily basis. However, even if one gives credence to her account, its objectivity is perhaps questionable given her position within the presidential office. It is the normal practice of politics for presidential staff to assess a president's decision-making capacity (including physical status) more favourably than non-staff members might; it is possible that Tóth's assessment is somewhat biased towards Göncz.

Indeed, according to articles published in the Hungarian press, there were signs that Göncz had health problems. In December 1997 Göncz was hospitalised for two weeks for the treatment of dyspnoea and a duodenal ulcer (Dobszay, 1998; *Népszabadság,* 20 December 1997). Since this sick leave did not last long, the issues associated with presidential incapacity were not seriously debated by political elites at the time. However, given that Göncz had no similar health problem at any time during the first term of his presidency,[39] it highlights the fact that there was a change in his physical condition. Göncz's ailing status could be attributed to his hard working lifestyle. It was noted in the Hungarian press that:

> Göncz works very hard from 8 am to 5 pm everyday. He reads almost all the available newspapers. He always writes speeches for himself. His [advisors] complain that they could not dissuade him from personally exchanging letters with Hungarian citizens.
>
> (Somos, 1997a)

Considering his advanced age (73–78 years old during the second term of his presidency), the performance of official and unofficial presidential tasks would not have been easy for him. A great number of Hungarian academics have pointed to this issue (interviews with Körösényi, Lánczi, Lengyel, Rainer, Somogyvári and Stumpf), but the following accounts are of particular relevance. János Rainer stated that: 'With the passage of time, one's activity diminishes . . . It is not possible that Göncz became suddenly exhausted. This was a process that started earlier, and something contributed to the development of this process' (interview with Rainer, 22 August 2007).Similarly but more explicitly, László Lengyel held the view that:

> During the Orbán government, many questioned why Göncz did not exhibit his proactive balancing role against this government. I think one of the most important [factors] indeed lay in his tiredness . . . The seven years of presiden[cy] made this old man feel extremely tired. During the first presidential term, he was terribly stressed out, [because of] political conflicts. This was an awful life.
>
> (Interview with Lengyel, 13 September 2007)

Thus, age or ill health could have been a factor which contributed to Göncz's reduced political activism. However, it is possible that this was not the primary factor and there are other elements to be taken into account.

A second, and perhaps more important, cause of Göncz's diminished political activities lies in the clarification of the president's constitutional competence.

190 *The post-Communist presidency*

The essence of this argument is that the Constitutional Court played a key role in curtailing presidential powers (Oltay, 1992: 19–20; Paczolay, 1993: 39—3; Pataki and Schiemann, 1991: 5–9; Schwartz, 2000: 83–5), and this contributed to the change in Göncz's perception of the president's role. In order to better understand why the Court's ruling was significant here, we need to step back and revisit the main points of the previous chapter. In Chapter 5, it was noted that during the first presidential term, Göncz undertook a proactive counter-balancing role to the Antall government. Far from being the symbolic figurehead that his ceremonial and nominal role might have suggested, Göncz became involved in a series of issues and events, and made clear that he had his own agenda to fulfil. This was expressed in his public statements, speeches, and through challenging various legislation passed in Parliament. As has been argued, this activism was informed by Göncz's desire to pursue his liberal and democratic beliefs that developed throughout his life.

However, his proactive presidential style became subject to controversy and sharp criticism with centred on whether Göncz had ever overstepped the constitutional boundaries of his role. In particular, two issues – who controls the Hungarian army and who has a right to appoint and dismiss state officials – were heavily disputed among political elites and legal experts alike. In both cases the Court concluded that these areas of interest fell under the jurisdiction of the prime minister or responsible ministers. With these decisions, the scope of presidential power was clarified and Göncz had to manoeuvre within newly delineated constitutional boundaries. Indeed, if one examines Göncz's understanding of the president's role by comparing his view of it before and after the Court's ruling, it becomes clear that the range and type of his subsequent political activism was influenced by the Court's decision.

In an interview with Hegedűs conducted on 14 July 1990, for example, Göncz stated his initial position regarding who had the right to mobilise the Hungarian army:

Hegedűs: Does the commander-in-chief belong to your jurisdiction or Parliament?
Göncz: It lies under the jurisdiction of the president.
Hegedűs: Does the parliamentary committee supervise the Hungarian army?
Göncz: Yes. I think the Prime Minister is also responsible for the supervision of Hungarian army.

(Hegedűs, 1990)

Considering the timing of the given interview, it is hardly surprising that Göncz, intervened in the taxi-drivers' strike (which took place in autumn 1990) with reference to the military mobilisation right. The Court, however, curtailed this power, stating that the president cannot rule on his own actions which implies that this responsibility is only nominal (see Section 5.2.1). Similarly, regarding the president's right to appoint and dismiss the heads of public media institutions, Göncz adhered to the position that it fell within his constitutional competence or at least he thought that consensus-based decision making was required. Before the Court brought its decision over the president's right to implement personnel management, Göncz thought that: 'Regarding the appointment of national media [institutions' heads] or the right of being the commander-in-chief, [a decision] can be reached only through consensus between the president and the premier' (Debreczeni, 2003: 304).

This once again highlights the fact that Göncz indeed considered the president's right of appointment to be operative. According to Göncz's understanding, the Law on Appointment – at the suggestion of the prime minister, the president appoints and dismisses the heads of public media – was a shared role; thus the president could legitimately participate in decisions regarding the distribution of frontline media appointments. However, the Court again curtailed this power, reasoning that 'the president should not withhold his signature from the appointments and dismissals of leaders of state institutions requested by the prime minister, unless those suggestions endanger the democratic functioning of the state institutions involved' (see Section 5.2.5). With these decisions, the vagaries associated with the president's constitutional competency and the overlaps with other political players were clarified and, this contributed to the change of Göncz's initial position on the president's role. In response to my question,[40] political scientist Attila Ágh reaffirmed the contention, stating:

> Let's look at history. Göncz was the first [post-Communist] president. There was no established constitutional rule regarding the president's role. There was a general rule in the Constitution but it was not clarified regarding the [extent of the] president's powers . . . . For example, according to the Constitution, the president is the commander-in-chief. But the question was what this meant in practice? The Court decided that the president is not politically responsible for his action, so he cannot make a real decision . . . As far as the right to appoint the heads of public radio and television goes, the Court once again decided in favour of the government's [position]. Or the [concept] of a passive presidency was born . . . The Court ruled that in Hungary there is a strong government but no dual executive. The president is not part of the Executive. This is almost a symbolic president. After this ruling, very few political conflicts arose because the president's competence had been clarified . . . With this clarification, Göncz said, '*it is all right. I understood my role and moved within his constitutional boundaries*'.
> (Interview with Ágh, 3 October 2007, my emphasis).

As Ágh contended, if the scope of presidential power was clarified by the Court's ruling, Göncz would move within narrowly defined constitutional boundaries. Moreover, this newly regulated and comparatively weak presidential model would remain in his political consciousness. Göncz's own view was put across in the Hungarian press and, indeed, supports the argument that the Court's decisions altered Göncz's perception on the role of the president.[41] In an interview with *168 Óra,* Göncz stated his position regarding what the Court's rulings meant for him:

> The Constitutional Court narrowed down [the scope] of my jurisdiction . . . I was only allowed to make my decision with the counter-signatures of Ministers . . . With the passage of time, it became clear to me that the president *has no power but only a voice [szó]*.
>
> (Mester, 2000, my emphasis)

Similarly, but more explicitly, in response to a reporter's question – 'How have you enjoyed your role as president of the Republic?' – Göncz upheld the position, stating that:

> In my opinion, *the president has no power* . . . If the role [comes with any power] then that is a reflection of the existing [power] relations [between other political actors] . . . There were two occasions [of jurisdictional disputes] in which I confronted the government. One concerned the question of being the commander-in-chief. This was clarified by the Court's [ruling]. Another was the Right of Appointment and this was also forwarded to the Court. But who would expect that this kind of fierce dispute could have occurred as a consequence of the taxi blockade and the issue of appointment of public media bosses . . . In any case, *within the first four years the Court [clearly] demarcated the scope of presidential manoeuvre*.
>
> (Wisinger and László, 2007: 327–8, my emphasis)

Thus, it can be concluded that the change in Göncz's conception of the president's role and power was informed by the Court's decisions.

The final element contributing to the alteration of Göncz's presidential role can be found in the nature of Hungarian democracy. More precisely, Göncz's earlier proactive role was a function of Hungary's inexperience vis-a-vis democracy. To better comprehend why this factor influenced Göncz's thinking on the presidential role, it is worth briefly looking into the country's prior democratic history. Traditionally, Hungary had little experience of the presidential governance (Kukorelli, 1995: 210; Sükösd, 1996: 347; Szoboszlai, 1996: 122). The first presidential model came to being on 11 January 1919 with the election of Count Mihály Károly (Feitl and Kende, 2007: 197). Károly's Republic, however, was short-lived; owing to the subsequent establishment of the Soviet Republic under Béla Kun (which itself lasted only 100 days). Thereafter, Admiral Miklós Horthy ruled as regent along with numerous prime ministers until the end of the Second World War. With the end of the War, the so-called Little Constitution – formalised as Act I of 1946 – was adopted as a fundamental form of the presidency (Kovács, 2001: 352; Sükösd, 1996: 347). According to this Act, the president was to be elected by Parliament for four years. The ISP chairman, Zoltán Tildy filled the position and was succeded by a Social Democrat leader, Árpád Szakasits (Feitl and Kende, 2007: 198–201). Their presidencies, however, only lasted for three years until 1949, as the Little Constitution was superseded by the first codified Constitution – the Communist Constitution. Thus, from 1919 until 1989, the conception of the president's role and power was not entrenched in the minds of political elites or the Hungarian population. Instead, as Taras notes, 'the succession of undistinguished prime ministers may have, if anything, moulded Hungarian political culture into a less leadership-conscious system than elsewhere in the region' (Taras, 1993: 165).

In this circumstance, Göncz, who was elected as the first post-Communist president had no prior example to follow. Despite the fact that the amended Constitution of Act XX of 1949 provided a set of general rules and stipulations regarding presidential powers on paper, the practical meaning of these remained unclear. The main issue was, however, that defining or interpreting the Constitutional texts was problematic, as the first generation of post-Communist elites themselves had no prior experience or established norms of practice to follow. Consequently, during the initial stage of the so-called 'democratic institution-building' process (Ágh, 1998: 84–96, 2001a: 90–3),[42] conflicts among political players would be more likely to occur. Political scientist David Olson observed the inherent characteristics of Eastern European democracies:

> In the new democracies . . . nothing is settled: neither the powers of offices within the regime, nor the relationship among them – especially among the major offices and institutions of president, parliament, and prime minister . . . The executive office is a temporary arrangement grafted on a residual constitution of the Communist era. The powers of the office are largely undefined, and the options available to it are more a function of contemporary exigencies than established practice.
> (Olson, 1994: 36)

Thus, 'in a consolidated democracy, the rules of politics have been fixed and, debate over constitutional change mostly relates to fine-tuning' (Henderson and Robinson, 1997: 175), whereas in post-Communist states, 'this stage has yet to be reached' (ibid). In this respect, it is hardly surprising that Göncz became involved in conflicts and confrontations with other political actors. According to Olson, political skirmishes and jurisdictional disputes among political elites would continuously occur until routinised political practice or the code of political behaviour came to be fairly established in the political culture. Within the Hungarian context, by a process of trial and error under the first term of Göncz's presidency, such a step was more or less completed. As has already been discussed, during this period, the Constitutional Court played a key role in settling jurisdictional disputes among political players which, in turn, led to the clarification of constitutional competences. Subsequently, Göncz, who had also identified and located his own role and position within the new democratic constitutional order, became less involved in political frictions. István Somogyvári aptly captured the way in which the issue of 'newness'– or the country's lack of democratic experience – developed into conflicts among political actors when they variously interpreted the Constitution. Somogyvári noted:

> All institutions tried to find their roles . . . When political institutions began to operate, Parliament, the Constitutional Court and the president tried to find their roles and boundaries through interpretation of the Constitution . . . When the president interpreted the Constitution to mean that he had a real right to oppose the premier's decisions, the text of the Constitution provided such a basis which could develop into a jurisdictional debate. It was not clear what the roles of the prime minister and the president meant. The president judged that he had a real right to veto the premier's decisions. But the Court ruled that it is not so . . . It is natural to see that the prime Minister, government, Parliament, the Court and the president tried to find their roles. A new constitutional order had to be put into operation and through this process, the increase [in the number] of conflicts was natural, [because] the real function of each institution was shaped through conflicts . . .[43] *I am saying this because in a new democracy, this was not at all surprising.*
>
> (Interview with Somogyvári, 22 May 2007, my emphasis)

Thus, having completed the initiation period that Hungary's transitional democracy had to face, Göncz – along with other political players – gradually became familiar with their roles, functions and limitations of power which, in turn, contributed to the establishing patterns of political practice and behaviour. In fact, Göncz also pointed to the 'newness' issue as a fundamental question that Hungary's nascent democracy had to address at the time. Göncz recounted that:

> The Constitution in use today – the modified version of the old one – was created by three parties, those who sat down at the Round Table Negotiation . . . It was not possible to know who would win the [founding general] election. But it was to their credit that they succeeded in creating such a Constitution which was correct and served as guarantees against excessive power which might give an opportunity to upset the established political balance arbitrarily . . . [But] there is no perfect Constitution. It was not possible to think of every condition and to [presuppose] all [possible] situations to determine every necessary precise regulation about the complicated [matters] . . . In particular, this was the case [with regard to] the presidential post which up to that point had no established tradition, [in terms of] what is possible, not possible and what is allowed and not allowed. Also, what concrete problems this situation might raise?
>
> (Wisinger and László, 2007: 327–8)

It is clear that the country's lack of democratic experience remained as a question in Göncz's political consciousness. On the one hand, Göncz took the view that in the course of the political transformation to democracy, Hungary managed to formulate basic law which was not overtly weighted towards one particular political force. On the other hand, he considered that such a balanced constitutional arrangement contained inconsistencies regarding the delineation of presidential compe-

The second presidency (1995–2000)   195

tences. According to Göncz, the locus of the existing problem lay in the country's inexperience vis-a-vis presidential governance. Göncz did not directly mention that the issue of newness arising from the country's inexperienced democracy was an inherent weakness and challenge that needed to be overcome. However, it is fair to suggest that the first transitional period of post-Communist democracy carried an importance, as it would pave the way for establishing a fundamental framework and blue-print for the next generation of political elites to follow. In fact, in an interview with *Magyar Hírlap*, Göncz stressed how significant the first four years of the post-Communist democratic experience were:

Göncz: Previously, Hungary was not a Republic, so there was no tradition of the presidency and no example of the president's [role] or [what] power the president [possessed]. The Constitution circumscribed the president's powers very [tightly] and left him [certain room for] manoeuvre in order to make decisions and [take] action. [But] these were again curtailed by the Constitutional Court during the Antall government [. . .].

Newspaper interviewer: In legal terms, this is a weak presidency.

Göncz: Yes. By the end of the Antall government, *[politicians] eventually learned by experience and understood the scope for manoeuvre [available to them]* . . . It became clear that the only [effective] instrument of power that remained available to the president was his voice.

(Szále, 2003, my emphasis)

Thus, if 'a nation's politics is tamed or [consolidated] only when broad support for democratic procedures and institutions, as well as a shared acceptance of norms of accommodation and cooperation, develop among political elites' (Higley, Kullberg and Pakulski, 1996: 133), the first four years' transitional period was the rite of passage that post-Communist Hungary's politics had to undergo. This basic but essential experience ultimately contributed to the refining of a set of new rules, roles and ideas that post-Communist elites conceived differently at the initial stage of democratic transformation. Taking all these into account, it can be concluded that all three factors discussed above – the issues of ill health, of the country's democratic inexperience and the clarification of constitutional competences refined by the Court's decisions – were all behind Göncz's diminished political activism or his weak presidential role. Göncz's own views and thoughts regarding his experience as the head of state, delivered in his retirement speech, are appropriate for concluding this exploration of Göncz's post-Communist presidency:

Ten years ago, Parliament [elected] me to the Office of the President of the Republic – the first servant of the Hungarian population . . . The Constitution precisely defined the character of the Office and task of the Office-holder. The president represents the unity of the nation and safeguards the democratic functioning of state institutions above party politics. [The right] to represent and safeguard – is not the [same as the exercise of] power. Even the Constitution obliges the president to [have] a minister's counter-signature [for the exercise] of [issuing] a pardon. [When] the president has reservations about the constitutionality of laws, he can only [express this] [through] sending it to Parliament [for reconsideration] or the Constitutional Court. The Constitution vests the president with real power only in extraordinary circumstances or [in the event of the outbreak] of war [. . .].

His [voice] – the convincing power of the truth – thus only supports confidence in the [presidential] service. This voice expresses the desires and anxieties of the Hungarian population, the majority of whom are the rich and poor and the literate and illiterate alike. If he does [this], the president is the living conscience of the country, and possibly become a mediator of the people. He is responsible for the people in terms of moral aspect [. . .].

. . . The only instrument to me was [my] voice. It is possible that I made mistakes more than once. It is possible that I spoke out in [a situation] in which I should not have done so. It is possible that I remained silent when I had to say. But, silence sometimes speaks louder than words [. . .].

I worked with four governments altogether. I did not agree with any of them in every regard. But there is no reason or right to doubt their goodwill . . . I am indebted to the achievement the four governments have made. I am indebted to the country for its resolute [attitude] towards the future. And I am grateful for the citizens who living beyond our border, my Hungarian brothers for their [respect] and love.

Finally let me say one sentence. With the help of the God, in the last day of my ten years' working day, I can say this:

Thank you Hungary!

(*Népszava*, 4 August 2000)

Conclusion

In reminiscing about his life, Göncz came to the following conclusion:

> I was often asked later why an agronomist had needed to be a welder, why welding called for a law degree. These questions were often coming up. I was a loner throughout my life. I went everywhere *without the grounding*, but *always by outside compulsion*.
>
> (Tóth, 2009, my emphasis)

It appears from Göncz's statement that he wished to suggest that the life course he chose was forged as a result of the external pressure he experienced and the circumstances which surrounded him, as he merely drifted into the situation he now occupies. Perhaps, to some extent, this was true as Göncz's life has been marked by the many twists and turns of his career; by his mid thirties, he had already experienced the life of a student in the resistance movement, a junior politician, a steelworker, an agriculturalist and a 1956 revolutionary (Chapters 1 and 2). For this varied career, the social and political circumstances such as the outbreak of the 1956 Hungarian Revolution were certainly an important factor which influenced his subsequent life course (imprisonment and the pursuit of a literary career thereafter).

The important decisions that Göncz made, however, were neither coincidental nor simply a result of a nebulous external pressure. As an intellectual, he had his own principles and beliefs and there was always room for Göncz to make his own decisions. In fact, when analysing Göncz's life particularly in terms of the values he committed to consistently, it becomes apparent that he strove after his ideals throughout his life. The practical application of these ideals resulted in his attempts to address different social issues of the age (as discussed in Chapters 1, 2 and 3), Göncz sought to realise his ideals by finding, and applying himself to, specific roles in the key social and political movements. In order to understand why Göncz struggled for democracy and its values, this chapter revisits the main arguments of preceding chapters and assesses them critically in order to draw them together as a conclusion. Ultimately, the chapter probes the significance of Göncz's political experiences and their implications for the understanding of contemporary Hungarian politics and its democratic development. To this end, I will begin the conclusion by addressing the main research questions raised in the introduction of the book.

Göncz's political developments before his election to the post-Communist presidency

The following questions have been identified and raised in this book: First, from where did Göncz's political ideals originate and what form did they take? Second, in which ways did Göncz seek to translate his political ideals into practice? Last, with regard to Hungary's transformation to democracy, what did Göncz seek to achieve and what did he actually accomplish as the first post-Communist president of the Republic of Hungary?

In contrast to József Antall, whose intellectual and political foundation originated in and was significantly informed by his privileged family tradition, especially from his father's success as a politician (Debreczeni, 2003: 15), the genesis of Göncz's political beliefs was not in his family but the circle, clubs and social movement in which he participated and his first-hand experiences of the struggle against the autocratic rule of the age. Interestingly, the first important activity in which Göncz engaged during his formative period and which had a crucial impact on the shape of his social and political outlook was his scouting experience. Fostering a constructive social basis of well rounded and responsible citizens was the main goal and founding percept of the Scout movement when it was established in the United Kingdom (as discussed in Section 1.1). The Hungarian version of scouting in which Göncz participated, however, had a different significance for him especially in terms of the development of his social consciousness.

Born in Budapest, Göncz had not had an opportunity to observe the situation of rural society and discover the living conditions and social milieu in which the vast majority of the Hungarian population (landless peasants) lived during the inter-war period. Göncz's scouting experience in rural areas and, more importantly, his access to the literature of populist writers, had a crucial impact on him in this regard. The peasant populist literature Göncz accessed suggested that the structure of Hungarian society was largely semi-feudal in character and rural areas particularly fell outside the scope of modernisation. By virtue of wealth and superior education, the aristocracy and landed nobility held important posts in the state administration and possessed the significant portion of arable land. In contrast, the peasants had no land to cultivate and no access to credit and social benefits; in effect, their interests had been unjustly denied in the existing social order (The Horthy Regency March 1920–November 1944). 'The land of three million beggars' (Tóth, 1999: 145) was well representative of the unbearable living conditions of the pauperised peasantry and the indifference of ruling elite towards the issue. Above all, Göncz realised that there was a moral imperative for radical social change and, land reform was seen as the key to resolving pressing social need. As concluded in Chapter 1, the impact of the ideas of peasant populism on Göncz's political views remained enduringly significant, leading him to pursue peasant populist ideas thereafter. Göncz's attendance at the PTWG social debate forum, his decision to become a member of the ISP, his agricultural study and his career as an agronomist and, more importantly, his emphasis on the importance of education for peasants as well as his critique regarding the inadequacy of Soviet farming model in Hungary which delivered a speech in the Petőfi Circle, all testify to Göncz's attachment to the significance of peasant populism during early years of his life.

Concerning the origin of Göncz's liberal values, his first-hand experiences of the struggle against Nazism during the inter-war period and the Hungarian variant of Communism has been discussed in depth. As a whole, the analysis conducted in Part I of the book led to the conclusion that Göncz's resistance to these extreme forms of political ideology contributed to the shaping of his liberal democratic beliefs. Moreover, it became evident that Göncz's liberal political beliefs did not fit neatly into a particular political ideology or clear-cut platform; something that was expressed through his preference for the free market rather than the state's interventionist economic policy. Göncz's conception of liberal values was universal which, from the perspective of today, is representative of civic or human rights. The common values which were evidenced and highlighted by Göncz's actions in the anti-Nazi student movement and his role following the suppression of the 1956 Revolution lay in his commitment to the realisation of an independent, democratic and socially responsible society. As concluded in Part I, Göncz's desire to pursue liberal values in these resistance activities remained of the utmost significance, while his earlier political preference for the ideas of peasant populism receded into the background. In turn, the process of the shift in his political orientation towards liberal values was very visible.

Thus, by the late 1980s, Göncz was able to draw his own conclusion that, for him, peasant populism had lost its contemporary relevance, although his emotional attachment to its ideals remained in his political beliefs (as evidenced by his participation in the founding of the re-constructed ISP at the Pilvax Coffee House). Instead, Göncz's preference for liberal values over peasant populism was marked and this was clearly expressed by his participation in the founding of the NFI (an alliance of civic groups and associations) and his statement on liberal democracy. According to Göncz, liberal democracy referred to an institutional system in which different political visions and varied values could co-exist (as discussed in Section 3.2). At the core of his conception of democracy, pluralism based on mutual understanding and tolerance of varied values appreciated by members of society was thus deeply entrenched within it. Göncz expressed this conviction when he took the initiative for the founding of the NFI, where he stressed the importance of the promotion of political plurality in the wider Hungarian society.

From the analysis of Göncz's political beliefs, it became apparent that the populist-liberal elements were entrenched in his political beliefs and his desire to pursue its ideals was expressed through his actions. But then what does the co-existence of these values mean in practice in understanding Göncz's contribution to Hungarian politics?

When analysing the main features of Göncz's political beliefs, what distinguishes him from any other Hungarian politician is that the formation of his democratic ideals was neither informed by a particular political ideology nor took a specific form that might have fitted into Hungarian political tradition. Certainly, his attachment to the ideas of peasant populism and those of liberal democracy were expressed by his actions, decisions and proactive role undertaken during his life. Göncz's leaning towards the 'populist-liberal' or rural–urban values, however, is interesting in itself as these two values have been considered as oppositional or antithetical in character in Hungarian intellectual and political culture. In fact, according to the literature pertaining to Hungary's political system, this division has been considered as one of the defining political cleavages established in Hungarian politics (Elster et al., 1998: 131–6; Körösényi et al., 2003: 135–46; Szarvas, 1994: 12–5).

The populists who saw themselves as a successor to the populist movement in the 1930s largely constituted 'self-educated provincial intellectuals' of peasant origins (Tőkés, 1996: 176). At the core of their values, Hungarian tradition based in the virtue of agriculture, peasants and 'of rural and village life' was deeply entrenched; politically they were of a 'nationalist and anti-capitalist' outlook (Falk, 2003: 431). Their primary concern was the fate of the Hungarian minority who lived beyond its neighbouring border. For the representation of their interests and values, the populist founded the HDF at Lakitelek in 1987 (as discussed in Section 3.1). In contrast, the liberals broadly 'drawing on the bourgeois urbanist tradition of political thought and literature' (Romsics, 1999: 415) were 'disproportionally Jewish' (Falk, 2003: 126) and politically they were of a liberal and cosmopolitan outlook. The guarantee of human rights including press freedom and the freedom of speech was placed at the core of their values and, the Hungarian minority issue was dealt with as a matter of universal human rights. As discussed in Section 3.1, in reaction to the founding of the HDF, the liberals founded their own political platform through the NFI and later transformed into the AFD. In brief, given their different political orientations and varied values established in their political and intellectual culture, the populist-liberal combination is inherently incompatible or irreconcilable.

In the fabric of Göncz's political beliefs, however, these two oppositional elements had been deeply entrenched and consistently remained as defining features for him and his beliefs. Of course, as noted above, Göncz's attachment to the ideas of peasant populism was overtaken by his pursuit of liberal democracy (prominently so after his involvement in the resistance of 1956 and dissident movements of the 1980s). Despite this, it is important to remember that along with his evident political preference for liberal values, the significance of peasant populism remained consistently within his political beliefs. András Körösényi noted the peculiarity of Göncz's political orientation:

> Göncz was a person who had a link to the populist and liberal camp. He had the link to the sub-culture of the populist intellectuals and that of the liberal intellectuals. It is true the populists founded the HDF, whereas the urbanists

founded the AFD. But there were people who did not entirely fit into each camp, rather an odd mixture . . . Indeed, Göncz was the figure who could fall within both camps.

(Interview with Körösényi, 11 July 2007)

Similarly, András Lánczi held the view that:

Göncz brought the populist element to the AFD. Within the AFD, it had never been nurtured naturally. In its platform, the populist line is not visible. But Göncz had the capability to make a link to this direction and indeed it was gleaned through him . . . The populist-liberal is not a usual concept. It is an unusual combination . . . and it is Göncz's phenomenon.

(Interview with Lánczi, 12 July 2007)

In practice, this means that the co-existence of populist-liberal values gave rise to an image of Göncz the image of him *not* as the figure who represented the narrow interests of a party or its programme, but who might act as mediator between the two oppositional camps. Indeed, as discussed in Section 4.2.3, this perceived image of Göncz was one of the most important contributory factors that led to his election as president of the Republic. According to the result of the first post-transitional parliamentary election, the HDF could have elected their presidential candidate, Sándor Csoóri (the leading figurehead of the populist writers). Yet, Antall considered that the presidential post chaired by Csoóri could be misused to challenge his authority and instead found an alternative figure. Given Göncz's previously populist leaning (in view of Göncz's working experience as a junior politician at the ISP) and their joint actions during the resistance of 1956 (in the matter of the collection of signatories to support Bibó's Draft Proposal), Antall had good reason to assume that Göncz's position in the AFD could be acceptable. Thus, even if Göncz's proactive role in the founding of the AFD (the HDF's rival) was somehow acknowledged by Antall and his camp, Göncz was accepted as the president. Antall expected Göncz to play a symbolic presidential role, while leaving the real affairs of state to his government. However, as we have seen in Chapter 5, Göncz did not interpret the role of the president in the manner that Antall expected. On the contrary, Göncz clearly demonstrated his liberal political principles and that he had his own agenda and issues and would not simply undertake a ceremonial presidential role. The main characteristics of Göncz's presidency including his interpretation of the presidential role and responsibility and the significance of his values are re-assessed in terms of his contribution to Hungary's democratic development in the conclusion of the book. Before then, having examined the nature of Göncz's political beliefs and its practical meaning, it is necessary to explore the significance of the way in which he sought to realise his political beliefs.

In terms of Göncz's pursuit of liberal and democratic political beliefs, prior to his election to the post-Communist presidency, Göncz had two chances to translate his ideals into practice. One was through his participation in the anti-Nazi student resistance movement and another was in resistance that followed the defeat of the 1956 Revolution. On both occasions, his ideals were defeated but his resistance to the inequity of the established order highlights the values that he upheld.

First, as concluded in Section 1.3, Göncz's involvement in the student armed-resistance movement served as a catalyst which contributed to the development of his liberal and democratic beliefs. Near the end of the Second World War, during the Hungarian fascist Szalási regime, Göncz was conscripted into the Hungarian army. He served in the 25th Infantry Battalion but, upon realising that this was not a war he wished to commit to, he soon deserted his military posting. Instead, he found his role in the civil resistance movement which consisted of a few hundred individuals hailing from a wide range of political and social backgrounds. Different groups conceived differing strategies to fight against the German troops and their varying political affiliations were barely subjugated to their anti-Nazi sentiment. According to Göncz, however, a common denominator which bound them together existed; this was their desire to create a free, independent and humane society. Having appreciated these goals and shared the sense of responsibility, Göncz decided to commit himself to the resistance movement.

Similarly, and more importantly, in autumn 1956 when the Hungarian population posed a revolutionary challenge to the ruling Communist regime, Göncz once again clearly demonstrated the stance he stood with and the goals he sought to achieve. Initially Göncz was uncertain about whether the events of 1956 were serving the interests of a particular group or a national upsurge that arose from the aspirations of the Hungarian population. Upon realising that the Revolution was the genuine manifestation of popular will (the will of which sought to construct an independent, democratic and socially responsible society), Göncz decided to commit himself to the resistance that followed the suppression of the Revolution. Beginning with conveying István Bibó's Draft Proposal to the Indian Embassy, continuing with the smuggling of Imre Nagy's manuscript out to the West to the launch of the secret donation movement for the families of arrested revolutionaries, all these proactive roles highlight the fact that Göncz's desire to pursue the ideals of the Revolution was indeed expressed by his actions. The result of these actions was not successful as it neither changed the Soviet leadership's intentions for Hungary, nor attracted practical support and assistance from the West. As Göncz observed, the *real politik* which followed the suppression of the Revolution was well representative of 'the ruthless logic of the balance of power' (Békés et al., 2002: XIV) and the Cold War contested between the West and the Soviet Union.

Despite this, Göncz's resistance to the established order of the Kádár regime clearly demonstrated his stance and the values he upheld. As Gough notes, Kádár was able to consolidate his power only after brutal reprisals against those who struggled for freedom (Gough, 2006: 250) and the condemnation of their crushed ideals (Lendvai, 2008: 242) as well as the forcing 'national amnesia' (the depoliticisation of social life) concerning the memory of 1956. In contrast, those with whom Göncz strove to bring together during the resistance movement proved to be vigorous debating partners who preserved their defeated but victorious ideals. Even during imprisonment Göncz, along with the 1956-ers, defended their revolution retrospectively through their rumination on the events and significance of the Revolution. They kept their faith and envisaged the future of Hungary and waited for the appropriate time and circumstances in which they could realise their crushed ideals.

Having established this, Chapter 3 further examined the way in which Göncz sought to realise his political ideals by exploring the significance of Göncz's participation in the dissident movement of the late 1980s. The analysis presented in the chapter once more highlights the contention that Göncz's desire to pursue his liberal ideas was clearly expressed by his actions in the founding of the NFI and the CHJ. As noted in Section 3.1, the second half of the 1980s in Hungary was a time in which internal and external circumstances moved favourably towards democratic change. Gorbachev's accession to the Soviet leadership, the growing influence of reform Communists' position within the hierarchy of the Hungarian Communist leadership and the emergence of democratic forces and their outspoken demands for radical economic and political change, all contributed to the erosion of the Kádár regime and his removal thereafter. Göncz, along with his friends, sensed this atmosphere and took the lead in the process of reviving the dissident movement through taking initiatives regarding the formation of grass-root social organisations. Göncz's proactive role in the drafting of the NFI founding statement and his participation in its social debate forum (where he shared his opinion and experience with younger generation) was exemplary in this regard; his pursuit of liberal political beliefs was more prominently evidenced by his action in the founding of the CHJ. As clearly stated in its founding statement, the main objective of the CHJ lay in dealing with the past. Having realised that the truth about the events and memories of the 1956 Revolution had been concealed for three decades during the Kádár regime, Göncz along with 1956 veterans appealed to Hungarian society regarding the iniquity of the system. Redressing past wrongs was the main issue to be addressed and this in practice meant the reburial of Nagy and his associates as well as their subsequent rehabilitation which needed to be dealt with as a matter of urgency. To this end, on 5 June 1988, the CHJ was founded and during this process Göncz, as a vice-president of the organisation, undertook a proactive role in mediation between the regime and society. Above all, Göncz stressed the regime's open approach towards its past as a potential path towards a process of societal reconciliation. As noted in Section 3.3, this intention was well evidenced by the CHJ founding statement (which emphasised the opening of previously sealed legal cases and secret files) and more prominently by the letter Göncz wrote to the general secretary of the HSWP, Károly Grósz. In the letter, Göncz emphasised that the regime's dishonest attitude towards its past resulted in disharmony between Hungarian society and the government and proposed that a dialogue with society be started. This endeavour was not successful as the proposition was rejected, but on 16 June 1989 – the thirty-second anniversary of Nagy's execution – the long cherished desire shared by Göncz and the 1956 veterans came to fruition. As Rainer notes, '16 June 1989 the day of Nagy and his associates' reburial in no way constituted the end of the reworking of the history of the Soviet system in Hungary, especially with respect to the Kádár era' (Rainer, 2009: 195).[1] Nevertheless, as history tells us it was this very day that marked the beginning of the end of Communism and catalysed Hungary's transition to democracy; it is fair to suggest that, while he was reacting to historical events and external forces, Göncz made an important contribution to Hungary's democratic transformation and its move towards that direction.

Göncz's political achievements as the first post-Communist president

Having noted the importance of Göncz's contribution to Hungary's transformation to democracy, the remaining chapters (Part II) were devoted to examining the significance of his political achievements as the first post-Communist president of Hungary. As a whole, the analysis of Göncz's presidency presented in Part II led to the conclusion that Göncz contributed to the consolidation of democracy in two ways. Firstly, he advanced the establishment of the Office of the Presidency and secondly he advocated the promotion of liberal and democratic values in the political as well as social sphere of Hungarian society.

In terms of the democratic institution-building process, Göncz played a key role in shaping the role of the presidency. As noted in Section 6.3, in its history, Hungary did not have a well established tradition of presidential governance or template for the role of the president. The presidencies held by three heads of state during the inter-war period – Mihály Károly, Zoltán Tildy and Árpád Szakasíts – lasted only four years in total. After the political transformation of 1989, Göncz's years as president were thus a time (at least at first) of hopeful creativity. Göncz had his own conception regarding the presidency and the newly amended Constitution provided an institutional basis and guideline. Some stipulations within the Constitution were, however, inconsistent and vaguely defined (as discussed in Section 4.3); each political actor who had different ideas about the president's role and responsibility came into jurisdictional dispute both with Göncz and one another. These disagreements concerned, for example, the president's right to lead the Hungarian army, that of international representation and the right to appoint and dismiss state officials (Chapter 5). These issues all arose during Göncz's first presidential term where the first democratically elected Antall government was in power. Göncz interpreted these issues as ones that fell under the jurisdiction of the president or, at least, he believed that they gave rise to decisions that ought to be shared by president and prime minister. In contrast, Antall and his cabinet members understood that the president's constitutional powers were titular, thus Göncz did not have a right to claim such interests. In effect, this jurisdictional dispute caused constitutional debate among political elites and legal experts over the scope of presidential powers and the post holder's role and responsibility. As noted in Sections 5.2.1 and 5.2.5, during this jurisdictional dispute, the Constitutional Court played a central role in delimiting presidential powers. In effect, the Court concluded that the president is not held accountable for his political actions, thus he did not have powers to exercise. As a result, much of the vision and motivation that had initially inspired Göncz to act as a proactive president was dissipated. This perception ultimately contributed to the change of Göncz's presidential style, in which a less active and conflict-averse presidential approach was prevalent during his second presidency (see Section 6.3). There was a partial exception to this pattern – the question of presidential pardon – but, in his retirement speech as Göncz made clear, this issue once again contributed to reinforcing his conviction that granting a pardon did not fall within the presidential competences. Thus, in terms of the process of political institution building and its subsequent routinised practice in Hungarian political culture, it is possible to say that, while he was constrained by external forces beyond his control, Göncz played a key role in the shaping of the basic attributes of presidency. From today's perspective, there is little doubt as to what is the main role of the president within Hungary's constitutional framework: the central task lies in the performance of ceremonial and symbolic duties.

Second, Göncz contributed to the rooting of liberal and democratic values in Hungary's political culture. As stated above, Göncz's political preference for these values derived from his first hand experience in fighting against the autocratic rule of the age. The common values that Göncz embraced in these activities were his commitment to the realisation of a free, democratic and socially responsible society. Having said that, Chapters 5 and 6 probed whether Göncz successfully represented and embodied such values when he became the president of Hungary. On the whole, the analysis presented in these chapters led to the conclusion that Göncz was indeed committed to his principled liberal and democratic beliefs throughout his presidency. In particular, the following democratic elements underpinned in the fabric of Göncz's political beliefs were highlighted: consensus-based democracy, the principle of equality, the rule of law and the freedom of expression and press freedom. There was a difference of emphasis in his value system (media freedom was the most significant during his first presidency, whereas it was the principle of equality that was highlighted during his second presidency), but the four democratic values were well embodied by his presidency.

First, Göncz's desire for a consensus-based democracy was explored within the framework provided by the following events and issues: the taxi-drivers' strike, dealing with the Laws of Privatisation and of Organised Crime. While these events took place under three different governments, Göncz consistently stressed that consensus-based decision be sought in order to address the point in question. During the taxi blockade, Göncz took on a mediation role, negotiating between strikers and the government, and he emphasised that the strike be settled through mutual agreement. In this event, Göncz's desire for seeking a peaceful and non-coercive solution was ultimately highlighted by his public statement. Similarly, dealing with the Law of Privatisation and the Anti-Mafia Package, Göncz stressed that the disagreement be resolved by consensus. In the former situation, Göncz returned the law to Parliament to provide an opportunity for MPs to settle the existing legal dispute themselves. In the latter, Göncz forwarded the package to the Constitutional Court to help clarify the point of contention between the governing party and the opposition. The letter Göncz sent to the Court clearly underscored the fact that the lack of clarity of the decision-making rule – whether the law which required a two-thirds majority vote could be amended with a simple majority was differently interpreted by the governing party and the opposition – was Göncz's main reservation about signing the law.

Second, and more prominently, the significance of the egalitarian principle was evidenced by Göncz's actions in dealing with the following issues: the question of the Communist past, the granting of a pardon in the Kunos case, and the Laws of Arable Land and of Incompatibility. These issues were once again raised under three successive governments, but regardless of this regime change, Göncz stressed how important the principle of equality was. Dealing with the Law of Compensation, Göncz made clear that the distinction between land and other forms of property for claiming monetary compensation from the state ought to be resolved before its enforcement. Similarly, dealing with anti-Communist legislation, Göncz constantly emphasised that the perpetrator who should have been duly punished for past crimes under the new regime also be equally treated before the law. Any retroactive justice which undermined the egalitarian principles of the new Hungarian Republic was inadmissible to Göncz; he stressed that past injustice ought to be corrected strictly within the framework of a state built upon the principle of the rule of law. The equal treatment of criminals before the law was again highlighted in the Kunos trial. In this issue, Göncz consistently underscored the value that the convicted banker ought to be treated equally before the law. The majority opinion of Hungarian society was against Kunos' release. In his decision-making capacity, however, Göncz displayed his firm belief that the wrongdoer who had not been granted a right to legal redress ought to be treated fairly. The same stance was again expressed by Göncz in dealing with the Law of Arable Land and of Incompatibility. In the former case, Göncz stressed that domestic and foreign investors alike be granted the right of land ownership. In the latter, Göncz urged that discriminatory measures within the law (initially only dependent on the length of time that MPs had held their parliamentary seats) be reconsidered in the legislative process.

Finally, the significance of the principle of press freedom and the freedom of expression was the highlighted in the issue pertaining to control over the broadcast media, the *La Stampa* affairs and the Law of Radio Frequency. All these situations arose during the Antall government; a government which attempted to place the public media under their control. Göncz, however, stated his firm position that under no circumstances should the freedom of expression and media freedom be violated by political and personal influence. His liberal political conviction was most strongly demonstrated in this issue, the extent to which some members of the conservative leadership attempted to impeach Göncz for his controversial stance and interpretation of his role and responsibilities. Despite this, Göncz made clear that in so far as the press freedom and the freedom of expression are concerned, he would not concede his position to the government's demands.

However, this is not to suggest that Göncz's pursuit of liberal and democratic values always had a positive effect on Hungarian politics. As noted in Chapter 5, the political division that existed between the conservative and the liberals came to be widened further by Göncz's involvement and, subsequently, this widening gap developed into the polarisation of politics. In effect on the side of the liberal camp, Göncz was seen by his camp as a symbol of democracy (as epitomised by the formation of the Democratic Charter). In contrast, among the conservatives, he was thought of as a partisan and divisive figurehead who failed to represent the unity of the nation. However, even if Göncz's political role could not be assessed favourably in all aspects, it should be noted that four democratic elements underpinning his political beliefs were important values *per se*. Göncz was not the father of this value system but its champion and a symbol of its continuity; the picture of Hungary's democracy would have been different without him.

Two decades have passed since Hungary's transition to democracy and Göncz's election to the presidency. Ferenc Mádl (formerly a law professor, now deceased),[2] László Sólyom (an ex-president of the Constitutional Court), Pál Schmitt (resigned during his term in office due to the discovery of plagiarism in his doctoral thesis)[3] and currently János Áder (a founding member of the Alliance of Young Democrats), all of whom came from distinctive backgrounds have succeeded to the presidency and pursued their political goals and agendas. It is perhaps too early to discuss and evaluate Göncz's political legacy in regard to how his successors view Göncz and his political achievements as a role model for approaching the presidential post however, this is a potential topic and avenue for future research.[4] Yet, it is fair to suggest that the political activism and the presidential activity that Göncz undertook during this pivotal transitional period is already an important integral part of Hungary's history. During this process, Göncz firmly stood by his liberal principles and democratic values and made them the central tenets of his presidency. As Pridham notes, if the path to democratic consolidation 'requires the gradual removal of uncertainties that usually surround transition and then the full institutionalisation of a new democracy, the internalisation of its rules and the dissemination of democratic values' (Pridham, 2000: 20), Göncz at least brought the virtue of liberal values into Hungarian politics. He did not, and was not able to, harmonise the three pluralistic values which he espoused, but played his part in the consolidation of Hungary's democracy. In an essay on the role of politicians and intellectuals, Göncz stated his opinion that:

> The three kinds of values, let us call them conservative, liberal and socialist for simplicity's sake, are not isolated but are simultaneously present in everybody, much like chips of glass of different colours in a kaleidoscope. As it turns, so the pattern changes. It is not us but history that turns the kaleidoscope ... We can count on the fact that, depending on how the kaleidoscope turns, the colours are rearranged even for individuals, creating a conservative, liberal or socialist pattern. The same is true for societies [...].
>
> Democratic institutions built from the grassroots up, social autonomy, would properly ensure that the individual's, that is everybody's natural need for equality and justice was satisfied, since that is its very purpose: ensuring everybody freedom of thought and an institutional framework for the equality of all citizens.

Is all that a dream? If the growth of our infant democracy continues uninterrupted, this will perhaps become established truth after two or three parliaments . . . This can of course only happen if conservatives and socialists accept freedom as a legitimate need, if liberals and socialists do not doubt the legitimacy of faith and tradition, and liberals and conservatives accept equality and solidarity as legitimate needs as well. And if the three kinds of values are present in every man, and in every party, albeit in different proportions. The only open question is whether the [three] values are always supportive of progress, all of them, and always. This is where the responsibility of politicians comes in, and that of the intellectuals, artist or writer who moves on the fringe of politics.

(Göncz, 1994: 9–10)

Through conducting in-depth interviews with Göncz and those elites who directly or indirectly became involved in politics, this research laid the groundwork of a political biography of Göncz. The analysis of accounts based on interviewing was instrumental in understanding Göncz's political beliefs, his value system and his own interpretation on the key events and issues of the age. Given his ailing physical status, Göncz would not and could not have engaged in political and public matters. Göncz stated: 'I have received numerous invitations but my physical condition does not allow me to meet these [requests]. I would attend the events which are the most important to me but my priority is spending time with my family' (Gréczy, 2006).[5] In this regard, this book makes a valuable contribution to the body of literature concerned with Göncz's own views on, and experiences of, post-Communist transitional presidencies. Göncz was certainly a strong advocate of liberal democracy and played an important part in the process of delineation of powers in an ever-evolving context provided by the process of political transformation. The opening of archives and the disclosure of Göncz's personal documents to research in the future, however, may suggest differing perspectives and assessments regarding Göncz's political philosophy and his achievements; this political biography is not – and cannot be – finite. Nevertheless, as Francis Bacon observed, 'it is the true office of history to represent the events themselves, together with the counsels, and to leave the observations and conclusions thereupon to the liberty and faculty of every man's judgement'.[6] Thus I do hope that this first English language scholarly biography provides some insights into, and answers to, questions raised in this book, and contributes to the wealth of knowledge of contemporary Hungary's history.

Notes

Introduction

1 Online Available HTTP: http://ftp.resource.org/gpo.gov/papers/1999/1999_vol1_899.pdf (accessed on 25 October 2010).
2 With the termination of Göncz's tenure as president, more material has become available for research. However, these materials are only available for consultation at the 1956 Institute.
3 Online Available HTTP: <Http://www.rev.hu> (accessed on 26 October 2010).
4 According to telegram exchanged between U.S State Department and U.S Embassy, in April 1982 Göncz visited to U.S and during this time he met Mildred Patterson, an official of the State Department. But this report does not detail the nature of his visit, not least what discussion went on between them. Unclassified telegram, Case ID: 200403498, United States Department of State Review Authority.
5 Representative translation works are Thomas Wolfe's of *Time and the River*, Ernest Hemingway's *Islands in the Streams*, J.R.R. Tolkien's *the Lord of the Rings*. Aside from translation work, Göncz wrote a number of pieces of dramas, among them, *Magyar Medea* and *Iron Bars* were successful plays performed in Central and Eastern Europe (Wilson and Wilson, 1989: 10).
6 To deal with daily requests of researchers, the Hungarian libraries and archives based in Budapest use a quota system. To access archived newspapers, each researcher can apply for a maximum of 5 items each time and subsequent requests can be made after these returns of the items.
7 According to the 2007 version of Pressdok – the database covering 150 Hungarian periodicals – there were more than 3500 articles that directly and indirectly related to Göncz's presidency.
8 It is only open to the researchers who hold European Union citizenship. Researchers outside this category can access this archive only if they secure a letter of clearance from the appropriate official.
9 The secretary to Göncz, Zsuzsánna Tormássy (now deceased) explained to me that, thirty years after Göncz's death, his personal documents (currently are held in the Library of Presidential Office) will be available to researchers (interview with Tormássy, 21 August 2007).
10 Online Available HTTP: <http://www.gla.ac.uk/lbss/research/ethics> (accessed on 30 September 2010).
11 For the publication of this book, three interviewees asked to be anonymous.

Chapter 1: Beginnings

1 As a consequence of Hungary's defeat in the First World War, this treaty dismembered the territory of Austro-Hungary Empire.

2 'The Association of Hungarian Boy Scouts', Online Available HTTP: <http://www.cserkesz.hu> (accessed on 9 July 2010).
3 'Boy Scouts', Online Available HTTP: <http://www.britannica.co.uk> (accessed on 10 July 2010).
4 '*Kéziiratok*' (Manuscripts) in HU OSA 302-0-5, Fonds 302: Samizdat Publication of Gábor Demszky.
5 Piarists is the name of Catholic educational order. Found by Saint Joseph Calasanctius, the Piarits provided free education for poor children. In Hungary, the Piarists were introduced by the Polish Duke, Szaniszló Lubomirski in 1674, and were officially founded in 1721 by electing their own first head of fathers, Lénárd Zajkáni. For full details, see: 'A Magyar Piarista Rendtartomány Története' (The History of the Hungarian Piarist Province), Online Available HTTP: <http://www.piarista.hu/kivagyunk/piaristak> (accessed on 10 July 2010).
6 'The NÉKOSZ Legend',Online Available HTTP: <http://ww.rev.hu> (accessed on 10 July 2010).
7 'Magyar Értelmiség!' (Hungarian Intellectuals!), presented by the National Archive of Hungary.
8 'A Teleki Pál Munkaközösség, a magyar értelmiség demokratikus szervezetének munkaterve' (The Pál Teleki Work Group, the work plan of the democratic organisation of Hungarian intellectual), presented by the National Archive of Hungary.
9 'Teleki Pál Munkaközösség, magyar értelmiség semokratikus szervezetének külpolitikai tanfolyama' (Pál Teleki Work Group, the coursework of foreign policy of the Democratic Organisation of Hungarian Intellectuals), presented by the National Archives of Hungary.
10 For a biographical file of Tibor Hàm, see *The New York Times* (9 July 1990).
11 For biographical data, see Fekete (2000) and Online Available HTTP: <http://mek.niif.hu/00300/00355/html/index.html> (accessed on 11 July 2010).
12 For instance, there were forced dissolutions of the Social Democrats and the Smallholders.
13 The Györffy College operated between 1940 and 1948, primarily for peasant children.
14 '*Levente-mozgalom*' (Levente movement), Online Available HTTP: <http://mek.niif.hu> (accessed on 11 July 2010).
15 In terms of domestic and foreign policy towards the Nazis, the Lakatos government sought policies different from those of his predecessors. In essence, it stopped anti-Jewish policy and attempted to conclude an armistice with the Soviet Union (Izsák and Pölöskei, 2003: 129).
16 The Rákosi Hill is located near the Ferihegy International Airport in Budapest.
17 '*Kéziiratok*' (Manuscripts) in HU OSA 302-0-5, Fonds 302: Samizdat Publication of Gábor Demszky.
18 The populist writers could be largely divided into three groups: one was that of those individuals who sympathised with the idea of a third road between socialism and capitalism (László Németh); another was that the bourgeois democrats or centrists (Imre Kovács and István Bibó), and finally there were the socialists (Géza Feja, Gyula Illyés and Ferenc Erdei) (Kontler, 2002: 359;Romsics, 1999: 172).
19 A series of sociological monographs – 'The Discovery of Hungary' (*Magyarország Felfedezése*) – is a good example (Romsics, 1999: 172).
20 Most arable land belonged to the aristocracy and the Catholic Church (Molnár, 2001:271–2).
21 Online Available HTTP: <http://www.rev.hu/sulinet56/online/szerviz/kislex/biograf/goncz.htm> (accessed on 12 July 2010).
22 Treaty of Peace with Hungary (1947), *The American Journal of International Law*, Vol. 42, No.4.
23 'The 1949 XX Law of the Hungarian Peoples' Republic of Constitution', Online Available HTTP: <http://www.complex.hu> (accessed on 12 July 2010).

24 Online Available HTTP: <http://www.rev.hu> (accessed on 12 July 2010).
25 Online Available HTTP: <http://www.rev.hu> (accessed on 12 July 2010).
26 During the 1956 Revolution, Kovács assumed the post of state secretary of the Imre Nagy government. With the defeat of the Revolution, he undertook mediation between the Revolutionary Workers' Council and the Kádár regime, but his arbitration failed and in November 1958, he died from heart attack (Palasik, 2002; Vida, 2002).
27 '*Kéziiratok*' (Manuscripts) in HU OSA 302-0-5, Fonds 302: Samizdat Publication of Gábor Demszky.
28 In his Oral History and in his interview collections, Göncz stated that his visit to Romania was concerned with the matters of peace, but no detailed information regarding this matter was given.

Chapter 2: The 1956 Hungarian Revolution

1 Göncz did not mention the title of book, but considering the time of interview given, the relevant book authored by Lomax would be *Hungary 1956* published in 1976.
2 In an interview with Kossuth radio, Göncz mentioned that in his life he met Nagy three times (on a tram and in Parliament). But this is far from clear how he was able to work at Parliament at the time (Wisinger and László, 2007: 34).
3 'Mi a börtönben négyévig győztesnek éreztük magunkat' (In the prison for four years, we considered ourselves as victors), Online Available HTTP: <http://www.bibotarsasag.hu> (accessed on 22 July 2010).
4 It functioned as an alternative education provider primarily for peasants' children.
5 Khrushchev's Secret Speech is generally considered as the beginning of the de-Stalinisation process; a thaw in rigid political climates which had dominated during the Stalin era and the opening of a wedge for 'different national paths to Communism' (Kontler, 2002: 425). For the full text of speech, see 'Khrushchev's Secret Speech' Online Available HTTP: <http://www.soviethistory.org> (accessed on 22 July 2010).
6 Online Available HTTP: <http://www.mult-kor.hu> (accessed on 22 July 2010).
7 In Göncz's Oral History, there was an indication that Göncz came to know about the Circle through his friends, but he was unable to reconstruct the circumstances of his initial introduction clearly.
8 Indeed this was published in the following journal – the *New Voice* (Varga, 2006: 89).
9 'Extensive and intensive farming', Online Available HTTP: <http://www.britannica.com> (accessed on 22 July 2010).
10 For the list of 16 points, see László (2006: 187–9).
11 The chronology of the Revolution was reconstructed according to Litván's books (1991, 1996) and a documentary film directed by Kóthy and Topits (2006).
12 For the details of the Yugoslavian reactions to the Revolution and Nagy's matter, see Swain (2011: 122–9).
13 For the full content of the Proclamation, see Izsák and Nagy (2004: 243–4).
14 K.P.S. Menon is not the same figure as an ambassador Vengalil Krishnan Krishna Menon (V.K.K. Menon). V.K.K. Menon led the Indian delegations in UN and later served as a minister of defence to Nehru.
15 The Non-Aligned Movement (NAM) is the principle of which stresses India's independence from any major power blocs' influence. The following five principles served as a basis for the NAM: Mutual respect for each other's territorial integrity and sovereignty, mutual non-aggression, mutual non-interference in domestic affairs, equality and mutual benefit and peaceful co-existence.
16 On 30 November 1956, Kádár replied to Nehru. In essence, Kádár refused to accept Nehru's proposition, claiming that allowing the UN observers' entry into Hungary would contribute to the development of social unrest and would go against his regime's efforts to restore normality (Huszár, 2002: 24–6).

17 Upon the rejection of the Indian leadership's mediation in the Hungarian question, Nehru increasingly became embittered with the Soviet leadership's intransigence. In numerous speeches, interviews and international conferences, Nehru consistently stated his position against the Soviet Union's aggression and their military occupation in Hungary as well as its subsequent reprisals taken by the Kádár regime. The Hungarian issue ultimately contributed to reinforcing Nehru's political beliefs that the right of self-determination and national independence be guaranteed in any countries. For details, see Hasan,Prasad and Damodaran (2005, 2006a, 2006b, 2006c, 2007).
18 Göncz explained that the Draft Proposal was handed over to Molotov, but according to documentary evidence, it was actually delivered to Bulganin. See Kenedi (1996: 142).
19 For the details of the programme and their analyses, see Békés, Byrne and Rainer (2002: 4–8).
20 Founded in 1955, the Nagy Group was constituted from those Communists who supported Nagy's New Course. The main goal they sought to achieve were Nagy's reinstatement and the facilitation of the implementation of reform programmes (Litván, 1989: 991). The key figures of the group were Miklós Gimes, Miklós Vásárhelyi, Losonczky Géza, Sándor Szilárgyi and Sándor Haraszti (*Népszabadság*, 16 June 1989a).
21 In his Oral History, there is an indication that in 1957, Göncz met Kardos at Júlia Soós's flat (a sociologist and friend).
22 '*Kéziiratok*' (Manuscripts) in HU OSA 302-0-5, Fonds 302: Samizdat Publication of Gábor Demszky presented by the Open Society Archive.
23 See also '1956 Revolution', Online Available HTTP: <http://hungaria.org/1956> (accessed on 25 July 2010).
24 They were, for example, Sándor Kelemen, István Oláh, Júlia Soós, Judit Gyenes (Pál Máléter's wife), Domokos Varga's wife, István Kemény's wife, István Bibó's wife and Göncz's wife.
25 This place is in Gyorskocsi Street, a few blocks away from Battányi Square.
26 '*Kéziiratok*' (Manuscripts) in HU OSA 302-0-5, Fonds 302: Samizdat Publication of Gábor Demszky presented by the Open Society Archive.
27 They were Menon's diaries (Menon, 1963, 1967) and biographies, autobiographies and Nehru's works written or edited by (Brown, 2003; Gopal, 1989; Hasan, Prasad and Damodaran, 2006a, 2006b, 2006c, 2007; Nehru, 1942; Stein, 1969).
28 According to official data, 418 people were convicted in summary proceedings for their direct involvement in the Revolution and before September 1958, the number of convicted for political reasons reached 16, 798 (Congdon and Király, 2002: 534–5). But above all, the most extreme acts of violence perpetrated against innocent people were the volley of gunshots at Eger, Miskolc, Salgótarján and Tatabánya (Szakolczai, 2002: 171).
29 This place is located in Kozma street, nearby Kőbánya on the Pest side.
30 'The testimony of Sándor Kopácsi' (the former chief of Budapest Police), Online Available HTTP: <http://eletfogytiglan.nolblog.hu/archives/2009/06> (accessed on 26 July 2010).
31 For the list of the prisoners, see Litván and Varga (1995: 470–2).
32 'Mi a börtönben négyévig győztesnek éreztük magunkat' (In the prison for four years, we considered ourselves as victors), Online Available HTTP: <http://www.bibotarsasag.hu> (accessed on 22 July 2010).
33 This is an ironic expression referring to the prison where the prisoners who received heavy penalties served their sentences.
34 '*Kéziiratok*' (Manuscripts) in HU OSA 302-0-5, Fonds 302: Samizdat Publication of Gábor Demszky presented by the Open Society Archive.
35 According to the letter exchanged between Kádár and Béla Biszku (the interior minister), Bibó was deprived of one year prison service commutation (which he was due) because of his participation in the Vác hunger strike. Biszkus reported to Kádár claiming that Bibó's attitude towards the regime and the Soviet Union had not been

changed and his leading role in the strike highlighted the fact that the commutation of his prion sentence would not be desirable (Huszár, 2002: 181).
36 According to István Tóth (the former chairman of the Workers' Council of Győr-Sopron County), Márianosztra was so rigorous that seeing any visitors and receiving letters and packages were banned and the beating of prisoners often occurred (Nagy, 1990).
37 Fekete Sándor was a leading journalist who published and distributed the underground publication of the 1956 Revolution under the pseudonym of Hungaricus. See '1956 Enciklopédiája' (Encyclopedia of 1956), CD ROM.
38 In reaction to the intervention of Soviet forces in Hungary, the UN adopted numerous resolutions condemning the Soviet aggression and urged the immediate withdrawal of troops and the admittance of UN observers in Hungary. However, the Kádár regime backed by Khrushchev refused to comply with the resolutions; in response, the UN set the Hungarian question as an agenda year after year until the autumn of 1962 (Lendvai, 2008: 193).
39 Hungary's membership in the UN was suspended in 1957 owing to Kádár's refusal to accept the entry of the UN special committee for the investigation of the situation (Kontler, 2002: 437).
40 The precise date of their release is not known but the general amnesty took effect on 21 March 1963 and Bibó was released thereafter.
41 The HSWP was founded on 31 October 1956. Given the leading role of Kádár in the founding of the party, it tends to be associated with Kádár's era. However, in his Oral History, Göncz made a clear distinction that the HSWP he envisaged was not related to Kádár but Nagy.
42 In an essay Göncz wrote, he remembered between 1953 and 1956, the country was not full of poverty but full of lies regarding its own tradition and history. Göncz asserted that this moral indignation over the derogated image of the country was an important factor in leading people to take to the streets in 1956, more so than people's demands for economic improvement (Göncz, 1991: 273).
43 In László Regéczy-Nagy's Oral History, Göncz is quoted as saying that socialism could be combined with 'democratic civic rights and a formal social arrangement'. Considering the time this comment was made, Göncz thought in this way after Imre Nagy's speech regarding the New Course was delivered. Moreover, in his Oral History, Göncz said that 'if it had been possible, he would have joined the Nagy-led HSWP'. Given this, it seems to me that in Göncz's political ideals, the idea of reform socialism or democratic socialism was embodied. You have known Göncz for a long time, so could you tell me whether the idea of democratic socialism had a place in Göncz's political ideals?

Chapter 3: Dissidence in the 1980s

1 For an empirical data on this see Linz and Stepan (1996: 303).
2 In March 1988, even two months before his removal from power, Kádár still failed to recognise the existing critical status, claiming that 'there is no crisis in Hungary' (*Népszava*, 18 March 1988).
3 The first sign appeared on 14 June 1985 at the Monor Conference where 45 Hungarian intellectuals with different social backgrounds gathered, and raised their voices in favour of change (Koppany, 1986).
4 The essence of the political programme lay in the arrangement of power-sharing which limited the monopoly of power of the party. Instead, it stressed the strengthening of the role of Parliament and the creation of responsive government to social demands. But the significant limit of the programme was that it did not seek the dismantling of the existing system but attempted a constitutional revision within it. For fuller details see Bihari (2005: 351–61).

5 The AYD was founded on 30 March 1988 by 37 university students. The initial founding goal of the AYD lay in the formation of the independent youth organisation to its counterpart, the Hungarian Young Communist League, and 'testing the limits of the already-crumbling Communist regime' (Kiss, 2002: 741).
6 They were, for example, the future leaders of the AYD, László Kövér and Viktor Orbán; those of the AFD, Gábor Demskzy, Miklós Haraszti and János Kis; the 1956 veterans, György Litván, Imre Mécs, Miklós Vásárhelyi and Árpád Göncz (Miszlivetz, 1995: 233).
7 For the list of signatories, see 'A felhívással egyetértek é stámogatom a Hálózat létrehozását' (I agree with the [proclamation] and support the creation of the Network) in HU OSA 302-0-6, presented by the Open Society Archive.
8 'Vázlat a Hálózat működéséről' (Draft on the functioning of the Network), in HU OSA 302-0-6, presented by the Open Society Archive.
9 For the contents of document, see Kis, Kőszeg and Solt (1992: 399).
10 A similar view was held by a former editor of *Beszélő*, Ferenc Kőszeg (Bába, 2007: 37–8).
11 A multi-party system in Hungary was introduced only after February 1989 and until then organisations could not call themselves political parties.
12 The statement was revised and elaborated by Göncz (interview with Göncz and Göntér, 10 January 2008).
13 Göncz expressed a similar view in an interview with Gábor Demszky, in 'Demokrácia reménye' (Hope of democracy), HU OSA 302-0-5, Fonds 302: Samizdat Publication of Gábor Demszky presented by the Open Society Archive.
14 The question asked was as follows: The fact that with the end of the Second World War, Göncz worked at the ISP, particularly for Béla Kovács. But before the systemic change of 1989 when the party was re-organised, Göncz did not join the ISP but the AFD. I assume that there would be numerous accounts explaining the change of Göncz's political orientations or his political interests. Could you tell me what was primarily responsible for Göncz's joining the AFD?
15 They were, for example, Tibor Hám, István Csicsery-Rónay and Kálmán Saláta.
16 The question asked was as follows: According to my research, the Hungarian populist movement was influential in the shaping of Göncz's political views. From the perspective of today, among political parties which were close to the idea of peasant populism, they were the HDF or the ISP. But Göncz joined one of the most liberal parties, the AFD. In your opinion, what could be a factor responsible for Göncz's joining the AFD?
17 For example, they were Erzsébet Nagy (the daughter of Imre Nagy), Judit Gyenes (the widow of Pál Maléter), Mária Haraszti Újhelyiné (the widow of Géza Losonczy), József Szilágyiné (the widow of József Szilágy), Miklós Vásárhelyi (the press secretary of the Nagy government), Tibor Zimány, György Litván, András B. Hegedűs, Imre Mécs, Sándor Rácz (the chairman of Budapest Workers' Council) and others.
18 The final revision of this was made by Göncz (Kozák, 2008).
19 Even after Kádár's removal from power, Károly Grósz still held the view that the events of 1956 were a counter-revolution (*Népszabadság*, 12 July 1988).
20 This is located in Gerlóczy street 11 on the Pest side of the capital.
21 They were as follows: Aliz Halda, András B. Hegedűs, Ferenc Donáth, Ferenc Mérei, György Litván, Imre Mécs, Jenő Széll, Miklós Vásárhelyi and Árpád Göncz. Three historians – Gyula Kozák, Miklós Szabó and Zsolt Csalog– participated in this talk as interviewers.
22 For a brief biographical account, see Tőkés (1996: 221–2).
23 Göncz Árpádlevele Grósz Károlyhoz (The letter of Árpád Göncz to Károly Grósz), manuscript, presented by the 1956 Institute.
24 Göncz Árpádlevele Grósz Károlyhoz (The letter of Árpád Göncz to Károly Grósz), manuscript, presented by the 1956 Institute.

25 Grósz Károly Miniszterelnök levele Göncz Árpádhoz (The letter of the prime minister Károly Grósz to Árpád Göncz), manuscript, presented by the 1956 Institute.
26 Grósz Károly Miniszterelnök levele Göncz Árpádhoz (The letter of the prime minister Károly Grósz to Árpád Göncz), manuscript, presented by the 1956 Institute.
27 The official account given by the regime was as follows: 'In order to satisfy the demands of duty and humanity and with a view at all time to social reconciliation, it assents to the reburial of those executed on 16 June 1958' (Kiscsatári, 2009: 11).
28 'Ez az én legbelsőbb, személ yes ügyem' (This is my deepest and most personal affair), Online Available HTTP: <http://www.c3.hu/scripta/beszelo/99/10/02besz,htm> (accessed on 30 July 2010).
29 For the reconstruction of the event and capturing the moment of the day, see (Gough, 2006: 248; Molnár, 2009: 121–45; Papp, 2002; Vásárhelyi, 2006: 160–2) and (*Magyar Hírlap*, 17 June 1989; *Magyar Nemzet*, 16 June 1989; *Népszabadság*, 16 June 1989b, 17 June 1989; *Népszava*, 16 June 1989).
30 Before the opening of border, the Foreign Minister Gyula Horn requested an opinion from the Soviet leadership, to which they replied 'this is not an affair that concerns the Soviet Union' (Brown, 2000: 194–5), indicating that the dismantling of the Soviet Union was just around the corner.
31 'Göncz Árpáddal Mink Andrásés Révész Sándorbeszélget 1989-ról' (András Mink and Sándor Révész discussed with Árpád Göncz about 1989), Online Available HTTP: <http://www.c3.hu/scripta/beszelo> (accessed on 30 July 2010).

Chapter 4: Development of post-Communist presidency in Hungary

1 The significance of this day was memorialised by the adoption of 'Act XXVIII of 1990 on the Significance of the 1956 October Revolution and Struggle for Freedom' (*Népszabadság*, 3 May 1990a, 1990b).
2 The third party, representatives of social organisations attended the RTN as observer but they did not have a right of decision.
3 They were the Alliance of Free Democrats, the Alliance of Young Democrats, the Democratic League of Independent Trade Unions, Endre Bajcsy-Zsilinszky Friendship Society, the Hungarian Democratic Forum, the Hungarian People's Party, the Hungarian Social Democratic Party, the Independent Smallholders' Party (Sajó, 1996: 73–4).
4 For further details, see Bayer (2005: 135–41); Bozóki (2002: 15–26); Bruszt (1990: 355–87); Bruszt and Stark (1991: 209–45); Kónya (2002: 267–85); Sajó (1996: 74–88) and Swain (2006: 145–52).
5 There was no agreement on the composition of the impartial Media Committees.
6 '1949 évi XX. Törvény a Magyar Népköztársaság Alkotmánya' (Act XX of 1949 on the Constitution of the Peoples' Republic of Hungary), Online Available HTTP: <http://www.1000ev.hu> (accessed on 10 August 2010).
7 The terminology of the former derives from French political scientist, Maurice Duverger, and the latter follows the American political scientists, Matthew Shugart and John Carey. For details, see Shugart (1993).
8 The reason for the change in their political stances was not clear. O'Neil suggested that 'a back-door arrangement with the Communist' could be responsible for the change of position taken by the HPP and the CDPP (O'Neil, 1997: 204). However, Schiemann asserted that the cautious position of the CDPP and the HPP towards the HSWP – they feared Communists may pull out of negotiations – was responsible for the shift of their position (Schiemann, 2005: 89–93).
9 In academic literature, there is no clear account explaining the change of the HDF's position. According to a view common to Ripp and Swain, however, there was regular contact between Antall and Pozsgay over the summer, which is highly indicative of the fact that there was a back-door arrangement between them (Ripp, 2006: 441–2; Swain, 2006: 150).

216 *Notes*

10 'Göncz Árpáddal Mink Andrásés Révész Sándorbeszélget 1989-ról' (András Mink and Sándor Révész discussed with Árpád Göncz about 1989), Online Available HTTP: <http://www.c3.hu/scripta/beszelo> (accessed on 30 July 2010).
11 On 9 October 1989, the HSWP was split into the HSP led by Imre Pozsgay and the Hungarian Communist Workers' Party led by Gyula Thürmer.
12 According to poll conducted in 1989, throughout the year, Imre Pozsgay's popularity constantly remained high above 90 percent (Kurtán, Sándor and Vass, 1990).
13 For the development of the referendum see *Népszabadság* (11, 18, 26 June 1990; 28 June 1990a, 1990b; 5 July 1990).
14 The key lists of the new legislation which required a two-thirds majority were as follows: the Law of Referendum, the Law of the Legal Status of the MPs, the Law of the Constitutional Court, the Law of using Public Forces, the Law of Assembly and Party, the Law of Media, the Law of Travelling and Asylum, the Law of Local Government, the Law of Strike, the Law of Electorate to name but a few (Bihari, 2005: 396).
15 Tölgyessy stated that although the AFD did not like forming a coalition with the HDF, they sought to do in consideration of the public opinion at the time: the general public wanted to see the formation of coalition government (emails with Tölgyessy, 14, 16 August 2010).
16 The president can dissolve Parliament only in these very unusual circumstances: first, when Parliament votes on no-confidence in government four times a year; second, if Parliament fails to appoint the premier within 40 days after parliamentary election.
17 '1946 évi I. Törvény Magyarország Államformájáról' (Act I of 1946 on the State Form of Hungary), Online Available HTTP: <http://www.1000ev.hu> (accessed on 10 August 2010).
18 The name of György Konrád was indeed mentioned in one of the AFD meetings that took place in Tihany (Wisinger and László, 2007: 77).
19 Initially, Antall offered the co-chairmanship of the HDF to Csoóri, but he refused it (*Népszabadság*, 4 June 1990).
20 'The Constitution of Hungary', Online Available HTTP: <http://www.parlament.hu> (accessed on 10 August 2010).
21 The Constitution does not detail the procedure of the appointment and dismissal of the heads of broadcast media. This process was detailed and adopted separately as 'Law No. LVII of 1990 on the Appointment Procedure of the Heads of the Public Media'.
22 It can be also activated under normal circumstances when parliamentary session reaches the end of a cycle. In this case, the president activates reserve function to aid a smooth transition to the next parliamentary session.
23 '1990 évi XL Törvény a Magyar Köztársaság Alkotmányának Módósításáról' (Act XL of 1990 on the Amendment of the Constitution of Hungary).
24 '2006 évi LIV Törvény a Magyar Köztársaság Alkotmányáról Szóló 1949 évi XX Törvény Módósításáról' (Act LIV of 2006 on the Amendment of Act XX of 1949 regarding the Constitution of Hungary).
25 Initially, the president only had a right to set the date of national referenda, but the constitutional amendment adopted as Act LXI of 2002 expanded this right to the point at which it currently remains.
26 The terminology of this follows the Hungarian political scientist, András Körösényi.

Chapter 5: The first presidency (1990–1995)

1 Hungary moved towards privatisation gradually. The direct sale state-owned properties and firms to private businessmen was preferred (Fowkes, 1999: 26, 112–17; Henderson and Robinson, 1997: 248–9).
2 This Agency fulfilled the role of 'supervising the privatisation processes' (Romsics, 2007: 322).
3 According to Orbán's speech delivered in Parliament, one of the reasons for the increase

of petrol prices lay in compensating for the deficit in the state budget which, in turn, highlights the fact that the increase of crude oil prices on the international market was not solely responsible for the government's action. For the speech, see: (Bozóki, 1992b: 482–3).
4 Horváth was in charge of the situation because Antall was in hospital for surgery at the time.
5 This was 'not effectively operated' until the beginning of the blockade. The main reason for this lay in the Antall government's reluctance to 'accept the trade unions as legitimate partners'. The Antall government did not consider the IRC as an important forum for political discussion (Cox and Vass, 1994: 164–5).
6 Moldoványi claimed there was no hard evidence because an order to dispatch military forces was never given (Moldoványi, 2001). However, there is still a possibility that the government might have given only a verbal order so as not to leave a paper trail of evidence; one cannot simply say that Göncz's judgement was wrong.
7 Göncz stayed in his office until the crisis was over (interview with Tölgyessy, 15 October 2007).
8 '1989 évi XXXI törvényaz Alkotmány módósításáról' (Law XXXI of 1989 on the Amendment of the Constitution).
9 '2002 évi LXI törvény a Magyar Köztársaság Alkotmányáról szóló 1949 évi XX törvény módósításáról' (Law No. LXI of 2002 on the Amendment of the Constitution of the Republic of Hungary regarding Law No. XX of 1949); The 'Constitution of Hungary'.
10 According to the Hungarian ambassador, András Gulyás, in foreign policy, Havel and Walesa could exercise wider powers than Göncz (interview with Gulyás, 3 July 2007).
11 Online Available HTTP: <http://www.complex.hu> (accessed on 23 August 2010).
12 If claims of compensation valued more than £3300, only 10 percent of the original value was compensated.
13 This cut-off date was chosen, because 'the first session of the fake Parliament' controlled by the Communists was held at the time (Okolicsanyi, 1991a: 8).
14 This was complemented by the adoption of the Third Compensation Act. According to this Act, those victims and heirs who were executed, imprisoned, and taken to labour camps between 11 March 1939 and 23 October 1989 were entitled to benefit from partial monetary compensation (*Népszabadság*, 2 November 1991).
15 The AFD claimed since all Hungarian people suffered from the Communist rule, 20,000 (HUF) should be equally distributed to everyone.
16 The second version of the Compensation Law was adopted after the Court ruled the first Compensation Act was unconstitutional. This expanded compensation coverage with the inclusion of those damages and losses incurred between 1 May 1939 and 8 June 1949 (*Népszabadság*, 2 June 1992).
17 Having found the number of beneficiaries covered by the first Compensation Act was arbitrarily reduced by the amendment of the law, Göncz sent it to the Court (Sólyom and Holló, 1994: 221).
18 Placing a limit on the holding of a cooperative's property for the purpose of compensation was not found to be unconstitutional.
19 These dates were chosen as they were the juncture of the new beginnings of Hungary's history. On 21 December 1944, the first provisional National Assembly was held at Debrecen. Similarly, on 2 May 1990, the first session of the post-Communist Parliament began.
20 'The ruling of the Constitutional Court', Case No. 42/1993, Online Available HTTP: <http://www.mkab.hu> (accessed on 24 August 2010).
21 The Geneva Convention stated that war crimes and crimes against humanity are not subject to the statute of limitations. See: 'Convention on the Non-Applicability of Statutory Limitations to War Crimes and Crimes against Humanity', Online

Available HTTP: <http://www2.ohchr.org/english/law/pdf/warcrimes.pdf> (accessed on 24 August 2010).
22 '1993 évi XC Törvényaz 1956 Októberi Forradalomés Szabadságharcsorán Elkövetett Egyes Bűncselekményekkel Kapcsolatos Eljárásról', Online Available HTTP: <http://www.complex.hu> (accessed on 24 August 2010).
23 According to a poll conducted by the Medián Institute, only 53 percent of respondents said the Communists who were accountable for their past misconducts should be called to account (through making those names to available to the public). Twenty-six percent of respondents said nothing should be done to these wrongdoers (Beck, 1992).
24 'Göncz Árpád Újévi Köszöntő Beszédei (1991–2000) az MTI sajtó adatbázisa alapján' (The New Year's Greeting of Árpád Göncz between 1991 and 2000 based on the MTI press data), presented by the Library of the Hungarian Parliament.
25 The meaning in English is 'no crime, no punishment without a previous penal law'.
26 'The ruling of the Constitutional Court', Case No. 11/1992, Online Available HTTP: <http://www.mkab.hu> (accessed on 24 August 2010).
27 The question raised was as follows: During the Antall government, numerous laws which often gave rise to dispute were passed in Parliament. For instance, in dealing with the Communist past, referring to moral responsibility, the Antall government passed the Laws of Compensation, of Justice and of Screening. However, on several occasions, Göncz vetoed these laws. Of these, how do you evaluate Göncz's actions or his role in dealing with the Law of Justice?
28 This model was in fact practised in the South Africa.
29 'The Law No. LV of 1994 on Arable Land', Online Available HTTP: <http://www.complex.hu> (accessed on 25 August 2010).
30 The maximum which an individual Hungarian citizen can buy is 300 hectares.
31 Hungary reached an agreement with the EU on the opening of land market. According to this, foreigners could buy arable land from 2011, albeit that it had been partially opened to those who were willing to making a living from agriculture ('Hungary restricts foreign access to farm land', *Agra Europe*, 2003).
32 Officially, on 1 April 1994, Hungary submitted its application to join the EU, Online Available HTTP: <http://www.mfa.gov.hu> (accessed on 25 August 2010).
33 This is a non-profit-making international organisation whose 'mission is to act as a global catalyst for change through the identification and analysis of the crucial problems facing humanity'. See: 'The Club of Rome', Online Available HTTP: <http://www.clubofrome.org> (accessed 25 August 2010).
34 The Promethée is a Paris-based think-tank association.
35 Initially, the Charter was the texts of '17 points composed by liberal Hungarian intellectuals' outlining the minimum conditions of democracy (interview with Konrád, 7 September 2007). After Kónya and Csurka formulated a radical idea in their essays on the way in which the government should govern the country, it gained an impetus to draw on public participation, increasingly turning into a peaceful civic movement (Bozóki, 1996: 178–213).
36 'The ruling of the Constitutional Court', Case No. 48/1991, Online Available HTTP: <http://www.mkab.hu> (accessed on 26 August 2010).
37 The question raised was as follows: During Göncz's Presidency, a number of controversial bills were passed. For example, in an attempt to deal with the Communist past, the Antall government introduced the Laws of Compensation and of Justice. However, these laws were challenged by Göncz. Similarly, in the issue of the control over broadcast media, Göncz persistently refused to sign the appointment and dismissal of the heads of media suggested by Antall. Of these, could you tell me in which event Göncz played the most important role? Secondly, how do you evaluate his action?
38 Oltay argued that among Hungarian newspapers, 'the government's views are reflected in these two dailies - *Új Magyarország* and *Pesti Hírlap*' (Oltay, 1992: 42).

39 'The Law No. LVII of 1990 on the Appointment Procedure of the Heads of the Public Media'.
40 (Körösényi *et al*., 2003: 528–31; Petrétei, 2001b: 148–52).
41 One possible account lies in the jurisdiction of the Constitutional Court. The Court does not have competences in the provision of a concrete ruling on jurisdictional disputes that arose among state institutions, but is limited to abstract 'norm control'.
42 Even in current politics, a new media law has been severely criticised by media experts, professionals and politicians at home and those of the members of the European Union. The new media law that was adopted by the Orbán government (which took into effect on 1 January 2011) places the governing parties in a strong position to control over media. This issue was even raised by the president of the European Commission; José Barroso, who stressed that media freedom is 'a fundamental and sacred democratic value' to be upheld. See Brand (2011) and 'EU speechless over Hungary's contentious media law', Online Available HTTP: <http://www.euraactiv.com> (accessed on 18 May 2011) and 'Hungary media free but press freedom declined, says Freedom House', Online Available HTTP: <http://www.politics.hu> (accessed on 18 May 2011).
43 A good example is found in the correspondence exchanged between Antall and Göncz; Göncz and the Constitutional Court and others. These letters had been exchanged over the period of the occurrence of controlling media and Göncz stressed that media be independent (Kurtán, Sandor and Vass., 1993: 186–205).
44 The 'No. LXII Law of 1993 on Radio Frequency Management' Online Available HTTP: <http://www.complex.hu> (accessed on 25 August 2010).
45 'The ruling of the Constitutional Court', Case No. 48/1993, Online Available HTTP: <http://www.mkab.hu> (accessed on 25 August 2010). See also *Magyar Dokumentáció* (July 1993).
46 'The ruling of Constitutional Court', Case No. 48/1993, Online Available HTTP: <http://www.mkab.hu> (accessed on 25 August 2010).
47 'The ruling of Constitutional Court', Case No. 48/1993, Online Available HTTP: <http://www.mkab.hu> (accessed on 25 August 2010).
48 The Court ruled that regulating radio frequencies is a technical matter and freedom of press and opinion is a secondary one, concluding that the question of technicality took precedence over the freedom of press and expression in this case.
49 The new media law was adopted in 1996 during the Horn government.
50 According to Boross, the direct cause of the 1956 veterans' protest lay in Göncz's refusal to accept András Márton's request. The chairman of the Military Section of the Committee for Historical Justice, Márton, asked Göncz to let him give a speech along with him, but this request was refused by Göncz (Somos, 1997a).
51 Swain asserts that the ISP could have been behind the organised event, with evidence for such involvement being the appearance of 'gangs of skinheads who had been invited up to Budapest' (Swain, 1993: 80).
52 The holding of an event can be prevented by the police only under the condition that the event would seriously 'interfere with undisturbed functioning of any representative organ or court or to cause a disproportionate disruption of traffic' (Kilényi and Lamm, 1990: 61).
53 The head of the Cabinet of the Interior Ministry András Gyekiczki said the full report of the case could not be made available to the public in the interests of national security.

Chapter 6: The second presidency (1995–2000)

1 Kiss suggested that one reason for the AFD's decision to enter a coalition with the HSP lay in their vested interests which in practice meant that it would be better for the party 'not to sit another term in opposition than to firmly distinguish themselves from the HSP and its chequered past' (Kiss, 2006: 933).

2 The offices of the president and the premier were located in the same bloc at Parliament, but they usually did not see one another. Exchange of letters was the preferred method of communication (interview with Lengyel, 13 September 2007).
3 For a detailed discussion regarding the concept of majoritarian and consensual democracies see Ágh (2001a: 89–112).
4 For a detailed discussion of the Orbán government's governing style and their concep of democracy see Bozóki (2008: 206–16).
5 According to Körösényi, 'presidentialisation' means the increase of the premier's independent decision-making powers and increased independence from the control of the governing party and Parliament alike. Conventionally, the premier's powers under parliamentarianism depend on whether the governing party supports or opposes the premier's decision. But, once the premier's power is centralised and he or she becomes less subject to the check of Parliament, in theory, becoming close to the presidentia model.
6 The essence of the ruling was that the legislature is entitled to transform the system of social supports, if it provides a transitional period for the introduction of a new system However, the Bokros package was unconstitutional, since it did not offer a proper preparatory period (Case 31/1995, and 43/1995, Online Available HTTP: <http://www mkab.hu> (accessed on 24 August 2010; *Magyar Dokumentáció*, July 1995).
7 For an analysis of the effects of adjustment package on Hungary's economy and its comparative perspective see Csaba (2000: 805–27).
8 For the details of Göncz's re-election see Babus (1995); Bodnár (1995); *Magyar Hírlap* (20 June 1995); *Népszabadság* (20 June 1995) and *Népszava* (20 June 1995).
9 Kövés and Matolcsy shared the view that the austerity programme was 'the result of incorrect diagnosis' of Hungary's economic ailments (Adam, 1999: 62).
10 This economic crisis took place in December 1994 prompted by radical devaluation of the Mexican Peso.
11 'Göncz Árpád újévi köszöntő beszédei 1991–2000' (New Years' Speech of Árpád Göncz 1991-2000), presented by the Library of Hungarian Parliament.
12 In Hungary's history, the first attempt to legislate this law was made in 1875. According to Bihari, this law became the foundation of following amendments, and it was the 1946 Hungarian Parliament that formalised it as the 'XXVI Law of Incompatibility' (Bihari, 1997: 6).
13 '1997 évi V. Törvényaz Országgyűlési Képviselők Jogállásról szóló 1990 évi LV. Törvény Módósításáról' (The Law No. V of 1997 on the Legal Status of Members of Parliament regarding the Amendment of the Law No. LV of 1990) Online Available HTTP: <http://www.complex.hu> (accessed on 25 August 2010).
14 (Case, No. 30/1997), Online Available HTTP: <http://www.mkab.hu> (accessed on 25 August 2010).
15 'The Incompatibility of Members of Parliament', Online Available HTTP: <http://www.complex.hu> (accessed in 25 August 2010).
16 The president's right to propose a draft of bill was to be removed (*Magyar Hírlap*, 2 June 1995).
17 According to poll, the socialist-liberal coalition's involvement in financial corruption was seriously questioned by the general public, and this was demonstrated by public distrust in the government (Szabó, 1997: 641).
18 The question raised was as follows: Concerning the Law on Incompatibility, you explained that three factors – the prevention of eroding Göncz's popularity, preparation for the 1998 parliamentary election and his leniency towards the Horn government – were primarily responsible for his veto. According to this, it appears that the seeking of self-interest was the main reason of Göncz's veto. What is your opinion?
19 The Horn government merged two privatisation agencies – The State Privatisation Agency and the State Holding Company – into a unit to streamline the bureaucratic procedure and accelerate the privatisation process (Fowkes, 1999: 156).

20 Indeed, the relevant legal framework was formulated as the '1991 XXXIII Law on Transferring certain State Properties into the Ownership of Local governments'.
21 'The Constitution of Hungary', Online Available HTTP: <http://www.parlament.hu> (accessed on 10 August 2010).
22 'The Constitution of Hungary', Online Available HTTP: <http://www.parlament.hu> (accessed on 10 August 2010).
23 Ágh upheld the view, asserting that the Law of Privatisation contributed to the fast reshaping of ownership structure, despite corruption problems plaguing the privatisation process (Ágh, 2001c: 482).
24 If the president requests a judicial review, the Court is obliged to take it as a priority. However, it is still unclear usually how long it takes time to proceed.
25 There is an interpretation that Göncz issued a pardon Kunos, because the AFD which received support from the AB persuaded Göncz to do so. It was claimed that during Kunos' trial the people who were close to the AFD attended and this showed how lobby activities were behind this case. What is your opinion about this?
26 'The Judicial System in Hungary' Online Available HTTP: <http://www.birosag.hu> accessed on 25 August 2010).
27 The relevant clause was included in the Article 45 (1) of the Constitution, Online Available HTTP: <http://www.parlament.hu> (accessed on 25 August 2010).
28 Arguing that the reform plan of the justice system 'was not well structured' (EECR, 1998 Fall), the Orbán government decided to delay the enforcement of the law.
29 'Act No. IV of 1978 on the Criminal Code', Online Available HTTP: <http://www.1000ev.hu> (accessed on 25 August 2010).
30 Until 1999, Göncz granted 1218 pardons in total (Bihari, 2000) and this case was the only one in which the president and the justice minister were unable to reach a consensus (Wisinger and László, 2007: 335).
31 The essence of the deal Kunos made with his client was that the AB gave a loan, in return the client's company had to allocate some portion of shares or incomes to them (Csák, Dániel and Zsubori, 2007).
32 The survey institute, Szonda Ipsos, conducted poll regarding the general public's sympathy towards Göncz and Antall. In every criterion, Göncz was judged much more favourably than Antall, including Göncz's integrity and modesty (Bakony, 2005: 20). Moreover, the sympathy of Hungarian population towards Göncz was evidenced by his consistently high level of popularity; around 80 per cent throughout his presidency (Babus, 2000). His popularity also contributed to the increase of public confidence in the presidential office compared to other any state institutions (Babus, 2001).
33 '1999 évi LXXV Törvény a Szervezett Bűnözés Valamint Azazzal Összfüggő egyes Jel enségek Elleni Fellépés Szabályairól és az Ehhez Kapcsolódó Törvény módosításról' (Act LXXV of 1999 on the Combat Against Organised Crime and the Related Phenomena and the Amendment of Related Acts of Parliament), Online Available HTTP: <http://www.complex.hu> (accessed on 26 August 2010).
34 These were Act XXXIV of 1994 on the Police, Act LXXXVI of 1993 on Aliens, Act on Asylum, Act on the Border Guards and Act XII of 1998 on Travelling Abroad.
35 The relevant provision is Article 40B of the Constitution.
36 'The Constitution of Hungary', Online Available HTTP: <http://www.parlament.hu> (accessed on 26 August 2010).
37 Until 1997, if MPs did not agree with the legislation adopted, they were entitled to request a priori judicial review from the Constitutional Court. To take this legal proceeding, at least, 50MPs were required to meet the quorum.
38 'The ruling of the Constitutional Court', Case No. 1/1999, Online Available HTTP: <http://www.mkab.hu> (accessed on 26 August 2010).
39 At least, the relevant information was not made available to the press.
40 The same question was consistently raised among my interviewees to probe different perspectives and opinions. Of 52 interviews, the question was raised with 23 interviewees.

Notes

The vast majority of them (20) pointed to the clarification of constitutional competence as the main factor responsible for Göncz's reduced political activism. Among them, Ágh's account was the most comprehensive and succinct thus, it is included as an example here. The questions raised were as follows: During Göncz's presidency, in the press numerous political analyses and critiques on Göncz were published. According to these, in terms of domestic politics, it would appear that during the first term of his presidency, Göncz relatively played more proactive and controversial role than his second presidency. Firstly, do you agree with this comment? If you do, I would like to ask you what was primarily responsible for Göncz's changed presidential style? Secondly, how do you evaluate his role and actions?

41 Göncz's interviews with (Bíró and Németh, 2000; Szálé, 2003).
42 Institution building is the first step towards the consolidation of democracy. Theoretically, it consists of three levels: macro-, meso- and micro-political institutions. The first refers to the fundamental form of state, such as to decide whether it takes on parliamentary or presidential form of government. The second means the 'modernisation of state administrations, central governments, nation-wide organisations'. The final process refers to local and municipal governments and civil organisations at grass-root level. The sequencing of institution-building from macro to micro-politics, however, does not proceed step by step but in fact complete at varying phases and degrees. According to Ágh, by the mid of 1990s, at least Hungary completed institution-building process at the macro-levels.
43 For a comparative study of how 'constitutional contestation and conflict settlement were instrumental in the development of president-cabinet relations' see Raadt (2009: 83–101).

Conclusion

1 This is because of the positive esteem in which Kádár is held by the Hungarian population. According to Gough, the Hungarian population was, and is, nostalgic for him even if they have acknowledged his role in the 1956 Revolution (Gough, 2006: 254). In fact, according to the polls conducted in April 1999 and August 2006, Kádár was regarded as one of the most positive personalities in twentieth century of Hungarian history. '*A 20. Század értékelése*' (Assessment of the twentieth century), Online Available HTTP: <http://www.median.hu> (accessed on 1 December 2010).
2 For obituaries, see *Heti Válasz* (29 May 2011); *Heti Világgazdaság* (29a, 30 May 2011); *Magyar Hírlap* (30 May 2011); *Magyar Nemzet* (29a, 30a May 2011); *Népszabadság* (29 May 2011); *Népszava* (30a May 2011). For more detail and assessment of his political achievements see *Heti Válasz* (7 June 2011); *Heti Világgazdaság* (29b May, 7 June 2011); *Magyar Hírlap* (29 May, 7 June 2011); *Magyar Nemzet* (29b, 30b May 2011); *Népszabadság* (7 June 2011) and *Népszava* (30b, 31a, 31b May, 7 June 2011).
3 For further details see *The Economist* (2 April 2012); *Heti Világgazdaság* (2 April 2012); *Magyar Nemzet* (2 April 2012); *Népszava* (3 April 2012) and Tóth (2012).
4 There are some articles of comparative analysis between Göncz and his successors (Fricz, 2010; Gréczy, 2005; *Magyar Hírlap*, 10 February 2007; *Népszabadság*, 6 August 2010; *Népszava*, 29 June 2010; Szomszéd, 2010). However, these are far from comprehensive which enables researchers to observe the process of how Hungarian population and political elites have considered the political achievements of three post-Communist presidents.
5 A similar view was expressed by Göncz when he politely refused to attend the twentieth anniversary of the founding of the AFD. Göncz said: 'his [advanced] age and [ill] health condition prevents him from attending the event to celebrate together' (*Hetiválasz*, 1 November 2010).
6 Online Available HTTP: <http://www.quoteworld.org/categories/history> (accessed on 3 December 2010).

Bibliography

In the interest of consulting the pictures of Göncz, see the website of the 1956 Institute and Oral History, at HTTP://www.rev.hu/fotodb/f?p=110:1:1204721176025679, accessed on 10 December 2012.

Chapters and articles with authors' names in English, German and Hungarian

Ablonczy, B. (2006) *Pál Teleki (1874–1941): The life of a controversial Hungarian politician*, New York: Columbia University Press.

Ács, N. (2000) Az államfő (The head of state) in *Országgyűlési választások, az országgyűlés és az államfő (The parliamentary elections, the parliament and the head of state)*, Budapest: Budapesti Közgazdaságtudományi és Államigazgatási Egyetem Államigazgatási Kar.

Adam, J. (1999) Transition to a market economy in Hungary, in Adam, J. *Social cost of transformation to a market economy in post-socialist countries: The case of Poland, the Czech Republic and Hungary*, Basingtoke: Macmillan.

Ágh, A. (1998) *The politics of Central Europe*, London: Sage Publications.

—— (2000) In the midst of systemic change, in Kostecki, W. *(eds.) Transformation of post- Communist states*, London: Macmillan.

—— (2001a) 'Early consolidation and performance crisis: The majoritarian-consensus democracy debate in Hungary', *West European Politics*, Vol.24, No.3.

—— (2001b) Early democratic consolidation in Hungary and the Europeanisation of the Hungarian polity, in Pridham, G. and Ágh, A. (eds.) *Prospects for democratic consolidation in East Central Europe*, Manchester: Manchester University Press.

—— (2001c) The socialist-liberal government 1994–1998, in Ormos, M. and Király, B. (eds.) *Hungary: Governments and politics 1848–2000*, New York: Columbia University Press.

Andor, L. (1998) 'New strikers in old team: Parliamentary elections in Hungary', *Labour Focus on Eastern Europe*, No.60.

Arato, A. (1994) 'Election, coalition and constitution in Hungary', *The Hungarian Quarterly*, Vol.35, No. 135.

—— (1995) 'Parliamentary constitution making in Hungary', *East European Constitutional Review*, Vol.4, No.4.

—— (1996) The Hungarian constitutional court in the media war: Interpretations of separation of powers and models of democracy, in Sajó, A. and Price, M. (eds.) *Rights of access to the media*, The Hague: Kluwer Law International.

Bibliography

Argentieri, F. (2008) Dealing with the past and moving into the present, in Curry, J. and Wolchik, S. (eds.) *Central and East European Politics: From Communism to democracy*, New York: Rowman & Littlefield Publisher.

Ash, T. (1990) *We the people: The Revolution of '89 witnessed in Warsaw, Budapest, Berlin and Prague*, London: Granta Books.

Bába, I. (2007) *Békés átmenet: Adalékok a kialkudott rendszerváltáshoz (Peaceful transformation: Data on the bargained systemic change)*, Budapest: Demokratikus Átalakulásért Intézet.

Bakony, A. (2005) *Köztársasági elnök kontra kormány: Az államfői intézmény kialakulása Magyarországon (The president of the republic versus government: The formation of the presidential institution in Hungary)*, Budapest: Hungarian political Science Association.

Báldy, P. (2003) *Az alkotmány magyarázata (The explanation of the constitution)*, Budapest: KJK-KERSZÖV Jogi és Üzleti Kiadó.

Barany, Z. (1999) 'Out with whimper: The final days of Hungarian socialism', *Communist and Post-Communist Studies*, Vol. 32, No.2.

Bayer, J. (2005) 'The process of the change of the political system in Hungary: Deepening crisis, emerging opposition', *East European Quarterly*, Vol.39, No.2.

Baylis, T. (1996) 'Presidents versus prime ministers: Shaping executive authority in Eastern Europe', *World Politics*, Vol. 48, No.3.

Békés, C., Byrne, M. and Rainer, J. (2002) (eds.) *The 1956 Hungarian Revolution: A history in documents*, Budapest: Central European University Press.

Benziger, K. (2008) *Imre Nagy, martyr of the nation: Contested history, legitimacy, and popular memory in Hungary*, Plymouth: Lexington Books.

Berki, R. (1992) 'The realism of moralism: The political philosophy of István Bibó', *History of Political Thought*, Vol.13, No.3.

Berry, J. (2002) 'Validity and reliability issues in elite interviewing', *Political Science and Politics*, Vol.35, No.4.

Bihari, M. (1997) 'A képviselők összeférhetetlensége és a hatalommegosztás' (The incompatibility of MPs and the seperation of power), *Politikatudományi Szemle*, Issue 1.

—— (2005) *Magyar politika 1944–2004: Politikai és hatalmi viszonyok (Hungarian politics 1944–2004: Political and power relations)*, Budapest: Osiris Kiadó.

Bölöny, J. and Hubai, L. (2004) *Magyarország kormányai 1848–2004 (The governments of Hungary from 1848–2004)*, Budapest: Akadémiai Kiadó.

Bonn, G. (1991) 'Indisches Tagebuch: Die ungarishe Revolution und der indische Diplomat M.A. Rahman – Herausforderung und Bewaehrung (Indian diary: The Hungarian Revolution and the Indian Diplomat M.A. Rahman – Challenge and accomplishment)', *Indo Asia*, Vol. 33, No. 2.

Bozóki, A. (1992a) Political transition and constitutional change in Hungary, in Bozóki, A., Körösényi, A. and Schöpflin, G., (eds.) *Post-Communist transition emerging pluralism in Hungary*, London: St. Martin's Press

—— (1992b) *Tiszta lappal: A Fidesz a magyar politikában 1988–1991 (With a Clean Record, Fidesz in the Hungarian politics 1988–1991)*, Budapest: FIDESZ.

—— (1996) 'Intellectuals in a new democracy: The Democratic Charter in Hungary', *East European Politics and Societies*, Vol.10, No.2.

—— (2002) Introduction: The significance of the Roundtable Talks, in Bozóki, A. (ed.) *The Roundtable Talks of 1989: The genesis of Hungarian Democracy*, Budapest: CEU Press.

—— (2003) *Politikai pluralizmus Magyarországon 1987–2002 (Political pluralism in Hungary from 1987–2002)*, Budapest: Századvég Kiadó.

—— (2008) 'Consolidation or Second Revolution? The emergence of the New Right in Hungary', *Journal of Communist Studies and Transition Politics*, Vol.24, No.2.
Bozóki, A. and Karácsony, G. (2002) The making of a political elite: participants in the Hungarian Roundtable Talks of 1989, in Bozóki, A. (ed.) *The Roundtable Talks of 1989: The genesis of Hungarian democracy*, Budapest: Central European University Press.
Brown, A. (2000) 'Transnational influences in the transition from communism', *Post-Soviet Affairs*, Vol. 16, No.2.
Brown, J. (2003) *Nehru: A political life*, New Haven and London: Yale University Press.
Bruszt, L. (1990) '1989: The negotiated revolution in Hungary', *Social Research*, Vol.57, No.2.
Bruszt, L. and Stark, D. (1991) 'Remaking the political field in Hungary: From the politics of confrontation to the politics of competition', *Journal of International Affairs*, Vol. 45, No. 1.
Bryman, A. (2004) *Social research methods*, Oxford: Oxford University Press.
Caine, B. (2010) *Biography and history*, New York: Palgrave Macmillan.
Calhoun, N. (2004) *Dilemmas of justice in Eastern Europe's democratic transitions*, New York: Palgrave Macmillan.
Cartledge, B. (2006) *The will to survive: A history of Hungary*, London: Timewell Press.
Chamberlayne, P, Bornat, J. and Wengraf, T. (eds.) (2000) *The turn to biographical methods in social science: Comparative issues and examples*, London and New York: Routledge.
Comisso, E. (1995) 'Legacies of the past or new institutions? The struggle over restitution in Hungary', *Comparative Political Studies*, Vol. 28, No.2.
Congdon, L., and Király, B. (eds.) (2002) *The ideas of the Hungarian revolution suppressed and victorious 1956–1999*, New York: Columbia University Press.
Cox, T. (2006) '1956-Discoveries, legacies and memory', *Europe-Asia Studies*, Vol.58, No.8.
Cox, T. and Furlong, A. (1994) 'Political transition in Hungary: An overview', *Journal of Communist Studies and Transition Politics*, Vol.10, No.3.
Cox, T. and Vass, L. (1994) 'Civil society and interest representation in Hungarian political development', *The Journal of Communist Studies and Transition Politics*, Vol. 10, No.3.
Crampton, R. (1997) *Eastern Europe in the twentieth century and after*, London and New York: Routledge.
Csaba, L. (2000) 'Between transition and EU accession: Hungary at the millennium', *Europe Asia Studies*, Vol.52, No.5.
Cservenka, J. (2000) 'A történelem alattunk van' (We are in the history), *Europai Utas*, April issue.
Csizmadia, E. (1995) *A magyar demokratikus ellenzék: Monográfia 1968–1988 (The Hungarian democratic opposition: Monography 1968–1988)*, Budapest: T-Twins Kiadó.
Deák, I. (1995) 'A fatal compromise? The debate over collaboration and resistance in Hungary', *East European Politics and Societies*, Vol. 9, No.2.
Debreczeni, J. (2003) *A miniszterelnök: Antall József és a rendszerváltozás (The Prime Mminister: József Antall and the systemic change)*, Budapest: Osiris Kiadó.
Dexter, L. (1970) *Elite and specialised interviewing*, Evanston: North Western University Press.
Dezső, M. and Bragyova, A. (2007) Az országos *Népszavazás* Magyarországon (The national referendum in Hungary), in Jakab, A. and Takács, P. (eds.) *A Magyar jogrendszer átalakulása 1985/1990–2005 (The transformation of Hungary's legal system 1985/1990–2005)*, volume 1, Budapest: Gondolat–ELTE ÁJK.

Bibliography

Ekiert, G. (1996) *The state against society: Political crises and their aftermath in East Central Europe*, Princeton: Princeton Univesity Press.

Elster, J. (1993) 'Bargaining over the presidency', *East European Constitutional Review*, Fall 1993/Winter 1994.

—— (1996) Introduction in Elster, J. (ed.) *The Roundtable talks and the breakdown of Communism*, Chicago and London: The University of Chicago Press.

—— (2006) Introduction in Elster, J. (ed.) *Retribution and reparation in transition to democracy*, New York: Cambridge University Press.

Elster, J., Offe, C. and Preuss, U. (1998) *Institutional design in post-Communist societies: Rebuilding the ship at sea*, Cambridge: Cambridge University Press.

Enriquez, C. (1998) Elites and de-Communization in Eastern Europe in Higley, J., Pakulsk, Y. and Wesolwski, W. (eds.) *Post-Communist elites and democracy in Eastern Europe*, New York: St. Martin Press.

Fahidi, G. (1994) 'Paying for the past: the politics and economics of compensation', *The Hungarian Quarterly*, Vol. 35, No. 136.

Falk, B. (2003) *The dilemmas of dissidence in East-Central Europe*, Budapest: Central and European University Press.

Feitl, I. and Kende, J. (eds.) (2007) *Demokratikus köztársaságok Magyarországon (Democratic republics in Hungary)*, Budapest: Napvilág Kiadó.

Fekete, M. (ed.) (2000) *Prominent Hungarians [at] home and abroad*: London: Fehér Holló Press.

Fleming, D. (1995) 'Compensation or restitution?: An analysis of the Hungarian Land Compensation Acts 1991–92', *Journal of Property Valuation and Investment*, Vol. 13, No.4.

Fowkes, B. (1999) *The post-Communist era: change and continuity in Eastern Europe*, London: Macmillan.

Fricz, T. (2001) The Orbán government, an experiment in regime stabilisation: The first two years (1998–2000) in in Ormos, M. and Király, B. (eds.) *Hungary: Governments and politics 1848–2000*, New York: Columbia University Press.

Göncz, Á. (1946) 'Baloldaliság és reakció' (Leftness and reaction), *Nemzedék*, 27 December.

—— (1991) *Gyaluforács: Esszék, jegyzetek, interjuk (Shaving: Essays, notes, interview)*, Pesti Szalon Könyvkiadó.

—— (1992) Europe rediscovering its own map, in Bressand, A. and Csáki, G. (eds.) *European reunification in the age of global networks*, The Institute for World Economics and Promethee.

—— (1993) 'Breaking the vicious circle', *Common Knowledge*, Vol.2, No. 1.

—— (1994) 'Intellectual or politician?', *The Hungarian Quarterly*, Vol.35, No.136.

—— (2004a) *Sodrásban I (In the mid-stream I)*, Budapest: Ulpius-ház Könyvkiadó.

—— (2004b) *Sodrásban II (In the mid-stream II)*, Budapest: Ulpius-ház Könyvkiadó.

Gopal, S. (1989) *Jawaharlal Nehru: A biography*, Oxford: Oxford University Press.

Gough, R. (2006) *A good comrade: János Kádár, Communism and Hungary*, London and New York: I.B. Tauris.

Granville, J. (2001) 'István Bibó after 1956', in István Bibó and the history of Hungary in the 20th century, *International Conference Papers*, Trento.

Gyarmati, G. (2005) Hungary in the second half of the twentieth century, in Tóth, I. (ed.) *A concise history of Hungary*, Budapest: CorvinaOsiris.

György, A. (1947) 'Post-war Hungary', *The Review of Politics*, Vol.9, No.3.

Guha, R. (2007) *India after Gandhi: The history of the world's largest democracy*, London Macmillan.

Hack, P. (2007) Az átmeneti igazságszolgáltatása (The transitional justice), Jakab, A. and Takács, P. (eds.) *A magyar jogrendszer átalakulása 1985/1990–2005, Kötét I (The transformation of Hungary's legal system 1985/1990–2005, vol. I)*, Budapest: Gondolat–ELTE ÁJK.

Halmai, G. (1998) 'The reform of constitutional law in Hungary after the transition', *The Journal of the Society of Legal Studies*, Vol.18, No.2.

—— (1999) Volt-e jogorvsolati joga Kunos Péternek? (Was there the right of legal redress to Péter Kunos?), in Halmai, G. (ed.) *A személyi szabadság és tisztességes eljárás (The personal freedom and fair proceeding)*, Budapest: Indok Kiadó.

—— (2004) *Alkotmánybírósági esetjog (The case-law of the Constitutional Court)*, Budapest: Indok kiadó.

—— (2002) Introduction: The end of activism after ten years' practice of the Sólyom Court, in Halmai, G. (ed.) *Constitution found? The first decade of Hungarian constitutional review on fundamental rights*, The Netherlands: Book World Publications.

Halmai, G. and Scheppele, K. (1997) Living well is the best revenge: The Hungarian approach to judging the past, in McAdams, J. (ed.) *Transitional justice and the rule of law in new democracies*, Notre Dame, IN: University of Notre Dame Press.

Hankiss, E. (1990) *East European Alternatives*, New York: Clarendon Press.

—— (1996) The Hungarian media war of independence, in Sajó, A. and Price, M. (eds.) *Right of access to the media*, The Hague: Kluwer Law International.

—— (1999) Média-ko-média avagy elnök a pagodában (Media vs. Comedia or the president in the pagoda) in *Proletár reneszánsz (Proletariat Renaissance)*, Budapest: Helikon Kiadó.

Hasan, M., Prasad, H. and Damodaran, A. (eds.) (2005) *Selected works of Jawaharlal Nehru: 1 September–30 November 1956*, volume 35, New Delhi: A Project of the Jawaharlal Nehru Memorial Fund.

—— (2006a) *Selected works of Jawaharlal Nehru: 1 December 1956–21 February 1957*, volume 36, New Delhi: A Project of the Jawaharlal Nehru Memorial Fund.

—— (2006b) *Selected works of Jawaharlal Nehru: 22 February 1957–30 April 1957*, volume 37, New Delhi: A Project of the Jawaharlal Nehru Memorial Fund.

—— (2006c) *Selected works of Jawaharlal Nehru: 1 May 1957–31 July 1957*, volume 38, New Delhi: A Project of the Jawaharlal Nehru Memorial Fund.

—— (2007) *Selected works of Jawaharlal Nehru: 1 August–31 October 1957*, volume 39, New Delhi: A Project of the Jawaharlal Nehru Memorial Fund.

Hegedűs, A. (1994) *A petőfi kör vitái: hiteles jegyzőkönyvek alapján (Debates of the Petőfi circle: based on reliable records)*, Budapest: 1956-os Intézet.

—— (1997) The Petőfi Circle: The Forum of Reform in 1956 in Cox, T. (ed.) *Hungary 1956: Forty years on*, London and Portland: Frank Class.

Held, J. (ed.) (1980) *The modernisation of agriculture: Rural transformation in Hungary 1848–1975*, New York: East European Monographs, Boulder.

—— (ed.) (1996) *Populism in Eastern Europe: Racism, Nationalism and Society*, New York: Boulder.

Henderson, K., and Robinson, N. (1997) *Post-Communist politics: An introduction*, London: Prentice Hall.

Higley, J., Kullberg, J. and Pakulski, J. (1996) 'The persistence of post-Communist elites', *Journal of Democracy*, Vol.7, No.2.

Holmes, S. (1993) 'A forum on Presidential Powers', *East European Constitutional Review*, Fall 1993/Winter 1994.

Huszár, T. (2002) *Kedves, Jó Kádár Elvtárs: Válogatás Kádár János levelezéséből*

1954–1989 (Dear a Good Comrade Kádár: selection from János Kádár's letter 1954–1989), Budapest: Osiris Kiadó.

Huyse, L. (1995) 'Justice after transition: On the choices successors elites make in dealing with the past', *Law and Social Inquiry*, Vol. 20, No. 1.

Isaacs, J. and Downing, T. (1998) *Cold War*, London: Bantam Press.

Ishiyama, J. and Velten, M. (1998) 'Presidential power and democratic development in post- Communist politics', *Communist and post-Communist Studies*, Vol. 31, No.3.

Izsák, L. (2001) The Kádár regime and its collapse, in Ormos, M. and Király, B. (eds.) *Hungary: Governments and politics 1848–2000*, New York: Columbia University Press.

Izsák, L. and Nagy, J. (2004) *Magyar történeti dokumentumok 1944–2000 (Hungarian historical documents 1944–2000)*, Budapest: Nemzeti Tankönyvkiadó.

Izsák, L., Pölöskei, F. Romsics, I. and Urbán A. (2003) *Magyar miniszterelnökök 1848–2002 (Hungarian Prime Ministers from 1848–2002)*, Budapest: Kossuth Kiadó.

Jenkins, R. (1995) 'Politics and the development of the Hungarian non-profit sector', *International Journal of Voluntary and Nonprofit Organisations*, Vol. 6, No.2.

Josselson, R., and Lieblich, A. (1995) Introduction in Josselson, R. and Lieblich, A. (eds.) *Interpreting experience: The narrative study of lives*, London: Sage Publications.

Kenedi, J. (ed.) (1996) *A fogoly Bibó István vallomásai az 1956-os forradalomról (The confessions of the prisoner, István Bibó about the 1956 revolution)*, Budapest: 1956- os Intézet.

Kenez, P. (2006) *Hungary from the Nazis to the Soviet: The establishment of Communist regime in Hungary*, Cambridge: Cambridge University Press.

Kidwai, M. (1984) 'India's stance on the Hungarian crisis', *Indian Journal of Politics*, March issue.

Kilényi, G. and Lamm, V. (eds.) (1990) *Democratic changes in Hungary: Basic legislations on a peaceful transition from Bolshevism to democracy*, Budapest: Public Law Research Centre of the Hungarian Academy of Sciences.

Kiscsatári, M. (2009) 'Annus mirabilis', *The Hungarian Quarterly*, Vol.50, No.194.

Kis, J. (1991) 'Post-Communist politics in Hungary', *Journal of Democracy*, Vol.2, No.3.

—— (2003) *Constitutional democracy*, Budapest: Central European University Press.

Kis, J., Kőszeg, F. and Solt, A. (eds.) (1992) *Beszélő: Összkiadás, III. Kötet (Speaker: compilation, vol. III)*, Budapest: AB-Beszélő Kiadó.

Kis, J. and Vida, I. (eds.) (2005) *Magyarországi pártprogrammok 1988–1990 (Hungary's party programmes 1988–1990)*, Budapest: ELTE Eötvös Kiadó.

Kiss, C. (2002) 'From liberalism to conservatism: The Federation of Young Democrats in post-Communist Hungary', *East European Politics and Societies*, Vol.16, No.3.

—— (2006) 'The misuses of manipulation: The failure of transitional justice in post-Communist Hungary', *Europe-Asia Studies*, Vol.58, No.6.

Kiss, S. and Vitányi, I. (1983) *A Magyar diákok szabadságfrontja (The Freedom Front of the Hungarian Students)*, Az Antifasiszta Ifjúsági Emlékmű Szervezőbizottsága.

Kontler, L. (2002) *A history of Hungary: Millenium in Central Europe*, New York: Palgrave Macmillan.

Kónya, B. (2000) 'Hungary', *The American Journal of Economics and Sociology*, Vol.59, No.5.

Kónya, I. (2002) Hungary's negotiated revolution in Congdon, L. and Király, B. (eds.) *The ideas of the Hungarian Revolution, suppressed and victorious 1956–1999*, New York: Columbia University Press.

Koppany, S. (1986) 'Hungarian opposition groups hold meeting to discuss nation's future', *Radio Free Europe Background Report*, presented by the Open Society Archive.

Kornai, J. (1996) 'Paying the bill for Goulash Communism: Hungarian development and macro-stabilisation in a political-economy perspective', *Social Research*, Vol. 63, No. 4.
Körösényi, A. (1992) The decay of Communist rule in Hungary, in Bozóki, A., Körösényi, A., and Shöpflin, G. (eds.) *Post-Communist Transition: Emerging pluralism in Hungary*, New York: St. Martin Press.
—— (1999) *Government and politics in Hungary*, Budapest: Central European University Press.
—— (2006) Mozékony patthelyzet (Agile stalemate), in Gombár, C. (ed.) *Túlterhelt demokrácia: Alkotmányos és kormányzati alapszerkezetünk (Overburdened democracy: Our constitutional and basic governing structure)*, Budapest: Századvég Kiadó.
Körösényi, A., Tóth, C. and Török, G. (2003) *A Magyar politikai rendszer (The political system of Hungary)* Budapest: Osiris Kiadó.
—— (2007) *A magyar politika rendszer (The political system of Hungary)*, Budapest: Osiris Kiadó.
Kőrösi, Z. (1991) Névjegyzék (Register), in Litván, G. (ed.) *Az 1956-os magyar forradalom: reform, felkelés, szabadságharc and megtorlás (The 1956 Hungarian Revolution: reform, uprising, freedomfight and reprisal)*, Budapest: Tankönyvkiadó.
Kőrösi, Z. and Molnár, A. (2003) *Carrying a secret in my heart: Children of the victims of the reprisal after the Hungarian revolution in 1956*, Budapest: Central and European University Press.
Kovács, Á. (2006) *Viták a köztársasági elnök jogköréről (Debates on the scope of the presidential powers)*, Debrecen: Debreceni Állam és Jogtudományi Kar.
Kovács, É. (ed.) (1993) Marionettbábu vagy félisten?: A köztársasági elnökkel kapcsolatos hatásköri viták a Magyar sajtóban (Marionette or demigod: Debates over the scope of the president's [powers] in the Hungarian press), Politikai Tanulmányok, presented by the 1956 Institute.
Kovács, V. (2001) 'A köztársasági elnök: a végrehajtó hatalomon kívűl és a politika felett?' (The president of the Republic: outside of the power [branch] of the executive and above the party?), *Magyar Közigazgatás*, Vol.51, No.6.
Kovrig, B. (1984) Hungary in Harmstone-Rakowska, T. (ed.) *Communism in Eastern Europe*, Bloomington, IN: Indiana University Press.
Kozák, G. (1991) A forradalom utóvédharcai (Rearguard struggles of the Revolution), in Litván, G. (ed.) *Az 1956-os magyar forradalom: reform, felkelés, szabadságharc and megtorlás (The 1956 Hungarian Revolution: reform, uprising, freedomfight and reprisal)*, Budapest: Tankönyvkiadó.
Kramer, M. (1998) 'The Soviet Union and the 1956 Crises in Hungary and Poland: Reassessment and new findings', *Journal of Contemporary History*, Vol.33, No.2.
Kukorelli, I. (1995) The presidency in Király, B. (ed.) *Lawful revolution in Hungary 1989–94*, New York: Columbia University Press.
Kurtán, S., Sándor, P. and Vass, L. (eds.) (1991) A taxi blokád (The taxi blockade), in *Magyarország politikaiévkönyve 1990 (The 1990 year book of Hungary's politics)*, Budapest: Demokrácia Kutatások Magyar Központja Alapítvány.
—— (1990) A közvélemény 1989-ben (The public opinion in 1989) *in Magyarország politikai évkönyve* 1989 (The 1989 year book of Hungary's politics), Budapest: Demokrácia Kutatások Magyar Központja közhasznú Alapítvány.
—— (1992a) 'Az MDF Frakció Elnökségének Állásfoglalása Tervezete: Igazságtételt Alkotmányosan és Törvényesen' (The Draft of the Standpoint of the MDF Factional Presidium: Justice [must be done] constitutionally and legally), in *Magyarország*

politikai évkönyve 1991 (The 1991 year book of Hungary's politics), Budapest: Demokrácia Kutatások Magyar Központja közhasznú Alapítvány.

—— (1992b) (eds.) 'Göncz Árpád, a Magyar Köztársaság Elnökének Beszéde az Alkotmánybíróság Teljes Zárt Ülésen 1991 December 17-én' (The Speech of the President of the Republic of Hungary, Árpád Göncz in the Closed Session of the Constitutional Court on 17 December 1991), in *Magyarország politikai évkönyve* 1991 (The 1991 year book of Hungary's politics), Budapest: Demokrácia Kutatások Magyar Központja közhasznú Alapítvány.

—— (1993) Médiavita: a levelézesek éve (A media debate: The year of correspondence)', in *Magyarország politikai évkönyve* 1992 (The 1992 year book of Hungary's politics), Budapest: Demokrácia Kutatások Magyar Központja közhasznú Alapítvány.

—— (1999) A Fidesz-Magyar Polgári Párt választási negyven pontja (40 election points of the Fidesz-Hungarian Civic Party), in *Magyarország politikai évkönyve* 1998 (the 1998 year of Hungary's politics), Budapest: Magyar Központja közhasznú Alapítvány.

Lánczi, A. and O'Neil, P. (1996) 'Pluralisation and the politics of media change in Hungary', *Journal of Communist Studies and Transition Politics*, Vol.12, No.4.

László, E. (2006) *The Hungarian Revolution of 1956: myths and realities*, New Jersey: East European Monographs.

Lázár, G. (ed.) (1992) A politikai közvélemény a Medián kutatásinak tükrében (The political public opinion as reflected by the polls of Medián) in Kurtán, S., Sándor, P. and Vass, L. (eds.) *Magyarország politikai évkönyve* 1992 *(The 1992 year book of Hungary's politics)*, Budapest: Demokrácia Kutatások Magyar Központja közhasznú Alapítvány.

Lendvai, P. (2008) *One day that shook the Communist world: The 1956 Hungarian uprising and its legacy*, Princeton and Oxford: Princeton University Press.

Lewis, P. (1994) *Central Europe since 1945*, London and New York: Longman.

Lilleker, D. (2003) 'Interviewing the political elite: Navigating a potential minefield', *Politics*, Vol.23, No.3.

Linz, J. and Stepan, A. (1996) *Problems of democratic transition and consolidation*, Baltimore and London: The Johns Hopkins University Press.

Litván, G. (1989) 'A Nagy Imre-Csoport' (The Imre Nagy group), *Századvég*, 1–2 issue.

—— (ed.) (1991) *Az 1956-os magyar forradalom: reform, felkelés, szabadságharc and megtorlás (The 1956 Hungarian Revolution: reform, uprising, freedomfight and reprisal)*, Budapest: Tankönyvkiadó.

—— (ed.) (1996) *The Hungarian Revolution of 1956: Reform, revolt and repression 1953–1963*, London and New York: Longman.

—— (2008) *Maradunk a tényeknél: Történeti-politikai írások (Let's remain in the facts: Historical-political writings)*, Budapest: 1956-os Intézet.

Litván, G. and Varga, K. (1995) *Bibó István életút dokumentumokban (Path of life of István Bibó in documents)*, Budapest: 1956-os Intézet Osiris-Századvég.

Lomax, B. (1993) Hungary at the crossroads in Whitefield, S. (ed.) *The new institutional architecture of Eastern Europe*, Basingstoke: Macmillan.

Lukács, G. (1992) A Teleki Pál Munkaközösség rövid története (Brief history of the Pál Teleki Panel), in Csicsery-Rónay, I. and Vígh, K. (eds.) *Teleki Pál és kora: A Teleki Pál emlékév előadásai (Pál Teleki and his era: The memorial lectures of Pál Teleki)*, Budapest: Occidental Press.

Marer, P. (1999) Economic transformation, 1990–1998, in Braun, A. and Barany, Z. (eds.) *Dilemmas of transition: The Hungarian experience*, New York: Rowmanand Littlefield.

McGregor, J. (1994) 'The Presidency in East Central Europe', *RFE/RL Research Report*, Vol.3, No.2.
Menon, K. (1963) *The flying troika*, London: Oxford University Press.
—— (1967) *The lamp and the lampstand*, London: Oxford University Press.
Mészáros, I. (1993) *Teleki Pál nemzetnevelő programja (The programme of Pál Teleki's national educator)*, Gödöllő: Teleki Pál Egyesület.
Mézes, F. (1992) 'The media war', *The New Hungarian Quarterly*, Vol.127, No.33.
Mihály, P. (1997) 'A kárpótlás' (The compensation), *2000*, Vol.9, No. 3.
—— (2004) *A kárpótlás (The compensation)*, Budapest: Kulturtrade Kiadó.
Milton, A. (2000) *The rational politician: Exploiting the media in new democracies*, Aldershot: Ashgate.
—— (2001) 'Bound but not gagged: Media reform in democratic transitions', *Comparative Political Studies*, Vol.34, No.5.
Miszlivetz, F. (1995) *Vadkelet-party (Wild Eastern-party)*, Szombathely: Savaria University Press.
Mitchell, W. (1981) Foreword in Mitchell, W. (ed.) *On narrative*, Chicago and London: The University of Chicago Press.
Molnár, A. (2009) *Ötvenhatosok a rendszerváltásról ('56-ers about the political transformation of 1989)*, Budapest: 1956-os Intézet.
Molnár, M. (2001) *A concise history of Hungary*, Cambridge: Cambridge University Press.
Monori, Á. (2005) Mediaháborúk (Media Wars) in Bajomi-Lázár, P. (ed.) *Magyarország mediatörténet: A késő Kádár-kortól az ezredfordulóig (The history of Hungarian media: From the late Kádár period to the millennium)*, Budapest: Akademiai Kiadó.
Morlang, D. (2003) Hungary: Socialists building capitalism, in Curry, J. and Urban, J. (eds.) *The left transformed in post-Communist societies: The cases of East Central Europe, Russia and Ukraine*, Lanham, MD: Rowman and Littlefield.
Mudde, C. (2001) 'In the name of the Peasantry, the Proletariat, and the People: Populism in Eastern Europe', *East European Politics and Societies*, Vol.15, No.1.
Nagy, G. (1990) 'Felsőfokú nyelvtanfolyam a börtönben' (Advanced language course in the prison), *Új Tér-kép*, 30 May.
Nehru, J. (1942) *Jawaharlal Nehru: An autobiography*, London: John Lane.
—— (1961) *India's foreign policy: Selected speeches, September 1946–April 1961*, Delhi: The Publications Divisions, Ministry of Information and Broadcasting Government of India.
Némedi, D. (1995) 'Remarks on the role of peasants in the Hungarian ideology', *Journal of Popular Culture*, Vol.29, No.2.
Okey, R. (2004) *The demise of Communist East Europe 1989 in context*, London: Arnold.
Okolicsanyi, K. (1990) 'President Árpád Göncz and the Office of the Presidency', *Report on Eastern Europe*, Vol.1, No.42.
—— (1991a) 'The compensation law: Attempting to correct past mistakes', *Report on Eastern Europe*, Vol. 2, No. 19.
—— (1991b) 'Compensation law finally approved', *Report on Eastern Europe*, Vol.2, No.36.
—— (1993) 'Hungarian compensation programs off to a slow start', *RFE/RL Research Report*, Vol.2, No. 11.
Olson, D. (1994) The new parliaments of new democracies: The experience of the Federal Assembly of the Czech and Slovak Federal Republic, in Ágh, A. (ed.) *The emergence of East Central European Parliaments: The first steps*, Budapest: Hungarian Centre of Democracy Studies.

Oltay, E. (1992) 'Hungary', *RFE/RL Research Report*, Vol. 1, No. 39.
—— (1992) 'Towards the rule of law: Hungary', *RFE/RL Research Report*, Vol.1, No.27.
—— (1993a) 'Hungary attempts to deal with its past', *RFE/RL Research Report*, Vol.2, No.18.
—— (1993b) 'Hungarian radio and television under fire', *RFE/RL Research Report*, Vol. 2, No. 38.
O'Neil, P. (1993) 'Presidential power in post-Communist Europe: The Hungarian case in comparative perspective', *Journal of Communist Studies and Transition Politics*, Vol.9, No.3.
—— (1997) Hungary: political transition and executive conflict: the balance or fragmentation of power, in Taras, R. (ed.) *Post-Communist Presidents*, Cambridge: Cambridge University Press.
—— (1998) 'Revolution from within: Analysis, transition from authoritarianism, and the case of Hungary', *World Politics*, Vol.48, No.4.
Paczolay, P. (1992) 'Judicial review of the compensation law in Hungary', *Michigan Journal of International Law*, Vol.13, No.4.
—— (1993) The new Hungarian constitutional state: Challenges and perspectives, Howard, D. (ed.) *Constitution making in Eastern Europe*, Washington: The Woodland Wilson Centre Press.
Palasik, M. (2002) *Kovács Béla: 1908–1959 (Béla Kovács: 1908–1959)*, Budapest: Occidental Press.
Pál, L. (1991) '1956 és ami utána következett' (1956 and which followed thereafter), *Kapu*, Issue 12.
Pataki, J. (1992a) 'Dealing with Hungarian communists' crimes', *RFE/RL Research Report*, Vol.9, No.1.
—— (1992b) 'Political battle in Hungary over broadcasting dismissals', *RFE/RL Research Report*, Vol. 1, No. 30.
—— (1993) 'Power struggle over broadcasting in Hungary', *RFE/RL Research Report*, Vol. 2, No. 11.
—— (1994) 'Hungarian radio staff cuts cause uproar', *RFE/RL Research Report*, Vol.3, No.19.
Pataki, J. and Schiemann, J. (1991) 'Constitutional Court limits presidential powers', *Report on Eastern Europe*, 18 October.
Peabody, R, Webb Hammond, S., Torcom, J., Brown, L. P., Thompson, C. and Kolodny, R. (1990) 'Interviewing political elites', *Political Science and Politics*, Vol.23, No.3.
Petrétei, J. (2001a) A köztársasági elnök (The president of the Republic), in *Magyaralkotmányjog II: Államszervezet (The law of the Hungarian Constitution II: State organisation)*, Budapest-Pécs, Dialóg Campus Kiadó.
—— (2001b) Az alkotmánybíróság (The Constitutional Court), in *Magyaralkotmányjog II: Államszervezet (The law of the Hungarian Constitution II: State organisation)*, Budapest-Pécs, Dialóg Campus Kiadó.
—— (2005) 'A köztársasági elnök vétójogáról' (About the veto of the Republic of the President of [Hungary]), *Jogtudományi Közlöny*, Vol. 60, No. 4.
Pimlott, B. (1999) 'Is contemporary biography history?', *Political Quarterly*, Vol.70, No.1.
Pittaway, M. (2003) Hungary, in White, S., Batt, J. and Lewis, P. (eds.) *Developments in Central and East European politics*, London: Palgrave Macmillan.
Pokol, B. (2003) 'Separation of powers and parliamentarism in Hungary', *East European Quarterly*, Vol.37, No.1.

Pridham, G. (2000) *The dynamics of democratisation: A comparative approach*, London and New York: Continuum.
Raadt, J. (2009) 'Contestable constitutions: Ambiguity, conflict, and change in East Central European dual executive systems', *Communist and post-Communist Studies*, Vol. 42, No. 1.
Rainer, J. (1993) 'István Bibó – A great political diagnostician', *Hungarian Quarterly*, Vol. 34, No. 132.
—— (2002a) A progress of ideas: The Hungarian Revolution of 1956, in Congdon, L. and Király, B. (eds.) *The ideas of the Hungarian revolution suppressed and victorious 1956–1999*, New York: Columbia University Press.
—— (2002b) The reburial of Imre Nagy: A symbolic act of democratic transformation in Hungary, in Congdon, L. and Király, B. (eds.) *The ideas of the Hungarian revolution suppressed and victorious 1956–1999*, New York: Columbia University Press.
—— (2009) *Imre Nagy: A biography*, London and New York: I. B. Tauris, pp. 166–198.
Révész, S. (1995) *Antall József távolról 1932–1993 (József Antall from a bird's eye view, 1932–1993)*, Budapest: Síkkiadó.
—— (2000) *Beszélő évek 1957–1968 (Years of speaker 1957–1968)*, Budapest: A Beszélő Politikai és Kulturális Folyóirat Kiadása.
Richards, D. (1996) 'Elite interviewing and approaches and pitfalls', *Politics*, Vol.16, No.3.
Ripp, Z. (2006) *Rendszerváltás Magyarországon 1987–1990 (Political transformation in Hungary from 1987–1990)*, Budapest: Napvilág Kiadó.
Robert, P. (1998) 'The politics of history: some methodological and ethical dilemmas in elite- based research', *British Educational Research Journal*, Vol.24, No. 1.
Roberts, B. (2002) *Biographical research*, Buckingham: Open University Press.
Romsics, I. (1999) *Hungary in the twentieth century*, Budapest: Corvina and Osiris.
—— (ed.) (2000) *Magyar történeti-szöveggyűjtmény 1914–1999. I (Text collection of Hungarian history between 1914 and 1999 Vol. I)*, Budapest: Osiris Kiadó.
—— (2001) The first four years of democratic transformation in Ormos, M. and Király, B. (eds.) *Hungary: governments and politics 1848–2000*, New York: Columbia University Press.
—— (2005) Hungary in the two world wars, in Tóth, I. (ed.) *A concise history of Hungary*, Budapest: Corvina·Osiris.
—— (2007) *From dictatorship to democracy: The birth of the third Hungarian republic 1988–2001*, New York: Columbia University Press.
Rose-Ackerman, S. (2005) *From elections to democracy: Building accountable government in Hungary and Poland*, New York: Cambridge University Press.
Rothschild, J. and Wingfield, N. (2000) *Return to diversity: A political history of East Central Europe since World War II*, Oxford: Oxford University Press.
Schwartz, H. (1993) 'The new courts: An overview', *East European Constitutional Review*, Spring issue.
—— (2000) *The struggle for constitutional justice in post-Communist Europe*, Chicago and London: The University of Chicago Press.
Sajó, A. (1996) The Roundtable Talks in Hungary, in Elster, J. (ed.) *The Roundtable Talks and the breakdown of Communism*, Chicago and London: The University of Chicago Press.
Saláta, K. (1989) *Fejezetek a Független Kisgazda Párt 1945 – ös küzdelméből (Chapters on the Independent Smallholders' Party from the 1945 struggle)*, Washington D.C: Occidental Press.

Schiemann, J. (2005) Presidentialism, parliamentarism and opposition intransigence: The Presidency, in *The politics of pact-making: Hungary's negotiated transition to democracy in comparative perspective*, New York: Palgrave Macmillan.

Schöpflin, G. (1977) Hungary in McCauley, M. *(ed.) Communist power in Hungary 1944–1949*: London: Macmillan.

—— (1991) 'Conservatism and Hungary's transition', *Problems of Communism*, Vol. 40, No. 1/2.

Shugart, M. (1993) 'Of Presidents and Parliaments', *East European Constitutional Review*, winter issue.

Sólyom, L. and Holló, A. (1992) *Az alkotmánybírósági határozatai 1991 (The rulings of the constitutional court in 1991)*, Budapest: Triorg Kiadó.

—— (1993) *Az alkotmánybírósági határozatai 1992 (The rulings of the Constitutional Court in 1992)*, Budapest: Triorg Kiadó.

—— (1994) *Az alkotmánybírósági határozatai 1993 (The rulings of the Constitutional Court in 1993)*, Budapest: Triorg Kiadó.

—— (1995) *Az alkotmánybírósági határozatai 1993 (The rulings of the Constitutional Court in 1993)*, Budapest: Triorg Kiadó.

Stanger, (2004) 'How important are new Constitutions for democratic consolidation? Lessons from the post-Communist states', *Democratization*, Vol. 11, No. 3.

Stark, D. (1996) 'Recombinant property in East European capitalism', *The American Journal of Sociology*, Vol.101, No.4.

Stein, A. (1969) *India and the Soviet Union: The Nehru era*, Chicago and London: University of Chicago Press.

Sükösd, F. (1996) Az elnöki intézmény, a Magyar köztársasági elnöke (The presidential institution, the president of the Republic of Hungary), in Kiss, L. (ed.) *Válogatott fejezetek a rendszeres alkotmánytan köréből (Selected chapters from the systematic studies of constitution)*, Pécs: Janus Pannonius Tudományegyetem Állam és Jogtudományi Kar Kiadó.

Sükösd, M. (2000) Democratic transformation and the mass media in Hungary: From Stalinism to democratic consolidation, in Gunther, R. and Mughan, A. (eds.) *Democracy and the media: A comparative perspective*, Cambridge: Cambridge University Press.

Surányi, G. (2000) A bizalom elnöke (The president of reliability), in Borbíró, Z. (ed.) *Göncz Árpádnak (To Árpád Göncz)*, Budapest: Helikon.

Swain, G. (2011) *Tito: A biography*, London: I.B. Tauris.

Swain, N. (1993) Hungary, in White, S., Batt, J. and Lewis, P. *(eds.) Developments in East European politics*, London: The Open University.

—— (2006) Negotiated revolution in Poland and Hungary, 1989, in McDermott, K. and Stibbe, M. (eds.) *Revolution and resistance in Eastern Europe: Challenges to Communist rule*, Oxford: Berg Press.

Swain, N. and Swain, G. (2003) *Eastern Europe since 1945*, London and New York: Palgrave Macmillan.

Szabó, C. (1997) Átalakulófélben: A kormány és tevékenységének közmegítélése 1996ban (In the process of transformation: Public opinion on the government and its activities in 1996), in Kurtán, S., Sándor, P. and Vass, L. (1997) (eds.) *Magyarország politikai évkönyve 1996 (The 1996 year book of Hungary's politics)*, Budapest: Demokrácia Kutatások Magyar Központja közhasznú Alapítvány.

Szakolczai, A. (2002) Repression and restoration 1956–1963, in Congdon, L. and Király, B. (eds.) *The ideas of the Hungarian Revolution, suppressed and victorious 1956–1999*, New York: Columbia University Press.

Szarvas, L. (1994) 'Parties and party factions in the Hungarian parliament', *Journal of Communist and Transition Politics*, Vol.10, No.3.
Szilágyi, S. (1991) István Bibó, Central Europes political therapist, in Nagy, K. (ed.) and Boros, A. (trans.) *Democracy, revolution, self-determination: Selected writings*, New York: Boulder.
Szoboszlai, G. (1996) Parliamentarism in the making: crisis and political transformation in Hungary, in Lijphart, A. and Waisman, H. (eds.) *Institutional design in new democracies: Eastern Europe and Latin America*, Colorado: Westview Press.
Szomszéd, O. (2005) 'Államfői jogkörök alkalmazása a gyakorlatban' (Application of the presidential powers in practice), *Politika Tudományi Szemle*, Vol. 14, No.1.
Taras, R. (1993) Leaderships and executives, in White, S., Batt, J. and Lewis, P. (eds.) *Developments in East European politics*, London: Macmillan.
Tőkés, R. (1970) 'Popular front in the Balkans: 3. Hungary', *Journal of Contemporary History*, Vol.5, No.3.
―――― (1997) Party politics and political participation in post-Communist Hungary, in Dawisha, K. and Parrott, B. (eds.) *The consolidation of democracy in East-Central Europe*, Cambridge: Cambridge University Press.
―――― (1996) *Hungary's negotiated revolution: Economic reform, social change and political succession*, Cambridge: Cambridge University Press
Tölgyessy, P. (1999b) *Elégedtlenségek egyensúlya: Válogatott írások (Balance of discontentment: Selected writings)*, Budapest: Helikon Kiadó.
Tóth, M. (ed.) (1990) *A magyar írószövetség közgyűlése: Jegyzőkönyv (The general meeting of the Hungarian Writers Association: Record)*, Budapest: Magyar Írókszövetsége.
―――― (1999) *Árpád Göncz in mid-stream*, Budapest: CORVINA·UNESCO.
Varga, Z. (2006) Paraszti követelések 1956-ban (Peasant demands in 1956) in Estók, J. (ed.) *1956 és a magyar agrártársadalom (1956 and the Hungarian agricultural society)*, Budapest: Magyar Mezőgazdasági Múzeum.
Vásárhelyi, M. (2006) *A történelemben: válogatott beszédei és írásai a nyolcvanas- kilencvenes ékből (In the history: select speeches and writings from the 80s–90s)*, Budapest: Élet és Irodalom Kiadása.
Vida, I. (2002) 'Parasztpolitikus az úri Magyarországgal szemben' (Peasant politician [who was] against the gentry Hungary), *História*, 2002/2003 issue.
Vigh, K. (1992) *Bajcsy-Zsilinszky Endre 1886–1944: A küldetéses ember (Endre Bajcsy-Zsilinszky 1886–1944: A man with mission)*, Budapest: Szépirodalmi Könyvkiadó.
Vitányi, I. (2002) 'Göncz Árpád' (Árpád Göncz), *Essay*, presented by Iván Vitányi.
Unwin, P. (1991) *Voice in the wilderness: Imre Nagy and the Hungarian Revolution*, London: Macdonald.
Welsh, H. (1996) 'Dealing with the communist past: Central and East European experiences after 1990', *Europe-Asia Studies*, Vol. 48, No.3.
Weydenthal, J. (1991) 'The Visegrád Summit', *Report on Eastern Europe*, 1 March.
Whitehead, L. (1994) East Central Europe in comparative perspective in Pridham, G., Herring, E. and Sanford, G. (eds.) *Building democracy? The international dimension of democratization in Eastern Europe*, London: Leicester University Press.
Wilson, K. and Wilson, C. (1989) *Voices of dissent: Two plays by Árpád Göncz*, London and Toronto: Associated University Presses.
Wisinger, I. and László, G. (1994) *Göncz Árpád: Beszélgetések az elnökkel (Árpád Göncz: Talks with the president)*, Budapest: Pesti Szalon Könyv Kiadó.
―――― (2007) *Visszanézve: Beszélgetések Göncz Árpáddal (Looking back on: Talks with Árpád Göncz)*, Budapest: Gloria Kiadó.

Wisniewski, R. and Hatch, J. (1995) Life history and narrative: Questions, issues, and exemplary works, in Wisniewski, R. and Hatch, J. (eds.) *Life history and narrative*, London: The Falmer Press.

Journal articles without authors' names

'Constitutional Watch', *East European Constitutional Review*, Spring 1995, Vol. 1, No. 1.
'Constitutional Watch', *East European Constitutional Review*, Winter 1997, Vol. 6, No.1
'Constitutional Watch', *East European Constitutional Review*, Fall 1998, Vol.7, No. 4.
'Constitutional Watch', *East European Constitutional Review*, Winter/Spring 1999, Vol. 8, No. 1–2.
'Constitutional Watch', *East European Constitutional Review*, Summer 1999, Vol. 8, No.3.
'Hungary restricts foreign access to farm land', *Agra Europe*, 2003, Vol. 4, No.1.
'Treaty of Peace with Hungary', *The American Journal of International Law*, 1947, Vol.42, No.4.

Newspapers with authors' or editors' names in English and Hungarian

Babus, E. (1995) 'Újra Göncz Árpád, az államfő: Szimpla duplázás' (Again Árpád Göncz, the head of state: Simple repetition), *Heti Világgazdaság,* 24 June.
—— (1996a) 'Alkotmánykoncepcio-vita: A szentek keze' (The debate on the conception of a new constitution: We all favour ourselves), *Heti Világgazdaság,* 18 May.
—— (1996b) 'Átszerkesztett alaptörvény-koncepció: Újra itt van' (The concept of a redrafted constitution: Here it is again), *Heti Világgazdaság*, 9 November.
—— (1996c) 'Alkotmánykoncepcio-vita: Az elnök új ruhája' (The debate on the concept of a new constitution: The president's new clothes), *Heti Világgazdaság,* 30 November
—— (1997) 'Államfői vétók: Taktikai fault?' (The veto of the head of state: Tactical fault), *Heti Világgazdaság*, 11 January.
—— (2000) 'A Gönczi dekád' (A decade of Göncz), *Heti Világgazdaság*, 10 June.
—— (2001) 'Egydimenziós elnök' (The one dimensional president), *Heti Világgazdaság,* 4 August.
Bak, M. (1995) 'Távozik a kormány két minisztere' (Two government's ministers leave their posts), *Népszava*, 13 March.
Barabás, T. (1989) 'A "Bibó-tanszék" tanitványa' ('Disciple of the Bibó-department'), *Est Hirlap*, 7 July.
Beck, L. (1992) 'Nem az igazságtétel a legfontosabb feladat' (Justice is not the most important task), *Magyar Hírlap*, 21 October.
Bihari, T. (2000) 'Göncz Árpád egy elnöki évtizede' (A decade of Árpád Göncz's presidency), *Népszava*, 1 July.
Bíró, L. (2000) 'Erkölcsi tőkémet nem élhetem fel a napi politikában' (I cannot use my moral [authority] in daily politics), *Népszava*, 30 December.
Bíró, L. and Németh, P. (2000) 'A társadalmi felemelkedés megteremtése a legsürgetőbb (The creation of social progress is the most urgent), *Népszava*, 14 March.
Bodnár, L. (1991) 'Az alkotmánybírósághoz fordult Göncz Árpád' (Árpád Göncz turned to the Constitutional Court), *Népszava*, 14 May.
—— (1995) 'További öt évre Göncz Árpád a köztársasági elnök' (For another five years, the president of the Republic of Hungary [is] Árpád Göncz), *Magyar Nemzet*, 20 June.

Buják, A. (2000) 'Göncz Árpád: Tiz éve' (Árpád Göncz: ten years), *168 Óra*, 8 June.
Csák, C., Dániel, A. and Zsubori, E. (2007) 'Agrobank-ügy: példát statuáltak' (Agricultural bank affair[s]: set as an example), *Figyelő*, 3 September.
Csuhaj, I., and Kéri, T. (1998) 'Az ellenzék bírálja az új parlamenti munkarendet' (The opposition criticises the new parliamentary work order), *Népszabadság*, 28 December.
Dobszay, J. (1998) 'Gyendelkedő köztársasági elnök: Recept nélkül' (Ailing the president of the Republic: Without prescription), *Heti Világgazdaság*, 10 January.
Dornbach, A. (1992) 'A rendőrség tudott a skinheadek mozgósításáról' (The police knew about the mobilisation of the skinheads), *Népszabadság*, 28 October.
Fahidi, G. (1999) 'Egykézés' (Only child), *Heti Világgazdaság*, 3 July.
Farkas, G. (1990) 'És mit mond a Festő?' ('And what the painter says?'), *Népszabadság*, 21 October.
—— (1991) 'Lépés a körkörös barátság felé' (Step towards a multi-lateral friendship), *Népszabadság*, 15 February.
—— (1991) 'Nem vissza, előre kell menni!' (No step back, but must go forward!), *Népszabadság*, 29 October.
Fekete, A. (1991) 'Alkotmánybírósághoz fordult az elnök' (The President turned to the Constitutional Court), *Népszabadság*, 19 November.
Félix, P. (1994) 'Földönkívüliek' (Outsiders from [the law] of arable land), *Héti Világgazdaság*, 29 April.
Fricz, T. (2010) 'Jó köztársasági elnök lehet Schmitt Pál' (It is possible that Pál Schmitt would be a good president of the Republic), *Magyar Nemzet*, 23 July.
Gréczy, Z. (2005) 'A kiteljesitett elnöki örökség' (The fulfilled president's legacy), *Népszabadság*, 30 July.
—— (2006) 'Én már láttam válságban az országot, a mostani nem az' (I have already seen that the country was in crisis [but] that is not [our] present [situation]), *Népszabadság*, 24 July.
György, B. (1997) 'Bumerángparti' (Boomerang party), *Magyar Narancs*, 9 January.
Halmai, G. (1991) 'A köztársasági elnök kifejezi a nemzeti egységet' (The president of the Republic represents the unity of the nation), *Magyar Hírlap*, 22 July.
—— (1995) 'Hogyan (ne) bíráljuk az államfőt?' (How can or cannot we criticise the head of state?), *Élet és Irodalom*, 30 June.
Hámor, S. and Bárfai, G. (1991) 'Ninch elévülés' (There is no [statutory] limitation), *Népszabadság*, 5 November.
Hegedűs, A. (1998) 'Visszatekintés 1988-ra' (Retrospect about 1988), *Magyar Nemzet*, 13 June.
Kéri, T. and Zsoldos, A. (1997) 'Göncz részletezte alkotmányos aggályait' (Göncz detailed his constitutional anxieties), *Népszabadság*, 7 January.
Kis, J. (1990) 'A megállapodás' (The agreement), *Beszélő*, 5 May.
Komor, V. (1989) 'Történelem és igazságtétel' (History and justice), *Magyar Nemzet*, 8 February.
Kovács, L. (1992) 'Göncz Árpád: Megkérdőjelezhetetlen az alkotmánybíróság döntése' (Árpád Göncz: The decision of Constitutional Court cannot be questioned), *Népszabadság*, 6 March.
Kozák, G. (2008) 'TEB-ből TIB' (From TEB to TIB), *Élet és Irodalom*, 13 June.
Kurcz, B. (2010) 'A szolidáritás zenéje: a váci börtönsztrájk' (The music of solidarity: The Vác prison [hunger] strike), *Népszava*, 22 October.
Lengyel, G. (1992) 'Mindenki kapod utána, de csak kevesen érik' (Everyone tries to get this thing but not everyone has the chance to get it), *Magyar Hírlap*, 6 November.

238 Bibliography

Lengyel, L. (2000) 'Az utolsó munkanap két elnöki ciklus után' (The last working day after two presidential term), *Népszabadság*, 3 August.

Lovas, I. (2002) 'Ha Mádl Göncz lenne' (If Mádl would become Göncz), *Magyar Nemzet*, 26 June.

Mátraházi, Z. (1989) 'Drámákba foglalt börtönnapló' (Prison diary [depicted] in dramas), *Magyar Nemzet*, 11 November.

Mester, Á. (2000) 'Maradtam, aki voltam' (I remained as I was), *168 Óra*, 21 December.

Moldovány, T. (2001) 'Elnök, blokád és szerepzavar' (President, blockade and interfering role), *Hetiválasz*, 5 October.

Petri, A. (2002) 'Ez volt történelemünkben az a rövid pillanat, amikor a társadalom egységes volt' (In our history, this was the brief moment when the society was united), *Népszava*, 22 October.

Pogány, S. (1997) 'Göncz Árpád nem írta alá a privatizációs törvényt' (Árpád Göncz did not sign the law of privatisation), *Magyar Hírlap*, 4 January.

Rádai, E. (1990) 'Elnök is járhat villamossal' (The president also can use the tram)', *168 Óra*, 8 May.

Sereg, A. (1991) 'Göncz Árpád az alkotmánybíróságon' (Árpád Göncz is in the Constitutional Court), *Népszabadság*, 18 December.

—— (1999) 'Alkotmánysértő a maffiaellenes törvénycsomag' (The Anti-Mafia Package violates the Constitution), *Népszabadság*, 24 February.

Somos, A. (1994) 'Halottnak a beöntés' ('Pears before swine'), *Magyar Narancs*, 8 December.

—— (1997a) 'A köztársasági elnök hét éve: Díszmagyar' (The seven years of the president of the Republic: Honourable citizen), *Magyar Narancs*, 20 March.

—— (1997b) 'Díszmagyar' (Honourable Hungarian), *Magyar Narancs*, 20 March.

Stefka, I. (2000) 'Támogatás a politikai üldözötteknek' (Support to the victims of political persecution), *Magyar Nemzet*, 4 November 2000.

Stépán, B. (1997) 'Jog és etika' (Law and ethics), *Magyar Hírlap*, 7 January.

Sükösd, M. (1992) 'Médiaháború' (Media war), *Magyar Narancs*, 27 May.

Szálé, L. (2003) 'Egy hatalmi eszközöm volt: a szó' (My power instrument was [my voice]), *Magyar Hírlap*, 12 April.

—— (2006) 'Beszélgetés Göncz Árpáddal, a magyar köztársaság volt elnökével' (Talk with Árpád Göncz, the former president of the Republic of Hungary), *Magyar Hírlap*, 20 October.

Szász, I. (2010) 'Elnököktől az elnökig' (From presidents to the president), *Népszava*, 3 July.

Szegő, M. (2010) 'Mementó 1990: Göncz Árpádot elnökké választják' (Memento 1990: Árpád Göncz is elected to the [office] of the president), *Heti Világgazdaság*, 3 August.

Szerető, S. (1993) 'A frekvenciagazdálkodási törvény normakontrollját kéri az elnök' (The president asks for the norm control of the Law of Frequency Management), *Magyar Hírlap*, 26 May.

Szily, L. (1997) 'Nem lesz fennakadás a magánosításban' (There will be no delay in privatisation), *Világgazdaság*, 6 January.

Szomszéd, O. (2010) 'Sólyom László rendhagyó öt éve' (Five years of László Sólyom['s] non-conformist [presidency]), *Magyar Nemzet*, 4 August.

Tódor, J. (1997) 'A legfőbb ügyészség titkosított jelentése' (The classified report of the chief prosecutor), *Magyar Narancs*, 27 March.

Tölgyessy, P. (1993) 'Tette, mint lehetett' (He did his best that he could do), *Népszabadság*, 18 December.

—— (1999a) 'Mire jó az államfői hatalom?' (What is good for the power of the head of state?), *Magyar Nemzet*, 24 December.
Tóth, Á. (2012) 'Bukás' (Downfall), *Népszabadság*, 3 April.
Vajda, P. (1991) 'Göncz Árpád ott lesz Visegrádon' (Árpád Göncz will be in Visegrád), *Népszabadság*, 14 February.
Varga, I. (1995) 'Az ellensúlyozó' (The counter-balancer), *Magyar Fórum*, 15 June.
Varró, S. (2000) 'Az elnök tíz éve: Göncz Árpád távozik' (The ten years of the president: Árpád Göncz is off from the Office), *Magyar Narancs*, 1 June.
Veress, J. (2010) 'Teaforrdalom' (Tea revolution), *Népszava*, 22 October.

Newspapers without authors' or editors' names in English and Hungarian

Beszélő (1993) A botrány legalitása (The legality of the scandal), 3 July.
Beszélő (1990) A köztársaság börtönviselt ideiglenes elnöke (The ex-convict interim president of the Republic), 5 May.
Budapest Sun (1998) Why offer a presidential pardon?, 19 November.
Economist, The (2012) Schmitt quits, 2 April.
Élet és Irodalom (2008) Ötvenedik évforduló, huszadik évforduló (50th anniversary [of the execution of Imre Nagy], 20th anniversary [of the founding of the Committee for Historical Justice], 13 June
Esti Hírlap (1995) Dr. Göncz Árpád életrajza (Dr. Árpád Göncz's biography), 20 June.
Göncz Árpád újévi köszöntő beszédei (1991–2000) az MTI sajtóadatbázisa alapján (The new year's greeting of Árpád Göncz between 1991 and 2000 based on the MTI press data), presented by the Library of Hungarian Parliament.
Hetek (1999) Vége az Agrobank-sztorinak (The end of the Agricultural Bank's story), 24 April.
Heti Válasz (2010) Göncz Árpád fogadta az indiai nagykövetet (Árpád Göncz accepted the Indian ambassador), 1 November.
Heti Válasz (2011) Így búcsúztak el Mádl Ferenctől ([We] say farewell to Frenc Mádl in this way), 7 June.
Heti Válasz (2011) Mádl Ferenc halálára (For the [occasion] of Ferenc Mádl's death), 29 May.
Heti Világgazdaság (1994) Földtörvénykezés (Dealing with the law of [arable] land), 16 April.
Heti Világgazdaság (2011a) Elhunyt Mádl Ferenc: Schmitt Pál csendes tiszteletadása (Ferenc Mádl passed away: Pál Schmitt's silent tribute), 29 May.
Heti Világgazdaság (2011b) Orbán: megrendülten állunk a hír hallatán – reakciók Mádl Ferenc halálára (Orbán: we were shaken by the news – reactions to the death of Ferenc Mádl), 29 May.
Heti Világgazdaság (2011) Elhunyt Mádl Ferenc: a Sándor-palota előtt róhatják le kegyeletüket (Ferenc Mádl passed away: we pay tribute to him in front of the Alexander's Palace), 30 May.
Heti Világgazdaság (2011) Eltemették Mádl Ferencet (Ferenc Mádl was buried), 7 June.
Heti Világgazdaság (2012) Ilyen volt Schmitt Pál 20 hónapja (It was like this Paul Schmitt's 20 months), 2 April.
Irodalmi Újság (1988) Történelmi igazságtételt!: Felhívás a magyar társadalomhoz (Historical justice! Proclamation to the Hungarian society), 16 June.
Kis Újság (1945) Gyöngyösi külügyminiszter nyitotta meg a Teleki Pál Munkaközösség

240 *Bibliography*

külpolitikai tanfolyamát (The Foreign Minister Gyöngyösi opened the coursework of foreign policy of the Teleki Pál Work Cooperative), 26 May.

Kossuth Népe (1945) A szovjet-Unió ma a leghatalmasabb világpolitikai tényező (The Soviet Union is now the most powerful factor of world politics), 27 May.

Magyar Dokumentáció (1991) Göncz Árpád az alkotmánybírósághoz fordult (Árpád Göncz turned to the Constitutional Court), May.

Magyar Dokumentáció (1991) Vita a bűnök elévüléséről (Dispute over the statue of limitation of crimes), October.

Magyar Dokumentáció (1991) Göncz Árpád az igazságtételről (Árpád Göncz [speaks out] about the justice), November.

Magyar Dokumentáció (1992) Alkotmányellenes a Zétényi-Takács felé törvény (The law of Zétényi-Takács is against the Constitution), March.

Magyar Dokumentáció (1992a) Antall József kérdései az alkotmánybírósághoz (The questions of József Antall to the Constitutional Court), June.

Magyar Dokumentáció (1992b) Az alkotmánybíróság a köztársasági elnök kinevezési jogkörről (The Constitutional Court [made its decision] about the scope of the president's right of appointment), June.

Magyar Dokumentáció (1992) Vita a Kossuth téri incidensről (Dispute over the incident of the Kossuth Square), October.

Magyar Dokumentáció (1993) Alkotmánybírósági határozat a frekvenciagazdálkodási törvényről (The ruling of the Constitutional Court concerning the Law of Frequency Management), July.

Magyar Dokumentáció (1995) Alkotmánybírósági döntés a Bokros csomagról (The decision of the constitutional court on the Bokros package), July.

Magyar Dokumentáció (1998) Törvény a szervezett bűnözés elleni fellépésről (Law is about the [combat] against organised crime), December.

Magyar Hírlap (1988) Hálózat helyett Szabad Demokraták Szövetsége (Instead of the Network, Alliance of Free Democrats), 14 November.

Magyar Hírlap (1989) A nemzet méltósággal rótta le kegyeletét a mártírok előtt (With nation's dignity, [people] paid tribute to the martyrs), 17 June.

Magyar Hírlap (1990) Göncz Árpád nyilatkozata (The statement of Árpád Göncz), 27 October.

Magyar Hírlap (1991) Göncz Árpád négy kérdése a kárpótlásról (The four questions of Árpád Göncz about the compensation), 14 May.

Magyar Hírlap (1991) Göncz elnök nem nevezett ki alelnököket (The president, Göncz did not appoint the vice presidents of [the broadcast media]), 13 July.

Magyar Hírlap (1992) Göncz Árpád kinevezte az alelnököket (Árpád Göncz appointed the vice-presidents [of the broadcast media]), 3 March.

Magyar Hírlap (1992) A elnök az alkotmány szerint nem vonható politikai felelősségre (According to the constitution, the president is not [held] responsible for his political [actions]), 25 May.

Magyar Hírlap (1992) Nyilatkozattervezet az elnöki hatáskörről (The draft of [resolution] regarding the scope of the president's power), 26 May.

Magyar Hírlap (1992) Vita a Kossuth téri tüntetésről (Debate over the demonstration of the Kossuth Square), 27 October.

Magyar Hírlap (1992) Az előzményekre csak a bizottság nem kíváncsi (The committee is not interested in the antecedents), 29 October.

Magyar Hírlap (1993) Göncz Árpád a sajtószabadság ügyét szívügyének tekinti (Árpád Göncz considers the freedom of the press to be of utmost significance), 2 November.

Bibliography 241

Magyar Hírlap (1993) A koalíció levele Gönczhez (The letter of the coalition to Göncz), 23 November.
Magyar Hírlap (1993) La Stampa: Ügyetlen kísérlet az elnök bajba keverésére (La Stampa: Clumsy attempt to get the president in a trouble), 26 November.
Magyar Hírlap (1993) Elvetélt MIÉP-javaslat a Parlamentben (The proposal of the MIÉP was aborted in Parliament), 7 December.
Magyar Hírlap (1995) Leértékelték a forintot (The Forint has been devalued), 13 March.
Magyar Hírlap (1995) Kifütyülték a pénzügyminisztert ([People] catcalled the minister of finance), 23 March.
Magyar Hírlap (1995) Az országgyűlés előtt a titoktörvény (The secret law is before the parliament), 1 June.
Magyar Hírlap (1995) Alkotmáyozás: A Magyar köztársaság új alkotmányának koncepciója (Constitutionalisation: The new concept of the Hungarian Constitution), 2 June special edition.
Magyar Hírlap (1995) Göncz Árpád aláírta a stabilizációs törvényt (Árpád Göncz signed the law of stabilisation), 14 June.
Magyar Hírlap (1995) Újra Göncz Árpád a Magyar köztársaság elnöke (Again Árpád Göncz [is elected] to the president of the Republic of Hungary), 20 June.
Magyar Hírlap (1997) Göncz alkotmányos szabályozást kíván (Göncz wishes constitutional regulation), 7 January.
Magyar Hírlap (2000) Göncz állította le a taxisblokád katonai felszámolását (Göncz stopped the military [intervention] in the blockade), 24 October.
Magyar Hírlap (2007) Államfők köszöntötték Gönczöt (The heads of state thank Göncz), 20 February.
Magyar Hírlap (2011) Elhunyt Mádl Ferenc volt köztársasági elnök (The former president of the Republic, Ferenc Mádl passed away), 29 May.
Magyar Hírlap (2011) Elhunyt Mádl Ferenc (Ferenc Mádl passed away), 30 May.
Magyar Hírlap (2011) Schmitt Pál: Mádl Ferenc erős jellemű ember volt (Pál Schmitt: Ferenc Mádl was a strong personality [in terms of his moral authority and political principle]), 7 June.
Magyar Hírlap Observer (1992) TV 2 Interview, 2 July.
Magyar Narancs (1998) A Kunos-ügy: Nincs kegyelem (The Kunos affair: No pardon), 19 November.
Magyar Nemzet (1988) Szabad Demokraták Szövetságévé alakult a Szabad Kezdeményezések Hálózata (The Network of Free Initiatives is [trans]formed into Alliance of Free Democrats), 14 November.
Magyar Nemzet (1989) Ma temetik a mártírokat (Today the martyrs are buried), 16 June.
Magyar Nemzet (1990) Drámai légkörben megegyezés született (Agreement was reached in a dramatic atmosphere), 29 October.
Magyar Nemzet (1991) A kárpótlási törvény több pontja alkotmányellenes (In several aspects, the law of compensation is against the Constitution), 30 May.
Magyar Nemzet (1992) Alkotmányellenes az elévülési törvény (The obsolete law is against the constiution), 4 March.
Magyar Nemzet (1992) Az államfő nem írta alá a médiaelnökök felmentését: Göncz Árpád beszéde a rádióban és a televízióban (The head of state did not sign the dismissal of the heads of media: The speech of Árpád Göncz on radio and television), 2 July.
Magyar Nemzet (1992) Vizsgálóbiztottság alakul? (The investigation committee is formed?), 26 October.

Magyar Nemzet (1992) Éles viták a Kossuth téren történtekről (Sharp debates over the incident of the Kossuth Square), 27 October.
Magyar Nemzet (1993) Göncz Árpád az alkotmánybíróság véleményét kéri (Árpád Göncz asks for the opinion of the Constitutional Court), 26 May.
Magyar Nemzet (1993) Göncz Árpád válaszlevele a koalíciós pártoknak (The letter of Árpád Göncz to the coalition parties), 24 November.
Magyar Nemzet (1995) Kemény gazdasági döntéseket hozott a kormány (The government made a harsh decision in economic [matters]), 13 March.
Magyar Nemzet (1995) A család védelemre szorul ([The Bokros package] is for the protection of family), 3 April.
Magyar Nemzet (1995) Göncz Árpád súlyos dilemma előtt áll (Árpád Göncz is [in] a serious dilemma), 1 June.
Magyar Nemzet (1995) Göncz Árpád aláírja? (Is Árpád Göncz signing [the package?]), 3 June.
Magyar Nemzet (1995a) Göncz Árpád aláírta a stabilizációs törvényt (Árpád Göncz signed the stabilisation law), 14 June.
Magyar Nemzet (1995b) Az ellenzék bírálja de megérti az államfői döntést (The opposition criticises but understands the decision of the head of state), 14 June.
Magyar Nemzet (1996) Ütközőpont a hatályba lépes (Point of [issue] is the [date of law enforcement]), 17 June.
Magyar Nemzet (1997) Az összeférhetetlenségi törvényt visszakapta a T. Ház (The T House [parliament] received the Law of Incompatibility), 3 January.
Magyar Nemzet (1997) A privatizációs törvénymódósítást sem írta alá Göncz Árpád (Árpád Göncz did not sign the amendments to the Law of Privatisation), 4 January.
Magyar Nemzet (1997) Csiha Judit megfelelő jogi konstrukciót vár (Judit Csiha expects an appropriate legal construction), 7 January.
Magyar Nemzet (1997) Parlament vétó az ingyenes szövetkezeti vagyonjuttatásra (Parliament's veto to the free handover of the state property to the [agricultural] cooperative), 26 February.
Magyar Nemzet (1998) Kunos kegyelmet kapott Göncztől (Kunos was granted a pardon [by] Göncz), 10 November.
Magyar Nemzet (1999) Normakontrollt kér az államfő (The head of state asks for a norm control), 9 January.
Magyar Nemzet (2000) Tíz év után elköszönt Göncz Árpád (After ten years, Árpád Göncz took leave), 4 August.
Magyar Nemzet (2011a) Elhunyt Mádl Ferenc (Ferenc Mádl passed away), 29 May.
Magyar Nemzet (2011b) Schmitt: A nemzet nevében, fájó szívvel búcsúzom (Schmitt: In the name of the Republic, with heart breaking [mind] I say goodbye to [him]), 29 May.
Magyar Nemzet (2011a) A miniszterelnök is lerótta kegyeletét Mádl Ferenc emléke előtt (The prime minister also pays tribute to Ferenc Mádl), 30 May.
Magyar Nemzet (2011b) Minden magyar elnöke volt ([Mádl] was the president of all Hungarians), 30 May.
Magyar Nemzet (2012) Schmitt-től jobbra: Áder? (From Schmitt further to the right: Áder?), 2 April.
Magyar Távirat Iroda (2001) Októberben várható ítélet a volt Agrobank-elnök ügyében (In October, the verdict is expecting in the affair of the former president of the Agricultural Bank), 26 September.
Napi Magyarország (1998) Göncz megkegyelmezett Kunosnak (Göncz [granted a] pardon to Kunos), 10 November.

Bibliography 243

Napi Magyarország (1998) Maffiaellenes törvény (Anti-maffia law), 28 December.
Népszabadság (1988) Célunk megismertetni Magyarországot (Our goal is to have Hungary be known [to the world]), 12 July.
Népszabadság (1988) Szabad Demokraták Szövetsége alakult (Alliance of Free Democrats was formed), 14 November.
Népszabadság (1989) A végtisztesség legyen a nemzeti megbékélés jelképe (Giving the last respect to [Nagy Imre and his associates] would be the symbol of the national reconciliation), 1 June.
Népszabadság (1989a) Nagy Imre (Imre Nagy), 16 June.
Népszabadság (1989b) Ma: Gyászszertartás a Hősök terén (Today: Funeral service at the Heroes' Square), 16 June.
Népszabadság (1989) A nemzet megrendülten búcsúzott Nagy Imrétől és Mártírtásaitól ([With] devastation, the nation said good bye to Imre Nagy and the martyrs of his associates), 17 June.
Népszabadság (1989a) Megállapodás a háromoldalú politikai egyeztető tárgyalásokon (Agreement on the tripartite political negotiations), 19 September.
Népszabadság (1989b) Megállapodás: a politikai egyeztető tárgyalások 1989 június 13-a és szeptember 18-a közötti szakaszának lezárásáról (Agreement: about the closing off the political negotiations which took place during the period between 13 June 1989 and 18 September), 19 September.
Népszabadság (1990) A Demokrata Fórum alakít kormányt (The Hungarian Democratic Forum forms the government), 10 April.
Népszabadság (1990a) Május közepén már lesz új kormány (In the middle of May, there will be [a] new government), 3 May.
Népszabadság (1990b) Október 23 nemzeti ünnep (23 October is a national holiday), 3 May.
Népszabadság (1990) A kormány szociális piacgazdaságot ígér (The government promises a social market economy), 23 May.
Népszabadság (1990) Bíró Zoltán: Csoóri nem vállalta (Zoltán Bíró: Csoóri did not accept [the co-charimanship of the MDF], 4 June.
Népszabadság (1990) A nép válassza-e az államfőt? (Whether the people elect the head of state?), 11 June.
Népszabadság (1990) Sokkal több mint százezer aláírás (Much more than 100,000 signatures), 18 June.
Népszabadság (1990a) Július 29: Népszavazás az elnökválasztásról (29 July: Referendum about the presidential election), 28 June.
Népszabadság (1990) 160 ezer aláírás hiteles (160, 000 signatures are valid), 26 June.
Népszabadság (1990b) Népszavazás az elnökválasztásról (Referendum about the presidential election), 28 June.
Népszabadság (1990) Hogyan válasszunk elnököt? (How do we choose our president?), 5 July.
Népszabadság (1990) Nem szavazott a nép (The people did not vote), 30 July.
Népszabadság (1990) Átlagosan 65 százalékkal drágult (On average, oil price is increased by 65 percent), 26 October.
Népszabadság (1990a) A kormány bűnös hibát követett el amikor erőszakkal fenyegetőzött (The government committed crime when they threatened with coercion), 27 October.
Népszabadság (1990b) A köztársasági elnök az erőszak ellen: Bénult közutak, ninch megállapodás (The president of the republic is against the [exercise] of the public force: National roads are paralysed, there is no agreement), 27 October.

244 Bibliography

Népszabadság (1990) Vége a blokádháborúnak (End of the blockade war), 29 October.
Népszabadság (1991) A parancsnok marad (The general remains), 3 April.
Népszabadság (1991) Göncz Árpád nem nevezi ki az alelnököket (Árpád Göncz does not appoint the Vice-Presidents of [broadcast media]), 13 July.
Népszabadság (1991) A radikális reformer (The radical reformer), 7 August.
Népszabadság (1991) A politikai üldözöttek kárpótlásáról (About the compensation of the politically persecuted [people]), 2 November.
Népszabadság (1991) Lépésem segítheti Gönczöt (My action can help Göncz), 18 November.
Népszabadság (1992) Kárpótlás (Compensation), 2 June.
Népszabadság (1992a) Alkotmányellenes az 1974-es kormányhatározat (The 1974 Government Decree is against the Constitution), 9 June.
Népszabadság (1992b) A köztársasági elnök nyilatkozata (The statement of the President of Republic), 9 June.
Népszabadság (1992) Javaslat parlamenti vizsgálatra (Proposal for the parliamentary examination), 26 October.
Népszabadság (1992) Demokráciában a szólásszabadság az államfőt is megilleti (In a democracy, the freedom of speech also applies to the head of state), 27 October.
Népszabadság (1992) Az elnök nem sértődött meg (The president was not offended), 28 October.
Népszabadság (1992) Bodrácska János ismét célpont (János Bodrácska is the target again), 30 October.
Népszabadság (1993) Göncz az alkotmánybírákhoz küldte a frekvenciatörvényt (Göncz sent the law of frequency to the constitutional judges), 26 May.
Népszabadság (1993) Göncz Árpád aláírta az igazságtétel törvényt (Árpád Göncz signed the law of justice), 25 October.
Népszabadság (1993) Göncz Árpád jobboldali veszélyre figyelmeztet (Árpád Göncz warned of right wing danger), 22 November.
Népszabadság (1993) A MIÉP vizsgálatot kér az államelnök ellen (The MIÉP asks for an examination against the president), 24 November.
Népszabadság (1994) Göncz Árpád nem írja alá a földtörvényt? (Doesn't Árpád Göncz sign the law of arable land?), 30 April
Népszabadság (1995) Súlyos stabilizációs kormánycsomag ([The] serious stabilising government package), 13 March.
Népszabadság (1995) A parlament ismét Göncz Árpádot választotta meg köztársasági elnöknek (The Parliament again elected Árpád Göncz for the president of the Republic of Hungary), 20 June.
Népszabadság (1996) Az ellenzék alkotmányellenesnek tartja a privatizációs törvényt (The opposition considers the law of privatisation to be unconstitutional), 21 December.
Népszabadság (1996) Göncz Árpád mérlegeli a privatizációs törvény aláírását (Árpád Göncz thinks over giving his signature to the law of privatisation), 30 December.
Népszabadság (1997) Összeférhetetelenség: Göncz visszaküldte a törvényt (Incompatibility: Göncz returned the law to [parliament]), 3 January.
Népszabadság (1997) Göncz a privatizációs törvényt is visszaküldte a parlamentnek (Göncz also returns the law of privatisation to parliament), 4 January.
Népszabadság (1997) Nem lesz előrehozott parlamenti ülésszak (There will not be an [extraordinary] parliamentary session), 7 January.
Népszabadság (1997a) Nem változott az összeférhetetelenségi törvény (The Law of Incompatibility is not changed), 26 February.

Népszabadság (1997b) A szövetkezetek nem juthatnak ingyenes állami vagyonhoz (The free transfer of state property cannot be [made] to the cooperatives), 26 February.

Népszabadság (1997) Az államfő orvosi kivizsgálásra jár (The head of state went to see a doctor), 20 December.

Népszabadság (1998) A kormány szigorítaná a BtK.-t (The [Orbán] government would tighten the criminal law), 10 November.

Népszabadság (1998) Kunos börtönben marad (Kunos remains in prison), 11 November.

Népszabadság (1998) Az ellenzék szerint kétharmados a maffiaellenes törvénycsomag (According to the opposition, the anti-maffia package is [the law which requires] a two-thirds [majority vote]), 22 December.

Népszabadság (1999) Az AB-hez fordult Göncz (Göncz turned to the Constitutional Court), 9 January.

Népszabadság (2000) A honvédség nehézjárművei elindultak (The heavy vehicles were dispatched from the Hungarian army), 24 October.

Népszabadság (2010) TGM: Sólyom elnökségének mérlege zéró ([According to] Mikós Gáspár Tamás, the balance of Sólyom Presidency is zero), 6 August.

Népszabadság (2011) Elhunyt Mádl Ferenc (Ferenc Mádl passed away), 29 May.

Népszabadság (2011) Schmitt: Mádl Ferenc erős jellemű ember volt (Schmitt: Ferenc Mádl was a strong personality [in terms of his moral authority and political principle]), 7 June.

Népszava (1945) A nép és a külügyi szolgálat (The people and the foreign policy service), 27 May.

Népszava (1988) Kádár János nyilatkozata (Statement of János Kádár), 18 March.

Népszava (1989) Ma: végső tiszteletadás Nagy Imrének és mártírtársainak (Today: last tribute to Imre Nagy and the martyrs of his associates), 16 June.

Népszava, (1989) Az MDF elnöke Antall József, köztársaságielnök-jelöltje Für Lajos (The president of the MDF, József Antall, the presidential nominee of the Republic Lajos Für), 23 October.

Népszava (1991) Az alkotmánybírósághoz fordult Göncz Árpád (Árpád Göncz turned to the Constitutional Court), 19 November.

Népszava (1993) Göncz mondta, de nem így (Göncz said it but not in this way), 24 November.

Népszava (1995) Göncz Árpád aláírja a Bokros-csomagot (Árpád Göncz signs the Bokros package), 3 June.

Népszava (1995) Bokros száz napja (Hundred days of Bokros), 14 June.

Népszava (1995) Újra Göncz Árpádot válaszotta köztársasági elnöknek az országgyűlés (The Parliament again elected Árpád Göncz for the president of the Republic of Hungary), 20 June.

Népszava (1997) Az MSZP várhatóan újra megszavazza az összeférhetetlenségi törvényt (Expectedly, the MSzP again votes for the law of incompatibility), 9 January.

Népszava (1998) Göncz Árpád aláírta Kunos kegyelmi kérvényét (Árpád Göncz signed the petition for [granting] a pardon [to] Kunos), 10 November.

Népszava (2000) Köszönöm Magyarország (Thank you Hungary), 4 August.

Népszava (2009) A szabadságot mindennap meg kell védeni ([We] must protect freedom everyday), 16 June.

Népszava (2010) Nehéz államfői örökség vár Schmittre (Difficult presidential [task] lies ahead Schmitt), 29 June.

Népszava (2010) A szolidaritás zenéje: a váci börtönsztrájk (The music of solidarity: the Vác strike), 22 October.

Népszava (2011a) Elhunyt Mádl Ferenc volt államfő (The former head of state, Ferenc Mádl passed away), 30 May.
Népszava (2011b) Emlékezés Mádl Ferencre – Szili: a volt államfő halála a magyar demokrácia súlyos vesztesége (Remembrance of Ferenc Mádl – Szili: The death of the former head of state is the big loss of Hungarian democracy), 30 May.
Népszava (2011a) Emlékezés Mádl Ferencre – Egyesült Államok: a volt államfő jelentősen hozzájárult Magyarország demokratikus átalakulásához (Remembrance of Ferenc Mádl – The United States: the former head of state made a significant contribution to the democractic transition of Hungary), 31 May.
Népszava (2011b) Emlékezés Mádl Ferencre – Gyászol a Magyar Polgári Együttműködés Egyesület (Remembrance of Ferenc Mádl – The Association of the Hungarian Civic Cooperation mourns), 31 May.
Népszava (2011) Búcsú Mádl Ferenctől (Farewell from Ferenc Mádl), 7 June.
Népszava (2012) Schmitt Pál megerősítette, a nemzet egysége érdekében mondott le (Paul Schmitt affirms that he resigned from [the presidential post] in the interest of the unity of nation), 3 April.
Pesti Hírlap (1992) Göncz Árpád este nem ment operába: Tüntető távollét (Árpád Göncz did not go to the Opera House: Absence of protest), 26 October.
Pesti Hírlap (1993) Az elnök (is) nemzetközi segítséget kér médiaügyben (Dealing with media issue, the President asks for international helps), 22 November.
Szabad Szó (1945) A népből fakadó erőkre szeretnénk építeni Magyarország külpolitikáját (We would like to build the Hungarian foreign policy which arises from the people), 27 May.
The Baltimore Sun (1990) Árpád Göncz: steelworker, lawyer, playwright and President, 24 September.
The New York Times (1989) In Hungary, a prophet honored, 16 June.
The New York Times (1990) Parliament elects formerly imprisoned writer as president, 3 May.
The New York Times (1990) Dr. Tibor Hám, a politician in Hungary and physician in U.S., 9 July.
Új Magyarország (1993) Topolino vörösben ás feketében (Topolino in red and black), 25 November.
Új Magyarország (1997) Göncz Árpád visszaküldte (Árpád Göncz returned [the law of incompatibility to parliament]), 3 January.
Új Magyarország (1997) Összeférhetetlen osztogatás? (Incompatible distribution?), 7 January.
168 Óra (1990) Elnök is járhat villamossal (President can also commute by tram), 8 May.
168 Óra (1991) Aki megmentette Göncz Árpádot ([The person] who saved Árpád Göncz), 23 April.
168 Óra (1991)'56 eleven emléke (1956 is [in] a living memory), 22 October.
168 Óra (1992) Kinek a forradalma? (Whose the revolution is?), 27 October.
168 Óra (1993) A vizsgálat lezárult, felejtsük el? (The investigation is closed, shall we forget about it?), 6 July.
4 × 4 (1997) Litván György beszélget a 75 éves Göncz Árpáddal (György Litván talked with 75 years old Árpád Göncz), 20 February.

Unpublished archival data

'A felhívással egyetértek és támogatom a Hálózat létrehozását' (I agree with the [proclamation] and support the creation of the Network) in HU OSA 302-0-6, presented by the Open Society Archive.

'A Teleki Pál Munkaközösség, a magyar értelmiség demokratikus szervezetének munkaterve' (The Pál Teleki Work Group, the work plan of the democratic organisation of Hungarian intellectual), presented by the National Archive of Hungary.

'Demokrácia reménye' (Hope of democracy), HU OSA 302-0-5, Fonds 302: Samizdat Publication of Gábor Demszky presented by the Open Society Archive.

'Göncz Árpád levele Grósz Károlyhoz' (The letter of Árpád Göncz to Károly Grósz), manuscript, presented by the 1956 Institute.

'Grósz Károly Miniszterelnök levele Göncz Árpádhoz' (The letter of the Prime Minister, Károly Grósz to Árpád Göncz), manuscript, presented by the 1956 Institute.

Hegedűs, A. (1985) An Oral History of Göncz, volume 1, presented by the 1956 Institute.

Hegedűs, A. (1990) An Oral History of Göncz, volume 2, presented by the 1956 Institute.

'Kéziiratok' (Manuscripts) in HU OSA 302-0-5, Fonds 302: Samizdat Publication of Gábor Demszky.

'Magyar Értelmiség'! (Hungarian Intellectuals!), documentary leaflet presented by the Hungarian National Archive.

'Teleki Pál Munkaközösség, Magyar Értelmiség Demokratikus Szervezetének külpolitikai tanfolyama' (Pál Teleki Work Group, the coursework of foreign policy of the Democratic Organisation of Hungarian Intellectuals), presented by the National Archives of Hungary.

Tóth, M. (2009), 'Göncz Árpád: Az eszmék felezési ideje' (Árpád Göncz: Ideas have a longer half-life), abridged version of the Oral History of Árpád Göncz.

'Vázlat a Hálózat múködéséről' (Draft on the functioning of the Network), in HU OSA 302-0- 6, presented by the Open Society Archive.

Official documents: The following documents are presented by the librarian of Hungarian Parliament, Helga Kardos.

De-classified telegram, Case ID: 200403498, United States Department of State Review Authority.

1989 évi XXXI törvény az alkotmány módósításáról (Act XXXI of 1989 on the amendment of the Constitution).

1990 évi XL törvény a Magyar Köztársaság Alkotmányának módósításáról (Act XL of 1990 on the amendment of the Constitution of Hungary).

2002 évi LXI törvény a Magyar Köztársaság Alkotmányáról szóló 1949 évi XX törvény módósításáról (Act LXI of 2002 on the amendment of Act XX of 1949 regarding the Constitution of Hungary).

2006 évi LIV törvény a Magyar Köztársaság Alkotmányáról szóló 1949 évi XX törvény módósításáról (Act LIV of 2006 on the amendment of Act XX of 1949 regarding the Constitution of Hungary).

Audial and visual data

'A forradalom nem kisajátítható' (The revolution cannot be appropriated), Göncz's interview with Kossuth Radio (1990) 22 October, CD-ROM, presented by the Open Society Archive.

Göncz's interview with Bartok Radio (2002) 12 July, CD-ROM, presented by the Hungarian archivist, Krisztina Kulcsár. Hungarian National Archive.

Kóthy, J. and Topits, J. (2006) 'Forró ősz a hidegháborúban' (A fiery autumn in the Cold War), documentary film, directed by Judit Kóthy and Judit Topits.

Papp, Z. (2002) 'Göncz', portrait film, part 1 and part 2, directed and presented by Zsigmond Gábor Papp.
'1956 Enciklopédiája' (Encyclopedia of 1956), CD-ROM, presented by the 1956 Institute.

Interviews

Ágh, A. (2007) 3 October, A leading political scientist at the University of Corvinus.
Babus, E. (2007) 19 May, A chief political editor of *Heti Világgazdaság*.
Bíró, Z. (2007) 10 December, A founding member and the former President of the HDF.
Bod, Á. (2007) 8 November, A former head of the Hungarian National Bank, currently a professor in economics at the University of Corvinus.
Csaba, L. (2007) 5 July, A former economic advisor to Mihály Kupa, currently a professor in economics at the Central European University.
Elias, S. (2007) 6 December, A former social policy advisor to Göncz.
Gombár, C. (2007) 1 October, A former head of the Hungarian national radio, currently a sociologist at the Eötvös Loránd University.
Göncz, Á. (2006)18 June, A former president of Hungary.
Göncz, Á. and Göntér, Z. (2008) 10 January, A former president of Hungary and the First Lady.
Gulyás, A. (2007) 3 July, A senior diplomat, foreign policy advisor to three former Hungarian Presidents, Árpád Göncz, Ferenc Mádl – at the time of the interview – László Sólyom, currently the head of secretariat of Árpád Göncz.
Gyenes, J. (2007) 23 August, The widow of the former minister of defence to the Nagy government Pál Maléter and a founding member of the Committee for Historical Justice.
Hack, P. (2007) 6 July, A former MP of the AFD, currently a professor in law at the Eötvös Loránd University.
Halmai, G. (2007) 15 November, A former chief counsellor of the Constitutional Court, currently a professor in law at the Eötvös Loránd University.
Hegedűs, A. (2007) 29 October, A former MP of the AYD, currently the head of the Hungarian Europe Society.
Ilonszki, G. (2007) 16 October, A political scientist at the University of Corvinus.
Kéri, L. (2007) 12 June, A leading political commentator.
Kende, P. (2007) 5 October, A historian, veteran of the 1956 and currently the chairman of the 1956 Institute.
Konrád, G. (2007) 7 September, A former chairman of International Pen Club.
Kónya, I. (2007) 11 December, A former parliamentary factional leader of the HDF.
Körösényi, A. (2007) 11 July, A leading politician scientist at the Corvinus University, currently the head of the Association for Hungarian political scientists.
Kozák, G. (2007) 19 September, A former head of the Oral History Section of the 1956 Institute.
Kulin, F. (2007) 14 November, A former factional leader of the HDF.
Lánczi, A. (2007) 12 July, A leading political scientist at the University of Corvinus.
Lengyel, L. (2007) 13 September, An economist and political commentator at the Institute of Financial Research.
Litván, G. (2006) 22 July, A historian and former director of the 1956 Institute.
Miszlivetz, F. (2007) 16 July, A founding member of the Network of Free Initiatives and a head of the Institute of Social and European Studies Foundation.
Rádai, E. (2007) 11 October, A chief political editor at *Élet és Irodalom*.

Rainer, J. (2007) 22 August, A leading historian and the head of the 1956 Institute.
Regéczy-Nagy, László. (2007) 5 October, A former military officer, 1956 veteran and co-convict of Bibó's trial, currently the head of the Committee for Historical Justice.
Salamon, L. (2007) 24 October, A former MP of the HDF, currently, an MP of the AYD.
Somogyvári, I. (2007) 22 May, A former general secretary of the Parliamentary Constitution-Drafting Committee, currently a chief advisor to the Hungarian National Audit Office.
Stumpf, I. (2007) 3 July, A former minister of the Office of the Prime Minister, currently a judge of the Constitutional Court.
Szomszéd, O. (2007) 14 June, A political commentator at the Institute of Perspective.
Szunyog, K. (2007) 19 August, The former head of the Office of the President.
Tölgyessy, P. (2007) 15 October, A former president of the AFD.
Tormássy, Z. (2007) 21 August, a former secretary of Göncz.
Tóth, M. (2007) 4 September, A former chief secretary of the Presidential Office.
Varga, L. (2007) 27 August, A historian and member of the Screening Committe.
Varró, S. (2007) 15 August, A journalist at the *Magyar Narancs* and currently, at the *Hírszerző*.
Vitányi, I. (2007) 23 November, a veteran of the Hungarian anti-fascist movement and an MP of the HSP.
Wisinger. I. (2007) 7 June, A former head of the Hungarian Journalist Association.
A former senior judge of the Constitutional Court (2007) 9 May.
A former member of the democratic opposition and ex-chairman of the AFD (2007) 27 September.
A leading political scientist at the Péter Pázmány Catholic University (2007) 16 November.

E-mail correspondence

Faragó, A. (2008) 'Kérdésem a Glasgow-i Egyetemről' (My question from the University of Glasgow). E-mail (21 and 25 August 2008), A former Spokesman of the Office of the President.
Kis, J. (2010) 'Kérdésem a Glasgow-i Egyetemről' (My question from the University of Glasgow). E-mail (4 and 10 August 2010), A former President of the AFD, currently a professor in political science at the Central European University.
Tölgyessy, P. (2010) 'Kérdésem a Glasgow-i Egyetemről' (My question from the University of Glasgow). E-mail (14, 16 August 2010), A former chairman of the AFD, currently a political commentator.

Internet Resources

Laws and Acts adopted: The following Acts are accessible via the websites HTTP://www.1000ev.hu and HTTP://www.complex.hu.

'A Magyar Népköztársaság Alkotmánya' (Act XX of 1949 on the Constitution of the Peoples' Republic of Hungary).
'Act No. IV of 1978 on the Criminal Code'.
'1946 évi Törvény Magyarország Államformájáról' (Act I of 1946 on the State Form of Hungary).
'1990 évi XXVIII törvény az 1956 Októberi Forradalom és Szabadságharc Jelentőségének

Törvénybe Iktatásáról' (Act XXVIII of 1990 on the Significance of the 1956 October Revolution and Freedom Fights).

'1990 évi LVII Törvény a közszolgálati tájékoztatási eszközök vezetőinek kinevezési rendjéről' (Law No. LVII of 1990 on the Appointment Procedure of the Heads of the Public Media).

'1991 évi XXV Törvény a tulajdonviszonyok rendezése érdekében az állam által 1949 Június 8-a után az állampolgárok tulajdonában igazságtalanul okozott károk részeleges kárpótlásáról szóló elfogadott törvény' (Law No. XXV of 1991 on Partial Compensation for Damages Unlawfully Caused by the State after 8 June 1949 to Properties Owned by Citizens in the Interest of Settling Ownership Relations).

'1991 évi XXXIII Törvény egyes állami tulajdonban lévő vagyontárgyak önkormányzatok tuljadonába adásáról' (The 1991 XXXIII Law on Transferring certain State Properties into the Ownership of Local Governments).

'1993 évi LXII Törvény a frekvenciagazdálkodásról' (Law No. LXII of 1993 on Radio Frequency Management).

'1993 évi XC Törvény az 1956 októberi forradalom és szabadságharc során elkövetett egyes bűncselekményekkel kapcsolatos eljárásról' (Law No. XC of 1993 on the Procedure related to certain crimes committed during the 1956 Revolution and Freedom Fight'.

'1994 évi LV Törvény a termőföldről' (Law No. LV of 1994 on Arable Land).

'1997 évi V. Törvény az Országgyűlési Képviselők Jogállásról szóló 1990 évi LV. Törvény Módósításáról' (The Law No. V of 1997 on the Legal Status of Members of Parliament regarding the Amendment of the Law No. LV of 1990).

'1999 évi LXXV törvény a szervezett bűnözés valamint az azzal összfüggő egyes jelenségek elleni fellépés szabályairól és az ehhez kapcsolódó törvénymódosításról' (Act LXXV of 1999 on the Combat Against Organised Crime and the Related Phenomena and the Amendment of Related Acts of Parliament).

The rulings of the Constitutional Court: The following rulings are accessible via the official website of the Hungarian Constitutional Court, at HTTP://www.mkab.hu.

The rulings of the Constitutional Court in 1991 (Case No. 48/1991).
The rulings of the Constitutional Court in 1992 (Case No. 8/1992; Case No. 11/1992; Case No. 36/1992).
The rulings of Constitutional Court in 1993 (Case No. 4/1993).
The rulings of the Constitutional Court in 1993 (Case No. 42/1993; Case No. 48/1993).
The rulings of the Constitutional Court in 1994 (Case No. 35/1994).
The rulings of Constitutional Court in 1995 (Case No. 31/1995 and Case No. 43/1995).
The ruling of Constitutional Court in 1997 (Case No. 30/1997).
The ruling of Constitutional Court in 1999 (Case No. 1/1999).

Others

'A FKGP part története' (History of the Independent Smallholders' Party), Online Available HTTP: <HTTP://www.fkgp.hu> (accessed on 12 July 2010).

'A Magyar Piarista Rendtartomány története' (The history of the Hungarian Piarist Province), Online Available HTTP: <HTTP://www.piarista.hu/kivagyunk/piaristak> (accessed on 10 July 2010).

'A 20. Század értékelése' (Assessment of the twentieth century), Online Available HTTP: <HTTP://www.median.hu> (accessed on 1 December 2010).

'Börtöntörténetek: A Lordok Háza' (Prison story: The House of Lords), Online Available HTTP: <HTTP://eletfogytiglan.nolblog.hu/archives/2009/06> (accessed on 25 January 2010).
'Boy scouts', Online Available HTTP: <HTTP://www.britannica.co.uk> (accessed on 10 July 2010).
Brand, C. (2011) 'EU confronts Hungary over media freedom', Online Available HTTP: <HTTP://www.europeanvoice.com> (accessed on 18 May 2011).
'College of Social Science: Ethics Committee', Online Available HTTP: <HTTP://www.gla.ac.uk/lbss/research/ethics> (accessed on 30 September 2010).
'Convention on the Non-Applicability of Statutory Limitations to War crimes and Crimes against humanity', Online Available HTTP: <HTTP://www2.ohchr.org/English/law/pdf/warcrimes.pdf> (accessed on 7 May 2010).
'EU speechless over Hungary's contentious media law', Online Available HTTP: <HTTP://www.euraactiv.com> (accessed on 18 May 2011).
'Extensive and intensive farming', Online Available HTTP: <HTTP://www.britannica.com> (accessed on 22 July 2010).
'Ez az én legbelsőbb, személyes ügyem' (This is my deepest and most personal affair), Online Available HTTP: <HTTP://www.c3.hu/scripta/beszelo/99/10/02besz,htm> (accessed on 30 July 2010).
'Göncz Árpád', Online Available HTTP: <HTTP://www.rev.hu/sulinet56/online/szerviz/kislex/biograf/goncz.htm> (accessed on 12 July 2010).
'Göncz Árpáddal Mink András és Révész Sándor beszélget 1989-ről' (András Mink and Sándor Révész discussed with Árpád Göncz about 1989), Online Available HTTP: <HTTP://www.c3.hu/scripta/beszelo> (accessed on 30 July 2010).
'Hungarian encyclopedia' (Magyar Életrajzi Lexikon), Online Available HTTP: <HTTP://mek.niif.hu/00300/00355/html/index.html> (accessed on 11 July 2010).
'Hungary in the European Union', Online Available HTTP: <HTTP:// www.mfa.gov.hu> (accessed on 7 May 2010).
'Hungary media free but press freedom declined, says Freedom House', Online Available HTTP: <HTTP://www.politics.hu> (accessed on 18 May 2011).
'Khrushchev's secret speech', Online Available HTTP: <HTTP://www.soviethistory.org> (accessed on 22 July 2010).
'Levente-movement' (Levente-mozgalom), Online Available HTTP: <HTTP://mek.niif.hu> (accessed on 11 July 2010).
Majoros, D. (2000) 'A strategy to bring Hungarian land ownership legislation into conformity with European Community law', Online Available HTTP: <HTTP://commercialdiplomacy.org/pdf/ma_projects/majoras_dora.pdf> (accessed on 14 May 2010).
'Mi a börtönben négy évig győztesnek éreztük magunkat' (In the prison for four years, we considered ourselves as victors), Online Available HTTP: <HTTP://www.bibotarsasag.hu> (accessed on 22 July 2010).
Palasik, M. (2000) 'Affair of the Hungarian Community and its lessons' (A Magyar közösség ügy és tanulságai), Online Available HTTP: <HTTP://www.rev.hu/sulinet45/szerviz/szakirod/palasik2.htm> (accessed on 12 July 2010).
Papp, O. (2002) 'The path of one man in the twentieth century' (Egy férfi útja a XX. Században), Online Available HTTP: <HTTP://www.bibotarsasag.hu> (accessed on 9 July 2010).
Quoteworld: 'history', Online Available HTTP: <HTTP://www.quoteworld.org/categories/history> (accessed on 3 December 2010).
'Remarks at the welcoming ceremony for President Árpád Göncz of Hungary', Online

Available HTTP: <HTTP://ftp.resource.org/gpo.gov/papers/1999/1999_vol1_899.pdf> (accessed on 25 October 2010).

'The Association of Hungarian boy scouts', Online Available HTTP: <HTTP://www.cserkesz.hu> (accessed 9 July 2010).

'The Club of Rome', Online Available HTTP: <HTTP://www.clubofrome.org> (accessed on 25 August 2010).

'The Committee for Historical Justice in 1988' (A TIB 1988-ban), Online Available HTTP: <HTTP://beszelo.c3.hu/99/09/16kozak.htm> (accessed on 26 February 2009).

'The Constitution of Hungary', Online Available HTTP: <HTTP://www.parlament.hu> (accessed on 10 August 2010).

'The Institute of the 1956 Institute', Online Available HTTP: <HTTP://www.rev.hu> (accessed on 10 July 2010).

'The Judicial System in Hungary', Online Available HTTP: <HTTP://www.birosag.hu> (accessed on 25 August 2010).

'The NÉKOSZ Legend', Online Available HTTP: <HTTP://ww.rev.hu> (accessed on 10 July 2010).

'1956 Revolution', Online Available HTTP: <HTTP://hungaria.org/1956/> (accessed on 25 July 2010).

'1956. November: volt egyszer egy forradalom' (1956 November: Once there was a revolution), Online Available HTTP: <HTTP://www.mult-kor.hu> (accessed on 22 July 2010).

Index

Note: The following abbreviations have been used – f = figure; n = note; t = table

'*A beszélgetések az elnökkel*'
 ('Conversation with the President') 3
ACC *see* Allied Control of Commission
Ács, N. 105
Act on Asylum 186, 187, 221n
Act I (1946 Constitution) 92, 98, 99, 192
Act LIV (2006) 104, 216n
Act LXXV of 1999 on the Combat Against Organised Crime and the Related Phenomena and the Amendment of Related Acts of Parliament *see* Law on Organised Crime
Act LXXXVI of 1993 on Aliens 186, 221n
Act XL (1990) 104
Act XX (1949) (Communist Constitution) 90, 193
Act XXXIV of 1994 on the Police 186, 221n
Adám, Antal 141
Áder, János 207
A DiákEgység Mozgalom (Movement of Student Unity) 24
AFD *see* Alliance of Free Democrats (AFD)
Ágh, A. 160, 191, 221n
Agricultural Bank 179, 180
Agricultural Cooperatives and Producers, National Association of 131
agriculture 19–20, 27–31, 133; Göncz's own view regarding Soviet farming models 39, 41–2, 43, 199; Hungarian tradition deeply entrenched 200; *see also* land-ownership and reform; Law on Arable Land; Law on Compensation
agronomy: Göncz's study and work in 37, 62, 66, 67, 199

Alliance of Free Democrats (AFD) (formerly Network of Free Initiatives (NFI)) 170–6, 84, 101, 199, 200–1; Antall government and 108, 109; broadcast media 135, 143; coalition government with HSP 158, 159, 160–1, 162t, 163t, 219n; Göncz's allegiance to 151, 162, 163, 203; Göncz's interrupted speech on 36th anniversary of the 1956 Hungarian Revolution 155; Göncz's second Presidency and 157; organised crime 186; pact with HDF 95, 96–100, 138–9, 216n; political interests of Members of Parliament 169; political separation from HDF 115, 146, 206; post-communist Presidency 92–3, 94, 95t, 96–8; privatisation 174–5; 'Taxi Blockade' (taxi-drivers strike) 111; transition justice 119, 123, 125–6, 217n
Alliance of Young Democrats (AYD) 70, 92–3, 95t, 96–7 214n; case of Péter Kunos 180; Orbán government 158, 159–60, 161t, 162t, 163; organised crime 185; political interests of Members of Parliament 169; privatisation 175; transition justice 119, 123; urged Göncz's intervention on economic issues 163, 164, 165
Allied Control of Commission (ACC) 31, 32
Antall Jr., József 48, 74, 92, 97, 189, 198; attempts to impeach Göncz 145; attempts to place broadcast media under state control 110, 134–5, 136, 137, 218n; drafting of new broadcast media law 143, 219n; Göncz's interrupted

Antall Jr., József (*cont.*):
  speech on 36th anniversary of the 1956 Hungarian Revolution 154–5, 219*n*; Göncz's refusal to comply with broadcast media restructuring plan 136–41, 143–4, 146, 151; government of 96, 98, 100, 108, 109–111, 161*t*; Law of Radio Frequency Management 147–50; singles Göncz out for the Presidency 100–3, 216*n*; 'Taxi Blockade' (taxi-drivers strike) 217*n*; transition justice 118, 119, 121, 122, 204; Visegrád Summit 116, 118
Antall Snr., József 100
anti-fascism 16, 20, 23*f*, 24–7
'Anti-Mafia Package' *see* Law on Organised Crime
arable land *see* Law on Arable Land
Arany, Bálint 35
Árpád Göncz in Midstream (*Göncz Árpád: Sodrásban*) 6–7
Arrow Cross (military unit) 25, 121
assembly *see* Law of Assembly
Austria: Hungary opens border with 83, 215*n*
AYD *see* Alliance of Young Democrats

Babits, Mihály (poet) 29
Babus, Endre 126, 159, 171, 172, 173, 220*n*
Bacon, Francis 208
Bajcsy-Zsilinszky, Endre 20
Bayer, J. 70
Beszélő 9
Bibó, István 16, 29–30, 35, 39, 64; arrested and detained by Soviet authorities 52, 53, 54, 56; Draft Proposal 44, 47, 100, 202, 212*n*; Göncz smuggles Draft Proposal out of country 50; Göncz takes Draft Proposal to Indian Embassy 48, 49; hunger strikes in Vác prison 60, 61, 212*n*; released from prison 61, 62, 213*n*; work in translation bureau of Vác prison 57, 59
Bíró, Zoltán (first President of the HDF) 97–8, 113, 127
Bod, Ákos Péter 166–7
Bognár, József
'Bokros Package' *see* economic policies
Bonn, G. 55
Boross, Péter 112, 153–4, 155, 219*n*
broadcast media: absence of new media legislation 142–3, 149, 219*n*; Antall attempts to place under state control 110, 134–5, 218*n*; appointment/dismissal of Presidents and Vice-Presidents of 100, 103–4, 138–9, 140, 204, 216*n*; Constitutional Court and 135, 137, 140–2, 146, 219*n*; drafting of new law 143, 219*n*; foreign press 150–3; Göncz's belief in press freedom 99, 144–6, 152–3, 206; Göncz's refusal to comply with restructuring plan 136–41, 143–4, 146; Göncz's view of the media in a democratic state 144–6, 152–3, 205; Hankiss and Gombár dismissed 136; newspapers as sources 6; presidential rights of control 118; *see also* Law of Radio Frequency Management
Brown, J. 45
Bruszt, L. 81
Budapest Police Department 52, 212*n*
Budapest Radio Station 43
Budapest Technical University 43
Budapest University 25
Bulganin, Marshall Nikolai Alexandrovich 46, 49, 212*n*

Caine, B. 7
Calhoun, N. 127
CDP *see* Civic Democratic Party
CDPP *see* Christian Democratic Peoples' Party
Central and Eastern Europe (CEE): European Union and 133; transition justice and 118–19
CHIR *see* Special Commission for Historical Investigation
Christian Democratic Peoples' Party (CDPP) 91, 95*t*, 96, 119, 123, 215*n*; urges Göncz's intervention on economic issues 163
Civic Democratic Party (CDP) 31*t*
'Class Enemies' (idegen osztály) 60, 212*n*
Clinton, Bill 1–2
Club of Rome 132, 218*n*
Commander-in-Chief: role of 114, 172, 190, 191, 192, 204
Committee for Historical Justice (CHJ) 62, 68, 70, 76–85, 125, 214*n*; Göncz's activism in 84–5, 129, 203; *see also* Hungarian Revolution (1956)
Communism in Defence of the New Course (Nagy) 49–51, 202
Communist Party (CP) 31*t*, 32, 33, 34, 35, 36; bans Petőfi Circle 42; demand

for information and intelligence deriving from Western literature 57–8; Göncz interrogated and confined by 37; opposition groups and 71; people's distrust of 63, 213*n*; political prisoners 60; Roundtable Negotiations (RTN) 89–90
Communist rule 21, 24, 28; Constitution 192; fall of 1, 2, 83, 109, 215*n*; Göncz's resistance to extreme forms of political ideology 199; transitional justice 118–19, 206; *see also* post-communist Presidency; Soviet Bloc
compensation *see* Law on Compensation
consensus-based democracy: Göncz's belief in 158–9, 188, 191, 205–6; pardons 184–5; use of veto 177, 178
constitutional competences/powers *see* cross-signatory system; Presidential powers;Prime Ministerial powers
Constitutional Court 91, 114, 158, 193, 194, 221*n*; arable land 131–2; Bill on the Establishment of 90; broadcast media 135, 137, 140–2, 146, 219*n*; compensation 120, 121, 123, 124, 125, 126; curtailing of Presidential powers 171–2, 189–92, 195–6, 204–5, 220*n*, 221–2*n*; economic policies 164, 171; human rights 128, 218*n*; organised crime 185, 186–7, 205; privatisation 176; radio frequencies 148, 219*n*; Rules of the House 159–60; veto requests 177*f*, 221*n*
Constitution, The 92, 98, 99, 116, 117, 131; Act I (1946 Constitution) 92, 98, 99, 192; Article 19/D 148; Communist Constitution 90, 192, 193; drafting of new 171–2; economic policies 164, 170, 171, 220*n*; Little Constitution 192; privatisation 175–6; Rules of the House 159–60, 188; *see also* Republic of Hungary
'Conversation with the President' (*A beszélgetések az elnökkel*) 3
co-operatives 175, 176
Cope, Christopher Lee 49, 50
Corvinus University (Budapest) 41
Courts of Appeal 182
Cox, T. 39
Criminal Code (1998) 182, 221*n*
Criminal Procedure Act (1973) 124
'Crisis of Democracy, The' (Bibó) 35

cross-signatory system: economic policies 164, 165, 166, 169, 173, 205; Presidency and 104–6, 135, 138–9, 140–1, 153, 216*n*; Presidential pardons 178, 196; *see also* Presidential powers; Prime Ministerial powers
Csaba, László 167, 174
Csicsery-Rónay, István 5, 20, 21, 36, 74, 214*n*
Csiha, Judit 178
Csizmadia, E. 71
Csoóri, Sándor 83, 97, 98, 102, 216*n*
Csurka, István 97, 218*n*
Czech Charter (77) 69, 213*n*

DAHI *see* Democratic Alliance of Hungarian Intellectuals
Dávid, Ibolya (Minister of Justice) 179, 181
Debreczeni, József 114
de-Communisation 118–19
Democratic Alliance of Hungarian Intellectuals (DAHI) (formerly Pál Teleki Work Group (PTWG) 20–1
Democratic Charter 134, 218*n*
'democratic institution-building' 193, 204–5, 222*n*
Democratic League of Independent Trade Unions 92
democratic socialism 64, 66, 67, 68, 73–4, 213*n*; Göncz's approach to transition justice 121–2, 125, 126–7, 128, 147, 153; Göncz's intervention on economic issues 163, 173; Göncz's Presidency and 157, 190; Göncz's pursuit of democratic beliefs 201–4; Göncz's rooting of beliefs in political culture 205–8; strong influence on Göncz's political direction 75–6, 84, 108, 109, 110, 115
Déry, Tibor 56
Dexter, L. 9
dissident movements *see* Alliance of Free Democrats (AFl); Committee for Historical Justice (CHJ)
'divide and rule tactics' (salami tactics) 21
Donáth, Ferenc 77
Draft Proposal for a Compromise Solution to the Hungarian Questions (Bibó) 44, 47, 100, 202, 212*n*; Göncz smuggles proposal out of country 50; Göncz takes proposal to Indian Embassy 48, 49

East Germany: asylum seekers to flee to West 83
economic policies: Law of Incompatibility 169, 170*t*, 171–4; Law on Privatisation 174–6, 177*f*, 178; stabilisation programme ('Bokros Package') 164–9, 199, 220*n*
education: Göncz's belief in national system 19–20, 38, 42, 66, 199
Egypt 40, 43, 44–5
elections: parliamentary (1945) 31*t*, 32–7; parliamentary (1990) 95*t*, 96; presidential 90, 91, 92, 93, 94, 95
Elias, Sára 166
Elster, J. 118
Émigré Revolutionary Committee (Strasbourg) 50
equality, principle of 131, 132, 133, 170, 205, 206; privatisation and 175, 176, 178
Erdei, Ferenc 47
European Union 132, 133, 218*n*

Faragó, András 171, 176
Farkas, Ferenc 48, 49
Farkas, G. 55
Farkas, Imre 23
Farkas, Mihály 60
Fekete, Sándor 60–1, 213*n*
FFHS *see* Freedom Front of Hungarian Students
FFHY *see* Freedom Front of Hungarian Youth
First Presidency (1990–1995) 5, 108–9, 118–19, 157, 160; Antall government 109–111; Göncz expected to play symbolic presidential role 201; Göncz's interrupted speech 153–6; La Stampa affair 150–3, 206; Law on Arable Land 118, 145, 130–3; Law of Compensation (1991) 118, 119–22, 125, 217*n*; Law on Justice (1991) 118, 122–30; Law on Radio Frequency Management 118, 147–50, 206, 219*n*; main characteristics 201; political developments before election to President 198–204; 'Taxi Blockade' (taxi-drivers' strike) 111–15, 145, 190, 205, 216–17*n*; Visegrád Summit 116–18, 204; *see also* post-communist Presidency; Republic of Hungary; second Presidency
foreign policy rights: Presidential 116–18
foreign press 150–3

Forsyte Saga (Galsworthy) 58–9
'476-ers' (political prisoners) 56–7, 58
'Four Yes-es' (Négy Igen-es) referendum 93–5, 97, 115
France 40, 43, 44–5
freedom of expression: Göncz's belief in 109–10, 205, 206
Freedom Front of Hungarian Students (FFHS) 23*f*, 24–7
Freedom Front of Hungarian Youth (FFHY) 24
free economic competition, principle of 170
French Fifth Republic model of Presidency 91
Fricz, T. 159
Für, Lajos 94, 98, 113, 114

Gál, Zoltán (Speaker of the House) 169
'Garden Hungary' (Kert Magyarország) 42, 211*n*
Generation, The (*Nemzedék*) 34–5
Geneva Convention (1949) 124, 217*n*
Germany 2, 15, 20, 24, 25, 26
Gerő, Ernő 43
Gimes, Miklós 76
Gödöllő Agricultural University 29, 37
Gombár, Csaba 134, 135, 136
Göncz, Árpád: commitment to civic values 184–5, 199, 221*n*; described as 'non-hero' 1; early political influences 2, 15–19, 38, 39, 66, 73; experiences of skilled manual work 37; family background and early years 16–19; health problems 158, 188–9, 208, 222*n*; influence of great-great-grandfather 16–17; literary work/writing 2–3, 5–6, 21, 40, 209*n*, 211*n*, 213*n*; moral authority of 84–5, 101–2; moral principles 185; reminisces about his life 197; retirement 195–6; sense of social consciousness 165–6, 167
Göncz, Ilona *see* Heimann, Ilona (mother)
Göncz, Kinga (daughter) 40
Göncz, Lajos (father) 16, 17–18
Göntér, Zsuzsánna (wife) 5, 19–20, 50, 53, 58, 63; Göncz's political instinct 145; on reorganisation of ISP 74, 214*n*; Special Care Foundation (Fogyatékos Alapítvány) 166
Gorbachev, Mikhail 69, 203
Gough, R. 4, 5
Great Britain 40, 43, 44–5

Grósz, Károly: end of sole leadership of HSWP 83; Göncz writes letter of protest about Kádár regime to him 79–80, 203
Gyarmati, G. 41
Gyenes, Judit 78
Gyöngyösi, János 20
Györffy College (Györffy Kollégium) 24, 210*n*
Gyűjtő jail (*Gyűjtő fogház*) 56–7, 60–1
Gyurcsány, Ferenc

Halmai, G. 131, 137, 141, 142, 182
Hám, Tibor 5, 21, 22, 74, 214*n*
Hankiss, Elemér 134, 135, 136, 147
Hasznos, Miklós 123
Hatch, J. 7
Havel, Vaclav 116, 155, 217*n*
HBC *see* Hungarian Brotherly Community
HDF *see* Hungarian Democratic Forum
Head of Government/State: broadcast media rights 134–5; foreign policy rights 116–18
Hegedűs, A. 17, 32, 33, 77, 214*n*; Göncz's moral principles 185; Hungarian Revolution (1956) 42, 46, 47, 49, 53, 62; Hungarian Socialist Workers' Party (HSWP) 63; Viktor Orbán 72–3
Heimann, Ilona (mother) 16, 17, 18
Heroes' Square 81, 82
HF *see* Hungarian Front
Hirszerző (internet daily) 128
Historical Archives of the Hungarian State Security 6, 209*n*
Historical Investigation, Special Commission for *see* Special Commission for Historical Investigation
Historical Justice, Committee for *see* Committee for Historical Justice (CHJ)
HJLP *see* Hungarian Justice and Life Party
Holmes, S. 84, 107
Horn, Gyula 1; economic stabilisation programme 164–9; government of 158–60, 161*t*, 162*t*, 163, 219*n*; government involvement in corruption scandals 172, 220*n*; opening of Austrian/Hungarian border 215*n*; organised crime 185; privatisation 174–6, 177*f*, 178
Horthy, Admiral Miklós 192
Horváth, Balázs 111, 113, 217*n*
HRP *see* Hungarian Radical Party
HSWP *see* Hungarian Socialist Workers' Party

human rights: Göncz's views on 127–8, 218*n*; liberal democracy and 200
Hungarian Aid (HA) (*Magyar Segély*) movement 51, 212*n*
Hungarian Armed Forces: Göncz's position on role 190, 191, 192; role of Commander-in-Chief 102, 114, 172, 204
Hungarian Army: Göncz joins after German occupation 25, 67, 202
Hungarian Brotherly Community (HBC) 35–6
Hungarian Communist Workers' Party 216*n*
Hungarian Democratic Forum (HDF) 69–70, 92, 95*t*, 200, 215*n*; case of Péter Kunos 180; Constitutional Court and 141–2; Göncz's election to the Presidency 100, 101, 102, 216*n*; *La Stampa* affair 150–1; pact with AFD 95, 96, 97–100, 138–9, 216*n*; political separation from AFD 115, 146, 206; privatisation 175; transition justice 119, 123; urges Göncz's intervention on economic issues 163, 164; Zoltan Bíró 97–8, 113, 127
Hungarian Front (HF) 23–4, 33
Hungarian Justice and Life Party (HJLP) 150, 151
Hungarian National Bank 166, 167
Hungarian News Agency 99, 103–4
Hungarian Peoples' Party 91, 215*n*
Hungarian Radical Party (HRP) 31*t*
Hungarian Revolution (1848) 16
Hungarian Revolution (1956): '1956' (essay by Göncz) 2; arrest and trial of Göncz 51–3; chronology of key events 43–4, 211*n*; convictions for involvement in 212*n*; counter-revolutionary attempt to restore capitalist order 77, 214*n*; Göncz's hunger strikes while in prison 60–1, 212*n*; Göncz's interrupted speech on the 36th anniversary of 153–6, 219*n*; Göncz's involvement in 38, 39–41, 63–7, 84, 101–2, 202; Göncz's liaison role between István Bibó, India and the West 44–51, 54–5, 56, 202; Göncz's release from prison 62–3, 213*n*; Göncz's work at translation bureau 57–60, 68; imprisonment of Göncz 56–7, 67, 68, 203; Petőfi Circle (*Petőfi Kör*) 41–3 spec char; 'popular uprising' 81; transition justice 124; *see also* Committee for Historical Justice (CHJ)

Hungarian Revolution, Institute for the History of the 1956 *see* Institute for the History of the 1956 Hungarian Revolution
Hungarian Socialist Party (HSP) (formerly Hungarian Socialist Workers' Party (HSWP)) 94, 95*t*, 119, 151, 155, 216*n*; coalition government with AFD 158, 159, 160–1, 162*t*, 163*t*, 219*n*; organised crime 186; political interests of Members of Parliament 169
Hungarian Socialist Workers' Party (HSWP) (later Hungarian Socialist Party (HSP)) 63, 79, 82, 83, 213*n*; 'Four Yes-es' (Négy Igen-es) referendum 93–4, 115; Göncz writes letter of protest to about Kádár regime to Károly Grósz 79–80, 203; post-communist Presidency and 89, 90, 91, 92, 93, 94
'Hungarians' Proclamation (Magyarok) 44, 211*n*
Hungarian Workers' and Peoples' Party 43
Hungarian Writers' Association (HWA) 83
Hungary 1956 (Lomax) 40, 211*n*
Hungary 19, 22, 27; democratic history of 192–6; unity of nation valued by Göncz 65–6, 85, 108; *see also* People's Republic of Hungary; Republic of Hungary
HWA *see* Hungarian Writers' Association

Ilonszki, Gabriella 115, 141–2, 156, 180, 184–5
immigrants 186, 221*n*
incompatability *see* Law on Incompatability
Independent Smallholders' Party (ISP) 2, 5, 15, 16, 20, 21; dissolves after Second World War 35, 36; Draft Proposal 48; Göncz undertakes editorship of weekly party magazine 34–5; Göncz works as parliamentary secretary 22, 32, 33–4, 36–7, 100, 137; Hungarian Front (HF) and 23; parliamentary election (1945) 31*t*, 32–7; parliamentary election (1990) 95*t*; platform for Göncz to pursue ideals in politics 30, 38, 63–4, 199; political interests of Members of Parliament 169; privatisation 175; reorganises in 1980s 74, 75–6, 199, 214*n*; student resistance groups and 24; transition justice 119, 122; Zoltán Tildy as President 192

India 39, 44–51, 54–5, 56, 202
Institute for the History of the 1956 Hungarian Revolution 3, 6, 77
intellectual movement 19–23
International Colloquium on the European Agreement on Human and Cultural Rights 127–8
Irodalmi Újság (newspaper) 76
Ishiyama, J. 107
Izsák, L. 94–5

Játzkó, Pál 20, 22
Josselson, R. 7
judicial system 180–1, 182
Justice, Law on *see* Law on Justice

Kádár, János 44, 46, 50, 51, 54, 55; 1956 veterans 77–8; cultural policy of government 58, 102; death of 83; denies crisis in Hungary 69, 213*n*; economic policies 167; end of regime 20, 82, 203; Göncz's resistance to regime 202; Göncz writes letter of protest about regime to Károly Grósz 79–80, 203; Hungarian population holds in positive esteem 222*n*; Hungarian Socialist Workers' Party (HSWP) 213*n*; India and 211*n*; pardons 183; political prisoners 60, 61, 77–9; United Nations and 61, 213*n*
Kardos, László 23, 49, 50, 56, 212*n*
Kárl Marx Economic University (Budapest) 42
Károly, Count Mihály 192, 204
Kende, Péter 64, 129–30
Kenedi, J. 48
Kéri, László 151–2, 155, 162, 163, 167
Khrushchev, Nikita 41, 61, 211*n*, 213*n*
Kilényi, Géza 90–1, 132, 141
Király, Zoltán 95
Kis fogház (prison cell) 56, 57, 59
Kis, J. 111, 115
Kiss, Sándor 23, 50, 159
Konrád, György 101, 216*n*
Kónya, Imre 96, 113, 150–1, 218*n*
Körösényi, András 74–5, 105, 136–7, 146, 159, 214*n*; Göncz's presidential style 161*t*, 162*t*; peculiarity of Göncz's political orientation 200–1; Rules of the House 188
Kőrösi, Z. 77
Kosa, Lajos 165
Kossuth Radio 315, 28–9, 40, 120,

122; broadcast media 144; case of
Péter Kunos 183; Göncz's political
careerism and ambition 173; radio
frequencies 149
Kovács, Béla 15, 16, 21, 22, 74, 76;
Göncz works as secretary for 22, 32,
33–4, 36–7, 100
Kovács, É. 114
Kovács, János 53–4
Kövér, László 72–3
Kozák, Gyula 77
Kulcsár, Kálmán 90–1
Kulin , Ferenc 94
Kun, Béla 192
Kunos, Péter 178–85, 206, 221*n*
Kurtán, S. 123

Lánczi, András 108–9, 115, 201
land-ownership and reform 27, 28, 29, 38, 66, 210*n*; *see also* agriculture; Law on Arable Land ; Law on Compensation
La Stampa (Italian newpaper) 150–3, 206
László, G. 29, 37, 59, 75, 102, 109; broadcast media 144; case of Péter Kunos 178, 181, 183; democracy 194; Göncz's political careerism and ambition 173; *La Stampa* affair 152; presidential powers 192; radio frequencies 149; student resistance movements 25, 26; transition justice 120, 122
Law on Appointment 191, 192
Law on Arable Land 110, 118, 130–3, 206, 218*n*; *see also* agriculture; land-ownership and reform; Law of Compensation
Law of Assembly 154, 219*n*
Law of Compensation (1991) 118, 119–26, 206, 217*n*; *see also* agriculture; land-ownership and reform; Law on Arable Land
Law of Incompatibility 169, 170*t*, 171–4, 206, 220*n*
Law on Justice (1991) 118, 122–30, 218*n*
Law No. I of 1993 Compensation 120, 217*n*, 218*n*
Law No. LVII of 1990 on the Appointment Procedure of the Heads of the Public Media, The 103–4, 216*n*
Law No. V of 1997 on the Amendment of the Legal Status of Members of Parliament *see* Law on Incompatibility
Law No. V of 1997
Law No. XC of 1993 on the Procedure

Index 259

related to Crimes committed during the 1956 Revolution and Stuggle for Freedom 124
Law No. XXV of 1991 on Partial Compensation for Damages Unlawfully Caused by the State to Properties Owned by Citizens in the Interest of Settling Ownership Relations *see* Law of Compensation
Law on, Organised Crime 159, 185–8, 205, 221*n*
Law on Privatisation 174–6, 177*f*, 178, 205, 221*n*
Law on Radio Frequency Management 118, 147–50, 206, 219*n*; *see also* broadcast media
Law XXXI of 1989 104
Law XXXIX of 1995 on the Sale of State-Owned Entrepreneurial Assets *see* Law on Privatisation
Law of Zétényi-Takács *see* Law on Justice
League of Hungarian University Students 41
legal security, principle of 123, 124
Lengyel, G. 47
Lengyel, László 3, 97, 100, 189
Levente (paramilitary unit) 24
liberal democracy: co-existence of populist-liberal values 200–1; Göncz's approach to transition justice 121–2, 127–8, 147, 153, 190; Göncz's intervention on economic issues 163, 171, 173; Göncz's pursuit of liberal beliefs 201–4; Göncz's resistance to extreme forms of political ideology 199, 200; Göncz's rooting of beliefs in political culture 205–8; Göncz's second Presidency 161; influence on Göncz's political direction 108, 109, 110, 111, 115, 157
Lieblich, A. 7
Little Constitution 192
Litván, György 22, 47, 52; imprisonment 56, 57, 59, 60–1; joins AFD 75
Lomax, Bill 40, 211*n*
Looking Back (*Visszanézve*) 3
Losonczy, Géza 76
Lukács, G. 21

McGregor, J. 104
Mádl, Ferenc 106, 207
Magyar, Bálint 71
Magyar Dokumentáció 140

260 *Index*

Magyar Forum (HDF daily newspaper) 143
Magyar Hírlap 114, 121, 195
Magyar Hírlap Observer 137
Magyar Nemzet 149, 152–3, 165, 175–6
Magyar, Pál (newswriter) 47
Maléter, Pál 76, 78
March Front 27–8, 29, 85
Márianosztra prison 60, 61, 213*n*
Matyasovszky, Jenő 47
Mécs, Imre 56, 59, 70, 77, 102, 123
Medgyessy, Péter 81, 164–5
Members of Parliament: political interests 169, 170*t*, 171–4, 206, 220*n*
Menon, K. P. S. 45, 49, 211*n*, 212*n*
Mester, Á. 192
Mihály Táncsis Brigade (MTB) 24–6
Milton, A. 140
Mindszenty, József 183
Ministry of Justice (MOJ) 179, 183
Miszlivetz, Ferenc 70, 71–2
Mitchell, W. 7
Molnár, A. 77
Molnár, M. 27
Monori, Áron 138, 142, 143
Movement of Student Unity (A DiákEgység Mozgalom) 24
MTB *see* Mihály Táncsis Brigade
Municipal Court of Budapest 182

Nagy, Ferenc 33, 36
Nagy, Imre 39, 40, 43, 44, 48, 211*n*; arrested and tried 49, 50–1, 52; case against overturned 83; Communism in Defence of the New Course 44, 49–51, 202, 212*n*; execution 56, 76, 78; exhumation and reburial 81, 82; Göncz's sympathy with Nagy's political vision 63, 64, 65; makes speech regarding New Course 63, 64, 213*n*; memorial service for 79, 80, 214*n*; rehabilitation of 62, 81, 84, 203–4; research on subject of banned 77; tribute to deceased at Heroes' Square 81–2
National Alliance of People's Colleges 20
National Association of Agricultural Cooperatives and Producers 131
National Association of Peoples' College 41, 211*n*
National Bank of Hungary 103
National Guard (*Nemzetőr*) 24–5
National Interest Reconciliation Council 112, 217*n*

National Peasant Party (NPP) 27, 29, 30, 31*t*, 48
national populism *see* peasant populism
'national reconciliation' (Népszabadság) 82
Nazism 215, 20, 24, 153–4, 199; *see also* student resistance movements
Négy Igen-es referendum *see* 'Four Yes-es' referendum
Nehru, Jawaharlal 44–5, 46–7, 54–5, 211*n*, 212*n*
Németh, László (populist writer) 29
Németh, Miklós 81, 83, 167
Népszabadság (socialist daily newspaper) 55, 111, 146, 175
Népszava (daily newspaper) 127, 151, 168, 195–6
Network of Free Initiatives (NFI) *see* Alliance of Free Democrats
New Course 49–51, 63, 212*n*
New Peoples' College 30
New York Convention (1968) 124
New York Times, The 82
'1956' (essay) (Göncz) 2
1974 Decree 142
No. LV Law of 1994 on Arable Land *see* Law on Arable Land
No. LXII Law of 1993 on Radio Frequency Management *see* Law of Radio Frequency Management
Non-Aligned Movement (NAM) 211*n*
NPP *see* National Peasant Party
Nyers, Rezső 83

Office of Audit 91
Okolicsanyi, K. 119
Olson, David 193
Oltay, E. 138
'On Communism in Defence of New Course' (Nagy) 44, 49–51, 202, 212*n*
168 Óra (political weekly) 26, 56, 65–6, 191
O'Neil, P. 92
Opposition Roundtable (OR) 89, 90, 95, 215*n*; establishment of Presidency 91, 92, 93
Oral History (Göncz) 2–3, 6, 21, 40, 209*n*, 211n; arrest and interrogation by Soviet authorities 52–3; founding of Committee for Historical Justice (CHJ) 68; Hungarian Revolution (1956) 45, 49, 50, 212*n*; Viktor Orbán 72–3
Oral History (Regéczy-Nagy) 213*n*
Orbán, Viktor 72–3, 97, 100, 216–17*n*;

case of Péter Kunos 180, 183; Criminal Code (1998) 182, 221*n*; Göncz's reduced political activism 189; government of 108–9, 157, 158–60, 161*t*, 162*t*, 163*t*; organised crime 185–8
organised crime *see* Law on Organised Crime

Pál Teleki Work Group (PTWG) 15, 29, 32, 33, 35, 38; influence on Göncz's political vision 73, 199; profile of 19–23
Pandit, Vijaya Lakshmi Nehru 45
pardons (presidential) 178–85, 205, 206
Paris Peace Treaty 32
Parliamentary Constitutional Committee (PCC) 143, 177, 178
parliamentary election (1945) 31*t*, 32–7
Peasant Alliance 48
peasant populism 15, 32–3, 38, 39, 66, 74; co-existence of populist-liberal values 200–1; Göncz believes no longer relevant in 1950s 75, 199; Hungarian Writers' Association (HWA) and 83; impact on Göncz's political views 198–9, 200–1; overview 27–31; *see also* populist writers
Peoples' Republic of Hungary 32, 48, 89; communist Constitution 103; political and social changes in 1980s 1, 69–70; Soviet leadership 31; *see also* Hungary; Republic of Hungary: Soviet Bloc
personal data and privacy 170, 171
Péter, Gábor 60
Pet[ő]fi Circle (*Petőfi Kör*) 39, 41–3, 66, 199, 211*n*
Petrétei, J. 106
Piarists 19, 22, 210*n*
Pimlott, B. 3
Pintér, Péter 23
pluralism 73, 74, 84, 199, 214*n*
Poland 1, 71
police 186, 221*n*
political enfranchisement 27, 28
political prisoners 60, 61, 77–9, 119
populist writers (*népi írok*) 16, 69, 75, 83, 85, 210*n*; crucial impact on Göncz 198–9; overview 27–31; *see also* peasant populism
post-Communist Presidency: bargaining over the Presidency 90–3, 99–100, 195, 216*n*; constitutional powers 103–7; 'Four Yes-es' (Négy Igen-es) referendum 93–5, 97, 115; Göncz's selection for the Presidency 100–3; Roundtable Negotiations (RTN) 89–90; pact between HDF and AFD 95*t*, 96, 97–100, 138–9, 216*n*; puzzle of the AFD 96–8; *see also* Communist rule; first Presidency; Republic of Hungary; second Presidency
Pozsgay, Imre 81, 83, 92, 93, 94–5, 216*n*
Presidency *see* first Presidency; post-communist Presidency; second Presidency
'Presidentialisation' 160, 220*n*
Presidential powers 103–7, 135, 139–40, 141, 146, 149–50; curtailing of 171–2, 189–92, 195–6, 204–5, 220*n*, 221–2*n*; history of 192–6, 204, 216*n*; *see also* cross-signatory system; Prime Ministerial powers
presidential style 161*t*, 162*t*, 190, 205
press freedom: Göncz's belief in 99, 144–6, 152–3, 205, 206
Pridham, G. 207–8
Prime Ministerial powers 139, 193, 194; *see also* cross-signatory system; Presidential powers
privatisation: political interests 169, 170*t*, 171–4, 205, 220*n*; post-Communist 110–11, 174–6, 177*f*, 178, 216*n*, 221*n*
Privatisation, Law on *see* Law on Privatisation
PTWG *see* Pál Teleki Work Group

qualified majority rule 186–7
'quasi-majoritarian democracy' 160

Rádai, Eszter 160, 184
radio frequencies *see* Law on Radio Frequency Management
Rahman, Mohamed Attaur 45–6, 48–9, 55, 56
Rainer, J. 27, 30, 66, 75, 77, 126; Göncz's health problems 189
Rákosi, Mátyás 33, 42
Rákoskeresztúr Cemetery (Lot 301) 76, 79
Regéczy-Nagy, László 49, 52, 53, 61, 62; 'democratic socialism' 64, 213*n*
Republic of Hungary 89, 215*n*; transition to market economy 110–11, 216*n*; *see also* Constitution, The; first Presidency; Hungary; People's Republic of Hungary; post-communist Presidency; second Presidency

Revolutionary Council of Hungarian Intellectuals 44
Richards, D. 8
Right of Appointment 191, 192
right of legal redress 182–4
Ripp, Zoltán 92
Roberts, B. 5
Romania: Göncz makes illegal visit 36–7
Romsics, I. 24, 42, 60
Roundtable Negotiations (RTN) 89–90, 134, 194, 215n
rule of law: Göncz's belief in 205, 206
Rules of the House 159–60, 188

Salamon, László 113, 139, 180, 183
Saláta, Kálmán 22, 35–6, 74, 214n
Sansa, Tito 150
Sárközy, Tamás 172
Sátoraljaúhely prison 61
Schmidt, Péter 141
Schmitt, Pál 207
Schwartz, Herman 177
Scouting movement 18, 19, 22, 28, 38, 51; crucial impact on Göncz's social/political outlook 198
SDP see Social Democratic party
Second Presidency (1995–2000) 51, 57–8; case of Péter Kunos 178–85, 205, 206, 221n; economic stabilisation programme 164–9, 220n; Göncz's diminished political activism 188–96; Göncz's political activities (1990–2000) 161t; Horn and Orbán governments 158–60, 161t, 162t, 163; Law of Incompatibility 169, 170t, 171–4; Law on Organised Crime 185–8; Law on Privatisation 174–6, 177f, 178; main characteristics 201, 204; political achievements as first post-Communist President 204–8; see also first Presidency; post-communist Presidency; Republic of Hungary
'Secret Speech' (Khrushchev) 41, 211n
Serov, Ivan Aleksandrovich 55
Social Contract (Társadalmi Szerződés) (1987) 69, 213n
Social Democratic party (SDP) 23, 24, 31t
Soil Improvement Firm 37, 47
Sólyom, László (President of the Constitutional Court) 137, 141, 207
Somogyvári, István 90–1, 172, 193–4
Somos, A. 189
Soós, Júlia 212n
Soros, George 166

Soviet Bloc 67; 'democratic socialism' and 64; fall of 1, 2, 83, 109, 215n; farming model 39, 41–2, 199; Gorbachev in power 69; intervention of Soviet forces in Hungarian Revolution (1956) 43–4, 48, 54–5; United Nations and 61, 213n; see also Communist rule; Peoples' Republic of Hungary
Special Care Foundation (Fogyatékos Alapítvány) 166
Special Commission for Historical Investigation (CHIR) 124, 129, 218n
speeches 6–7, 30, 153–6; Göncz's retirement 195–6; Göncz's views on agriculture 39, 40, 41–2, 43, 66
SPPMC see State Privatisation and Property Management Corporation
Stark, D. 81, 110
State Privatisation and Property Management Corporation (SPPMC) 174, 176, 178, 220n
State Property Agency 110
State Security Authority 35
Stefka, I. 112
Stein, A. 46
Sticker, Kati 57
Strasbourg European Court of Human Rights 182
student resistance movements 16, 20, 32, 33, 38, 39; Freedom Front of Hungarian Students (FFHS) 23f, 24–7, 49; influence on Göncz's political development 66, 67, 84, 199, 201–2; see also Nazism
Stumpf, István 163, 180, 181
Suez Crisis (1956) 40, 43, 44, 45
Sükösd, F. 105, 142
Supreme Court 179, 182
Surányi, György 167–8
Szabó, György 23
Szakasits, Árpád 23, 192, 204
Szálé, L. 195
Székely, Tamás 25
Szekfű, Gyula 20
Szenpétery, Kálmán 25
Szilárgyi, József 76
Szomszéd, Orsolya 173–4
Szűcs, Ferenc 23
Szűr, Miklós 25
Szűrös, Mátyás 81

Takács, Péter 122
Tamás, Lábady 186–7
Tánczos, Gábor 56

Taras, R. 193
'Taxi Blockade' (taxi-drivers strike) 111–15, 145, 190, 205, 216–17n
'There Is a Way Out' (Network of Free Initiatives) 71
Think Tank Network 133, 218n
Third Compensation Act 217n
three Ts system (cultural policy) 58
Thürmer, Gyula 216n
Tildy, Zoltán 23, 34, 48, 56, 192, 204
Tito, Josip Broz 46–7
Tódor, J. 155
Tőkés, R. 28, 97
Tölgyessy, Péter 1, 90, 91, 101, 155, 216n; leaves AFD 158
Torgyán, József 74
Török, G. 161t, 162t
Tóth, M. 15–16, 22, 29, 30, 63, 65; European Union 132; founding of Committee for Historical Justice (CHJ) 68; Göncz reminisces about his life 197; Göncz's health problems 188–9; Göncz's imprisonment 53, 58; Göncz's presidential style 161t, 162t; Heroes' Square 82; inauguration speech 165; translation work 62; Göncz works in Vác prison translation bureau 57–60, 68
Treaty of Trianon 17, 24, 209n

Union of Working Youth 41
United Nations 43, 45, 46–7, 60, 61, 213n
United States 61; Göncz's visit (1982) 4–5, 209n
Unwin, Peter 50

Vác prison ('House of Lords') 57–60, 61, 212n

Varga, Béla 22, 47, 56
Varga, László 121
Várhelyi, József 24, 25
Varró, Szilvia (political editor) 128, 160
Vásárhelyi, Miklós 56, 77, 101
Velten, M. 107
Veszprém Chemical Heavy Industry Research Institute 62
veto (presidential) 105–6, 149–50, 216n; economic policies 171, 172, 173, 174, 221n; organised crime 187, 188; privatisation 176, 177f, 178
Vígh, Károly 15
Visegrád Summit 116–18, 204
Vitányi, Iván 15, 26
Voroshilov, Kliment 31, 32
Vörös, Imre 141

Walesa, Lech 116, 217n
Werbőczy Gimnazium (school) 18
Whitehead, L. 69
Wisinger, I. 29, 37, 59, 75, 102, 109; broadcast media 136, 144; case of Péter Kunos 178, 181, 183; democracy 194; Göncz's political careerism and ambition 173; *La Stampa* affair 152; Presidential powers 192; radio frequencies 149; student resistance movements 25, 26; transition justice 120, 122
Wisniewski, R. 7
Wittner, Mari 57
World Hungarian Association 102

Yugoslav Embassy 43, 211n

Zétényi-Takács, Law of *see* Law on Justice
Zétényi, Zsolt 122
Zimányi, Tibor 23